D1739601

GLOBAL PERSPECTIVES ON PRESS REGULATION
VOLUME 1: EUROPE

In this ground-breaking two-volume set, world-leading experts produce a rich, authoritative depiction of the world's press, its freedom and its limits.

We want press freedom but we also want freedom from the press. A powerful press may expose a corrupt government or aid it. It may champion citizens or unfairly attack them. A vulnerable press may lack supporters and succumb to conformity. It may resist and overcome tyranny. According to common belief, press freedom involves social responsibilities to equip public debate and render government transparent. Is this attitude valid given that the press is usually a private, commercial actor?

Globally, the health, authority and viability of the press varies dramatically. These patterns do not conform to traditional divisions between North and South, East and West. Instead, they are much more complex. How do we measure successful press regulation? What concessions can the state and/or society demand from the press? What constitutes the irreducible core of press freedom?

The contributions in Volume 1 look at key jurisdictions in Europe, whereas Volume 2 goes beyond Europe to analyse the situation in key jurisdictions in Asia, Africa, the Americas and Oceania. Each volume can be used independently or as part of the complete set.

This work will be incredibly valuable to policymakers and academics who seek to capture the global picture for the purposes of effecting change.

Global Perspectives on Press Regulation

Volume 1: Europe

Edited by
Paul Wragg
and
András Koltay

·HART·
OXFORD · LONDON · NEW YORK · NEW DELHI · SYDNEY

HART PUBLISHING

Bloomsbury Publishing Plc

Kemp House, Chawley Park, Cumnor Hill, Oxford, OX2 9PH, UK

1385 Broadway, New York, NY 10018, USA

29 Earlsfort Terrace, Dublin 2, Ireland

HART PUBLISHING, the Hart/Stag logo, BLOOMSBURY and the Diana logo are
trademarks of Bloomsbury Publishing Plc

First published in Great Britain 2023

A catalogue record for this book is available from the British Library.

A catalogue record for this book is available from the Library of Congress.

ISBN:	HB:	978-1-50995-034-8
	ePDF:	978-1-50995-036-2
	ePub:	978-1-50995-035-5

Typeset by Compuscript Ltd, Shannon

To find out more about our authors and books visit www.hartpublishing.co.uk.
Here you will find extracts, author information, details of forthcoming events
and the option to sign up for our newsletters.

To Sam, Daniel and Joey (PW)

To Orsi, Zalán and Zétény (AK)

PREFACE

This two-volume set invites readers to assess the conceptual, practical and doctrinal issues arising in realisation of a press freedom ideal in which the press may act as public watchdog without undermining the rights of others. Through careful, systematic evaluation of the differing perspectives on this ideal, as it relates to the various political, cultural and social climates around the world, this collection presents an unparalleled catalogue of world thought on the problem.

Volume I focuses on the European experience, in which, blighted by its history, a complex series of soft and hard law provides the press with the means to challenge state power whilst seeking to restrain it from unduly interfering with hard-fought human rights. In this ecosystem, we see that voluntary press regulatory schemes are common, such that the question becomes how far the state may go to enforce human rights norms without compromising press freedom.

Volume II provides viewpoints from the larger world, in which regulation is viewed with justified suspicion; from the USA, whose historic experience of suppression under oppressive colonial rule colours its view of press freedom to this day, to China, Latin America and Africa, where repressive regimes continue to hold considerable influence. Even in those commonwealth countries, lacking the same overt histories of repression, we find stubborn resistance to regulation despite a more general embrace of human rights culture. Here, then, we see the continuing challenges that realisation of the press freedom ideal must face.

ACKNOWLEDGEMENTS

The editors would like to thank all the contributors to this volume. Thanks are also due to our colleagues who helped with the publication of the book, especially Édua Reményi, who did a sterling job editing it, and to Stephen Patrick, who helped with the English proofreading of some of the original drafts. We are also grateful for the enormous support of the publisher. Without them this work would never have been born.

TABLE OF CONTENTS

LIST OF CONTRIBUTORS

Peter Coe is Associate Professor in Law, Birmingham Law School, University of Birmingham; Senior Visiting Research Fellow, School of Law, University of Reading; Associate Research Fellow, Institute of Advanced Legal Studies and Information Law and Policy Centre, University of London.

Pietro Dunn is a PhD Researcher, University of Bologna and University of Luxembourg.

Udo Fink is Professor, Chair for German Public Law, Public International Law, European Law and International Commercial Law, Johannes Gutenberg-University, Mainz.

Guilhem Gil is Senior Lecturer, Aix-en-Provence Law School, Aix-Marseille University.

András Koltay is Research Professor at the University of Public Service (Budapest) and Professor of Law at the Pázmány Péter Catholic University (Budapest).

Joanna Kulesza is a Professor of Law, Faculty of Law and Administration, University of Łódź.

Daithí Mac Síthigh is the Head of Research at Institute of Art, Design + Technology in Dún Laoghaire.

Sten Schaumburg-Müller is Professor of Law, Law Department, University of Southern Denmark.

Jan Oster is Professor of Civil Law, Business Law, Media Law, Data and Digital Law, University of Osnabrück.

Oreste Pollicino is Professor of Constitutional Law, Bocconi University, Milan, and Member of the Executive Board of the European Union Agency for Fundamental Rights, Vienna.

Andrei Richter is a Professor Researcher of Journalism at Comenius University in Bratislava.

Andrej Školkay is Director of Research at the School of Communication and Media, Bratislava.

Paul Wragg is Professor of Law at the University of Leeds.

1

On European Press Freedom: An Introduction

ANDRÁS KOLTAY

This introductory chapter will outline some of the elements of the Pan-European concept of the freedom of the press, while respecting the individual characteristics of each European state as regards the details of press freedom. I will work on the assumption that freedom of the press has elements in common in democratic European states that make it possible to identify a 'European' doctrine. It is important in this context to understand freedom of the press as a right that generally guarantees the freedom of all media. I will not cover issues of 'media regulation', although television, radio and on-demand media services are subject to a separate regulatory regime and slightly distinct constitutional doctrines. Similarly, the freedom of online platforms that have characteristics other than those of legacy media but which play a similar role in the public sphere is treated as a separate issue. Freedom of the press is therefore the freedom of all channels of communication that can be covered by the notion of 'press' or generally the 'media', but it does not include media or Internet (platform) regulation.

1. Freedom of the Press and Freedom of Expression

According to Jacob Rowbottom, the concept of the press can be defined in several ways, and definitions can be either 'institutional' or 'functional' in nature.[1] To this we can add an approach to the press as a 'technology', as Eugene Volokh argues that freedom of the press is nothing more than the right to freely use various technologies that facilitate mass communication, and thus the press is not privileged or burdened with additional obligations, and its boundaries coincide with those of freedom of expression.[2]

---

[1] J Rowbottom, *Media Law* (Oxford, Hart Publishing, 2018) 27–31.
[2] E Volokh, 'Freedom for the Press as an Industry, or for the Press as a Technology?' (2012) 160 *University of Pennsylvania Law Review* 459. For a summary of similar views of other authors, see

If the press is considered an important institution of a democratic social order, then the question arises as to whether it is necessary for the legal system to provide the press with additional rights, or possibly impose additional obligations in return. If the press is an 'institution', this seems inevitable, but as Tom Gibbons notes, 'their association with truth and participation in a democracy is only incidental'.[3] Gibbons' tactful words highlight the fact that the press cannot be obliged at all to act in accordance with the justifications underlying the protection of freedom of expression, just as individuals cannot always be obliged to exercise their freedom of expression in the interests of democracy or truth, or possibly with a view to self-fulfilment, in accordance with one philosophical justification for freedom of expression.

It would be tempting to define the press or media in terms of its technological characteristics, and just a few decades ago this would not have raised any particular difficulties; at most there may have been some controversy over the legal status of freelance or citizen journalists.[4] However, with the development of technology, previous frameworks have loosened, and public information is now provided not only by legacy media journalists but also by bloggers, vloggers, influencers, youtubers and, of course, any individual who has access to a public forum, typically online. It is not necessary for the speaker who provides information to be a professional journalist, nor is it necessary for him to carry out his activity on a for profit basis at all. The press can no longer be defined on the basis of purely formal criteria. It is worth determining whether it is reasonable to approach the press on the basis of its functions. Three functions can be identified that may bring us closer to establishing a useable definition of the press, and these are:

- informing the public about important and newsworthy events;
- monitoring the government as a public watchdog;
- promoting democratic dialogue, providing a platform for individual opinions.

Providing information to the interested public is essential in a democracy, and is a key element of the press's self-image and self-reinforced image. The press is a symbolic agora of today's society;[5] it is the space where individual opinions may appear and clash, and which also helps those interested in making informed opinions and making decisions. Individuals need the help of the press without which they would not have access to the necessary information. It would be a mistake to idealise the relationship between the press and its audience, as the former does not necessarily provide information properly and the latter does not necessarily take an interest in public affairs information.[6] The former problem can be dealt

---

P Coe, 'Redefining "Media" Using a "Media-as-a-constitutional-component" Concept': An Evaluation of the Need for the European Court of Human Rights to Alter its Understanding of "Media" Within a New Media Landscape' (2017) 37 *Legal Studies* 25, 37–39.

[3] T Gibbons, *Regulating the Media* (London, Sweet & Maxwell, 1998) 28.

[4] See P Coe, *Media Freedom in the Age of Citizen Journalism* (Cheltenham, Elgar, 2021).

[5] TG Tucker, *Life In Ancient Athens: The Social and Public Life of a Classical Athenian from Day to Day* (London, Macmillan, 1906).

[6] Rowbottom (n 1) 18–19.

with in part through legal regulation, while the latter has nothing to do with press regulation.

The idea of the press keeping watch over the government can be linked to the 'Fourth Estate' metaphor Thomas Carlyle attributes to Edmund Burke:

> Burke said there were Three Estates in Parliament; but, in the Reporters' Gallery yonder, there sat a Fourth Estate more important far than they all … Literature is our Parliament too. Printing, which comes necessarily out of Writing, I say often, is equivalent to Democracy: invent Writing, Democracy is inevitable … Whoever can speak, speaking now to the whole nation, becomes a power, a branch of government, with inalienable weight in law-making, in all acts of authority.[7]

The metaphor that the press is the Fourth Estate next to the clergy, the aristocracy and the commoners is undoubtedly captivating. However, Carlyle may have been wrong in attributing the term to Burke, whose published works do not include it. Presumably it was Thomas Macaulay who first published it in print in 1828:[8]

> The gallery in which the reporters sit has become a fourth estate of the realm. The publication of the debates, a practice which seemed to the most liberal statesmen of the old school full of danger to the great safeguards of public liberty, is now regarded by many persons as a safeguard tantamount, and more than tantamount, to all the rest together.[9]

According to this, the press exercises control over the current power, revealing the functioning of state bodies and government, exposing its anomalies and providing the members of society with sufficient information in order to be able to make informed decisions in democratic procedures. It should be noted, however, that Jeremy Bentham had recognised this before Carlyle[10] and James Mill[11] also highlighted the supervisory role of the press. This is an idea that has its roots in Europe, where government control of the press is identified as an important function of the press,[12] and the European Court of Human Rights (ECtHR) often refers to the press as the public watchdog of the public if it wants to justify extending its freedom.[13]

---

[7] T Carlyle, *On Heroes, Hero-Worship, and the Heroic in History: Six Lectures* (New York, Wiley and Putnam, [1841] 1846) 147.

[8] L Blom-Cooper, 'Press Freedom: Constitutional Right or Cultural Assumption?' [2008] *Public Law* 260, 261–62.

[9] TB Macaulay, 'Hallam's Constitutional History' (1828) 4 *Edinburgh Review* 96, 165. For the sake of completeness, we recall that Henry Fielding in a 1752 newspaper article meant the masses, the mob under 'Fourth Estate'. See H Fielding, 'O Ye Wicked Rascallions' *Covent Garden Journal* (13 June 1752).

[10] J Bentham, 'Letter to the Spanish People I on the Liberty of the Press, the Approaching Eight Months' Sleep of the Cortes, and the Exclusion of Experience from the Succeeding Cortes' in J Bentham, *On the Liberty of the Press and Public Discussion* (London, William Hone, 1821) 12.

[11] J Mill, 'Liberty of the Press' in *Encyclopaedia Britannica* vol VIII, 7th edn (Edinburgh, Adam and Charles Black, 1842) 278.

[12] Rowbottom (n 1) 19–20.

[13] *Lingens v Austria* [1986] App no 9815/82, [44]; *Jersild v Denmark* [1994] App no 15890/89, [31] and [35]; *Bladet Tromsø and Stensaas v Norway* [1999] App no 21980/93, [59] and [68]; *Observer and Guardian v the United Kingdom* [1991] App no 13585/88, [59(b)]; *The Sunday Times v the United Kingdom (No 2)* [1991] App no 13166/87, [50(b)]; *Dalban v Romania* [1999] App no 28114/95, [49]; *Bergens Tidende and Others v Norway* [2000] App no 26132/95, [49] and [57]; *Thoma v Luxembourg* [2001] App no 38432/97, [45]; *Goodwin v the United Kingdom* [1996] App no 28957/95, [39].

The third essential function of the press is to promote democratic dialogue by providing a channel for different opinions. This idea was formulated long before the emergence of democracies in today's sense.[14] It can also mean that journalists report on individual positions themselves and that they allow room for other speakers. It is important that the press does not transmit individual opinions to the audience 'raw' without sorting and processing them, but arranges them, puts them in context and confronts them with other opinions. The press is the principal organiser of public dialogue.[15] However, it should also be noted that tensions may arise between the individual wishing to express his views and the press, due to the latter's decision-making role as an organiser.[16]

After reviewing the most important functions of the press, it is clear that simply listing them is not sufficient to distinguish the press from other public speakers who are also able to perform one or all of these functions. These may be individual speakers, bloggers or social media users, but they can also be the service providers themselves, such as a blogger, video sharing, or social media platform. It is welcome if, for example, a court grants an individual speaker who is engaged in information activities strong protection similar to that of the professional press,[17] but it raises the question of whether it is necessary to grant him privileges as well, and whether such a speaker has any responsibility to the public.

In order to clarify the concept of the press, it is not enough to define its functions; it is also necessary to identify other distinguishing features. Some of these can be found – all of which will be features that an individual speaker or, for example, an online platform may have, but which are entirely specific to the press, and presumably only to a part of it. One of the most obvious such features is mass communication, which is undoubtedly one of the peculiarities of the press: its purpose and life force is to address many people.[18] The professional nature of the operation, and the knowledge of and adherence to standards of conduct specific to the activity, is another distinguishing feature.[19]

It is important to keep in mind that defining a concept of the press, one which is acceptable in principle and can be used in practice, is important only in so far as the legislation distinguishes between the press and other public speakers; if the press enjoys special privileges, access to those rights must be restricted so that the rights can be used in practice for the purposes established in principle. Therefore, in the age of mass public speech it may be necessary to identify which speakers qualify as the 'press', based on the nature of the information they publish.

---

[14] D Defoe, *An Essay on the Regulation of the Press* (London, 1704); Mill (n 11).

[15] D Anderson, 'The Press and Democratic Dialogue' (2013–14) 127 *Harvard Law Review Forum* 331, 333. See also D Anderson, 'The Press and Political Community' in A Koltay (ed), *Comparative Perspectives on the Fundamental Freedom of Expression* (Budapest, Wolters Kluwer, 2015).

[16] Rowbottom (n 1) 22.

[17] Jan Oster gives examples of this from the practice of the ECtHR, see J Oster, *European and International Media Law* (Cambridge, Cambridge University Press, 2017) 11–12.

[18] J Oster, *Media Freedom as a Fundamental Right* (Cambridge, Cambridge University Press, 2015) 60–61; Coe (n 2) 39–40.

[19] Coe (n 2) 40–41.

2. Regulation of the Press

The regulation of the press, although not completely uniform, is largely similar in most European countries (with notable exceptions). Freedom of the press is enshrined in the codified constitutions as an independent right, and either a separate press law or a uniform media law covering media services and also press products settles specific issues relating to the press. In addition, laws of general application and certain special laws may affect the conduct of the press. However, it is common for the content of freedom of the press to emerge not only from codified legislation but also from the case law of courts and constitutional courts. When reviewing the sources of regulation, other forms of regulation beyond state regulation, such as co-regulation and self-regulation, must also be taken into account. The latter is also common in Europe and rests on similar foundations in several countries.

In European states, constitutions identify and protect freedom of the press in addition to freedom of expression. These provisions are concise in their wording, in keeping with the 'genre' of constitutions, and do not seek to delimit or define the content of freedom of expression and the press. The clarification of these issues is left to lower-level legislation as well as for constitutional or higher courts and case law. However, it is difficult to argue that it would follow mandatorily from European constitutions protecting freedom of the press that the press must necessarily be afforded privileges. Even if a constitutional court or tribunal reaches this conclusion, it does not imply that it stems from the text of the constitution, but from the values and approach of the relevant decision-maker.

Even without a uniform European press regulation, the European Convention on Human Rights (ECHR), aiming to protect human rights and political freedoms in Europe, is very influential, and has a unifying effect between party states. Drafted in 1950 by the Council of Europe, the Convention entered into force in 1953. It established the ECtHR, thereby broadening the possibilities for the protection of human rights around Europe (states behind the Iron Curtain joined after the fall of Communism). Any person who feels their rights have been violated under the Convention by a State party can take a case to the ECtHR.

Article 10 of the ECHR provides the right to freedom of expression and information, subject to certain restrictions that are 'in accordance with law' and 'necessary in a democratic society'. This right includes the 'freedom to hold opinions and to receive and impart information and ideas without interference by public authority and regardless of frontiers'.

The Helsinki Final Act, another influential human rights document, was signed at the Conference on Security and Co-operation in Europe (CSCE) held in Helsinki in 1975. The document provides for the respect of human rights and fundamental freedoms, freedom of expression and the press among them. In 1994, the Organisation for Security and Cooperation in Europe (OSCE) was established as a successor to the CSCE. Within this framework, a number of commitments of the participating States were published in the fields of freedom of the media, freedom of expression and the free flow of information.[20]

The European Union (EU) does not regulate the press in general, as it does for audiovisual media services and video-sharing platform services.[21] However, many of the rules created by the EU can be applied specifically to press activities, even directly, such as the General Data Protection Regulation (GDPR),[22] or through their obligatory implementation in the Member States, as is the case with directives on copyright law[23] and on the fight against terrorism,[24] as well as other directives in similar specific fields. Some EU standards provide for certain restrictions on freedom of expression, such as the Framework Decision prohibiting the denial of genocide.[25] The most important of these rules, however, are the EU's general rules on the free movement of goods and services,[26] which also affect certain press markets, thus creating greater business opportunities and increased competition between players in the European press market. State aid rules[27] and general competition law, as established by the EU, are also relevant to media markets.

Article 11(1) of the Charter of Fundamental Rights protects 'the freedom of information and expression' and states in the second paragraph that '[t]he freedom and pluralism of the media shall be respected'. The fundamental rights enshrined in the Charter apply only within the scope of EU law, and as such the rights enshrined in the Charter cannot be invoked against the decisions of individual Member States in the absence of any other EU legal basis, that is connection to EU law. According to Article 51(1) of the Charter, its provisions 'are addressed to the institutions and bodies of the Union with due regard for the principle of

---

[20] *Commitments: Freedom of the Media, Freedom of Expression, Free Flow of Information, 1975–2017*, 4th edn (Vienna, OSCE Representative on Freedom of the Media, 2017), available at: www.osce.org/representative-on-freedom-of-media/99565.

[21] Directive 2010/13/EU of the European Parliament and of the Council of 10 March 2010 on the coordination of certain provisions laid down by law, regulation or administrative action in Member States concerning the provision of audiovisual media services [2010] OJ L95/1 (AVMS Directive).

[22] Regulation (EU) 2016/679 of the European Parliament and of the Council of 27 April 2016 on the protection of natural persons with regard to the processing of personal data and on the free movement of such data, and repealing Directive 95/46/EC [2016] OJ L119/1 (General Data Protection Regulation, GDPR).

[23] Directive 2001/29/EC of the European Parliament and of the Council of 22 May 2001 on the harmonisation of certain aspects of copyright and related rights in the information society [2001] OJ L167/10. Directive (EU) 2019/790 of the European Parliament and of the Council of 17 April 2019 on copyright and related rights in the Digital Single Market and amending Directives 96/9/EC and 2001/29/EC [2019] OJ L130/92.

[24] Directive (EU) 2017/541 of the European Parliament and of the Council of 15 March 2017 on combating terrorism and replacing Council Framework Decision 2002/475/JHA and amending Council Decision 2005/671/JHA [2017] OJ L88/6, Art 5.

[25] Council Framework Decision 2008/913/JHA of 28 November 2008 on Combating Certain Forms and Expression of Racism and Xenophobia by Means of Criminal Law [2008] OJ L328/55.

[26] The Treaty on the European Union and the consolidated version of the Treaty on the Functioning of the European Union 2012/C 326/01.

[27] See Communication from the Commission on the application of State aid rules to public service broadcasting [2009] OJ C 257/1.

subsidiarity and to the Member States only when they are implementing Union law'.[28] The provisions of the Charter do not standardise the level of protection of fundamental rights in the Member States and thus, as freedom of the press is only tangentially covered by EU standards, Article 11 of the Charter is also only marginally applicable to press matters. It is therefore up to the Member States to define the content of freedom of the press, to distinguish it from freedom of expression and to remove restrictions from it.

In September 2022, the European Parliament and the Council tabled a proposal for a European Media Freedom Act which would cover a number of aspects of media regulation and bring them under common EU rules, as opposed to the current approach of not including press products in EU media regulation.[29] The fate of the proposal is still uncertain, but it is in any case indicative of what the EU Commission considers to be among the fundamental issues of media freedom: protection of editorial freedom; protection of journalistic sources; protection against surveillance; independent and balanced public service media; protection of media service providers against arbitrary decisions by online platforms; action against media market concentration; fair and transparent spending of state advertising budget, etc.

In many European countries, the press is regulated by statutory law. Europe's press laws present a varied and colourful picture, and a review of them suggests that, in general, the existence or non-existence of a stand-alone press law is not necessarily directly related to the degree of freedom of the press in a given country. So far no comprehensive analytical work comparing European press regulations has been published, but the text of the laws and the collections summarising the essential elements of each regulation are sporadically available.[30] Press laws do not necessarily contain rules restricting content directly; where one exists, it typically establishes a criminal act or private law tort, such as a ban on hate speech or defamation, and does not establish a separate liability system for the press, instead ordering the application of general rules of criminal or civil procedure.[31] That is, these rules do not put the press in a more difficult position than if they were contained in criminal or civil codes. While press laws may include privileges granted to the press, these are not necessarily enshrined in such laws.[32]

---

[28] See also C-617/10 *Åklagaren v Hans Åkerberg Fransson*, ECLI:EU:C:2013:105.

[29] Proposal for a Regulation of the European Parliament and of the Council establishing a common framework for media services in the internal market (European Media Freedom Act) and amending Directive 2010/13/EU (Text with EEA relevance) (SEC(2022) 322 final) – (SWD(2022) 286 final) – (SWD(2022) 287 final).

[30] See 'Press Law and Practice: A Comparative Study of Press Freedom in European and Other Democracies' (London, Article 19 – International Centre Against Censorship, 1993); (2019) *Media and Entertainment Law Review*.

[31] See, eg, loi du 29 juillet 1881 sur la liberté de la presse (French Press Act); Disposizioni sulla stampa, legge 8 febbraio 1948, no 47 (Italian Press Act); Laki sananvapauden käyttämisestä joukkoviestinnässä, 460/2003 (Finnish Media Act).

[32] eg, the right to source protection may also be included in the press law and in the laws on criminal and civil litigation, compare section 5.1 below.

However, with very few exceptions, it can be stated that the press laws do not stipulate an obligation of the press to inform the public, or the possible responsibility of the government for supervising such provision of information or any task in the public interest. The common content of press laws is to lay down certain detailed rules relating to press activities, such as rules for the mandatory registration of press products, the appointment of the editor-in-chief, the provision of legal deposit copies and other formal requirements for the smooth application of the law (such as imprint content).[33] As compliance with legal requirements can be investigated by civil and criminal courts, media authorities that would otherwise have extensive oversight of television and radio media services usually have no jurisdiction over press outlets.

The media laws for these broadcast services are in most cases separate from the press laws, forming an independent set of rules, although uniform, comprehensive regulation exists in some legal systems.[34] The possibility of authority supervision is created exclusively by the Hungarian regulation which also attempts to ensure that decisions are taken in a special co-regulatory system, in which the decision-maker is a body appointed by the professional organisation operated by the publishers of press products, which is independent of the authority.[35] In addition to stand-alone press laws, there are a number of other statutory requirements for the press. They include the general private and criminal codes already mentioned which may also impose mandatory bans on the press, as well as sectoral rules such as data protection, copyright or advertising law.

Self-regulation can also help to achieve the goals of press regulation, as evidenced by the widespread use of press self-regulation across Europe. There is no clear definition of self-regulation – instead, it serves as an umbrella term for alternative (extra-legal) regulatory approaches. By self-regulation, here I mean a system of rules created and/or supervised by bodies set up by market and industry actors, but which formally operate independently of them.

Self-regulation is a bottom-up model, the essence of which is that each sector develops its own rules of conduct and ethics, which each recognises as binding upon itself, and where those who violate the rules are threatened with sanctions. The main characteristic of self-regulation is its voluntary nature: the industry players concerned are free to decide whether they want to participate in self-regulation or submit themselves to the self-regulatory mechanism. They may have not only moral reasons for subjecting themselves to such a regime – in the free market these

---

[33] See French Press Act (n 31); Italian Press Act (n 31); Tiskový zákon, no 46/2000 Coll (Czech Press Act); Bekendtgørelse af medieansvarsloven, lov no 1719 of 27 December 2018 (Danish Law on the Liability of Media).

[34] Example of the latter, Bundesgesetz vom 12 Juni 1981 über die Presse und andere publizistische Medien (Mediengesetz, the Austrian Media Act); and Zakon o medijih – ZMed (Uradni list RS, št 35/01 z dne 11. 5. 2001) (Slovenian Media Act). In the case of post-Soviet states, see, eg, A Richter, 'Post-Soviet Perspective on Censorship and Freedom of the Media: An Overview' (2008) 70 *International Communication Gazette* 307.

[35] 2010. évi CLXXXV. törvény a médiaszolgáltatásokról és a tömegkommunikációról (Hungarian Media Act) arts 190–202.

reasons usually have little influence anyway – but also a well-conceived material interest in participating. By submitting to self-regulation, they may project the image of a socially responsible company to their audience or hope that effective self-regulation creating such a positive image can avoid stricter – and then binding and mandatory – state measures or legislation. The advantages of self-regulation over codified law are its flexibility and ability to adapt more rapidly to changing technology or market conditions. At the same time, it may suffer from a lack of credibility – since self-regulation is created according to the intentions of industry actors, and decisions are left to bodies that are not completely independent of these actors – and uncertain effectiveness. Due to the lack of actual binding force, participation and also submission to decisions made as a result of supervision is left to the discretion of stakeholders.

Self-regulation supported by codified legal regulation can also be considered to be a form of self-regulation, where legal rules prescribe the framework, but self-regulatory organisations are entrusted with both the creation of norms (codes) and their supervision, and the state cannot control their operation. However, as Paul Wragg notes, self-regulation and voluntary regulation are commonly used as interchangeable concepts. Similarly, the terms mandatory and statutory law are also used interchangeably. This is not the case for other highly regulated professions such as doctors, lawyers and accountants whose professional organisations themselves adopt mandatory regulations for their members, and for some of whom membership in such professional bodies is mandatory and is a condition for carrying out a particular activity, so the rules are also generally binding.[36]

Voluntary self-regulatory solutions essentially sacrifice a measure of efficiency.[37] In her study, Lara Fielden provides a thorough overview of each European system of self-regulation.[38] Based on this, the key issues in terms of efficiency are:

- defining the range of bodies setting standards;
- the composition of the decision-making bodies;
- sanctions applied by these bodies;
- funding of the scheme;
- the voluntary or compulsory nature of participation.

As long as the publishers themselves delegate or co-delegate members to the bodies and the funding comes from them, they cannot be subject to substantive sanctions, such as fines, and their participation in the scheme can be suspended or withdrawn at any time, and as such these schemes cannot be considered effectively independent or effective.[39] Their goal is primarily to maintain independence

---

[36] P Wragg, *A Free and Regulated Press* (Oxford, Hart Publishing, 2020) 53–54.
[37] ibid 65–66.
[38] L Fielden, *Regulating the Press: A Comparative Study of International Press Councils* (Oxford, Reuters Institute for the Study of Journalism, 2012), available at: reutersinstitute.politics.ox.ac.uk/sites/default/files/2017-11/Regulating%20the%20Press.pdf.
[39] Wragg (n 36) 61–71.

from public bodies, which they also fulfil, but which comes at a price. Wragg's clear conclusion is that only a regulatory body that is independent of publishers in terms of staffing and funding, whose decisions are binding on publishers and which is capable of imposing substantive sanctions, can be truly independent and effective, whether it be under purely statutory regulation or possibly in co-regulatory systems that exist under state supervision.[40]

3. Possibilities of Prior Restraint

Licensing, that is, a separate, official permit, issued by the state, cannot be required for the issue, distribution and sale of press products in democratic legal systems. Nevertheless, registration requirements, widely known in European legal systems, are somewhat similar to licensing. Registration can be a simple administrative act and usually involves providing important information about a press product (or media service). If the regulation makes it a condition for entering the market, then it can be compared to licensing, because the act creates the right to provide the service and in the absence of such registration commencing publication is not allowed.

Reviewing the regulations of some European states, it can be concluded that where there is an obligation to register, this requirement for press products is a condition for starting the activity (commencing publication).[41] Registration is an administrative act, but in principle, in the case of arbitrary application of the law, it can have censorious effects. The reasons for its maintenance include the interest of different services, as this is the easiest way to prevent market problems arising from identity or similarity of names. It is also necessary for the official or judicial supervision of services to have an up-to-date, authentic register. Several European states reject this approach, while others have long used it, but, provided there are adequate legal guarantees, the obligation to register and censorship are well separated.

During the historical development of the notion of the freedom of the press, a consensus has grown up that prior and arbitrary intervention in the process of publication of opinions is impermissible, whereas *a posteriori* accountability or prosecution for the publication of unlawful content is acceptable, subject to appropriate legal safeguards. Formally, making the publication of newspapers conditional on a licence and thus the practice of official censorship ceased to exist in England in 1694, and after William Blackstone it has become a generally accepted view that the liberty of the press means the absence of prior restraints: 'The liberty of the

---

[40] ibid 255–77.

[41] Just a few examples, Italian Press Act (n 31), Legge in tema di editoria elettronica, no 62 del 7 marzo 2001, Art 1; Ustawa z dnia 26 stycznia 1984 r. Prawo prasowe (Polish Press Act) Arts 20–24; Tryckfrihetsförordning (1949:105) (Swedish Press Freedom Act) Art 5(5).

press is indeed essential to the nature of a free state; but this consists in laying no *previous* restraints upon publications, and not in freedom from censure for criminal matter when published.'[42] The prohibition of prior and arbitrary interference has become so fundamental to freedom of the press across Europe that it is seldom enshrined separately in individual state constitutions and laws.[43]

At the same time, prior restraint – along with legal guarantees that protect press freedom – is not in itself impermissible. The case law of the ECtHR does not preclude prior restraints from being a permissible restriction on freedom of expression either: in *The Sunday Times v the United Kingdom (No 2)*[44] and in *The Observer and The Guardian v the United Kingdom*[45] it expressly acknowledged this possibility, with the proviso that state courts should conduct the most thorough investigation possible in the cases that arise.

4. 'Duties and Responsibilities' of the Press

It is questionable whether the press has 'duties and responsibilities' when exercising its freedom. This wording is included in two documents that play an important role at the international level in the interpretation of freedom of expression and of the press: the European Convention on Human Rights (Article 10(2)) and the International Covenant on Civil and Political Rights (Article 19(3)). It is noteworthy that the texts do not mention these explicitly in relation to freedom of the press, but generally consider the freedom of expression. Nevertheless, the ECtHR, which monitors compliance with the Convention, clearly interprets these duties in relation to the press (media),[46] while it does not emphasise them for individual speakers.[47]

Peter Coe sums up the theory of the social responsibility of the press in his paper: according to this view, the press must act in the public interest, aiming to inform the public, as part of which it must follow standards of conduct that take into account the rights of others. In return it is entitled to additional protection compared with other persons exercising the freedom of expression or other press products not providing public interest information.[48] Damian Tambini argues that certain privileges are granted to the press 'based on a theory of the function and

---

[42] W Blackstone, *Commentaries on the Laws of England* Vol 4 (Chicago, IL, University of Chicago Press, [1765–69] 1979) 151.

[43] Examples of the constitutional prohibition of censorship, Grundgesetz (German Constitution) Art 5; Greek Constitution, Art 14; Dutch Constitution, Art 7; Luxembourg Constitution, Art 24.

[44] *Sunday Times (No 2)* (n 13).

[45] *Observer and Guardian* (n 13).

[46] *The Sunday Times v the United Kingdom (No 2)* [1979] App no 6538/74; *Observer and Guardian* (n 13); *Jersild v Denmark* (n 13) among other decisions.

[47] Oster (n 18) 36.

[48] P Coe, '(Re)Embracing Social Responsibility Theory as a Basis for Free Speech: Shifting the Normative Paradigm for a Modern Media' (2018) 69 *Northern Ireland Legal Quarterly* 403, 418–24.

role of the press in a democracy'.[49] The additional rights granted to the press and the additional duties associated with their exercise are thus in balance. According to Gibbons, private media companies can also have a public function in addition to their private interest activities.[50] Privately owned media enterprises need to both take into account the interests of their audiences and to impart diverse opinions.[51] Gibbons believes that the state cannot evade its responsibility to protect freedom of expression, especially with regard to fair participation in public discourse and access to opinions, and may use regulatory means to ensure this protection.[52] Eric Barendt notes that, by its nature, the media foster the exercise of freedom of expression,[53] and the regulation of the press must be judged in terms of its support for or inhibition of freedom of expression.[54] He refers to the right of reply as an example: if it expands the possibilities of public discourse, the regulation is acceptable despite the fact that it narrows the room for manoeuvre of the press.[55] In his later monograph, Barendt argues that the freedom of speech can be subject to regulation 'to make its exercise more effective'.[56] The social role of the press and the protection of freedom of expression can therefore confront each other, and the resolution of the conflict may only take place with a view to protecting public discourse.

The press not only reports on public debates but is also a catalyst for and participant in public discourse.[57] The press is a public forum; it is a place to publish thoughts and information that concern the public, but not in the sense of streets, squares and other public spaces – it is not open to anyone. An individual may not claim a right of access to the press for the purpose of publishing his opinion.[58] The public has a right of access to information on public affairs which involves much more than the right to freedom of information against the state. It is a strange kind of 'right': just as a right to access does not exist for the individual against the press, so this 'right to know' cannot be enforced; there is no duty to do so.

The press is free to report on what it wants, so it is possible to set up a newspaper to cover perfectly policy-free tabloid news or information on any topic, be it the culinary arts, DIY or imaginary superheroes. Nor does the theory of social

---

[49] D Tambini, *Media Freedom* (Cambridge, Polity Press, 2021) 67.

[50] T Gibbons, 'Free Speech, Communication and the State' in M Amos, J Harrison and L Woods (eds), *Freedom of Expression and the Media* (Leiden, Martinus Nijhoff, 2012) 33.

[51] ibid 39.

[52] ibid 42.

[53] E Barendt, 'Inaugural Lecture: Press and Broadcasting Freedom: Does Anyone Have any Rights to Free Speech?' (1991) 44 *Current Legal Problems* 63, 66.

[54] ibid 71.

[55] ibid 70–71.

[56] E Barendt, *Freedom of Speech* (Oxford, Oxford University Press, 2005) 69.

[57] E Carolan, 'Promoting Civic Discourse: A Form of Positive Free Speech under the Constitution of Ireland?' in AT Kenyon and A Scott (eds), *Positive Free Speech: Rationales, Methods and Implications* (Oxford, Hart Publishing, 2020) 76–79.

[58] G Marshall, 'Press Freedom and Free Speech Theory' [1992] *Public Law* 40, 50.

responsibility state that all press products must serve the public interest. Public interest content is indeed given greater protection by the courts, but this stems from the nature of the content and not from the identity of the speaker – the press has no additional rights over other speakers, just as it has no additional duties either.

Wragg argues that no duty can be imposed on the press, since there is no right to be set against it; the public cannot oblige the press to provide it with adequate information.[59] This is the weakness of the theory of social responsibility; the responsibility of the press is at best a moral expectation that cannot be enforced. Following Article 10(2) of the Convention, the ECtHR often refers in its decisions to 'duties and responsibilities', but this does not mean anything more than that the legal standards applicable to public speech must be complied with, both by the press or any another speaker.[60] At the same time, in the absence of an actual legal obligation, there are strong (and, in many cases, statutory) incentives for the media to report on public issues, which I will discuss later. Nevertheless, Jan Oster argues that the ECtHR actually takes the standards of 'ethical journalism' and 'responsible journalism' into account in its jurisprudence.[61]

After reviewing the case law of the Court, however, we cannot be sure that when it considers all the circumstances of the communication and applies ethical criteria in its decisions, it would indeed consider these criteria to be applicable only to the media and not to any speaker who exercises their general freedom of expression. The question arises whether the ethical standards for the street corner speaker is different from that of the media. The functioning and specific activities of the media (information gathering and its means, the use of effective language, editing, image selection, the tendency to use bombastic headlines, etc) naturally give rise to the need to comply with certain ethical standards, whereas these may not apply to the street corner speaker. The consideration of ethical aspects by the media is certainly not an 'obligation' in the legal sense because there is no legal right to be opposed to it. No one can demand that the media act ethically, and compliance with or failure to comply with ethical standards can only be a subsidiary consideration in determining the scope of media freedom.

The presentation of public issues and fostering of public discourse are not required by codified law or by any court, just as the right of individual access to the press is not guaranteed to anyone (which does not mean that access to the information published by the press shall not be guaranteed). The only exception to the latter, which is present in almost all European legal systems, is the right of reply. This right not only protects individual reputation – breached by the press – but

---

[59] Wragg (n 36) 83–109.
[60] ibid 91–92.
[61] See Oster, 'The Press Freedom Jurisprudence of the European Court of Human Rights', ch 11, section 4.2 in this volume.

also ensures that the public is informed of the false factual statements previously made by the press, and also of the truthful information relating to the given story. Such regulations are known Europe-wide, and they typically impose obligations on radio, printed and online press alike.[62] The legal systems of all EU Member States provide for a right of reply against the press[63] and Greece, Portugal and Slovenia even enshrine it in their constitutions.[64] The laws of most states are sufficient to ensure the right of reply in relation to false statements of fact, but in some states the applicant also has the right of reply to injurious statements (value judgements).[65] The compatibility of the right of reply and Article 10 has been confirmed by the ECtHR in several decisions.[66]

Mention should also be made of anti-concentration rules aimed at the diversity of press ownership, which restrict acquisition of ownership in the media market, including the press market.[67] Such restrictions are widespread across Europe, although they do not impose a duty directly on publishers of existing press products and can only prevent future acquisitions. The purpose of the restriction is to allow as many voices as possible to be present in the public arena, and as such it does not relate to the content but to the diversity of the proprietors. This may also imply a diversity of speakers and their opinions, but not necessarily.

The codes applied by the bodies implementing the self-regulation of the press may go beyond the legal regulation in prescribing the public interest tasks of the press. Accuracy and correctness and protection of privacy are typically included in European press self-regulatory codes,[68] albeit without actual binding force. However, the breach of ethical standards set in journalistic codes can indirectly influence the decisions of the courts. That was the case in *Stoll v Switzerland*,[69] where the manner in which the applicant obtained confidential

---

[62] K Ho Youm, 'The Right of Reply and Freedom of the Press: An International and Comparative Perspective' (2008) 76 *George Washington Law Review* 1017; A Richter, 'Right of Reply: International Standards and Slovak Press Law' (2019) 1–2 *Otázky žurnalistiky* 4.

[63] See, eg, French Press Act (n 31) Arts 12–13; Italian Press Act (n 31) s 8; Nederlands Burgerlijk Wetboek (Civil Code of the Netherlands) Book 6, Art 167.

[64] See Greek Constitution, Art 14(5); Portuguese Constitution, Art 37(4); Slovenian Constitution, Art 40.

[65] Finnish Media Act (n 31) c 3, Art 8; loi du 8 juin 2004 sur la liberté d'expression dans les médias (Luxembourg Media Act) Art 36; French Media Act (n 31) Art 13; Loi no 82-652 du 29 juillet 1982 sur la communication audiovisuelle (French Audio-visual Act) Art 6; Constitution of Portugal, Art 34(4); Lei no 2/99 de 13 de Janeiro, Art 24; Constitution of Greece, s 14; Ministerial Decree no 100/2000 on Private Purpose Audio and Audio-visual Media, Art 9; Act 1730/1987 on Public Service Radio and Television, Arts 3(12)–3(14); Act 1092/1938 on Printed Media, Arts 37–38; Att dwar l-istampa, XL (1974) (Maltese Press Act) Art 21.

[66] *Ediciones Tiempo SA v Spain* [1989] App no 13010/87; *Melnychuk v Ukraine* [2005] App no 28743/03; *Kaperzyński v Poland* [2012] App no 43206/07; *Eker v Turkey* [2017] App no 24016/05.

[67] Barendt (n 56) 429–33.

[68] Fielden (n 38) 65–70.

[69] *Stoll v Switzerland* [2007] App no 69698/01.

information and the form, tone and aim of the article were factors taken into account by the ECtHR in its decision that established no violation of Article 10 of the Convention.[70]

5. Privileges Granted to the Press

The public interest duties imposed on the press actually exist only to a limited extent in the legislation, yet the additional rights of the press are recognised by all legal systems. To whom should legal systems grant additional rights? Certain rules in some jurisdictions – such as the UK's law on the protection of journalistic sources[71] – are worded in general terms, protecting not only the press but also anyone who reaches out to the public and makes their views or some information known. This is not an unjustified approach, as not only the press but also an individual speaker can provide information to the public. However, most rules granting such privileges refer to the press or to journalists specifically. In this case, it is up to the courts to decide who is considered to be covered by the rule; only professional media actors or journalists, or instead even amateurs, lone bloggers or social media users, if they otherwise carry out regular information activities by the means available to them.

The case law of the ECtHR has also addressed the issue of the limits of these rights in a number of cases, and the Council of Europe's recommendation also mentions the granting of additional rights to the press by Member States as a matter of course.[72] An overview of European legal systems reveals a wide range of additional rights.

5.1. Protection of Journalistic Sources

The privileges of the press and journalists include their right not to be required to disclose their sources of information. A wealth of information comes to the press from confidential sources who only contribute to informing the public on condition that they remain anonymous. The maintenance of the confidentiality of sources is integral to the freedom of the press as, lacking such a guarantee, the media would be barred from a wide range of confidential information of public interest which, in turn, would impede the right of the public to information.

---

[70] ibid paras [140]–[152].
[71] Contempt of Court Act 1981, s 10.
[72] Recommendation CM/Rec(2011)7 of the Committee of Ministers to member states on a new notion of media, paras 42, 70–73.

The protection of the sources of information, however, may not be unlimited; in certain cases, the protection of the public interest may call for the revelation of the journalist's sources.[73]

Most European legal systems guarantee the freedom of journalistic sources. The case law of the ECtHR sets out the requirements that state regulations must meet:

- the opportunity to resort to preliminary court revision against the first decision;

- the statutory limitation shall be in accordance with the provisions of Article 10(2) of the Convention, that is, limitation shall be properly substantiated;

- the limitation is possible only when the authorities do not have alternative ways of obtaining the relevant information;

- the limitation should be proportionate, that is, revealing the identity of information sources should take place in exceptional cases only, when so justified by threat to human life or health or particularly significant public interest;

- in the context of protecting information sources, the opportunity to reject delivery of documents, deeds and data media shall also be provided for;

- no burden of proof may be required for the exercise of the right of information source protection.[74]

5.2. Protection against Search and Seizure

A right that is related to the protection of sources, which can also be interpreted separately from it, is that of protection against house searches and the seizure of tools and data carriers used by journalists. Such rules are also widespread, without which the right to protection of sources would be meaningless. Examples include the United Kingdom (UK), German or French rules,[75] each of which lay down the relevant rules as the rights of journalists and the press, subject to the necessary restrictions. The case law of the ECtHR on this right is also rich.[76]

---

[73] For national regulations see, eg, the UK's Contempt of Court Act 1981, s 10; and Germany's Strafprozeßordnung – StPO 7 April 1987 (law on criminal procedure) Art 53(1)5 and Zivilprozessordnung (law on civil procedure) Art 383(5)1.

[74] See, among other decisions, *Goodwin v the United Kingdom* no 17488/90; *Financial Times Ltd and Others v the United Kingdom* no 821/03; *Sanoma Uitgevers BV v the Netherlands* no 38224/03; *Voskuil v the Netherlands* no 64752/01; *Telegraaf Media Nederland Landelijke Media BV and Others v the Netherlands* no 39315/06; *Becker v Norway* no 21272/12.

[75] Police and Criminal Evidence Act 1984 (UK) s 13; Strafprozeßordnung 7 April 1987, Art 97(5)(1) (Germany); Code de procédure pénale (French Criminal Code) Art 56(2).

[76] *Nordisk Film & TV A/S v Denmark* [2005] App no 40485/02; *Roemen and Schmit v Luxembourg* [2003] App no 51772/99; *Ernst and Others v Belgium* [2003] App no 33400/96; *Tillack v Belgium* [2007] App no 20477/05; *Martin and Others v France* [2012] App no 30002/08; *Ressiot and Others v France*

5.3. Exemption from the Duty to Testify in Court Proceedings

In addition to the protection of sources, some jurisdictions provide, within certain limits, an exemption for journalists from the obligation to testify in court proceedings if the reason for the summons is related to their journalistic activities. This privilege is strongly linked to the right to source protection.[77]

5.4. Access Rights

The collection of news and information is supported by certain 'access rights' which grant journalists access to places that are otherwise closed to the public or to which they have limited access. These may include prisons, government buildings, press conferences, the otherwise restricted areas in courtrooms or parliament buildings, or any place or institution which, for some reason, even on a case-by-case basis, the press may need access to.[78] They may even have special access rights to public protests, disaster areas and crime scenes. Nor is this right of the press unrestricted, in fact, if necessary, it may be proportionately restricted: in *Pentikäinen v Finland*,[79] the request of a journalist who did not leave the scene of a violent demonstration despite a call from the police was rejected by the ECtHR.[80] The right of access is not always limited to the press: the Parliament's gallery and the courtroom are, as a general rule, open to all, but the press also has additional rights in these places (for example, the possibility of recording and interviewing). In other cases, such as in a prison or at a press conference, only members of the press may be present. A specific case of the right of access is the right to distribute a press product in places closed to the public: in one case, the ECtHR found that a ban on distribution at a military base that affected a magazine for no good reason violated the Convention.[81]

5.5. Protection of Investigative Journalism

Certain legal systems specifically protect investigative journalism and may even provide immunity from liability for wrongdoing. The ECtHR is reluctant to

---

[2012] App no 15054/07; *Saint-Paul Luxembourg SA v Luxembourg* [2013] App no 26419/10; *Nagla v Latvia* [2013] App no 73469/10; *Stichting Ostade Blade v the Netherlands* [2014] App no 8406/06; *Ivaschenko v Russia* [2018] App no 61064/10.

[77] See, eg, the German Criminal and Civil Procedural Law Rules: Strafprozessordnung, Art 53(1)(5), Zivilprozessordnung, Art 383(1)(5).

[78] eg, a refugee camp, as in *Szurovecz v Hungary* [2020] App no 15428/16.

[79] *Pentikäinen v Finland* [2015] App no 11882/10.

[80] See also *Butkevich v Russia* [2018] App no 5865/07.

[81] *Demokratischer Soldaten Österreichs and Gubi v Austria* [1994] App no 15153/89.

establish the breach of Article 10 in cases where the previous convictions were related to illegal preparatory acts of newsgathering.[82] At the same time an investigative journalist may choose the method of obtaining information which he uses, and in the meantime he has the right to keep the fact of his being a journalist secret.[83] A related issue is the possibility of publishing illegally obtained information and recordings. The law does not give a general permission to the press to do such things, but the courts may consider conflicting interests and may even decide that although a member of the press has obtained information illegally, its disclosure was not infringing.[84]

5.6. Anonymous Expression

The right of speakers (as opposed to 'sources') to remain anonymous in Europe does not necessarily follow from the constitutional protection of freedom of the press,[85] although this does not preclude it from being provided for by certain legislation or contractual arrangements. There are many examples of the latter in online communication – recognition of the right of journalists to remain anonymous is less frequent. Finnish law provides this right for publishers and media service providers, who may thus refuse to identify any of their authors.[86] On the contrary, other states may even oblige the press to reveal the identity of their authors.

5.7. Editorial Independence and 'Internal Freedom of the Press'

The essence of internal freedom of the press is that a journalist should not be obliged to do or refrain from doing something that would be contrary to the professional requirements of his profession or press ethical norms, or, if he resists such instructions, he should not be disadvantaged under labour law.[87] In certain cases, journalists and editors may be entitled – at least theoretically – to freedom of the press vis-á-vis the owner of the press product or media service. Only a few countries have introduced rules about this, and the rights they guarantee – the scope of the so-called 'internal freedom of the press', that is, within the organisation of the press, is not very wide. Editorial independence in this case is at most external – for instance, it may be exempt from government interference.

---

[82] *Erdtmann v Germany* App no 56328/10; *Brambilla and Others v Italy* [2016] App no 22567/09; *Salihu and Others v Sweden* App no 33628/15.
[83] *Nordisk Film & TV A/S* (n 76).
[84] *Radio Twist AS v Slovakia* no 62202/00; *Nagla* (n 76).
[85] E Barendt, *Anonymous Speech: Literature, Law and Politics* (London, Bloomsbury, 2016) 78–80.
[86] Finnish Act on Freedom of Expression in the Mass Media, s 16.
[87] CE Baker, *Human Liberty and Freedom of Speech* (Oxford, Oxford University Press, 1989) 262–66.

It can be argued that these rules may be contrary to the protection of freedom of the press, as they undoubtedly restrict the freedom of owners. In contrast, Gibbons argues that

> if freedom of the press has any significance, other than the owner's economic right to start a newspaper or his liberty to speak, it is in its identity with editorial autonomy conceived in this sense of serving a public interest in communication.[88]

According to Article 6(2) of the proposal of the European Media Freedom Act,

> media service providers providing news and current affairs content shall take measures that they deem appropriate with a view to guaranteeing the independence of individual editorial decisions. In particular, such measures shall aim to:
>
> (a) guarantee that editors are free to take individual editorial decisions in the exercise of their professional activity; and
>
> (b) ensure disclosure of any actual or potential conflict of interest by any party having a stake in media service providers that may affect the provision of news and current affairs content.[89]

The recital to the proposal states:

> Media integrity also requires a proactive approach to promote editorial independence by news media companies, in particular through internal safeguards. Media service providers should adopt proportionate measures to guarantee, once the overall editorial line has been agreed between their owners and editors, the freedom of the editors to take individual decisions in the course of their professional activity. The objective to shield editors from undue interference in their decisions taken on specific pieces of content as part of their everyday work contributes to ensuring a level playing field in the internal market for media services and the quality of such services.[90]

The Recommendation accompanying the proposal, which has already been published,[91] contains a catalogue of internal safeguards within media companies that could be used to implement the proposal. Among others, the Recommendation identifies the following: editorial mission statements; policies to promote a diverse and inclusive composition of editorial teams; rules to ensure the separation of commercial and editorial activities; procedures for reporting possible pressures (which may provide for the possibility to report pressures anonymously or confidentially); the right to object (which allows members of editorial teams to refuse to sign articles or other editorial content that has been changed without their knowledge or against their will); the possibility of invoking conscientious objection (which provides protection against disciplinary sanctions or arbitrary dismissal of

---

[88] T Gibbons, 'Freedom of the Press: Ownership and Editorial Values' [1992] *Public Law* 279, 289.

[89] Proposal for a regulation of the European Parliament and of the Council establishing a common framework for media services in the internal market (European Media Freedom Act) and amending Directive 2010/13/EU COM/2022/457 final.

[90] Recital (20) of the proposal.

[91] Commission Recommendation on internal safeguards for editorial independence and ownership transparency in the media sector C(2022) 6536 final.

members of the editorial board who refuse to carry out tasks which they consider to be contrary to professional standards); ethics or supervisory committees to monitor the implementation of internal rules; bodies responsible for the appointment, autonomy and independence of the editor-in-chief, etc.

The proposal has been the subject of a number of fundamental criticisms,[92] including the provisions of Article 6 cited above. If the proposal becomes law, the previously unsegmented right to freedom of the press would be differentiated according to the person exercising the right, and the freedom of media owners – who were previously the 'primary' holders of press freedom – would be subject to significant restrictions.

5.8. Tax and Other Benefits

Various tax benefits for the press can also be regarded as additional entitlements that indirectly and financially support the operation of the press. These include a sales tax rebate or reduced rate for printed products in some countries. Another such benefit is the setting of discounted postage rates for sending printed products which support the printed press.[93]

6. The Press as Primary Beneficiary of the Rules of General Application

The press is not only able to exercise the additional rights specifically granted to it; otherwise universal rights and exemptions from liability are in many cases primarily an actual advantage for the press. The obvious reason for this is that these rules are intended to protect public speech, and it is the press that exercises this right professionally on a day-to-day basis. In addition, the press can cause significant damage by violating the rights of others, and it naturally follows from these two characteristics that, even in the application of general legislation, the press is the one that exercises these rights most often or becomes a party to litigation.

6.1. Freedom of Information and Access to Government Information

Freedom of information laws are widespread in Europe and allow anyone to access data of public interest.[94] Information in the public interest is information held by

---

[92] 'We're fine as we are, Press tells EU as Brussels plans media freedom law' (*Politico.eu*, 16 September 2022), available at: www.politico.eu/article/eu-law-to-protect-media-freedom-scares-off-press-publishers.

[93] Barendt (n 56) 427–29.

[94] Freedom of Information Act 2000 (UK); Informationsfreiheitsgesetz, 5 September 2005 (Germany); Legge 6 novembre 2012, no 190, Decreto legislativo 14 marzo 2013, no 33 (Italy).

state bodies, local government or other bodies performing public tasks and relating to their activities or generated in the performance of their public task, the disclosure of which is not restricted (for instance, for the purposes of national security or for the protection of personal data). These laws do not explicitly grant additional rights to the press, but it is clear that it is the press which is able to exercise these rights in a truly effective way. It is the business of the press to concern itself with the procedure of obtaining the data, to interpret the information thus obtained and to use it in the course of its journalistic activities. Typically, the ECtHR invoked freedom of the press even when the applicant was not a journalist or publisher of a press product but a non-governmental organisation: refusing to provide information of public interest could infringe both freedom of expression and freedom of the press.[95] However, freedom of information laws do not generally require access to information held by governments; there is no such general right.[96]

6.2. Protection of Personality Rights and the Protection from their Excessive Application

Of the personality rights, the right to privacy and the right to reputation are those most often violated by public communication. This entails that an important element of freedom of the press is protection against the unjustified, excessive application of rules protecting these rights.[97] The court proceedings that have fundamentally shaped the case law in this area have typically been initiated following press communications. It makes sense that in proceedings to protect these rights, it is the press, and not individual speakers, which is most often on one side.

6.3. Data Protection

The protection of personal data can also be a barrier to public communication. Within the EU, the relevant issues are primarily governed by the GDPR which is directly applicable in all Member States,[98] but beyond that, there are additional statutory rules that are binding only in that particular State. The GDPR explicitly mentions, among other exceptions, the 'journalistic purposes', which may allow exceptions to be made to the strict data protection rules. Article 85(1) mentions journalism as a form of expression; in other words, it is clear that exceptions that can be defined by a Member State may also apply to speakers beyond the press.[99] The situation is similar for the right of erasure (also known as the right

---

[95] *Társaság a Szabadságjogokért v Hungary (TASZ)* [2009] App no 37374/05.
[96] Oster (n 18) 95–101.
[97] Recommendation CM/Rec(2011)7 (n 72) para 97.
[98] Regulation (EU) 2016/679 (n 22).
[99] For the overview of European regulations, see *Journalism and Media Privilege* (Strasbourg, European Audiovisual Observatory, 2017); B Wong, 'The Journalism Exception in UK Data Protection Law' (2020) 12 *Journal of Media Law* 216.

to be forgotten), where Article 17(3)(a) of the GDPR mentions, as an exception to the obligation to ensure the right to delete personal data, situations where the processing is necessary 'for the exercise of the right to freedom of expression and information'. It is clear, however, that these exceptions can most often be used by the press, due to the nature of its activities.[100]

6.4. Copyright

Copyright regulation is also a widely harmonised area within the EU. A member of the press may be exempted from the requirement to strictly protect copyrighted works and the obligation to acquire the consent of the copyright holder for the use of his work, in view of his information duties. The EU Directive also specifies the press and sets out the purpose of providing information and coverage of daily events, which form the basis for the free and complimentary use of copyright works.[101] This Directive gives Member States the option of granting exemptions, of which they do make use.[102] (Apart from EU regulation, several international treaties also exist in the field of copyright.)[103]

6.5. Protection for Whistle-Blowers

Whistle-blowers should not be retaliated against because they have exposed abuses, the exposure of which serves the public interest. Such notifiers, if they are determined to act, may contact either the public authority competent in the matter or the press. The French legal system provides protection for them in a separately identified way.[104] The protection of whistle-blowers is not a right of the press, as the press can in any case ensure their anonymity through the right to protection of sources, but the press is also the beneficiary of the rules protecting them, as it has a better chance of accessing important and worthwhile content. A particularly unique problem is when journalists themselves become whistle-blowers of abuses. The ECtHR has ruled in cases where journalists have drawn public attention to abuses by their own employers and ECtHR decisions have protected journalists from sanctions by their employer.[105]

---

[100] See also D Erdos, *European Data Protection Regulation, Journalism, and Traditional Publishers: Balancing on a Tightrope?* (Oxford, Oxford University Press, 2019).

[101] Directive 2001/29/EC (n 23) Art 5(3)(c).

[102] See the UK's Copyright, Designs and Patents Act 1988, Art 30(2); for the relevant regulation of further nine European countries, see *Journalism and Media Privilege* (n 99).

[103] Most importantly, the Berne Convention for the Protection of Literary and Artistic Works, from 1886.

[104] Loi no 2016-1691 du 9 décembre 2016 relative à la transparence, à la lutte contre la corruption et à la modernisation de la vie économique és Code pénal, Art L.122-9.

[105] *Matúz v Hungary* [2014] App no 73571/10; *Wojtas-Kaleta v Poland* [2009] App no 20436/02.

7. Regulating the Content of the Press Beyond the Limits of Free Speech

The general restrictions on freedom of expression should apply, *mutatis mutandis*, to press speech. The protection of reputation, safeguards on privacy, limitations on hate speech, etc are determined in each legal system by taking into account the extent to which a given speech act can be considered to be participation in the discussion of public affairs. The purpose and content of the speech, not the person of the speaker, determine the degree of freedom. Accordingly, the press as a speaker has no additional duties compared with other speakers, and the general restrictions on freedom of speech also apply to it. However, as Coe warns, ethical and bona fide conduct by the press and adherence to standards of conduct for its activities can be an important consideration in deciding whether a particular piece of content is permissible.[106] In order to assess whether the press can enjoy broad protection of freedom of expression at all, it may be necessary to take into account certain behavioural expectations. All this does not lead to any additional protection for the press or to additional duties or expectations being imposed on it, since acting in good faith, exercising diligence, taking steps with a view to exploring reality, etc may be relevant considerations for all speakers. However, objective duties may arise from the objective differences between speakers; it is clear that the press must act differently, for example in ascertaining the truthfulness of the information it conveys, to the individual speaker who, in his spare time, forms an opinion on certain public matters.

The press, like any other speaker, must adhere to the norms that restrict public speaking. However, operating in accordance with the legal regulations alone does not make the press, or the public sphere in general, suitable as a venue for thorough, multifaceted discussions and discussions on important public affairs that help the public to make the right decisions. This is due to the widespread protection of freedom of expression, which also allows – to a certain, and not insignificant extent – insults, expressions of hatred or the spread of untruths.

For the press, not only general legislation but also legal norms that are specifically binding on the press may impose a duty that directly affects the content they publish. 'Content regulation' is not the most reassuring term when it comes to freedom of the press, but it does not really mean anything more than the restrictions on freedom of the press that are specifically defined by the legislature to regulate the activities of the press. Standards aimed at regulating the specific content of the press are most often enshrined in the press laws of individual states, and violations of these laws may give rise to either criminal or civil liability. The use of press laws to define these rules can in fact only be seen as a simple legal means, and duties in criminal and civil proceedings could be enshrined in a country's criminal or civil law, so content regulation in press law alone does not impose

---

[106] Coe (n 48) 423.

a real additional burden on the press. Of course, it is very important what these rules are and how judicial practice can relax their potentially strict application to protect public discourses. Typical areas regulated by press laws include the protection of reputation[107] and privacy,[108] the restriction of 'hate speech'[109] or rules for the protection of minors.[110]

At the same time, the public interest duties and social responsibility of the press are usually not prescribed by special content regulations concerning the press. The exceptions to this are the Danish, Polish and Luxembourg regulations. These national legal systems impose certain obligations – with ethical content – at least in cases where the media outlet in question wishes to provide information in the public interest. Danish law requires compliance with general rules of press ethics without setting the ethical standards themselves, and only requires the publication of a condemnation decision of the Press Council as a sanction.[111] Polish press law requires the press to present the events it covers 'truthfully'.[112] It is the duty of the journalist to serve society and the state, and in doing so, he must exercise due diligence in his work, strive for accuracy, protect his informants, and use language correctly, avoiding profanity.[113] However, the Press Act does not provide for the liability of journalists in the event of non-compliance with the above provisions. Luxembourg media law also requires the press to verify the accuracy of the information obtained.[114] Failure to comply with this duty may result in a defamation procedure, that is, inaccuracy or error alone does not give rise to legal liability under the regulation.

In addition to press laws, other laws may apply specifically to the press. The range of these can be wide, so I will only mention two regulatory topics here. Special rules apply to reporting on ongoing court proceedings in order to protect the order of the judiciary. The UK's Contempt of Court Act 1981, for example, sets out detailed rules for what and how the press can report, and these duties may even prevent them from being present at trials.[115] The openness of the courtroom or the closure of the trial and recordings in the courtroom is a similar issue regulated by the legal systems.[116] Another area of regulation that is particularly important to the press is the regulation of advertising or, more broadly, commercial

---

[107] French Press Act (n 31) Art 29; Italian Press Act (n 31) Arts 12–13; Luxembourg Media Act (n 65) Arts 16–17; Maltese Press Act (n 65) Arts 11–12.

[108] Luxembourg Media Act (n 65) Arts 14–15.

[109] French Press Act (n 31) Arts 23–24.

[110] Italian Press Act (n 31) Art 14; Luxembourg Media Act (n 65) Art 18.

[111] Danish Law on the Liability of Media (n 33) ss 34 and 43.

[112] Polish Press Act (n 41) Art 6.

[113] ibid Arts 10 and 12.

[114] Luxembourg Media Act (n 65) Arts 10–11.

[115] Barendt (n 56) 145–48.

[116] See I Cram, *A Virtue Less Cloistered. Courts, Speech and Constitutions* (Oxford, Hart Publishing, 2002); on the British law, see also J Jaconelli, *Open Justice: A Critique of the Public Trial* (Oxford, Oxford University Press, 2002); J Bosland and J Townend, 'Open Justice, Transparency and the Media: Representing the Public Interest in the Physical and Virtual Courtroom' (2018) 23 *Communications Law* 183; P Wragg, 'Open Justice and Privacy' (2017) 22 *Communications Law* 90.

communication, which can contain specific norms relevant to the press. All this is reflected in EU law,[117] or may appear in national regulations in addition to harmonised issues.

In order to avoid the damage and dangers that can be caused by the exercise of freedom of the press, steps can be taken not only through mandatory legal regulation but also through self-regulation of the press. The codes of conduct applied by self-regulatory organisations seek to influence the activities of the press in a variety of ways, which are more varied than legal norms. These codes may contain content requirements, in areas such as respect for privacy, protection of minors and publication of information on criminal offences, as well as elements that are missing from the legal framework, chiefly because enforcing them as a legal norm would presumably be incompatible with the constitutional protection of freedom of the press. These rules may apply to the process of producing content, the information gathering activity of the press, and not necessarily the published content itself.

Under certain circumstances, the freedom of the press can be broader than the freedom of individual speakers, namely when the press reports on the speeches of others. If the press informs credibly and accurately that someone has said or communicated something relating to the discussion of a public matter, the press may be released from liability, even if the information it provides is otherwise infringing. For example, if a statement made by the press violates someone's right to protection of reputation, the original speaker can, of course, be sued, but the press, if it has remained within the terms of its coverage, cannot. This principle applies in many European countries,[118] and in the practice of the ECtHR.[119] It is not only the press that can rely on the defence of reporting, that is, the transmission of information from others, but in practice it typically protects the press, and courts and constitutional courts also loosen the framework of typically more rigid legal regulations where the press is concerned.[120]

8. On the Aims and Further Chapters of this Book

In this volume, we look at the legal systems of nine European countries to see how these democracies approach the fundamental right of freedom of the press and

---

[117] See, eg, Directive 2005/29/EC of the European Parliament and of the Council of 11 May 2005 concerning unfair business-to-consumer commercial practices in the internal market [2005] OJ L149/22 (the Unfair Commercial Practices Directive) s 11 of Annex I; Directive 2003/33/EC of the European Parliament and of the Council of 26 May 2003 on the approximation of the laws, regulations and administrative provisions of the Member States relating to the advertising and sponsorship of tobacco products [2003] OJ L152/16, Art 3.

[118] See the English Defamation Act 1996, ss 14–15 and sch 1 (Qualified privilege).

[119] *Thorgeirson v Iceland* no 13778/88; *Bladet Tromsø* (n 13); *Thoma* (n 13); *Selistö v Finland* [2004] App no 56767/00.

[120] See, eg, the Hungarian Constitutional Court Decision no 34/2017 (XII. 11.) AB. See also *Magyar Jeti Zrt v Hungary* [2018] App no 11257/16.

how they regulate it, and in another chapter we analyse the relevant case law of the ECtHR. The list of countries is by definition not exhaustive, but we have tried to select states from all geographical regions, whose overview gives an overall outline of the common European category of press freedom. Each chapter also provides a theoretical underpinning of press freedom and a historical overview. It is believed that the current concept of press freedom can only be understood in the light of different national histories, which vary considerably from country to country, but that the process of European unification that began at the end of the twentieth century has led to a convergence of national regulations which makes it meaningful to speak of 'European' press freedom. We are also aware that an adequate legal environment, including sufficient constitutional protection, legislation and consistent judicial decisions to ensure a sensitive balance between protection and restriction, is only one of the necessary but not sufficient conditions for the effective existence of press freedom, both to protect the press and to provide safeguards against excesses of the press. At the same time, we believe that jurisprudence fulfils its role by examining these issues and leaving the rest to other social sciences, democratic decision-making and the public itself, civil society more broadly, which can assert its expectations of the press and of the government of the day.

The authors of this volume present the legal system of their own countries (with the obvious exception of the case law of the ECtHR), and are therefore familiar with the rules they present from the inside. They are also internationally recognised scholars who present their subject of study in an unbiased manner, highlighting the achievements but not obscuring the difficulties. The volume does not seek to compare national legal systems but to present them side by side, and in this sense is comparative.

Along with Paul Wragg, the co-editor of this volume, we are convinced that the history of press freedom in Europe, however advanced and rich its regulation and practice, is not a closed story, and that not only the issues raised by new technologies but also the regulatory issues of traditional media are worthy of further reflection. It is a long time since international readers have had access to a volume that addresses the issues examined here in a comprehensive way, taking into account national specificities. The present volume – and its forthcoming companion which will cover the perception and regulation of press freedom in non-European countries – seeks to fill this gap, hopefully successfully. But that is for the reader to judge.

2

Danish Perspectives on Press Regulation

STEN SCHAUMBURG-MÜLLER

1. Introduction

Denmark belongs to the Northern European type of media system: there is a high level of journalistic professionalism, a low level of political parallelism (that is journalists pursuing political agendas), generous media subsidies, a large public service commitment and low level of ownership regulation.[1] As regards professionalism, most journalists have graduated from one (or more) of three schools of journalism, two of which are connected to universities. Based on my own experience,[2] which includes contact with journalists from a wide variety of media, Danish journalists are serious, genuine, often very good researchers and keen to get things right.[3] This does not, of course, imply that everything is perfect. Journalists make mistakes, they sometimes arrive at conclusions too quickly, they may be superficial, etc, but in general, Danish journalists are highly professional. They do score low when it comes to rankings of the public's trust in professions, – close to but higher than the ratings of second-hand car dealers and politicians[4] – but relatively high when it comes to trust in national newspapers and broadcasters.[5]

The Danish daily press is, by and large, not affiliated with political parties or interests. The three national omnibus newspapers originally emerged from the

---

[1] M Brüggemann et al, 'Hallin and Mancini Revisited: Four Empirical Types of Western Media Systems' (2014) 64 *Journal of Communication* 1037.

[2] For the present contribution I have carried out small-scale interviews with two media and journalist scholars, a lawyer from Danish media and the chairman of the Journalists' Union. Besides, I am in almost daily contact with journalists.

[3] According to the Press Ethical Rules, the press has an obligation to correctness, see section 4.2 below.

[4] The yearly trustworthiness measure 2021 by Radius, available at: radiuscph.dk/cases/trovaerdighedsanalysen.

[5] KC Schrøder, M Blach-Ørsten and M Kæmsgaard Eberholst, *Danskernes brug af nyhedsmedier 2020* (Roskilde, Roskilde Universitet, 2020).

party newspapers of the Conservatives, the Liberals and the Social Liberals. There is no longer any direct affiliation, but the approach of each is recognisable. The large public media institution, DR (Danmarks Radio) has a legal obligation to public service and neutrality,[6] and this is also true of the national television station, TV2. There are a few politically affiliated media, and a large number of magazines published by parties, organisations, trade unions, etc. Since the advent of social media, politicians often prefer to present themselves directly without the intervention of (potentially critical) journalists.

Subsidies for the media in 2022 amounted to a total of 4.3 billion Danish kroner (€578 million), a large part of which, 3.7 billion, went to the DR (the public Danish Broadcasting Corporation).[7] A substantial amount, 387 million is distributed to all sorts of media, including private media, which may apply for support according to politically agreed general criteria. In addition, the daily newspapers are VAT exempted (magazines are not).

As for public service commitment, the DR is legally required to offer a public service, and the same goes for other broadcasters, while most newspapers also largely take a public service approach. In return, Denmark has a low level of media ownership regulation. There are no specific rules on media ownership, including foreign ownership. Broadcasting from Denmark requires permission, but there is no restriction on broadcasting to a Danish audience from abroad.[8] The main relevant regulation is the Competition Act, which basically implements European Union (EU) law.

Summing up, and corroborated by the interviews, the press generally performs well when it comes to supplying the public with relevant information and analyses on societal issues, sport, art, culture, politics, etc, as well as critically digging into the (dubious) exercise of power (be it public or private) and providing space for opinions and discussions.[9] For this reason, I cannot recognise the picture painted by the call for contributions to this book:

> The press, especially the printed press, causes demonstrable harm to others. It vilifies groups and cultures; it invades, routinely, the privacy of individuals (whether famous or not); it traduces reputations; it neglects its status as a trusted source of information.

---

[6] With some Supreme Court cases dealing with equal presentation in connection with elections and referenda, U1960.33H and U1989.148H respectively (U for *Ugeskrift for Retsvæsen*, the weekly law report, 1960 for year, 33 for page and H for Højesteret, the Supreme Court; V indicates the Western High Court, Ø does the Eastern High Court, and B a city court. If the year is followed by a 'B', this indicates the literary part of the law report).

[7] The political media agreement, available at: www.regeringen.dk/aktuelt/publikationer-og-aftaletekster/medieaftale-for-2022-2025-den-demokratiske-samtale-skal-styrkes.

[8] The TV3 Channel broadcasts in Danish from Stockholm to Danish audience. See for more details on the various regulations section 4 and section 5 below.

[9] I use the term 'press' covering the printed press and broadcasting television and radio, unless otherwise indicated. For the present purpose I do not include social media.

By and large, the opposite is the case in Denmark.

This does not imply that everything works perfectly. In my judgement, the Danish press face the following problems and challenges. *Minorities* are underrepresented in the press, among journalists and even among journalism students. Minorities figures in the press when it comes to crime and special minority issues, but apart from that, minorities seldom appear. Perhaps the picture is improving, as the press realises that there is a problem with consequences for democracy, and that minorities may form a hitherto neglected market. *Political interference* is not a big problem; nevertheless it is a problem. The DR constitutes an important part of the press, and as an institution it is tax funded, while politicians tend to have difficulties in combining the protection of the freedom of the press with pursuing their own interests. As examples, a successful radio station was established in 2011, but closed in 2019. It appears that two large parties in Parliament were criticised and caricatured by the radio station more than others, and these two parties blocked the continuation of state support. Another example could be the attempts to interfere in DR's covering of Danish participation in the invasion of Iraq in 2004. This interference was not directly successful, but the mere existence of such an attempt by the politicians who are also the fund distributors may have had an adverse impact on the DR's prospect of delivering critical journalism.[10]

Probably the greatest challenge the media face in Denmark is the *development of digital media*. First, the press has been slow and even somewhat reluctant to adapt to the new technological developments. It seems to be a pervasive perception that paper print is somehow more serious and of a higher quality than web editions. At least initially, the web editions were indeed of lower quality – and free, with the result that it has been difficult to convince Danes to pay for quality online press. Secondly, non-Danish social media such as Facebook and TikTok have also been very successful in becoming the main sources of information for a large and seemingly growing part of the population.[11] This has direct repercussion for the press, as the social media companies appropriate large parts of their revenue from commercials. It also has repercussions for the public at large as the social media companies do not create public service content, do not fund independent journalism, and edit their content by means of untransparent algorithms, not by journalistic considerations.

---

[10] See, eg, Lisbeth Knudsen, 'Medierne og Irak-krigen' *Berlingste Tidende* (13 August 2013) (one of the three national omnibus newspapers), available at: www.berlingske.dk/internationalt/medierne-og-irak-krigen.

[11] See Ministry of Culture, 'Mediernes udvikling i Danmark' 2021, English summary, available at: mediernesudvikling.kum.dk/fileadmin/user_upload/dokumenter/medier/Mediernes_udvikling/2021/Overblik_og_perspektivering/Summary_and_discourse_2021.pdf; Danske Medier on young people's use of media, available at: danskemedier.dk/branchetal-statistik/unges-nyhedsvaner-paa-some.

2. Theory of Press Freedom

2.1. 'The Fourth State Power'

There seems to be no particular Danish theory of press freedom. In the Danish Constitution and in its legal doctrine, press freedom is understood as a part of freedom of expression[12] (see section 3 and section 4 below). It may be worth noting that the press is often referred to as the 'fourth state power',[13] which seems to be a mistranslation of the term 'fourth estate'. However, this may in fact be conceived of as more than an error.

First, it indicates that the press is paramount to the division of powers. In the Danish Constitution, as in many others, the tripartition of powers is established: 'Legislative authority shall be vested in the King and the Folketing conjointly. Executive authority shall be vested in the King. Judicial authority shall be vested in the courts of justice'.[14] To refer to the press as the 'fourth state power' seems to indicate that a proper division of power cannot function without a free press, where abuse of power can be brought to light, relevant matters can be discussed, etc. According to Montesquieu, there can be no freedom if there is no division of powers,[15] and there appears to be a more or less explicit assumption that freedom cannot be guaranteed solely through a tripartition of state powers. It also requires a forum for publicity, that is the press. Secondly, the term 'fourth state power' implies that it is not overly important whether a power is actually a state power or not, as long as it is a power. Thus, the press is conceived of as a necessary power, implying on the one hand that the role of the press is paramount to democracy and freedom, and on the other hand that the press is a power which in itself must be contained.

Perhaps it may also be relevant at this point to outline what could be called the Danish ideal of democracy, the 'dialogue democracy' (*samtaledemokrati*). The term was coined by the theologian Hal Koch, who in 1940 delivered some highly popular speeches which were published after the Nazi-German occupation.[16] According to Koch, democracy is not a system but a mode of life, and democracy is definitely not about voting down any minority but about listening, talking and exchanging views, etc. In this connection, it is worth noting that in Denmark majority governments are rare, and when they do occur, they never consist only of one party. For the press, this indicates that it is not so much a marketplace of ideas but rather a forum for distributing information and exchanging views, or a dialogue between different actors.

---

[12] I use the term 'freedom of expression' covering freedom of speech as well as freedom of information.
[13] In Danish: 'Den fjerde statsmagt'.
[14] Section 3; translation from the official website of the Danish Parliament, available at: www.ft.dk/-/media/pdf/publikationer/english/my_constitutional_act_with_explanations.ashx.
[15] Montesquieu, *De l'esprit des lois* (Paris, Garnier, [1758] 1973) Book 11, ch 6.
[16] H Koch, *Hvad er demokrati?* (1945).

2.2. Historical Background

Danish history, including the history of its press, has been relatively undramatic. From 1848 to 1849, there was a relatively calm transition from (soft) absolutism to (soft) democracy.[17] During the period of absolutism, the judiciary was highly independent, and the government administration was rule of law based. Freedom of the press, however, was limited, as it was necessary to acquire police authorisation in order to publish anything, be it newspapers, posters, books, etc. The 1849 Constitution institutionalised the tripartition of powers and guaranteed the freedom of the press (see more constitutional details in section 3 below). The relationship between the king, the government and the Parliament was not clearly spelled out, however, and in the latter part of the nineteenth century there was an increasing discrepancy between the majority of the Lower House (the Folketing) and the government. Over time, freeholder peasants increasingly began to organise themselves and became a major political power, including through the Venstre party (the 'Left' as opposed to the conservative Højre, the 'Right'). In 1901, the king gave in, appointing a Prime Minister who had the backing of the majority of the Lower House. At the same time, the workers' and the employers' organisations entered into an agreement recognising the workers' right to strike and the employers' right to direct and distribute work. This laid the foundations for a tradition of political compromises rather than political principles.

For the press, the Constitution meant no censorship, and newspapers flourished. By the turn of the century, the press was largely connected to parties, with three major parties operating: the party of the freeholder peasants (Venstre), another representing large proprietors (Højre) and a third one of the workers (the Social Democrats). Thus, most towns and counties had three newspapers. In 1905, the smallholders broke loose from Venstre and formed the Radikale Venstre, which literally translates into 'the Radical Left', but in fact is a Social Liberal party. As mentioned above, the three major Danish omnibus newspapers can trace their history to the Conservatives, the Liberals and the Social Liberals.[18] Throughout this period, it appears that the press was recognised as an important part of the democracy, and the regulation of the press was generally liberal and supportive – with two temporary exceptions: in the late nineteenth century, with its king-based minority rule including serious restrictions on freedom of speech and of the press; and during the Nazi-German occupation between 1940 and 1945 which largely overruled democracy and the protection of rights.

---

[17] This is true for the Kingdom of Denmark, less so for the Duchies of Schleswig and Holstein, where the Danish king was a duke.

[18] *Berlingske Tidende*, including *Weekendavisen, Jyllands-Posten and Politiken*. The Social Democrats lost their national omnibus paper in 2001.

2.3. Press Privileges and Obligations

Currently, the acknowledgement of the press as an important actor in a democratic society is apparent from a large bulk of regulatory elements, mainly supportive, but also including some which are more restrictive and aim to ensure accountability.

2.3.1. *Case Law: Protecting the Press when Reporting on Issues of Public Interest*

First, judgment U1989.726H is a case in point. A tabloid newspaper published a series of reports covering the situation in a psychiatric hospital, including pictures of inpatients. This no doubt constituted the disclosure of private information, which is criminalised under section 264(d) of the Penal Code. However, only 'unwarranted' disclosure is criminalised, and it was for the courts to consider whether the publication was unwarranted or not. As a point of departure, consent justifies interference with private life, and the newspaper had the consent and cooperation of the relatives as well as the staff. The problem was, of course, that the psychiatric patients were not legally able to consent, thus their consent was invalid, and for this reason the High Court issued a ban on further reporting. The Supreme Court, however, held that it was a matter of considerable societal concern, arguing that, considering the cooperation of the persons involved, their relatives and the staff of the institution, a ban could not be issued. In other words, when the press is reporting on issues of general interest, this interest may outweigh other rights such as the rights protecting private life. Of course, this does not grant general permission for the press to trespass on private life or in other protected areas, but it constitutes a protection of the press when it is dealing with matters of general interest. It is worth noting that the case was resolved without reference to the Constitution; instead, it was a matter of interpretation of the relevant criminal provision. Nor did the Court refer to the Convention for the Protection of Human Rights and Fundamental Freedoms (European Convention on Human Rights, ECHR), which Denmark ratified in 1953. In 1992, the Convention was incorporated into Danish law on an equal par with Danish legislation, and from then on the case law has regularly included references to it.

On the topic of the press's right to publish other person's illegal remarks, case law has been somewhat uncertain. On the one hand, in U1980.1056V, an editor was acquitted for publishing a double interview in which one of the interviewees made downright criminal remarks in relation to immigrants.[19] The editor had arranged a discussion between the person who had previously published criminal racist expressions and an opponent who had reported the

---

[19] s 266(b) of the Penal Code, criminalising grossly derogatory remarks in relation to group affiliation, ethnic, national, religious, etc. It is the Danish 'hate speech' clause, even though 'hate' is irrelevant for the application.

expressions to the police. The one expressing the criminal views was convicted, and the question in relation to the editor was whether he should be convicted for aiding and abetting the distribution of criminal expressions, which certainly was an option under the then prevailing Danish law. However, the editor was acquitted exactly because of his role as an editor.

Another case ended differently. In U1989.399H, a journalist conducted an interview with a gang of youths who had expressed racist views amounting to criminal expressions according to section 266(b) of the Penal Code. The interview was broadcast on the Danish public service television channel, the only one available at that time. In this case, the majority of the Supreme Court backed convicting the journalist for aiding and abetting the wider distribution of criminal expression. The journalist took the case to the European Court of Human Rights (ECtHR), and in *Jersild v Denmark*,[20] a plenary court ruled that Denmark had violated its obligations under Article 10 of the ECHR, the freedom of expression clause. This judgment, only the second where the Court held that Denmark had violated the Convention, was much debated, and with the incorporation of the Convention into Danish law in 1992, the Danish courts became acutely aware of the importance of the ECHR. However, it is worth noting that the concept of not criminalising press reporting was not foreign to Danish legal thinking.

Soon after the *Jersild* judgment, the Supreme Court faced a somewhat similar case, reported in U1994.988H. A group of demonstrators entered the garden of the Minister of the Environment who was responsible for the decision to establish a bridge between Denmark and Sweden. In order to make room for the bridge, some houses and allotment gardens were expropriated, and the protesters wanted to show how annoying it was to have one's garden dug up. Therefore, they entered the minister's garden and started digging. This, of course, constituted illegal trespassing, at the least. During the protest, a journalist and a photographer also showed up and took photos and made interviews with the demonstrators in the garden. They also entered the minister's garden, but it was questionable whether they also violated the Penal Code. The Supreme Court acquitted the two, arguing that reporting the event was of public interest, and that the infringement of private life was minor. Therefore, it did not amount to *illegal* trespassing.

This is now prevailing Danish law: the press is protected when reporting issues of public interest.[21] The difficult question has become that of balance: exactly when does the protection of the press reporting on issues of general interest outweigh the protection of private life or other relevant issues? In the latest Supreme Court judgment, U2021.5227H, the Court found that, in that case, the protection of private life outweighed the public interest. A television broadcaster made a report on the – deplorable – state of affairs at an old people's home. Cooperating with the relatives of an elderly and demented person, a hidden camera was installed,

---

[20] *Jersild v Denmark* [1994] App no 15890/89.
[21] U1994.998H was followed by U1999.1675H, U2008.2738Ø, TfK (*Journal of Criminal Science*) 2019.122Ø, U2010.1859H and other cases.

showing the unacceptable treatment of the patient, but also showing the patient in very precarious situations including when attending to intimate hygiene. The Supreme Court reiterated the prevailing law:

> The fact that a publication involves an infringement of private life is insufficient for issuing an injunction. This is only the case when the infringement is so gross that considerations for the offended party outweigh freedom of expression and information.

In the present case, the Court found that the publication was of obvious public interest, but that this did not justify the broadcasting of the most intimate recordings.

Similar considerations apply when journalists go undercover. If important information cannot be retrieved by other means, the courts will take this into consideration. The courts balance the interests involved, freedom of expression and information, including protection of the press on the one hand, and various other relevant interests on the other. In cases of forgery, for example, when the journalist forges documents in order to appear to be another person, according to case law, the journalist will be convicted, but the sentencing will be lenient. In U1990.71H, a journalist forged a birth certificate in order to pass himself off as an asylum seeker. After the publication of the reportage, which caused quite a lot of debate, the authorities changed the problematic procedures. The journalist was sentenced to 20 daily fines of 100 Danish kroner (€13.5) compared with the maximum penalty of two years, and six years under aggravating circumstances.

Danger can also be a relevant counter-consideration. In U2007.1673Ø, two journalists wanted to show how easy it was to purchase illegal fireworks. After the purchase they went directly to the police station. They were fined 5,000 kroner (€672) for the illegal possession of fireworks. Although the Court acknowledged the public interest, it balanced this against the danger of the men driving around with dangerous fireworks, so the fine was upheld.[22] In a somewhat similar case, a journalist and a photographer wanted to highlight the poor security situation at Kastrup airport. They had a steak at a restaurant in the airport where sharp cutting knives were freely available, and the journalist carried such a knife to the gate where he showed it to the staff after all the other passengers had boarded. The Supreme Court was divided. The majority held that the journalist could be convicted for illegal possession of a weapon, but with no fine or other sanction. A minority voted for acquittal. The entire Supreme Court seriously considered the public interest – after the reportage was published, knives were no longer freely accessible in the restaurant – but disagreed on the concrete balancing.

As to the question whether the same protection will apply to actors who are not formally attached to traditional media, the answer depends. On the one hand, everybody is covered by the general protection of freedom of speech, especially when it comes to bringing forward important societal issues. In U1980.1037H, an artist put up posters claiming: 'Danish pork is healthy – It bulges with penicillin'.

---

[22] The ECtHR dismissed a complaint, *Mikkelsen and Christensen v Denmark* [2011] App no 22918/08.

The slaughterhouses sought an injunction, claiming that the posters amounted to serious allegations of unlawful activities. The Supreme Court turned down the request, arguing that the issue was of general importance to the public and that the allegation was not totally unfounded as veterinary authorities had criticised the industry for excessive use of penicillin. In this case, the issue was of general societal interest whereas the status of the speaker was not of paramount importance. In the cases of the press overstepping the borders of private life etc, the situation is probably somewhat different. In the U1994.988H case, the demonstrators were all convicted of unlawful trespassing, and to my assessment it would not make a difference if one of them had been a famous blogger. In order to get the special protection in these cases, there is a need to distinguish the demonstrators from the reporters. If that distinction could be established in upcoming cases, special protection could be granted, but it would require a clear-cut case.

2.3.2. Statutory Law

In particular in the 1990s, a series of statutory Acts consolidated and expanded the protection of the press in various aspects. In 1991, the Media Liability Act (MLA) was enacted. As its title indicates, this piece of legislation regulates the special media liability regime (for more detail, see section 4.2 below) which until then had only covered the traditional printed press. The MLA expanded the group of media covered by it, to also cover broadcasting (compulsory) while other media can opt in to the MLA. Presently, more than a thousand online media have opted in. Besides the liability regulation, the MLA also includes certain obligations (see section 4 below), and it serves as a reference point for several press protection rules.

On *source protection*, section 172 of the Administration of Justice Act provides a detailed regulation of journalistic source protection. In the 1990s, this area was aligned so that the same considerations were relevant when dealing with questions of seizure, search, etc. Generally, the rules function well, and the threshold for cutting through the protection of sources is high.[23] For example, if a criminal offence consists of the revealing of secret information, the journalist has no obligation to reveal the source if the aim of the journalist or of the source was to reveal matters of public interest.[24] There are, however, still two problems relating to source protection, albeit none of them are serious: first, the protection only relates to media under the MLA, thus, the provision does not cover book publication or other publication that is not linked to an MLA media. This may be handled

---

[23] Hence, in accordance with the requirement according to ECtHR case law: journalistic source protection, 'unless it is justified by an overriding requirement in the public interest', *David Goodwin v the UK* [1997] App no 17488/90 and several others.

[24] This is most often the case. In a special case, U2015.1249H, dealing with a magazine reporting on well-known persons' holidays, the Supreme Court held that this was not a matter of public interest, well in line with ECtHR case law.

by the court who may apply the section via Article 10 of the ECHR.[25] Secondly, section 172 protection requires that there be a confidential relationship between the journalist and the source. In case U2021.5243H mentioned above, the Supreme Court ordered the broadcaster to hand over the unedited footage made in the old people's home. Since the recordings were made secretly, that is unknown to the staff, the situation did not fall under section 172.

If court hearings are to be held *in camera*, media under the MLA have the right to protest and argue before the court, and the media actor has the right to appeal against a decision to hear a case in camera. I would argue that this option has made in camera hearings less automatic than previously.

Access to court material. Since the 1990s, this area has become much more liberal for the public at large, including the press, of course, and with some special privileges for the media covered by the MLA.

Exemptions from personal data protection. Since the passage of the EU driven law on data protection,[26] the press has largely been exempted from this. Currently, the Danish regulation on the press and data protection is not altogether clear. On the one hand, personal data processing for journalistic purposes is exempted from the GDPR except Article 28 (regarding agreements with data processors) and Article 32 (safety measures). This is easy, it makes sense and it is quite lenient on the press. However, when the processing involves databases a 1994 act prevails, providing a special regime for media covered by the MLA. This implies, first, that media not covered by the MLA must apply the entire set of GDPR provisions, which is not in line with GDPR Article 85. Secondly, the 1994 act has quite strict requirements for databases that are also media, which nowadays probably includes all online media. These rules are almost impossible to follow, the media do not apply the rules, and nobody except for a few media lawyers seems to care.

Since the 1970s, an *Open File Act* has been in force as a point of departure giving the public access to documents within the administration. It is open to all, including the press, and is, of course, an important tool to help the press keep an eye on the executive. There are many exceptions, some of which are straight-forward, for instance, prohibiting revealing private information, while others are highly politically controversial. Thus, the 2013 version of the Act excludes correspondence between ministers and MPs and excludes any documents which may potentially be part of servicing ministers, also when this is done by external authorities. In my view, Danish administration remains bound by its absolutist origins. On the positive side, this includes the rule of law and very little corruption, but on the negative side, it also involves secrecy and a somewhat reluctant

---

[25] A city court judgment did exactly this, leaving a student of journalism free to protect his sources.

[26] Previously, Directive 95/46/EC of the European Parliament and of the Council of 24 October 1995 on the protection of individuals with regard to the processing of personal data and on the free movement of such data; and now, Regulation (EU) 2016/679 of the European Parliament and of the Council of 27 April 2016 on the protection of natural persons with regard to the processing of personal data and on the free movement of such data, and repealing Directive 95/46/EC [2016] OJ L119/1 (General Data Protection Regulation).

stance towards openness. For example, in 2017, the Minister of the Environment said that the quest for access to administrative documents was like a disease, and added that he would make the decisions as to which information should be made public and which should not.[27] In addition, the media are subsidised. Every fourth year, a media subsidies Act is enacted, stipulating the general principles according to which subsidies are allocated.

2.4. Obligations

Counterbalancing its privileges, the press also has certain obligations.[28] According to section 34(1) of the MLA, 'The content and conduct of the mass media shall be in conformity with sound press ethics',[29] and the MLA sets up a Press Council competent to receive complaints about media, covered by the MLA. The Press Council can sanction the media only by (1) expressing (at times 'strong') critique for not adhering to sound press ethics, and (2) by ordering the media in question to publish the decision. Thus, the Press Council cannot issue fines nor grant awards.[30] In addition to expressing critique, the Press Council may require the media to publish a reply, when the media have published inaccurate and potentially damaging information about a natural or legal person. According to the Press Ethical Rules, dealt with in more detail in section 4 below, the media have an obligation to correct incorrect information on its own motion, but there is an additional right to reply in sections 36–40.

As noted in section 2.3.2 above, the MLA is specific as to which media fall under the regulation: (1) traditional Danish print press; (2) radio and television broadcasting domiciled in Denmark; and (3) media receiving media subsidies. These three categories automatically fall under the MLA – and several other provisions of other statutory Acts, referring to the MLA. In addition (4) outlets of other types of media can opt in. This is highly relevant for online media, which do not automatically come under the MLA (and are therefore not automatically under the Press Ethical Rules) unless they receive media subsidies. Some media (in a very broad sense of the word) are not eligible under the MLA, for example, books, films and all non-Danish media, and this fact is relevant to both their obligations and privileges.

As indicated, the special obligations under the Press Ethical Rules regime are not compulsory for all media. However, a large number of online media have

---

[27] See, eg, Louise Reseke, 'Minister på lukket møde: Søgning om aktindsigt er en sygdom' (*MediaWatch*, 12 April 2017), available at: mediawatch.dk/Medienyt/TV/article9503420.ece.

[28] In accordance with Art 10(2) of the ECHR: 'The exercise of these freedoms ... carries with it duties and responsibilities'.

[29] Translation from the website of the Press Council, available at: www.pressenaevnet.dk/media-liability-act.

[30] See relevant constitutional constraints below, in section 3.

opted in, and all the online versions of daily newspapers, weekly magazines and Danish broadcasters have opted in, and are therefore subject to the special obligations as well as enjoying the resulting privileges. The Press Ethical Rules are of a peculiar nature. On the one hand, since they are regulated by the MLA they are statutory law and thus part of state law. On the other hand, the Press Ethical Rules themselves are negotiated and agreed upon by civil society organisations, presently Danske Medier (Danish Media, the owners) and the Dansk Journalistforbund (Union of Danish Journalists). Thus, the system constitutes a hybrid of state law and self-regulation.

In my view, this system functions quite well. The media, and especially the more professional elements of it, strive to act in accordance with the Press Ethical Rules, and it is not an obstacle to the running of the system that it is partly state driven. At times, there is political criticism of the regime, calling for stricter obligations and more severe sanctions. However, the criminal system deals with more serious infringements of private life, and as mentioned below, there are constitutional constraints to giving more powers to the Press Council.

3. Constitutional Press Freedom

The 1849 Constitution contained the following provision on freedom of the press: 'Any person shall be at liberty to publish his ideas in print, subject to his being held responsible in a court of law. Censorship and other preventive measures shall never again be introduced' (section 91).[31] In 1953, the Constitution was altered. The primary aims were the abolition of the Upper House and the option of female royal succession; the king at the time did not have any sons, and the king's brother and his son were not popular. The freedom of the press clause ended up as section 77 only included the additional wording 'to publish his ideas in print, *in writing, and in speech*' which was merely bringing the section up to date with the generally accepted interpretation. There has been no amendment of the Constitution since 1953.

The press was at the centre of the protection, with the 'press' in a broad sense including book printing, poster printing and, of course, newspaper printing. At the constituent assembly of 1848–49, the representatives found it most important to get rid of censorship. During the absolutist era, all printed matter had to be authorised by the police before being published, which was a highly unpopular system, leaving it to the whims of the local police directors to decide what could be published. They held discretionary power with no option of complaining against it. Hence the second sentence, with its banning of censorship and other preventive measures. Regarding this point, the absolute prohibition of censorship, the Danish constitution provides even stronger protection than the ECHR.

---

[31] Translation from the Parliament's website, available at: www.ft.dk/-/media/pdf/publikationer/english/my_constitutional_act_with_explanations.ashx.

However, the ban on 'other preventive measures' proved to be more problematic. Injunctions are clearly a preventive measure, but no one foresaw a constitutional problem in banning 'preventive measures' in relation to printed matter and at the same time allowing for injunctions, seizure, confiscation, etc. Several court cases have accepted injunctions on printed matter, without the courts – or the involved lawyers, for that matter – even considering their constitutionality.[32] Until the 1970s, pleading constitutional protection in freedom of speech cases was conceived of as if the defendant had run out of sound legal arguments.[33] However, in 1971 a legal dissertation on freedom of speech was published[34] arguing that the freedom of speech clause did in fact contain protection, if the expressions were of public interest. Even though its main arguments were not generally accepted, constitutional arguments began to appear in freedom of speech cases, and 'public interest' considerations gained weight. In U1980.1037H, the Supreme Court considered an injunction against a political poster, criticising Danish pork, a major export commodity, for containing penicillin. Seen from a purely libellous point of view, the author of the poster, an artist and political activist, could not prove his serious allegations, and the lower courts accepted the injunction. However, the Supreme Court held that the issue of veterinary drug use was of public interest, and that the charge was not totally made up but had some merit. Without any reference to the Constitution and as a simple interpretation of the libel clause, the Supreme Court rejected the injunction.[35]

Most likely triggered by this case, a Supreme Court judge wrote an article focusing on the problem:[36] injunctions are clearly preventive measures, since the Constitution prohibits preventive measures, but injunctions are also a necessary part of the legal system. His solution was to accept the possibility of injunctions also in freedom of the press cases but to require very close scrutiny of them by the courts involved and a serious balancing of interests with due concern for freedom of the press. At that time, injunctions were run by the bailiff courts which usually only deal with formal matters. Since the appearance of this article, the bailiff courts have seriously considered freedom of speech and freedom of the press issues,[37] and since 2012 injunctions cases have been heard by the city courts as first instance. In this way the rather clear wording of the Constitution and the practical needs

---

[32] As an example, U1949.922H, accepting police seizure of distributed political leaflets, the Supreme Court arguing that the distribution might cause public disorder. The leaflets did not have any criminal content, and there was no indication that the distribution actually did cause any public disorder.

[33] A Tylstrup, *Advokaten* (14 October 1983) 358.

[34] P Germer, *Ytringsfrihedens væsen* (Copenhagen, Juristforbundets, 1971).

[35] Somewhat similar is the case U1977.872V. The issue was a police order not to distribute leaflets against the military in the vicinity of military barracks. The High Court rejected a claim of unconstitutionality, but also rejected the police order, arguing that the legal backing, especially important in freedom of speech cases, was insufficient. A different outcome from the Supreme Court decision in U1947.922H – no *stare decisis* in Danish law – and a cautious approach: interpretation rather than constitutional provisions.

[36] M Munck, 'Trykkefrihed og forbud', U1982B.61.

[37] U1990.280Ø. The bailiff rejected the demand for an injunction, and the High Court upheld the decision, referring explicitly to the protection of freedom of speech.

of society were combined in what to my assessment amounts to a typical Danish legal pragmatic solution. Not overly principled, definitely not deductive, but a well reasoned and balanced approach. Critically, one may also point out that the problem was only properly addressed more than a hundred years after the Constitution came into force.

According to the wording, only the printing of ideas is protected. According to legal doctrine, though, the publication of any information is also covered. Seeking or receiving ideas and information is not included, however. The words 'subject to his being held responsible in a court of law' indicates that the legislature faced no constitutional barriers to concerning abridging the freedom of the press, nor did it have guidelines in this regard. At the constituent assembly it was taken for granted that the democratically elected Parliament was the best qualified body to decide the limits. Restrictions would be democratically decided and based on the will of the people and the common interest. This was also the view of constitutional scholars up until 1971, and by and large it proved correct, except for the two periods mentioned above, the late nineteenth century with legislation by decree, typically by the executive, and during the Nazi-German occupation from 1940 to 1945.

There is still a reluctance in Denmark to rely on constitutional provisions, including the freedom of speech clause. This is no doubt due to respect for the democratic, legislative process and the fact that the Danish Constitution is extremely difficult to alter.[38] However, the section on freedom of speech is mentioned in a number of Supreme Court cases, which is an indication, first, that the pleading lawyers now make use of the Constitution in court cases, and secondly, that the Supreme Court does not find the constitutional provision entirely irrelevant. In several cases, the Supreme Court has referred to 'the principles behind' the provision, but it never uses the constitutional provision as its sole or even main reasoning.[39]

The term 'in a court of law' implies that sanctions cannot be imposed by administrative bodies. This became apparent a couple of years ago when parliamentarians discussed the idea of authorising the Press Council to impose fines and provide compensation. The proposal had some backing until a judge pointed out its unconstitutionality. Thus, the constitutional provision is not totally without impact, but due to its wording and due to the Danish tradition of loyalty towards democratically made legislative acts, the constitutional provision does not play a major part in the protection of the freedom of speech, including the freedom of the press.

---

[38] Only in one case has the Supreme Court ever set aside a legislative provision as unconstitutional. In U1999.841H, the Parliament (with the executive's countersignature) had enacted a bill naming a specific school for non-eligibility for subsidies. The Supreme Court held that the Act breached s 3 of the Constitution, the division of powers clause, since the Act removed the option for the schools to have their case tried before a court of law. It should be noted that several members of Parliament had severely criticised the Act precisely for being unconstitutional.

[39] U2010.1859H, rejecting an injunction against a television broadcast (the infringement of private life being minor); U2022.5227H, accepting an injunction against a television broadcast (the infringement of private life being major).

4. Press Regulation

The following review is divided into three parts: general regulations especially important for the press; special legislation directed at the press; and soft law and local media regulation.

4.1. General Regulations of Special Importance for the Press

Like any other subject, the press falls under general legislation. However, two areas of the Penal Code are of special importance for the press: the protection of private life, and defamation.[40] The press regularly deals with issues which may involve the private life of individuals. This is the case for weekly magazines publishing information about and pictures of well-known people, and it is also relevant to that part of the press which strives to bring relevant information to the public in the sense of contributing to a debate of general interest, as the ECtHR would phrase it. For example, when publishing critical reports on the conditions in old people's homes, there are obviously relevant private life considerations for the elderly who may be depicted in very intimate situations.[41] Turning to defamation, one of the tasks of the press is certainly to bring to light information on dubious or illegal activities, but if the activities are neither illegal nor dubious, or they may be dubious but not illegal, the press may foresee defamation suits.

The provisions on the protection of private life underwent a more major revision at the beginning of the 1970s. Since then, there have been amendments, but the basic principles have remained the same.[42] Three provisions are of particular importance. Section 264 criminalises unwarranted trespassing. In the case law there have been numerous cases where journalists and photographers were acquitted with the following rationale. While it was true that they had entered private places, this was not deemed criminal because of the purpose of providing information to the public, and the infringement of private life was not gross.[43]

Section 264(a) criminalises the making of unwarranted visual recordings of persons at secluded places (private homes, private gardens, anywhere not open to the public). This may sound strange, as most people take pictures of others in

---

[40] I use the term 'private life' rather than 'privacy'. This follows the wording of the ECHR, and 'private life' seems to have broader connotation than 'privacy'. See *X v Iceland* [1976] App no 6825/74.

[41] U2021.5227H; U2012.1788H.

[42] In 2015, the Ministry of Justice asked the Penal Code Council [Straffelovrådet] to consider whether the provisions relating to private life and defamation ought to be altered. On the topic of private life, the Council had some suggestions, which by and large were enacted by the legislature, but the basic principles and the wording of most provisions remain the same.

[43] U1994.977H (demonstration in the private garden of a minister); U1999.1675H (demonstration on a small private island); U2008.2738Ø (demonstration at a secluded office at the Refugee Council); TfK 2019.122Ø (entering a restaurant out of hours with the purpose of speaking to the owner) and others.

secluded places, but an important requirement is the word 'unwarranted'. With consent, including tacit consent, the taking of photos and video recordings is not unwarranted and therefore perfectly legal. The same may be the case for the press if the information is of public interest. In U2021.5227H, the case where a television broadcaster had secretly recorded scenes from an old people's home, showing maltreatment, the case included a question of section 264(a). Wisely (in my assessment), the Supreme Court did not apply this section when accepting a ban on the publishing. It was the *publishing* of certain humiliating scenes which was the reasoning behind the ban. Thus, the recording itself was not outlawed. Section 264(d) criminalises the passing on of private information and pictures, including, of course, their publication. U2021.5227H is a case in point: exactly because of the passing on of highly intimate pictures of an elderly lady, the publication was banned even though the feature was of obvious public interest.

The area of defamation is regulated in sections 267–69, provisions which underwent substantial rephrasing in 2019, which removed an outdated approach which had relied heavily on 'truth' and 'proof'. The updated version is more in line with prevailing case law, including case law from the ECtHR. The press is protected when publishing information of public interest. However, when doing so the press may in fact charge someone with a criminal or illegal act. U1999.122H is a case in point. Some years ago, a man was convicted of murder. Two journalists dug into the verdict, and demonstrated that the police department had made some mistakes. So far, so good. However, in a television broadcast they also alleged that a named policeman had hidden important evidence, a serious charge even if it was framed as a question. The Supreme Court was divided on this question, with a majority voting in favour of sentencing the journalists because of the unwarranted accusation. This approach was later upheld by the ECtHR in *Pedersen and Baadsgaard v Denmark*,[44] also with a minority voting in favour of the journalists. The case illustrates the challenges facing investigative journalists: they enjoy special protection when dealing with issues of public interest, but the protection does not cover unwarranted accusations.

4.2. Special Regulation Directed at the Press

As mentioned above, the MLA regulates large sections of the press, and besides its formal approach to what constitutes the press it contains three relevant regulations. First, as the name indicates, it regulates liability. While its provisions are at times overly complicated, its principles are clear and well reasoned: for non-anonymous content, the author (for instance, the photographer) is liable, and the editor may also easily be complicit. For anonymous content, the editor is in most cases liable. Thus, the editor is the core actor, and she or he may be sentenced for content that she or he was not even aware of. In U1974.775B, the editor was sentenced to seven

---

[44] *Pedersen and Baadsgaard v Denmark* [2003] App no 49017/99.

days' imprisonment for the publishing of a nude young woman on the front page. It was during the summer holidays, while the editor was abroad, and apparently some rather inexperienced journalists had made the decision, obviously violating section 264(d) of the Penal Code. However, the editor was liable because the decision to print was made anonymously.

Secondly, the MLA contains the requirement that the press must abide by the Press Ethical Rules. This is an interesting hybrid. Legislation requires the press to follow rules that are professional rules, agreed upon by the relevant editor and journalist organisations. The MLA sets up a Press Council which is competent to deal with complaints. A council chamber consists of a Supreme Court judge as chair, representatives of the editors and journalists, and finally, a representative of the public, which in practice means a person from a relevant NGO. The Council, however, can only (1) express its critique and (2) require that the media in question publishes the decision. From 2012 to 2021, the Council received between 158 and 213 complaints a year, largely dealing with complaints about breaches of the Press Ethical Rules, with claims sustained in approximately one-quarter of the cases.[45] Without going further into details,[46] it may suffice to point out that sometimes the Press Ethical Rules and the decision taken by the Council are similar or close to the criminal judgment – this is mainly the case when dealing with the protection of private life and defamation. In other areas, the ethical regime puts stricter requirements on the press. For example, the Rules require 'correct information' (Rule A.1) whereas there is no general legal requirement for publishing the truth. When reporting on the proceedings of the criminal courts, the press is required to follow up on the outcome of cases, and to consider whether to indicate the identity of the criminal involved (Rules C.3 and C.6 respectively). Also, the Council has developed a set of rules dealing with hidden cameras, rules which in 2013 were incorporated into the written set of Press Ethical Rules (Rule B.7). Naturally, in some cases no infringement of the Press Ethical Rules will be found, for example, in cases where a journalist forges a document in order to retrieve relevant information. This constitutes good journalism, but is risky in relation to criminal law.

The third area regulated by the MLA is the right to reply in cases of 'information of a factual nature which might cause anyone significant financial or other damage … except where the correctness of the information is unquestionable'. The Council handles only a few cases dealing with the right to reply, either because the press itself tends to publish corrections if it has published wrongful information – which in itself is a requirement under the Press Ethical Rules – or because a reply must be 'limited to the necessary factual information' (MLA section 38(1)) which may be difficult or uninteresting for the complainants.

---

[45] Annual Report of 2021, 12–13, available at: www.pressenaevnet.dk/wp-content/uploads/2022/04/Aarsberetning-2021.pdf.

[46] For a more detailed account in English, see S Sandfeld Jakobsen and S Schaumburg-Müller, *Media Law in Denmark*, 2nd edn (Alphen aan den Rijn, Wolters Kluwer, 2019) ch 6.

4.3. Internal and Soft Law Regulation

In a way, the Press Ethical Rules are themselves soft law in the sense that they are agreed upon by the parties involved and there are no substantial sanctions connected to infringements. However, as mentioned above the Rules are lifted into Danish state law by virtue of section 34 of the MLA, and the Press Council, dealing with complaints, was established by the Act. DR, the all-important Danish broadcasting company, has a rather detailed set of rules, the Ethical Guidelines of 19 September 2019, dealing with all sorts of issues such as agreements with interviewees and other involved persons, staging and reconstructions, fictive identities, minorities, etc in addition to the areas already covered by statutory law, for example, protection of private life, defamation and press reporting. DR also has a complaints person, dealing with complaints and taking up cases on her own initiative. Other larger media bodies also have ethical rules, and some have more formalised complaints procedures.

5. Press and Media Freedom

5.1. Defining 'the Press': A Formal and a Functional Approach

As pointed out in section 3 above, there is no constitutional distinction between freedom of the press and freedom of speech. The relevant constitutional provision started out as an explicit protection of press freedom, although in legal doctrine this was rather quickly held to include freedom of speech. At any rate, the constitutional provision did not play any role in case law until the 1970s, and even thereafter it has never been decisive.

   In relation to protection of the press, prevailing statutory law follows a double track: a formal and a functional approach. The formal divide follows the MLA's categorisation of included media (see section 4.2 above): printed matter with a regular publication rate of twice a year or more, which includes newspapers, weeklies and magazines, falls under the MLA if they have a mixed content and are published in Denmark. Thus, paper editions of all magazines ranging from major daily omnibus newspapers, through specialised monthlies to local weeklies, all fall under the MLA. The same goes for whatever is broadcast from Denmark, and there is no opting out. The same goes for media which receive media subsidies. In addition, a special arrangement is in place for all other types of media; they can opt in, voluntarily to the MLA regime, and there is no substantial check on applications. This implies that all serious media, including the online versions of daily newspapers, magazines, etc, may be included. However, it also implies that less serious actors may be included. It remains to be seen whether the courts or the Press Council for that matter, will reject inclusion in cases where media are registered without having any of the normal features of a media. Danish courts have a knack of seeing through formalities and judging according to realities.[47] Significantly, media falling under the MLA enjoy various privileges (see section 2.3 above).

The other track is the functional approach. Freedom of speech and of information are protected, and in cases dealing with issues of public importance, strongly protected. This is the position taken by the ECtHR,[48] and since the Convention has been adopted into Danish law, the ECtHR case law is equally relevant. The Danish courts have rather easily taken the functional approach, which was recognisable even before the inclusion of the ECHR into Danish law in 1992. Since the late 1970s, the courts have consistently (although not irreproachably) protected freedom of speech when the speaker (or publisher, journalist, editor, artist, student, etc) delivered information of public interest. A case in point is the above-mentioned case U1980.1037H, which acquitted an artist who had published a poster criticising the use of penicillin in pork production by alleging unlawful behaviour on the part of the slaughterhouses.

Where there is a clash between the formal and the functional approach, according to my assessment the courts are likely to favour the functional approach. In a city court case, the court had to decide whether to allow journalistic source protection for a journalism student who was not attached to any media under the MLA.[49] He had written a student report on the PKK, a Kurdish organisation on the terror list of the EU and other international bodies. The student refused to reveal his sources, and the court reasoned that he was not covered by the relevant provision in the Administration of Justice Act, which takes the formal approach: only journalists (and others) connected to media under the MLA are covered. However, the Court decided that source protection falls under Article 10 of the ECHR (which is correct),[50] and consequently provided the student protection as if he were under AJA. The prosecution did not appeal the case.

5.2. Print and Broadcast

To a large extent, the print and the broadcasting media are subject to the same rules. All are, of course, accountable under penal law, and both the Danish press

---

[47] A case in point, totally outside media law, is the criminal case against a parliamentarian who was also a lawyer and who consistently constructed arrangements in order to avoid tax paying for himself and his clients. The Court set aside the arrangements even though they may formally fall under the relevant tax provision, justifying its verdict by pointing to fact that there was no reality whatsoever connected to construction, solely made up for tax evasion purposes. Three years' imprisonment, 1 million kroner fine (€120,000) and forfeiture of the right to function as a lawyer (advocate), U1983.205H. His parliamentary immunity was continuously lifted by the Parliament.

[48] See E Lexerød Hovlid, 'Finding a Judicial Definition of Journalism' in M Susi (ed), *Human Rights, Digital Society and the Law* (London, Routledge, 2019).

[49] Copenhagen City Court, decision of 19 May 2016.

[50] See, eg, *Goodwin* (n 23).

and television and radio broadcast from Denmark are automatically covered by the MLA. This entails, among other things, that the editor will often be the one responsible for unlawful content, that journalists enjoy certain privileges, and that the media actor in question has an obligation to abide by the Press Ethical Rules. Moreover, broadcasting has its own legislative Act, the BCA.[51] The present Act dates back to 2002, with 25 changes and amendments to date. This is a politically sensitive area. Historically, the DR had a monopoly of broadcast radio (from 1926) and later television. In the 1980s, the monopoly was abolished, however, the DR is still a large player – some would claim too large – with a special status and special obligations. Advertising, for example, is not allowed in the DR's productions, be they on radio, television, podcast, on-demand, etc. Of the many regulations within the BCA, three features ought to be mentioned. First, an authorisation is necessary. This is different from most other relevant areas: neither newspapers, magazines, podcasts nor social media need any authorisation. This also does not sit well with the constitutional ban on prior censorship (see section 3 above) but it has been accepted to date.

Secondly, the BCA covers broadcasting and audiovisual on-demand services, but not audio on-demand (podcasts), and there are special rules for the DR podcasts. Thirdly, the BCA provides for detailed regulation of advertising. The DR is totally prohibited from advertising (with a few exceptions in relation to, for instance, product placement in foreign productions broadcast by the DR), while other broadcasting, especially live television, is strictly regulated. Advertising on private television channels is permitted only in designated slots and is of rather brief duration, with no political advertising allowed etc.[52] The BCA also regulates advertising pertaining to audiovisual on-demand services, but is less strict. Thus, political advertising is permitted in on-demand television but not in traditional scheduled broadcasts, a difference which does not appear justifiable any more.

Advertising not covered by the BCA falls under the Market Competition Act, which to a large extent implements EU law in Denmark along with some further requirements. Media under the MLA have an obligation to draw a clear distinction between advertising and editorial content,[53] a rule that is taken seriously by the professional media. However, the rule is hardly sanctionable and the Press Council has never dealt with a case of this type. Previously, special press regulation was reserved for the printed press, but since the adoption of the MLA from 1991 and other legislative acts from the 1990s, liability rules, source protection, etc are treated identically for print and broadcasting alike.[54]

---

[51] Consolidated Act no 1350, 4 April 2020 amended by Act no 2212, 29 December 2020.

[52] This does not fit with the *TV Vest AS & Rogaland Pensjonistparti v Norway* ([2008] App no 21132/05) judgment. However, not even Norway has changed its legislation in order to comply with the judgment, and the judgment is not overly convincing.

[53] Press Ethical Rule, B.4.

[54] The former state of affairs was connected to the fact that the DR was the only broadcasting company, and it was regulated separately. With the opening of the market, it became obvious to treat the media and their journalists similarly.

6. Press Freedom and Platform Regulation

6.1. New Technologies

The advent of interactive media, including social media such as Facebook and TikTok, and online versions of traditional media, has caused a great deal of turmoil in the market, sparked some discussion but led to very few legal changes. Obviously, online media are also regulated under the penal code. According to section 9 and 9(a), 'An offence relating to text, sound or image data, etc, made generally available in Denmark through the Internet'[55] is under Danish law and under Danish jurisdiction. This implies that media with a basis abroad may fall under the Penal Code if they address a Danish audience (for instance, by using the Danish language). For example, TV3 is based in Stockholm and as a consequence does not fall under the MLA. However, the Penal Code applies to it.[56]

The Danish Penal Code employs a broad definition of aiding and abetting. Whoever takes part in a criminal act may be sentenced (here the MLA is highly relevant as it significantly confines the possible culprits to a few types of actors, especially the editor). This would imply that, for example, social media distributing criminal content could be punished. However, this has never happened to date. In a highly publicised set of cases, more than 1,000 youngsters were convicted for sharing videos of a young couple (under 18) who were involved in various sexual activities. Those actively sharing the illegal content were convicted,[57] but the company – the sharing was mainly carried out on Messenger – was never involved even though Facebook media were aware of it for more than a year, according to the available information. Thus, large social media companies seem to enjoy a kind of impunity.

The present government proposed a bill for regulating the liability of social media, inspired by the German Netzwerksdurchsetzungsgesetz. The idea was to rule out liability for at least 24 hours after posting, but then make it possible for aiding and abetting if the company does not do anything to remove the criminal content. However, the bill was stopped by the EU Commission.[58] Apparently, the Commission wants to curb national initiatives attempting to prosecute big social media companies.

Online media may fall under the MLA, and this Act, dating back to 1991, has proven to be very forward looking by allowing for 'other media', that is neither the printed press, nor the broadcasters, to opt in to the MLA regime. Opting in

---

[55] The Danish Penal Code in English, Karnov, available at: pro.karnovgroup.dk/b/documents/7000905337?tab=karnov_consolidations#LBKG20211851EN_P9A.

[56] See U2008.1565H.

[57] One case went to the Supreme Court, U2019.1232H, 40 days suspended imprisonment, tort payment of 10,000 kroner (€1,350) to the offended female and 2,000 kroner (€270) to the offended male. Payment in principle for each sharing.

[58] Email communication of 1 June 2022 from the EU Commission to the Permanent Representation of Denmark to the EU.

implies, amongst other things, that the media are subject to the Press Ethical Rules, that the Press Council is competent to handle complaints relating to that media actor, and that they enjoy certain privileges such as the protection of sources (see section 2.3 above).

The Press Council has struggled with the problem of user-generated content. The MLA is not very clear on this point – this is no surprise as the law was enacted in pre-social media and almost pre-Internet times. In 2013, the Press Ethical Rules were amended, emphasising that user-generated content falls under the rules but only if it is edited. The Press Council has interpreted this to mean that the mere selection and the deletion of a user contribution does not constitute 'editing',[59] and thus falls outside the Council's competence. I would argue that the question of 'editing' has not been properly solved, by the Press Council, Danish law, or EU law. It seems as if there is a poor understanding of the role of company-generated algorithms with regard to editing.

The MLA option solves a lot of problems. However, social media have not opted in to it, and neither have most bloggers, youtubers, etc. For these types of media, only the general regulation is relevant – that is if it is implemented (see above). For these media, there are no complaints procedures (except if the media itself has initiated any, see section 6.2 below), no obligations, for example, to procure correct information, no obligation to present incriminating material to the person(s) in question, etc. Recently, a proposal has been put forward to amend the Marketing Practices Act. At present, the existence of a commercial interest must be indicated, and the idea is to expand this indication obligation to include an indication of photoshopping.

6.2. Private Regulation of Online Platforms

Most, if not all, larger online platforms have their own set of regulations, internal in the sense that they are decided by the platform company, and internal in the sense that they contain rules for the users but not necessarily for external stakeholders such as the persons depicted or mentioned on the platform. Facebook, for instance, has a number of regulations, often referred to as 'community rules', indicating that they are for the Facebook community. However, these are not community rules in terms of how they are established, as they are decided entirely within the company. Facebook has also initiated a complaints body, the Oversight Board. Interestingly, the Board's terms of reference include international human rights as well as the 'community rules'. In relation to the latter, the Board has in several cases pointed to the incoherence of the internal rules.[60] I would suggest

---

[59] Somewhat in contradistinction to what was intended by the drafters.
[60] I made a closer study on case law from the Oversight Board in the sub-chapter titled 'Private Life, Freedom of Expression and the Role of Transnational Digital Platforms: A European Perspective' in S Hindelang and A Moberg (eds), *Yearbook of Socio-Economic Constitutions* Vol 2 (Cham, Springer, 2021).

that the large online platforms such as Facebook conceive of national law as a *lex inferior*, something which illegitimately interferes in the internal affairs of the 'community', and something which is irrelevant, at least when it comes to small countries like Denmark.[61]

Among the Danish public at large, a platform seems to be conceived of as a kind of public institution rather than as a private company selling services at a price. For example, the term 'censorship' is often used when user-generated content is deleted or blocked. For lawyers, it is obvious that the deletion practice of an online platform does not amount to censorship in a Danish constitutional sense. Still, it is often debated as if it were. As mentioned in section 6.1 above, the Danish government proposed a bill to further regulate the liability of platforms, a proposal that was blocked by the EU. In my view, the EU's proposal for a Digital Services Act will strengthen the area of impunity for the platforms, and in addition it is more focused on creating complaints procedures for users who have had their posts blocked than for other persons who may be depicted in pornographic settings or as victims of beheading, etc. Finally, it ought to be mentioned that the option of creating ethical guidelines for bloggers, etc has also been debated. The idea is to create rules corresponding to the Press Ethical Rules which normally does not cover bloggers, youtubers, TikTok'ers, etc. The idea seems to be more of a political wish from the legislators rather than one stemming from the bloggers themselves.

7. Conclusions

The Danish press functions reasonably well as providers of information and debates relating to culture, sport, local events, societal problems, etc. It is not perfect, of course, but not bad either.

Danish law pertaining to the regulation of the press functions reasonably well. There is a good balance between the protection of freedom of speech and information on the one hand and other considerations and interests on the other, such as the protection of private life. Again, it is not perfect, but not bad either.

Some problems remain unsolved in relation to a formal and a functional approach to the press. Statutory law often takes a formal approach: the divide is between the media under the MLA and other media. However, the courts seem to be able to handle the problem with a pragmatic, functional approach, and the friction that has arisen is more of a lawyers' problem than it is a pressing social problem.

---

[61] 'Governments sometimes order us to remove content they believe is illegal but does not violate our Community Standards … We fight to protect our community from unnecessary or overreaching government intervention'. Marc Zuckerberg, 15 March 2015. The quote no longer appears on *Facebook*.

The traditional printed press has been having economic difficulties lately. It is dependent on state subsidies and has entered the digital age reluctantly and belatedly.

There are unsolved problems in relation to online media and especially in relation to online platforms that are run not by editors but by algorithms. This is a general problem – or challenge – not specific to Denmark.

3

Freedom of the Press in France

GUILHEM GIL

1. Introduction

'Press freedom only wears out if it is not used'. This motto, printed on every issue of the satirical newspaper *Le Canard enchaîné* since its founding in 1915, conveys the fundamental idea that recognising press freedom as a legal principle is not enough. Its social and political value depends on the way it is used, which raises the question of whether the law should provide a legal framework for the exercise of this freedom. French domestic law has twice answered this question in the affirmative, in two of its founding instruments.

The first of these documents is the Declaration of Human and Civic Rights of 26 August 1789 which embodies the Rousseauist idea that statutes are the ultimate means of expressing the will of the people. It follows from this that if Article 11 of the Declaration explicitly protects free speech, this protection is granted subject to the general provisions of Article 4 which entrusts the law with the mission of determining the bounds ensuring and limiting the exercise of the natural rights of every man. This view, mainly supported by La Rochefoucauld and Mirabeau, was strongly opposed by other revolutionaries, such as Robespierre, who considered that such a freedom should never be restrained, even by law. These two opposite positions, one favouring a limited freedom while the other supported an absolute liberty, resurfaced when the second main legal pillar was crafted: the 1881 Act on Press Freedom. Once again, some of those involved, such as Clémenceau, argued that the best protection for press freedom lies not in the enactment of a specific statutory instrument but in the lack of it and in the application of ordinary law. This view did not prevail and, while the 1881 Act recognises press freedom as a general principle, it immediately attached to it a long list of limits, prohibitions and threats of sanctions.

Initially intended mainly to protect the interests of the state and its branches, these legal constraints progressively leaned towards the protection of individual rights, but a consistent theme ran through them: ensuring press freedom implies the submission of its activities to a wide set of derogatory rules. The domestic legal framework does indeed depend on the balancing of two ideas: on the one hand, granting the press an enhanced level of protection since a public freedom is at stake and, on the other, submitting it to an aggravated liability regime subject to criminal penalties.[1]

2. History of Press Freedom

The history of the French press is filled with numerous measures prejudicial to press freedom and which were mainly crafted by the ruling authorities to control the diffusion of ideas. Printing came to France some 30 years after its birth and was at first welcomed by the monarchy. However, it was soon realised that it had to be closely monitored and, on 20 October 1521, a royal order prohibited the selling of books without the prior approval of the university and the theology faculty. King Francis I, who was the target of many Protestant defamatory libels, declared by Letters patent on 13 January 1534 that any breach of this obligation was punishable by hanging. Due to the opposition expressed by Parliament, this order was not implemented, although the Sorbonne and the university worked hand in hand to destroy what was referred to as 'a diabolical invention giving birth every day to an infinity of pernicious books'. King Henry II, by Letters patent of 11 December 1547, decreed that the author's and the printer's names must appear on all books published, and renewed the ban on all publications not previously screened by the authorities. His son, Charles IX, took over this prohibition and made it punishable by death to print a book without authorisation. The system was formally instituted by the Moulins Ordinance in 1566, under which the permission for printing had to appear on the book itself, as well as the name and address of the printer, upon penalty of corporal punishment and forfeiture of the defendant's assets.

Under the reign of Louis XIII, a general regulation on printing and publishing was presented to Parliament on 16 July 1618: censors were officially appointed and were given the power, in the name of the king, of granting printing privileges. The same idea was revived by the Declaration of 12 May 1717 which outlawed printing any kind of book, leaflet, etc without general or special privileges bestowed by His Majesty. The death penalty for breaching this ban was instituted by a royal declaration of 16 April 1737 and was aimed at 'all those who had taken part in the composition, printing or distribution of written documents attacking religion, promoting unrest, undermining the authority of his majesty and causing turmoil against state public order'. Moreover, anyone who participated in the making of objectionable printed statements not covered by this list faced being sent to the gallows.

Besides this range of criminal sanctions, an administrative framework aimed at supervising printing activities was also established. A royal edict of August 1686

---

[1] B Ader, 'La vitalité de la loi du 29 juillet 1881' (2006) 35 *Legicom* 103.

provided that all those wishing to become printers or publishers had to produce a certificate from the university chancellor attesting that the applicant knew enough Latin and could read Greek. They also had to pass an examination administered by representatives of the printing profession. Those who were granted royal privilege also enjoyed a monopoly. The law specifically provided that no one, except printers and publishers, could engage in the book trade, whether wholesale or retail, even if they were the authors of the publication. Breaching this rule was punishable by a large fine, seizure of the publications and an exemplary punishment determined by the court. Printers were only permitted to work from the premises where their commercial sign was displayed. This building was allowed to have only one door which had to be fastened by a simple latch, so as to facilitate police controls.

This system lasted until a revolutionary decree, adopted by the Constituent Assembly on 17 March 1791, abolished all commissions, as well as all related licences.

This recognition of printing freedom was extremely short-lived and ended with the emergence of the Empire. An imperial decree of 5 February 1810 reinstated the printing monopoly. A fixed number of printers was authorised for each district (60 for Paris, later rising to 80). A licence was required to access the trade and it was granted to those who could not only prove their professional ability but also their morality and their affection for the fatherland and the emperor. The licensees had to take an oath, and could lose their right to print at any time. They had to keep a record of all the books they meant to publish, and inform the general director of printing, the local prefecture and the police minister, all three of whom had the power to defer printing of the book. The manuscripts of the book were to be sent to the censors appointed by the emperor. At their sole discretion, these censors could order changes and deletions. If the printer did not comply, the legal copies were to be seized and confiscated, and the equipment used to print the book could be destroyed. The same penalty of destruction was extended by the Act enacted on 21 October 1814 to all clandestine printing material, their owner facing a fine and a six-month imprisonment. This Act, while establishing aggravated penalties for various cases of non-compliance with the state control framework, also set censorship aside for some specific publications: those written in dead or foreign languages; pastoral letters; catechisms and prayer books; written observations made during a trial signed by a lawyer; memoirs of art or learned societies created and approved by the state; and opinions from members of both assemblies of Parliament.

The details of the system established in 1814 were frequently modified, sometimes making the penalties more severe, sometimes loosening the grip of the authorities on the press. However, even in those more lenient periods a long-lasting policy of the 'costly newspaper' was pursued, through the application of a stamp duty on each copy and the requirement that partners in press enterprises provide a personal security, which was a large sum of money, to cover the costs of potential judicial convictions. This suretyship system proved very effective, diminishing the number of publications while increasing the cost of each copy and therefore reducing the readership of publications, especially of opposition newspapers. This enforced financial burden was strongly criticised by Félicien Robert de Lamennais who, in 1848, had to close his newspaper, *Le Peuple constituant*, because of the high amount of the security and who said of it: 'one must have a lot of gold to have the right to speak. We are not rich. Silence to the poor!' These measures were backed by indirect means of encouraging the press to support the powers that be and to disadvantage the opposition. In times of shortages, the supply of paper was mainly directed in one way and not the other. State advertising, and its revenues, went to some and not to others. Moreover, a postal monopoly which had existed since the fifteenth century, as well as a rule prohibiting the sale of newspapers on the streets, allowed the ruling authorities to closely monitor the distribution of newspapers and periodicals.

The framework based on the 1814 Act was abolished by a decree issued on 10 September 1870 by the provisional Government of the Republic which was created after the defeat at Sedan and the ensuing capitulation of Emperor Napoleon III. Article 1 of this decree provided that the printing and publishing trades are free. A simple declaration to the authorities was still necessary, but the days of a system founded on a licence, a monopoly and an oath were over. The same principle of free printing and publishing is at the core of the legislative monument which is the Act of 29 July 1881 on press freedom. This text, as noted earlier, is probably the first statute that any Frenchman who is old enough to read encounters since its prohibition of 'wild posting' on public buildings is engraved on many structures constructed since the birth of the Third Republic and can still be read on most of them.[2] This Act was introduced by the then Minister of Justice as 'a freedom statute, such as the press never enjoyed in the past'. Often described as a true press code, this Act wholly replaced the previous legislation which had been scattered between more than 40 distinct statutory instruments. Aiming at presenting to all interested parties, professionals as well as citizens, all the boundaries set by law on the general principle of free speech, the Act includes five chapters dealing with printing and publishing, the periodical press, public posting, offences committed by the use of press or any other form of publication, and finally procedural rules.

This statutory instrument became the main pillar of press law, and its framework was later used as the backbone for the regulation of audiovisual media established in the 1980s.[3] The same principle of freedom was once again applied to digital communication. Article 1-IV of Law No 2004-575 of 21 June 2004 For Confidence in the Digital Economy (Loi pour la confiance dans l'économie numérique, LCEN) provides that

> public communication by electronic means is free. The exercise of this freedom may only be restricted to the extent required, on the one hand, by the respect of human dignity, of third parties' freedom and property, of pluralist expression of thoughts and

---

[2] ibid.
[3] Act of 29 July 1982; Act of 30 September 1986.

opinions and, on the other hand, by the protection of children and teenagers, by the preservation of public order, by the necessities of national defence, by the requirements of public services and by the constraints inherent in communication means.

The 1881 Act constitutes the basic structure of French media law which is made up of 'a ragbag collection of legal frameworks, some special and some general'.[4] Indeed, the content of the Act has since been frequently amended or supplemented, a process initiated by the Act of 2 August 1882 and which has continued ever since, some of the modifications being inserted in the founding Act while others remained separate. Because of the impediment of the specific procedural rules in the 1881 Act, and especially of the three-month time limit to introduce a complaint, the general tendency of the legislator was to remove from the scope of the 1881 Act the offences which were deemed to require more efficient prosecution. This process, which started with offences such as obscenity or the incitement to members of the armed forces to commit misconduct, has accelerated in recent times. For instance, public calls to commit acts of terrorism or the condoning of such acts was a press offence until the passage of the Act of 13 November 2014 which transferred it to the Penal Code. The explanatory statement accompanying the bill stated explicitly that the introduction of the offence in ordinary criminal law would allow for longer time limits and more appropriate procedural rules through the use of special investigative techniques. Moreover, the penalties for behaviour which was no longer seen as a free speech abuse but as a terrorist act are much harsher and include jail time.

It is widely agreed that French domestic law in this area lacks consistency, and this incoherence, in fact, dates back to the 1881 Act. For empirical reasons, some offences were set within the scope of the Act while others were excluded and the list of press offences is indeed 'more enumerative than rational'.[5] For instance, the incitement offences are sometimes regarded as press offences, such as with the offence of enticement to commit certain serious crimes, which falls under Article 24 of the Act, while others, such as public calls to commit suicide or to bear arms against the state authority or against sections of the population, are regulated by the ordinary provisions of the Penal Code. The same could be said concerning the offence consisting in revealing the identity of members of special law enforcement units which is treated as a press offence by Article 39(6) of the Act, but which could also have been prosecuted using ordinary provisions of the Penal Code or Defence Code protecting classified information. In the same way, revealing the fact that someone was adopted is considered a press offence even though the right to privacy protected by Article 9 of the Civil Code could have provided identical protection. The overall impression that emerges from examining the framework

---

[4] M Sénamaud, 'Le régime dérogatoire de responsabilité et de procédure' [2012] *Lamy droit des médias et de la communication* § 230–2.
[5] P Auvret, 'Eléments constitutifs des infractions à la loi de 1881' *JurisClasseur Communication*, fasc 3020, no 1.

built around the 1881 Act is one of a legislative monument affected by band-aid and incoherent reforms.[6]

3. Constitutional Press Freedom

In French domestic law, the principle of press freedom is enshrined in Article 11 of the Declaration of Human and Civic Rights of 26 August 1789. This text provides that

> the free communication of ideas and of opinions is one of the most precious rights of man. Any citizen may therefore speak, write, and publish freely, except what is tantamount to the abuse of this liberty in the cases determined by Law.

Replacing the previous system of censorship used under the monarchy, the writers of the Declaration established a so-called repressive system which, unlike its name might suggest, is the most liberal in the area of modelling fundamental rights. Therefore, if one sets aside the implementation of exceptional procedures justified by specific circumstances or by the nature of the publications, everyone may freely express his or her opinions without prior control by any authority. This control may only occur ex post facto, after publication and is to be implemented by the sole judicial authority which, according to Article 66 of the Constitution of 4 October 1958, is the 'guardian of the freedom of the individual'. This framework is the direct product of a speech made by Mirabeau on 24 August 1789 when the content of the future Article 11 was debated. As he asserted,

> if you have at your disposal a writing stand to write a slanderous letter, or a press for a libel, you must be punished when the deed is done. This is repression and not restriction. It is the offense which is punished, and one shall not restrain the freedom of men under the pretext that they want to offend.

The exact same principle governs the 1881 Act on Press Freedom. Article 5 of the Act provides that 'any newspaper or periodical may be published without prior declaration or authorisation, and without providing any security'. The framework is based exclusively on the repression ex post facto of offences predefined by law, that the publication might have committed. As one of the most famous commentators on the Act put it,

> to sum it up, no preventive measures and repression of only the deeds which fulfil the criteria of ordinary criminal offences, such are the two principles which lay the foundation for press freedom, and such are the ones which are fully entrenched in the 29 July 1881 Act.[7]

The Conseil constitutionnel, the authority in charge of ruling on the conformity of Acts of Parliament with the Constitution, declared that press freedom is

---

[6] ibid no 5.
[7] G Barbier, *Code expliqué de la presse* (Paris, Marchal et Billard, 1911) 3.

'a fundamental freedom which is all the more precious that its existence is one of the essential guarantees for the respect of other rights and freedoms and for national sovereignty'.[8] This approach implies that any statutory provision which would tend to establish a preliminary authorisation system, or which would produce similar effects, would be deemed to breach Article 11 of the 1789 Declaration.

However, this principle is applied differently depending on the nature of the media. According to some observers, while the printed press enjoys full protection, audiovisual communication is somewhat less protected, a situation which can be explained by its history and by its technical specificities. Indeed, the Conseil constitutionnel stated that 'concerning derogations to the broadcasting monopoly, the benefit of these derogations may be subjected by Parliament to prior administrative authorisation'. Nevertheless, the power thus granted to Parliament is valid only if the statutory provisions do not impart a discretionary nature to these derogations. The statute must therefore determine the conditions under which the administrative authority may grant these derogations and, specifically, statutory provisions must compel the administrative authority to ensure the free and pluralist expression of ideas and opinions. The aim of this duty is to ensure compliance with the constitutional principles of freedom and equality under the scrutiny of the competent judge.[9]

Concerning online communication, the approach taken is that of a ruling made by the Conseil on the Creation and Internet law (Haute Autorité pour la Diffusion de Œuvres et la Protection des droits d'auteur sur Internet, HADOPI) I Act in 2009. The Conseil held that

> based on the current situation of media, and considering the widespread development of public online communication services and the prominent role played by these services in the participation to democratic life and the expression of thoughts and ideas, free communication implies the freedom to access these services.

The same principle was renewed in a ruling in which the Conseil quashed most of the provisions inserted in the so-called Avia Act of 24 June 2020 on hate speech on the Internet. This statute had compelled platform operators, at the request of the administrative authorities, to remove, within the space of an hour, online material pertaining to terrorism or child pornography, and to remove, within 24 hours, patently unlawful hate speech material. Non-compliance was to be punished by a €250,000 fine for each breach, this amount being liable to be multiplied by five for legal persons. While welcoming the efforts made by Parliament to fight online hate speech, and recognising that the dissemination of child pornography or incitement to terrorism are abuses of free speech likely to seriously disturb public order, the Conseil reiterated that since the freedom of expression and communication is

---

[8] Conseil constitutionnel, 10 and 11 October 1984, n° 84-181 DC, Entreprises de presse, *Journal officiel de la République française*, 13 October 1984, 3200, para 37.

[9] Conseil constitutionnel, 31 October 1981, n° 81-129 DC, *Journal officiel de la République française*, 1 November 1981, 2997, paras 12 and 13.

a condition of democracy and is included among the guarantees for other rights and freedoms, all restrictions to its exercise must be necessary, appropriate and proportionate to the objective pursued.

In this instance, the Conseil considered that the legislator had utterly failed: not only was the characterisation of the content of the material as patently unlawful left at the discretion of the administrative authority, the platform operator, compelled to act within an hour, was deprived of his right to go to court, while no grounds for exemption for liability were provided. The Conseil considered that, in fact, this scheme would have been prejudicial to free speech as it would have prompted platform operators to systematically take down all notified material, whether patently unlawful or not, for fear of being held liable. The Conseil also underlined in this ruling that freedom to access online communication services also includes freedom to express oneself.

4. Regulation of Press Freedom

Despite what its title may suggest, the subject of the 1881 Act on press freedom is not the press but free speech. Its provisions apply to any and all forms of public communication. Therefore, the offences established by the Act may be applied to any material, both printed and disseminated to the public by any other means: public speech; circulated drawings or pictures; broadcasts or digital communication to unspecified recipients.[10] Focused as it is on shaping the extent of the liability incurred for abusing free speech, it ignores news organisations whose status was to be dealt with by ordinary law. This initial position proved untenable in the long run. Liberal economic principles, applied without any corrective treatment, were clearly bound to lead to growing industrial concentration. The creation of press groups which was often vital for the survival of some publications that could not last on their own, also represented a threat to free speech or at least to its pluralism.[11] To counteract the prejudicial impact of such mergers on press freedom, government interventionism greatly developed after the Second World War so as to thwart the influence of moneyed interests.

In the same way, and also modelled on Article 11 of the 1789 Declaration, the 1881 Act ignores the journalist as a specific political or economic player. The freedoms that are granted by the legal framework exist for all citizens, and no specific treatment is reserved for a given group. Although the first legal framework dealing with the journalistic profession was enacted in the 1930s, this professional status has gradually lost its specificities and is nowadays extensively similar to ordinary labour law. It has even been argued that the professional status of journalists 'is formally nonexistent since one cannot find in the law a coherent set of legal

---

[10] P Waschsmann, 'Liberté d'expression' *JurisClasseur Libertés*, fasc 800, no 39.

[11] E Derieux and A Granchet, *Droit des médias* (Paris, LGDJ, 2008) 73.

or decretal rules defining the conditions governing the admission to, the exercise of, and the termination of the occupation'.[12]

The purpose of the Act is to strike a fair balance between, on the one hand, free speech as enshrined in Article 11 of the 1789 Declaration and, on the other, the necessary prosecution of any abuses of this freedom. To achieve this, the Act first provides strong guarantees for press freedom. Besides excluding censorship as a general rule, it institutes a limited number of press offences which were originally far fewer than those included in the framework set by the 1819 Acts. In the initial version of the 1881 Act, there were nine offences: incitement to commit crimes or misdemeanours which were acted on; incitement to commit serious crimes, specifically against state authority, which were not acted on; seditious shouts or songs; incitement directed at a member of the armed forces to commit misconduct; insulting the President of the Republic; publication of false news causing public disorder; obscenity; defamation and insult; insulting foreign heads of state and diplomatic agents. Some specific types of publication were also prohibited in order to protect the functioning of the judicial system: it was forbidden to publish presentations of criminal charges; to report defamation trials; or to publish a fund-raising appeal meant to cover the costs of a criminal conviction.

Despite many subsequent changes, the initial framework of the Act has withstood the test of time. Defamation and insult still occupy a central place in this area of the law, backed by the offences punishing incitements to break the law that were adapted to keep up with the evolution of society so as to include the prosecution of material promoting hatred, discrimination, war crimes or crimes against humanity. Specific provisions were also added to increase the level of protection of vulnerable individuals such as minors, while some obsolete rules, such as obscenity, insulting the President of the Republic or incitement of soldiers' misconduct were repealed or transferred to ordinary criminal law. To protect the balance established in the 1881 Act and to prevent the circumvention of its provisions, the Cour de cassation has repeatedly prohibited the implementation of the rules of ordinary civil liability in the area of free speech. Even though some chambers within the Cour itself seem to play fast and loose with this rule,[13] it is faithfully implemented by the lower courts, which uphold the principle that

> when the alleged harm has its origin in one of the offences defined by the 1881 Act, the claimant cannot, even to escape the procedural restrictions set in this Act, use for the same facts different legal characterisations that would restrain the freedom protected by this Act outside its legal provisions.[14]

Following in the footsteps of the Acts enacted at the beginning of the nineteenth century, which started by defining the general principles governing the prosecution

---

[12] C Debbasch, *Droit des médias* (Paris, Dalloz, 2002) 341, § 1256.

[13] Cour de cassation, Chambre civile 1, 12 September 2019, n° 18-23.108, *Communication commerce électronique*, 2020, chr 4, no 3, note C Bigot.

[14] Cour d'appel de Paris, Pôle 1 Chambre 2, 28 January 2021, n° 20/07199.

of press offences, the 1881 Act also sets a binding procedural framework aimed at protecting press freedom. As the then Minister of Justice explained, the Act afforded the press a privileged situation by instituting specific derogatory rules concerning jurisdiction, criminal liability, procedure, seizure, pre-trial detention, recidivism, extenuating circumstances or aggregate sentences. One of the main features of this scheme is that, despite the principle set out in Article 47 which makes prosecution the sole preserve of the Public Prosecutor's Office, the leading roles in such trials are played by the parties. Indeed, Article 48 defines a long list of offences where the Public Prosecutor can only act if the prosecution was initiated by the victim's complaint. Thus, despite appearances, for most press offences only the victims may instigate criminal proceedings, the Prosecutor being deprived of his usual authority to act ex officio. Furthermore, the judge himself is relegated to playing a secondary role in the enquiry. Indeed, pursuant to Article 50 of the Act, he is bound by the characterisation of the facts as defined by the victim's complaint. This rule has two effects: first, the judge must circumscribe its ruling solely to the facts referred to in the complaint; and second, he is deprived of his usual authority to amend the characterisation. As the Cour de cassation put it, it is not for the trial judge to assess the extent to which the initial characterisation, set out in the complaint, was justified.[15]

This rule is especially important since the victim must, in his complaint, indicate which provision forms the legal basis of his action. Therefore, if the initial characterisation is erroneous, the judge will not be able to correct the mistake, and the case will be dismissed. Even though a correction of the characterisation is theoretically possible, the deadline for bringing a case set by the Act of three months from publication will, in fact, make it impossible to remedy the victim's initial mistake. The Cour de cassation refused to submit a priority preliminary ruling on the constitutionality of this rule to the Conseil constitutional, considering that it provides an adequate balance between the victim's rights and press freedom.[16] Moreover, when the Conseil constitutionnel faced a question concerning the similar provisions of Article 53, it ruled that the legislator had, in so doing, wanted the defendant to be able to prepare his defence as soon as he received the complaint notice and, especially if he is charged with defamation, could offer to present evidence within the required 10 days of the notice.[17]

Finally, as a counterbalance against numerous other derogatory rules which favour the press, and notably the fact that contrary to what is established in normal criminal law, the victim's discontinuance of his action brings the claim to an end, the 1881 Act also contains a very original feature – its cascading liability system, as enshrined in Article 42. This text was intended to ensure that the liability of the key players in a press trial could be established, which implied that a defendant could

---

[15] Cour de cassation, Chambre criminelle, 3 December 2013, n° 12-84.501.
[16] Cour de cassation, Chambre criminelle, 19 February 2013, n° 12-84.302.
[17] Conseil constitutionnel, 17 May 2013, n° 2013-311 QPC, Société Ecocert France.

always be found. As one observer put it, 'thanks to this provision, no press offence will go unpunished'.[18] This system is based on the idea that only some players may be held liable, according to a predetermined sequence. The publisher bears primary responsibility because he authorised the publication of the contentious material. If his liability cannot be established, which is uncommon, the author of the material then comes second. If the author's liability cannot be established, then in descending order come the printer, the retailers and the sellers of the contentious material. This statutory mechanism is quite original since, under common criminal rules, the printer, because he materially created the subject of the offence, and the author, because he intellectually created this material, should be the primary defendants. The implementation of ordinary criminal law would have been prejudicial to press freedom, however, by creating an incentive for censorship on the part of printers and for self-censorship by authors. Therefore, since the liability of the publisher is the key element of the Act, all press publications must identify their publisher whose name must be printed on all copies of the publication. The author, relegated to a secondary role, may only be charged as an accomplice and can avoid liability by producing evidence of the truth of the facts or of his good faith, which would exonerate both him and the publisher.

This cascading system was adjusted to the subsequent technological evolutions which the media underwent. The process started in the 1980s with the audiovisual sector. The Act of 13 December 1985 provided that, when one of the offences covered by the 1881 Act is committed through an audiovisual means of communication, the publisher will be prosecuted as the primary perpetrator when the contentious material was formulated before it was broadcast. Failing that, the author will be prosecuted, and, failing that, the producer. The requirement relating to the prior determination of the material was deemed essential from the traditional perspective of enforcing an editorial line while at the same time avoiding a situation where the publisher could be held liable for contentious speech made by the participants in a live show. In contrast, if the material was recorded before it was published, the publisher has a personal duty to monitor and verify everything that is broadcast.

A similar approach was taken first to telematic services and then to the Internet. Regarding the latter, the main difficulty concerned Internet access providers and hosting service providers. Unlike content providers, they were excluded from the cascading system because their role could not be compared to that of a publisher. Therefore, the legislator decided, in the LCEN of 2004, to place the burden of responsibility on those who provide the material which is posted, not on the technical intermediaries which cannot be legally defined as producers. They can, nevertheless, be held liable if, once made aware of the presence of unlawful material, they failed to act swiftly to remove the contentious content or to

---

[18] A de Briselainne, *La loi du 29 juillet 1881 sur la liberté de la presse* (Paris, Dupont, 1881) 167.

bar access to it. The courts have held that the materials including actions referred to by Article 6(I)(7) of the LCEN are to be regarded as being manifestly unlawful, which include public endorsement of crimes against humanity; incitement to racial hatred or hatred against individuals on grounds of their disability, gender or sexual orientation; endorsement of or incitement to commit acts of terrorism; assaults on human dignity; or child pornography. Hosting service providers must, then, set up a highly visible and easily accessible tool allowing any user to inform them of the presence of such offensive material; they must also swiftly notify the competent authorities. According to a Senate report,[19] however, the results of the legal framework concerning technical intermediaries were disappointing, this failure being due both to the inherent complexity of the liability regime and to the deterrent created by the existence of a specific offence of false denunciation of unlawful material.

This solution was reiterated when the interactive Internet emerged. HADOPI 1 provided that when an offence results from the content of a post sent by a web user to an online public communication service and made available to the public by this service in a personal contribution zone identified as such, the publisher cannot be held criminally liable as the main offender if it is demonstrated that he had no prior knowledge of the post before it was put online or if, as soon as he became aware of it, he swiftly acted to withdraw the post. As noted above, the requirement pertaining to the prior knowledge of the material is a hybrid between the 1985 condition concerning audiovisual media and the 2002 technical intermediaries' liability regime.[20]

While the legal framework ruling the printed press has evolved little since the end of the nineteenth century, and provides no significant clue concerning the duties of the press, modern statutes contain more explicit guidelines for audiovisual media organisations. The Act of 30 September 1986 compels all audiovisual services to comply with certain general obligations. Broadcast material must not breach human dignity or privacy, and must respect public order, in particular by avoiding hate speech and the promotion of violence. Children and teenagers must be protected from certain kinds of content thanks to a classification of the programmes aimed at preventing them from inadvertently coming into contact with inappropriate material. Moreover, the audience of audiovisual communication must enjoy programmes guaranteeing the expression of diverse socio-cultural trends so as to be able to exercise enlightened choices. As the Conseil constitutionnel underlined at the time,[21] free communication of ideas and opinions, protected by Article 11 of the 1789 Declaration of Human and Civic Rights, would

---

[19] F Pillet and T Mohamed Soilihi, 'Rapport relatif à l'équilibre de la loi du 29 juillet 1881 sur la liberté de la presse à l'épreuve d'internet' Sénat, 6 July 2016.

[20] N Mallet-Poujol, note on Cour de cassation, Chambre criminelle, 5 October 2021, n° 20-85.985 [2022] *Légipresse* 35.

[21] Conseil constitutionnel, 18 September 1986, n° 86_217 DC (1986) *Recueil des décisions du Conseil constitutionnel* 141.

be worthless if the people were unable to access, both in the public and private sectors, programmes that convey different points of view. From this perspective, the aim of the law is for viewers and listeners to be in a position to make their own choices without any undue influence from private interests or from public authorities. Of course, this requirement loses most of its relevance in connection with media organisations which do not deal with political matters and whose activity is exclusively devoted to areas such as sport or music. However, the need for diversity is not restricted solely to the political process but applies to each and every area of public communication.[22]

This need is explicitly met by broadcasting licence agreements in which private operators undertake to ensure the pluralist expression of currents of thought and opinion, until recently in line with the recommendations of the Conseil supérieur de l'audiovisuel (CSA), which was the public independent authority in charge of supervising the audiovisual sector and currently with those of its successor, the Autorité de régulation des communications (ARCOM). The reporters, anchormen or show hosts of these private broadcasters must make an honest presentation of controversial matters and ensure the expression of a range of different viewpoints.[23] Articles 28 and 33(1) of the 1986 Act mandate that these agreements must also contain the fundamental principle of honesty which aims at giving the audience reliable and trustworthy information. The importance of this principle was underlined by the CSA which stated that the honesty requirement applies to any and all programmes made available to the public. Their editors must check their sources and the reliability of the information they contain. As far as possible, they must indicate the origin of such information and must announce all unverified information in a conditional mood.[24]

To drive home this point, the Act of 14 November 2016 (Bloche Act) created a new statutory provision entrusting the CSA with the mission of ensuring honesty, independence and pluralism in the handling of information. The regulatory authority must specifically verify that the business interests of the shareholders of the networks, or of the audiovisual programme editors, do not breach these principles. In order to implement the honesty principle, private television networks which apply for broadcasting licences must undertake to employ professional reporters.[25] News-only networks must take further steps to safeguard their editorial independence. Their broadcasting licence agreements specify the existence of a specifically appointed directorate, the full personal liability of the director of the channel, an editorial office under the hierarchical authority of the channel

---

[22] C Haquet and D Malarski, 'Obligations générales de programmes des services de communication audiovisuelle' *JurisClasseur Communication*, fasc 251, no 80.

[23] Agreement TF1 and M6, Art 7; Agreement Canal +, Art 8; Agreement TNT, cable, satellite and ADSL, Art 2(3)(2).

[24] Conseil supérieur de l'audiovisuel, 20 December 2011, D, III.

[25] Agreement M6, Art 23; Agreement Canal +, Art 18; Agreement TNT, cable, satellite and ADSL, Art 2(3)(8).

manager and which are not subordinate to the controlling group of shareholders, as well as the existence of contracts, concluded in compliance with ordinary
market conditions, regulating all relationships between the news channel and all
the other companies belonging to the same group.[26]

One of the main components of the honesty requirement lies in the duty of
all audiovisual services to follow a rigorous approach in information processing
and spreading. This implies not only (and obviously) refraining from supporting
untrue or unfounded statements but also specifying the source, the date and the
circumstances in which the images were taken. Therefore, any use of archive footage must be shown by an on-screen overlay, which may have to be repeated. In the
same way, images created for the re-enactment of actual or alleged facts must be
displayed as such. Except when the material in question is a caricature or a pastiche,
any editing of sounds or images shall not misrepresent their original meaning or
mislead the audience. More generally, media organisations must make efforts to
avoid any confusion between, first, information and entertainment and, second,
between information and advertising. In this respect, when a private television
channel has capital links with companies which create or distribute audiovisual
material, the presentation of such material outside advertising slots must be done
in a strictly informative way, with moderation and by fully informing the audience
of the economic ties between the channel and the editor or distributor.

5. Press and Media Freedom

The regulation of public expression in French law is still based on an incomplete
body of ethical rules. An observation to this effect, made in a Senate report,[27]
conveys the inadequacies of the existing domestic framework, which are exacerbated by the specificities of public speech on the Internet. Admittedly, the national
collective agreement for journalists provides that its members acknowledge the
importance of professional ethics and the usefulness of these ethics for keeping
the public reliably informed. However, the professional principles enshrined in
this agreement do not constitute a true body of ethical rules because they do not
engage with major issues such as the seriousness of the investigation or the need to
seek reliable and verified information. These fundamental guidelines were, in fact,
crafted by the courts and, in this respect, defamation law was the main provider of
judge-made guidance.

Based on repeated court rulings, the sole fact that the defamation offence
occurred, that is to say that an allegation or an attribution of an act was expressed
that impugned the victim's honour or reputation, creates the presumption that its
author acted in bad faith. In the eyes of the justices of the Cour de cassation, if

---

[26] Agreement BFMTV, CNews, LCI, Art 17.
[27] Pillet and Mohamed Soilihi (n 19).

a malicious intent is legally attached to defamatory material this does not automatically breach the provisions of Articles 6 and 10 of the European Convention on Human Rights (ECHR) as long as the defendant benefits from the ability to produce contrary evidence.[28] Therefore, it falls upon the defendant to gather the elements allowing him to convince the judge that he acted in good faith, the courts having no legal standing to rule ex officio on this matter.[29] It is quite remarkable that, in the area of criminal law, which is governed by the legality principle, the good faith defence originated from a judicial creation, the courts considering the sole truth defence recognised by the 1881 Act as being insufficient to protect press freedom. This defence was belatedly acknowledged by Parliament in the Protection of Journalistic Sources Act of 4 January 2010 that added to Article 35 of the 1881 Act the provision that the defendant may, for the purposes of his defence, introduce evidence breaching a professional secret if it can prove his good faith or the truth of the defamatory allegations.

According to the explanation in the classical doctrine, good faith operates as an exonerating circumstance.[30] It does not erase the actus reus, which is the defamatory or slanderous material, nor the mens rea, which is the will directed towards this fact with the consciousness of its defamatory character, nor the *dolus specialis*, which is the consciousness of the harm that the defamatory material would cause the victim. It is the legal element of the offence which is set aside because, thanks to the proof of good faith, the act does not fulfil the requirements set by the law to criminalise the abuse of free speech. By setting aside the legal component of the offence, the law permits the establishment of a distinction between good and bad perpetrators.

Good perpetrators undertake beneficial activity because their action is useful to the political, intellectual or moral life of the nation. In contrast, bad perpetrators are only interested in satisfying the unhealthy curiosity of the public.[31] This approach was adopted by the courts which stated that 'the right to a fair trial and free speech justify that the defendant in a defamation trial should be allowed, for the purposes of his defence, to produce evidence of his good faith or of the truth of the facts'.[32] This justification derived from the protection of free speech explains why some press offences cannot be excused by the good faith defence because, in themselves, they are unable to contribute to a debate of public interest. Such is the case for insults or malicious accusations, which do not fall under the scope of Article 10(1) of the ECHR.[33] The good faith defence is therefore a tool which can settle the conflict between, on the one hand, reputation and honour and, on the other, the free flow of information and ideas.

---

[28] Cour de cassation, 16 March 1995, Bulletin des arrêts de la chambre criminelle, n° 115.
[29] Cour de cassation, 26 March 1996, Bulletin des arrêts de la chambre criminelle, n° 134.
[30] P Mimin, note Cour de cassation, Chambre criminelle, 27 October 1938, DP 1939, I, 77.
[31] ibid.
[32] Cour de cassation, Chambre criminelle, 11 February 2003, n° 01-86.685.
[33] Cour de cassation, Chambre criminelle, 12 April 2016, n° 14-87.124; Cour de cassation, Chambre criminelle, 19 June 2018, n° 17-84.153.

However, if democracy is fostered by the spread of ideas it does not need public debates fed by incorrect or misleading information. Therefore, some test had to be established to ensure, if not the truth of but at least the credibility of, the information. From this perspective, where democracy accepts the risk of allowing information to flow which is merely plausible, the same classical scholars identified in the interwar period the four elements which are deemed necessary to describe and characterise good faith: sincerity; a legitimate purpose; proportionality of the allegation to this purpose; and caution. As has been observed,[34] good faith weaves together two different components: one relates to man's qualities (lack of animosity, sincerity, caution) whose absence is a legal wrong; the other is made of extrinsic facts which may be objectively certified and over which the individual will has no control (such as the legitimacy of the purpose). These components are undeniably surrounded by a notorious legal uncertainty which led one scholar to state that, 'concerning good faith, the perpetrator can never be sure of anything but can always expect something'.[35]

These elements were adopted by the courts to establish what has become a general principle: defamatory allegations may be justified when the goal pursued by the journalist seems legitimate and when this journalist demonstrates that he wrote his words in compliance with certain requirements, specifically sincerity, caution and objectivity, that are likely to establish his good faith.[36] Traditionally, the courts were quite strict concerning the admission of good faith. The trial judges had to check that all four components were present before the prosecution could be ended. Therefore, rulings were quashed which exonerated the defendant on the ground of the lack of animosity if they failed to verify the requirements of caution, objectivity and a serious investigation.[37] The same applied to judgments which had admitted good faith on the sole grounds of the defendant's will to inform the public, which cannot by itself constitute an exonerating circumstance.[38] However, this classical approach has since been amended in two regards which are somewhat intertwined.

The courts first reassessed their position when the material at stake consists in the expression of an opinion on the functioning of a state institution. In a case adjudicated in 1978, the Cour de cassation held that the exonerating circumstance deriving from good faith is not, in this instance, contingent upon the proof of caution in the expression of thoughts.[39] In this case, a former Minister of Justice had violently attacked a judges' union and claimed that it was a syndicate driven by the will to subvert the judicial system. The Cour considered the context of the

---

[34] J Goulesque and J Michaud, 'Le parquet et le bon diffamateur' [1978] *Revue de science criminelle* 445.
[35] M Domingo, 'Atteintes à la réputation : la protection pénale' [1994] *Gazette du Palais* doctr 1002.
[36] TGI Paris, 17 November 1988, *Legipresse*, 1989, n° 58, III, 10.
[37] Cour de cassation, Chambre criminelle, 29 January 2008, n° 07-84.493, *Revue Lamy droit de l'immatériel*, 2008, n° 1207.
[38] Cour de cassation, Chambre criminelle, 12 October 1993, n° 92-81.538.
[39] Cour de cassation, Chambre criminelle, 23 March 1978, *Bulletin des arrêts de la chambre criminelle*, n° 115.

speech and underlined that the outrages were of the kind commonly used in political controversies. This liberal approach to good faith on a matter of public interest is in line with the second evolution, inspired by the judgments coming from the European Court of Human Rights and it was confirmed by the Cour de cassation at the turn of the millennium. Based on Article 10 of the ECHR, the Cour held that good faith had to be recognised when the allegations, made in the context of a political debate, concern the claimant's public activities, without any invasion of his privacy and provided that the information was not misrepresented.[40]

It seems that the traditional judicial implementation of the good faith doctrine has, for quite some time, begun to creak, and lost its uniform grip on press freedom. Indeed, its criteria have been applied differently by the courts depending on the context and the nature of the material. Many distinctions, with specific enforcements of the rule, were established in the fields of humour, interviews and reports, historical or political controversies, etc. The progressive disappearance of the initial coherence of the framework, which was speeded up by the increased importance of the ECHR principles, was also partly caused by taking into account the status of the defendant, taking into consideration whether he is a professional journalist or not. This last element does not have special weight concerning the first three components of good faith. The criteria for assessing the legitimacy of the purpose of a speech act are unaffected by the defendant's status: they are usually the same and consist in the will to inform and enlighten the public on matters of public interest such as the functioning of public services, the management of public institutions or any other subject matter on which there could be a right to know. The same neutrality of the status of the speaker applies when determining the lack of personal animosity which is often linked to the concept of abuse in the way in which opinions are expressed. An aggressive or vindictive tone, abusive language or vicious attacks all convey a lack of caution in the expression and are seen as signs of animosity, and it does not matter whether the feeling is mutual or motivated by ideological differences.[41] In contrast, the defendant's status has greater weight when dealing with the seriousness of the investigation which must be established independently of the caution in expression component.

This criterion implies that the journalist must have performed a due diligence on the allegations, using all available investigative means, documents or reports on the subject, must carry out systematic and comprehensive cross-checks of all relevant data and, when appropriate, must interview all those concerned by the publication. As has been pointed out elsewhere,[42] this requirement has an undeniable kinship with the European concept of adequate factual basis, and there is a trend for the courts to refer more and more frequently to the supranational concept rather than to the historical domestic one, both being probably set to merge in the

---

[40] Cour de cassation, Chambre mixte, 24 November 2000, *Bulletin mixte*, n° 4.

[41] Cour de cassation, Chambre criminelle, 30 March 2005, n° 04-83.543, *Bulletin des arrêts de la chambre criminelle*, no 109.

[42] E Raschel, 'Diffamation. Justification' *JurisClasseur Communication*, fasc 116, no 124.

future. In both systems, facts must be reported faithfully, without any misrepresentation, with a constant concern for objectivity and intellectual honesty. Since good faith cannot be established on facts occurring after the publication of the material, seriousness in the investigative process implies that the defendant had, at the time he published the allegations, sufficient evidence to believe in the truth of his own allegations.

As has been frequently emphasised, proof of the seriousness of the investigation must not be confused with the demonstration of the truth of the allegations. While the former implies that reasonable efforts were made to ensure the reliability of the information, the latter requires the proof of the reality of the facts. In other words, the truth defence concerns the allegation itself whereas the good faith defence is related to the behaviour of the author of the allegation. This difference explains why, on procedural grounds, a defendant who does not plan to prove the truth of the defamatory allegation does not lose the right to enter a good faith defence. The same applies when the truth plea was rejected by the court: this rejection does not prevent the defendant from introducing evidence of his good faith.[43]

Hence, when assessing the seriousness of the investigation the courts ascertain the level of professionalism of the journalist and the soundness of the work he accomplished, which thus make his conclusions reasonably reliable. Following these guidelines, the courts have made it clear that the duty of objectivity to which any journalist is subject compels him to verify, prior to any publication, the factual accuracy of what he claims.[44] Regardless of the length of the article or report, a serious investigation requires a personal journalistic involvement, and cannot be limited to mere phone calls to an unknown police source, without trying to meet the participants. In the same vein, the prior checking of the facts by a third party cannot be regarded as due diligence since any professional journalist has the duty to carry out serious enquiries to ensure that the information reflects the reality of the case.[45] This means, for example, that repeating information provided during a press conference does not exempt the journalist from his duties of prior investigation and caution in the expression of thought.[46] Furthermore, a true investigation requires that the adversarial principle be implemented to some degree, depending of course on the nature of the situation. This requirement embodies a fundamental ethical principle: truly informing the public demands that reporters must be neutral and objective and must therefore present various viewpoints on the facts, including first and foremost those of the individuals directly involved. Of course, the judge must apply this rule pragmatically. It is not required to take evidence directly from someone who has already publicly expressed his side of the story in various publications. Also, an attempt to contact an individual may be enough as long as it was made in earnest and the individual declined to present his version.[47]

---

[43] Cour de cassation, Chambre criminelle, 24 April 2001, n° 00-85.175.
[44] Cour de cassation, Chambre criminelle, 26 November 1991, n° 90-83.897.
[45] Cour de cassation, Chambre criminelle, 8 April 2008, n° 07-82.972.
[46] Cour de cassation, Chambre criminelle, 4 December 2007, n° 06-88.967.
[47] Cour de cassation, Chambre criminelle, 6 September 2016, n° 15-83.066.

To illustrate the position of the courts, the following conditions were considered as breaching the requirement of a serious investigation: the systematic amplification and broadening of unverified local facts; the biased presentation of some facts; carrying out a non-adversarial investigation by depriving some of the individuals of the ability to present their views; and the addition of unproven facts.

The concept of seriousness of the investigation has close ties with another component of the good faith doctrine – the notion of caution in the form of expression. Indeed, the tone used by the journalist must be proportionate to the seriousness of the charges and the credibility of the incriminating evidence. Hence, the good faith defence shall prevail where the journalist, who had enough sufficiently serious and tangible evidence to legitimately believe in the veracity of his allegations, did not present his case in a tendentious manner, did not spread any confusion, and did not dramatise the issue and the facts.[48]

Based on the case law coming from the courts, the media seem to have demonstrated a persistent reluctance to submit themselves to self-regulation. Indeed, all the attempts to formalise a corpus of ethical regulations have failed. The Press Summit of 2009 proposed, in its green book, inserting a Code of Conduct into the national collective agreement. This code would have been drafted by a Committee of Wise Men and its creation would have been accompanied by the institution of an Observatory of Press practices which would have served as a forum for the regular improvement of the rules. The text was modelled on numerous existing guidelines: the original professional charter of 1918, revised in 1938; the München Charter of 1971; and the charter on the quality of information drawn up in Lille in 2008. This code was to be completed by the ethical charters developed by each media enterprise. However, disagreement among journalists' unions scuppered the project. Its sole legal outcome was the provision of the Bloche Act of 14 November 2016 which compelled media organisations to draw up internally an ethical charter and provided for the creation, in the audiovisual sector, of committees on the fairness, independence and pluralism of news reports and programmes.

This process has been rebooted twice, most recently in a 2019 mission sponsored by the Ministry of Culture.[49] The proposal to create a self-regulation body met strong opposition, summed up in the assertion, written in the columns of *Le Canard enchaîné*, that this project was attempting 'to set up a small-scale court, entrusted with the mission to sift the printed and digital press, to tell right from wrong, correct from incorrect, ethical from rigged'.[50] Establishing self-regulation has indeed often been seen as a way to bypass the courts and a process which would lead to the development of a set of soft law rules, blurred and characterised by a

---

[48] Cour de cassation, Chambre civile 1, 3 April 2007, n° 05-21.344.
[49] E Hoog, 'Confiance et liberté' (March 2019), available at: www.culture.gouv.fr/Espace-documentation/Rapports/Confiance-et-liberte-Vers-la-creation-d-une-instance-d-autoregulation-et-de-mediation-de-l-information.
[50] *Le Canard enchaîné*, 'Macron, maréchal des déontologies' 6 February 2019, cited in Hoog, 'Confiance et liberté', 26.

holier-than-thou perspective. Moreover, it was often considered to infringe upon the discretion accorded to each publisher who bears the main legal liability, and therefore should be the sole judge of the essence of the content. Dismissing these reservations, the report strongly urged for the creation of a such a self-regulating body.

6. Press Freedom and Platform Regulation

In this domestic framework, media law applies to content rather than to its container. Therefore, if exchanges through social media, forums, blogs or other platforms are mainly regulated by press law, it is because a principle of technological neutrality prevails.[51] This implies that any piece of communication, irrespective of its medium or its broadcasting channel, is first and foremost communication which is subject to the general principles of media law. The key feature is that the statement was made in the public arena.[52] Hence, the entire set of rules aimed at protecting the rights and freedom of web users as well as the interests of third parties is transferrable to activities on blogs, forums, wikis and platforms. Even ordinary repressive provisions from the Penal Code are applicable to the participative web. Basically, the same rules apply to all forms of communication, within and out of the digital sphere, a principle which does not prevent the authorities from adjusting these rules so as to take into account the specificity of each media.[53]

According to these general guidelines, web users who participate in blogs, forums or social media are legally defined as publishers and incur full criminal and civil liability for the pieces of information or content they post. The law itself, in Article 6(III) of the LCEN provides that all individuals 'whose activity consists in publishing an online public communication service' are presumed to be publishers. This provision includes all those individuals who provide online content which is subject to the same rules applicable to content published on a physical medium or through other broadcasting devices. A web user, as a content provider, may therefore be prosecuted for all the traditional offences set out in the 1881 Act: defamation; insult; public calls to commit acts of terrorism and public justification of terrorism; public calls to commit crimes and criminal offences or their public justification; revisionism; breach of presumption of innocence, etc. This approach was initiated by the courts in the first days of the Internet and was legally sanctioned by Article 6(V) of the LCEN which lays down the principle that the provisions of Chapters IV and V of the 29 July 1881 Act, which determine various specific offences and the relating procedural rules, are applicable to online public

---

[51] P Achilleas, 'Internet et libertés' *JurisClasseur Libertés*, fasc 820, no 120.
[52] Cour d'appel de Toulouse, 5 September 2002, *Communication commerce électronique*, 2003, comm 10.
[53] B Barraud, 'Droit du web participatif' *JurisClasseur Communication*, fasc 600, no 11.

communication services. The conviction of web users as publishers is usually justified by the fact that they must exercise editorial control over the content of what is posted on the digital space they have created. As one court ruling clearly underlined, the defendant is responsible for the content of the website he created and for the information circulating on this network, he alone having the power to control the flow of its diffusion.[54]

However, this implementation of ordinary law had to be adjusted to the technical specificities of digital communication. In the same manner for audio-visual media services, it was considered that the web user could be held liable as a publisher only if the contentious content had been determined before it was transmitted to the public. As the Act of 12 June 2009 pointed out, when the offence results from the content of a post sent by a web user to an online public communication service and made available to the public by this service in a personal contribution zone identified as such (for instance, a comments section), the publisher cannot be held criminally liable as the main offender if it is demonstrated that he had no prior knowledge of the post before it was put online or if, as soon as he became aware of it, he swiftly acted to withdraw the post. As Boris Barraud has noted, one of the specificities of the participative web is its interactivity and its instantaneousness, which allow web users to react immediately to the posts made by other participants, making it unreasonable to punish an unaware publisher.[55] This adjustment of the cascading liability regime is combined with a unique feature which does not apply to other means of communication: the distinction between professional and non-professional actors of the Internet.

Professional publishers are submitted to strict requirements concerning their identification. Natural persons must give their name, surname, address, phone number and their registration number at the Trade or Commercial Registry. Legal persons must disclose their trade name, share capital, address of the head office, phone number and registration number at the Companies Registry. All professional publishers must also provide the name of their publishing director and the name or trade name, address and phone number of their hosting service provider. For non-professional publishers, only the name, trade name and address of the hosting company are to be indicated, provided that the non-professional publisher has already given his name, surname, address and phone number to the hosting service provider.

Besides considering the technical constraints of digital communication, the law, through the action of the courts, also seems to grant some weight to the status of the defendant. Some leniency is, at times, shown towards amateurs. The requirements that must be met in order to benefit from the good faith defence are indeed sometimes lowered when the defendant is not a professional journalist.

---

[54] TGI Toulouse, 5 June 2002, *Communication commerce électronique*, 2002, no 118, note L Grynbaum.
[55] Barraud (n 53).

As one ruling explained, a personal blogger is not required, prior to publication, to carry out a thorough, complete and objective investigation such as that expected of a reporter. The same idea was underlined by the Cour de cassation, which held that a private citizen cannot be subjected to the same requirements as an information professional. Therefore, the allegations made by the individual in this case, although clearly of an undeniably controversial nature, were free of personal animosity and were related to a raging debate of ideas, and as such they did not overstep the admissible boundaries of free speech.[56] It was also pointed out that a professional journalist, when hosting a blog in a purely personal and unpaid capacity, loses his professional status and in consequence was not compelled to carry out a thorough investigation of the facts he mentioned.[57] This should not be overstated, however. While the standards are somewhat lowered, the defendant still needs to fulfil the general requirements for a good faith defence: a legitimate purpose; the lack of personal animosity and caution; and restraint in the way of expression. These requirements will simply be adjusted and this customisation mainly concerns the seriousness of the investigation which is replaced by a bona fide belief in the seriousness of the sources. The courts will therefore examine whether the defendant left any glaring gaps in his evidence seeking process.

The application and adaptation to web users of the traditional legal standards governing press freedom has proven, in spite of legal or judicial adjustments, utterly inadequate. Such a danger was identified in the early years of the development of the Internet. As a former Minister of Justice put it,

> the technological evolutions have fundamentally changed the problem. We are no longer in the era of printed press! … We have to cope with a tool which is out of proportion with the printed press we knew and which was the standard in 1881. The Internet causes tremendous problems, and we must take adequate measures.

This appeal fell on deaf ears, however, and the sole effective measure consisted in extending the time limit for some specific offences. Aiming to fight hate speech on the Internet, the so-called Perben II Act of 9 March 2004 provided that the time limit to lodge a complaint was extended to one year for incitements to discrimination and for defamation and insults based on ethnicity or religion. This rule was later applied by the Act of 27 January 2014 to all incitements to commit aggravated discrimination or insult. This half measure could not, however, solve the inability of the judicial system to deal with the surge of litigation in recent years.

It is commonly pointed out that the implementation of press law to Internet users has produced a strange result: widespread litigation but few convictions. This outcome can be explained first of all by the lack of means of the courts. Traditionally, the bulk of press trials falls within the jurisdiction of the Seventeenth Chamber of the Paris tribunal judiciaire which is composed of only six judges. Therefore, cases are usually heard one year after the complaint was lodged, a delay

---

[56] Cour de cassation, Chambre criminelle, 15 March 2016, n° 14-88.072.
[57] Cour d'appel de Paris, 6 June 2007.

which conflicts with the spirit of press law which relies on very short time limits so as to put an end to unlawful situations as soon as possible. To remedy this situation, a recent statutory reform set aside a traditional rule which prohibited the implementation of summary trial procedures for press offences.[58] This derogation is limited in its scope, since it applies only to hate speech and concerns only material which had not been reviewed by a publisher prior to publication. Journalists are excluded from this new rule, which was crafted to target web users.

This case overload is not compensated by a high conviction rate, however, quite the opposite. Two main explanations have been suggested for this, one domestic and one international. First, one must consider the impediment created by the specific procedural rules of press law, especially the very short time limit and the court's lack of authority to change the characterisation of the facts defined in the complaint, leading to many inadmissibility rulings. Second, since the main Internet technical intermediaries are in the United States, the courts must often rely on the cooperation of the American Justice Department to obtain evidence. This relationship has sometimes proven difficult since the First Amendment protection of free speech has turned out to be a major impediment to the requests made by French courts on the basis of the Treaty on Judicial Cooperation of 10 December 1998.

Belatedly realising that acting on the web user end of the problem was, while not necessarily pointless, at least insufficient, the legislator eventually resolved to act against those who are accountable by design. This policy was explicitly recommended in a report sponsored by the Undersecretary for Digital Matters which stated that the prosecution policy had to be completed by a second component aimed at making platform operators more accountable through the establishment of diligence and transparency duties of social networks towards their members. In this view, the law should not rely solely on the removal of content but should act upstream and address the issue through the ability of the operators to accelerate or slow the dissemination of content and to regulate the behaviour of the users. This project was implemented by the Act of 24 August 2021 which seeks to involve platform operators in the fight against the dissemination of unlawful material. Reforming the LCEN, this new statute requires that platforms operators, which are now legally defined as components of the fight against unlawful content, insert in their terms and conditions a prohibition on posting unlawful content. These conditions must also precisely describe their moderation system, the contractual and legal measures applicable in the event of a breach, and their procedures, especially those concerning account deactivation. As has been observed, this Act compels the platform operators to comply with a legal specification, a method commonly used in contemporary law-making which consists of ordering private players to establish binding contractual norms while giving them some leeway as to the content of the rules.[59]

---

[58] Act of 24 August 2021, Art 46, amending Art 397(6) of the Penal Code.
[59] G Loiseau, 'Dissémination de contenus illicites: la pression monte vis-à-vis des opérateurs' *Communication commerce électronique*, 2021, comm 72.

7. Conclusion

In many ways, the French legal framework governing press freedom may seem to have reached the end of the line. Its many reforms have stripped it of the little clarity it had in the first place. There are too many offences, scattered all over the legal board and poorly articulated. The judicial system lacks the means to deal with new practices and is compelled to rely on ill-fitting statutory provisions, blurring even more legal solutions. The legislator, finally aware that making something new out of something old does not work, has thrown up his hands and delegated the mission to resolve them to private operators, who are themselves the source of some of the problems. The press itself, preoccupied by its own infighting, is unable to unite so as to address the challenges created by the digital era. Some believe that salvation will come from the outside, through the European Digital Services Act. One might well doubt it.

4

German Constitutional Rules Concerning the Press

UDO FINK

1. Introduction

Article 5(1) of the German Basic Law (Grundgesetz, GG)[1] protects free speech and freedom of information as basic rights (*Grundrechte*). It also addresses the related mass media, that is broadcasting, film and the press. There are no specific regulations concerning the Internet, however. Media, such as the press and media professionals including editors and journalists, enjoy a prominent position in the constitutional structure of the Basic Law. The reasoning for this is mentioned in many decisions of the Federal Constitutional Court (Bundesverfassungsgericht, BVerfG)[2] in conformity with a broad consensus of the academic community. Access to independent and trustworthy information and a free market of opinions is a prerequisite for social discourse that forms one of the fundamental basics of all democratic procedures.[3] As a former judge of the German Federal Constitutional Court, Ernst-Wolfgang Böckenförde once stated:

> Every liberal, secularised state lives from preconditions which it cannot guarantee itself. A liberal state can ... only succeed if the freedom which it grants its citizens is self-regulated from within, because of the moral substance of each individual and the homogeneity of its society.[4]

---

[1] The Basic Law has been the Constitution of the Federal Republic of Germany since 1949.

[2] BVerfG, judgment of 5 August 1966, 1 BvR 586/62, BVerfGE 20, 162; decision of 26 February 1969, 1 BvR 619/63, BVerfGE 25, 256.

[3] It is therefore no coincidence that only states with democratically constituted governments and a functioning separation of powers occupy the top places in the current press freedom ranking, see 'Close-up Germany' in *Press Freedom Ranking 2020* (Reporters Without Borders, 2020) 1. Germany currently occupies the eleventh place.

[4] English Translation of E-W Böckenförde, 'Die Entstehung des Staates als Vorgang der Säkularisation' in Recht, Staat, Freiheit: *Studien zur Rechtsphilosophie, Staatstheorie und Verfassungsgeschichte* (Frankfurt, Suhrkamp, 1991) 92, 112.

On the one hand, numerous examples from the past up to the present day impressively demonstrate the massive influence of media such as the press on public opinion.[5] The dissemination of misinformation and of opinions based on misinformation or of deliberate hate speech attacking the core values of the legal system are likely to weaken democratic structures and may violate fundamental rights. This leads to a specific challenge for the legal system regarding press organs. Most importantly, they must be independent, free from any control by the state, especially any pre-censorship which can prevent them from performing the functions necessary for democracy. On the other hand, the legal system must provide tools to protect human rights and other public values against attacks through content that exceeds the limitations of the Constitution.

At the same time, people nowadays have direct access to electronic platforms that can multiply their ideas. The Internet in particular gives each person a stage to disseminate their own views of the world. The traditional media no longer function as 'gatekeepers' controlling access to the public. In response, the Internet forms its own communities, some of which are becoming increasingly critical of 'mainstream' newspapers and broadcasting, even if the reputation of these media was traditionally undisputed. In many cases this exceeds the level of healthy scepticism and crosses over into hostility or even the use of violence.[6]

Among all these developments the press remains the archetype of all media.[7] It is the oldest type of mass media, and it is still one of the most important factors in building public opinion. Against this background, the present chapter will examine the constitutional structure of freedom of the press and the constitutional conditions for its supervision.

2. Federal Law and State Law

Article 20(1) GG establishes Germany as a federal state, which affects, among other matters, press law. At both federal and state level, there are constitutional and

---

[5] Headlines such as the attempt by right-wing politicians to exert financial influence on a major Austrian daily newspaper, the *Kronenzeitung*, make it clear that the media has a central influence on social discourse and demonstrates the value of an independent press. Last but not least independent journalists uncovered these machinations, as a consequence of the so-called 'Ibiza affair': Leila Al-Serori et al, 'Ein Jahr Ibiza-Affäre – Ein Beben, das andauert' (*Süddeutsche Zeitung*, 17 May 2020), available at: www.sueddeutsche.de/politik/ibiza-affaere-strache-1.4909474.

[6] This is exemplified by threatening letters from the now banned right-wing extremist group Combat 18, which were intended to intimidate journalists, see F Jansen, 'Neonazis bedrohen Journalisten – Ein Verbot der rechtsextremen Gruppe Combat 18 rückt offenbar näher' *Tagesspiegel* (4 July 2019), available at: www.tagesspiegel.de/politik/neonazis-bedrohen-journalisten-ein-verbot-der-rechtsextremen-gruppe-combat-18-rueckt-offenbar-naeher/24525316.html.

[7] The Verfassung des Deutschen Reiches from 1849 (Constitution of the Paulskirche) already provided a free press in Art 143. In the Verfassung des Deutschen Reiches of 1919 (Constitution of Weimar) this was enshrined in Art 118, see B Schmidt-Bleibtreu, H Hofmann and HG Henneke (eds), Grundgesetz, 15th edn (2022) Art 5, marginal no 1.

sub-constitutional regulations dealing with the press. In the light of Article 31 GG, which gives federal law supremacy over state law, the federal constitution must be the focus of the following analysis.

Some of the provisions of the various state constitutions, such as Article 10(1) of the Constitution of Rhineland-Palatine, Article 20(1) of the Constitution of Saxony or Article 10(1) of the Constitution of Saxony-Anhalt are in any case identical in wording to Article 5(1) GG. For the federal legal system as a whole Article 28(1)(1) GG sets the rule, that the constitutional order of the states must be in conformity with the principles of the Basic Law. The existence of a free press is without doubt one of these principles.

3. Freedom of the Press in an International Context

As a result of the Second World War, when Germany was solely responsible for a war of aggression against half of the world, the Federal Constitution of 1949 opens the German legal system to all kinds of influences from international law. Already in the process of drafting the GG the Western Allies – the United States, the United Kingdom and France – had a direct influence on Germany becoming a liberal and democratic state. This of course also affected the concept of press under the new Constitution.

Against this background it is not surprising that the provisions guaranteeing freedom of the press under German law have been highly influenced by international legal sources. First, this influences the topics covered by the media. In times of globalisation, journalists work and cooperate across national borders. The content of newspapers is not limited to national subjects. Moreover, the market of newspapers is international. Readers from Germany get information from newspapers edited in Switzerland as well as in France or the United States. This free flow of information across national borders is crucial for the functioning of the European Union (EU) that fundamentally requires an open market of information across the borders of its Member States.

Because Germany is a member of the EU and a party to the Convention for the Protection of Human Rights and Fundamental Freedoms, Article 5(1) GG must be harmonised with Article 11(2) of the Charter of Fundamental Rights of the EU (CFR) and Article 10(1) of the Convention for the Protection of Human Rights and Fundamental Freedoms (European Convention on Human Rights, ECHR). Although the press is not explicitly mentioned in either provision, it is comprehensively protected as a manifestation of the freedom of expression.[8] Among these

---

[8] See J Meyer-Ladewig, M Nettesheim and S Raumer (eds), *EMRK: Europäische Menschenrechtskonvention*, 4th edn (Vienna, Nomos, 2017) Art 10, marginal no 19 with further references. For a detailed discussion of media freedom under the Basic Law in relation to Articles 8 and 10 ECHR, T Giegerich (1999) 63 *RabelsZ* 472 ff.

international regulations, the ECHR is of specific importance because it forms the minimum standard of the CFR (its Article 52(3))[9] and it is applicable as a reference for the interpretation of all basic rights under the Basic Law of Germany.

4. Definition of the Press as a Mass Medium Among Others

The press is mentioned in Article 5(1) GG, which states that 'freedom of the press and freedom of reporting through broadcasting and film are guaranteed. Censorship does not take place'. The wording of the text makes it clear, that Article 5(1) GG covers several different types of media. The application of this law therefore requires manageable definitions of the terms press, broadcasting and film. In times of media convergence, driven by common platforms, notably the Internet, differentiating between the press and broadcasters is becoming more and more difficult.[10] Traditionally the concept of press in the German Federal Constitution is that, irrespective of its content, it is printed matter suitable and intended for distribution to an undefined group of persons. It is irrelevant whether the printed matter is published periodically.[11] Examples of the 'press' by this definition include, in addition to the daily newspapers covered by the conventional definition, company and school newspapers, books or leaflets.[12]

This concept, based on Johannes Gutenberg's invention of printing in 1450, has become too narrow. Nowadays this is only one way of disseminating press content. Press organs increasingly employ electronic platforms such as the Internet. With technical progress, increasing numbers of electronic ways of dissemination have become more and more dominant. These channels are more fast-moving and accessible to a wider audience while the prophets of doom conjure up the spectre of the 'death of newspapers' with regard to print media.[13] The exact definition of the so-called electronic press is quite complex, however, because the Internet also hosts other types of media. Concerning broadcasting, Article 5(1) GG contains a guarantee of development that allows broadcasters to leave behind traditional methods of using radio waves in order to disseminate content on electronical platforms instead.[14] Similar guarantees do not exist for the press, or at least the

---

[9] *Cf von Hannover v Germany*, App no 59320/00, judgment of 24 June 2004, NJW 2004, 2647.

[10] H Mangoldt, F Klein and C Starck, *GG*, 7th edn (Munich, CH Beck, 2018) Art 5, para 132.

[11] HD Jarass and B Pieroth, Grundgesetz, 16th edn (Munich, CH Beck, 2020) Art 5, marginal no 34.

[12] BVerfG, decision of 8 October 1996, 1 BvR 1183/90, NJW 1997, 386.

[13] M Steinbeis, 'Einige Gedanken zum Zeitungssterben' (*Verfassungsblog*, 17 November 2012), available at: verfassungsblog.de/einige-gedanken-zum-zeitungssterben. In fact, the circulation figures of classic print media have been declining for years, Federation of German Newspaper Publishers, quoted by statista.com 2021, available at: de.statista.com/statistik/daten/studie/72084/umfrage/verkaufte-auflage-von-tageszeitungen-in-deutschland/#professional.

[14] As early as 1991, the Federal Constitutional Court in E 83, 238 stated: 'The guarantee of continued existence and development for public service broadcasting also extends to new services using new technologies that can take over the functions of conventional broadcasting in the future'.

Federal Constitutional Court is yet to develop such a concept. The printing press, in the narrow technical approach taken by the Federal Constitutional Court at least, requires recording on physical carrier media such as CD-ROMs, disks or flash drives.[15]

However, several facts suggest that digitally published journalistic work should also be qualified as press products. Especially in the case of online magazines, online journals, news blogs or newsletters, it seems arbitrary to classify an article as being press or not, depending solely on the mode of publication. If one takes this idea *ad absurdum*, it means that an article in a conventional newspaper is regarded as being published in the press, while the same article would not be protected by freedom of the press when distributed via the Internet. Instead, as in the area of the protection of personality rights,[16] like personal data or pictures, the Basic Law is open to technological developments while the concept of the press is open to such an interpretation in order to ensure the most comprehensive protection of fundamental rights possible.[17] Ultimately, it will have to be differentiated in individual cases whether the characteristics of the 'press' are present or whether a medium is protected by other fundamental rights.[18] A purely formal approach is therefore inappropriate. As a result, the fact that it employs electronic media like the Internet is no longer enough to determine whether a specific piece of content is press or broadcasting.

The Federal Constitution does not provide a precise definition of electronic press, since Article 5(1) GG was never adapted to the era of the Internet. Such a definition can only be found in other legal sources, which take all the relevant technological developments into account. Definitions of broadcasting, tele-media in general and tele-media that are similar to broadcasting are given in the interstate agreement on media services (Medienstaatsvertrag, MStV). This treaty between all 16 States of the Federation is not part of the Basic Law, meaning that it cannot be used *ipso jure* as a tool for the interpretation of the Constitution. It is generally agreed that the definition of broadcasting given in this treaty is narrower than the definition used in the Constitution.[19] However, the essence of distinguishing electronic press from broadcasting in the sense of Article 5 GG is reflected in this treaty.

Tele-media are defined in the second sentence of section 1(1) MStV as all electronic information and communication services, insofar as they are not

---

[15] C Starck and A Paulus in Mangoldt, Klein and Starck, (n 10) Art 5, para 129.

[16] One may only think of the right to informational self-determination, on this fundamentally BVerfG, judgment of 15 December 1983, 1 BvR 209/83, BVerfGE 65, 1; or confidentiality and integrity of technical systems, on this BVerfG, judgment of 27 February 2008, 1 BvR 370/07, BVerfGE 120, 274.

[17] In conclusion, also BVerfG, decision of 21 December 2016, 1 BvR 1081/15, NJW 2017, 1537; in Schmidt-Bleibtreu, Hofmann and Henneke (n 7) Art 5, marginal no 18.

[18] For a more detailed overview of issues related to press work and freedom of expression on the Internet, in particular censorship and the responsibility of platform operators, see D Hauck et al, *International Report on Internet Censorship* 365 ff. In general on the regulation of electronic press products, W Lent, *ZUM* (Munich, CH Beck, 2013) 914 ff.

[19] Mangoldt, Klein and Starck (n 10) Art 5, para 178.

telecommunication services according to section 3(61) of the Telecommunications Act, which consist entirely of the transmission of signals, or telecommunications-supported services according to section 3(63) of the Telecommunications Act or broadcasting according to sentences 1 and 2.[20] In the light of this definition, electronic press must be qualified as tele-media.[21] Paragraph 17 ff of the MStV calls them tele-media with journalistic and editorially designed offerings reproducing periodical printed products. Thus, they are seen as tele-media in the sense that they are covered by the regulations of this treaty. Their content, however, is equal to traditional press products.

Nevertheless, these tele-media are different from broadcasting or tele-media similar to broadcasting. Radio and television as forms of broadcasting are defined in section 1(2) MStV as the presentation and dissemination of journalistic-editorial offerings in moving images or sound by means of telecommunication.[22] Tele-media with content that is similar in form and design to radio or television, and that is made available from a range specified by a provider for individual retrieval at a time chosen by the user (audio and audiovisual media services on demand), must share the same features. The essence of these definitions is as follows. Broadcasting and tele-media similar to broadcasting disseminate mainly moving images and sound. 'Mainly' means that broadcasters are also entitled to disseminate text. Overall, however, the whole content in broadcasting, moving images together with sound must be predominant. When there is published text, it has to have a close interrelation to the moving images. Section 30(7) MStV states that tele-media offers must not be press-like. They are to be designed primarily using moving images or sound, with text not being the main focus.[23]

Under this regulation 'press-like' is any publication, where text is 'the main focus'. Press may also include photographs but no moving images. However, the requirement that text must be predominant is related to content and not to the traditional definition of printing as a process of production. The distinction between these different types of tele-media is crucial because each of these media is subject to a different regulation regime. Broadcasting is very deeply and very precisely regulated. Private broadcasters need a licence, whereas public broadcasters are directly established by law. Their financing, specifically financing through advertisements, is restricted, and even their content is, at least in principle, prescribed. Sophisticated rules ensure that the broadcasting market guarantees a

---

[20] 'Tele-media are all electronic information and communication services, unless they are telecommunication services according to Paragraph 3 No 61 of the Telecommunications Act, which consist entirely in the transmission of signals, or telecommunication-based services according to Paragraph 3 No 63 of the Telecommunications Act, or broadcasting according to Sentences 1 and 2'.

[21] 'Telemedia with journalistic-editorially designed offerings in which, in particular, the contents of periodical print products are reproduced in full or in part in text or images'.

[22] 'Broadcasting is a linear information and communication service; it is the provision and dissemination of journalistic and editorial content in moving images or sound for the general public and for simultaneous reception along a broadcasting schedule by means of telecommunications'.

[23] 'Tele-media services must not be similar to the press. They are to be designed with a focus on moving images or sound, whereby text may not be in the foreground'.

certain pluralism of ideas. Tele-media which reproduce press products, such as those in the printed press need no licence and can be operated freely and their financing through advertisements is not limited, nor are there any requirements concerning their content. The regulation of this type of media is confined to the observance of journalistic standards (paragraph 19 MStV), the obligation to name the responsible publisher (paragraph 18 MStV, 'Impressumspflicht'), and the obligation to publish counterstatements (paragraph 20 MStV, 'Gegendarstellungsrecht').

5. Autonomy from the State

First and foremost, freedom of the press grants rights to individuals and companies working in that area to decide autonomously about the content they want to disseminate. Editors and journalists can defend themselves against state interference when disseminating any opinions and facts of any kind. For the same reason, the second sentence of Article 5(1) GG refers to press organisations that are independent from the state.[24] The press can only be organised privately, and any influence by the state and its subdivisions is prohibited. In the famous *Spiegel* decision the Federal Constitutional Court stated that the important role of the press for a functioning democracy cannot be fulfilled by the state. Press companies must be able to organise themselves privately. They must work according to private-sector principles and in private-law organised forms. Consequently, they are in intellectual and economic competition with each other, in which the public authorities are not allowed to intervene.[25]

6. Free Press as an Exclusive Right of Publishers?

As the journalist Abott Liebling once remarked: 'Freedom of the press is guaranteed only to those who own one'.[26] In a certain sense this is also true of press organisations under the German Constitution. A free and pluralistic market of information requires different press organs which stand for different opinions. Traditionally, the press includes a range of opinions: conservative, liberal, social and extreme. The approach of a specific publication is linked to the editor, no matter whether this is a company, a private owner or, as in the *Frankfurter Allgemeine Zeitung* case,

---

[24] G Dürig, R Herzog and R Scholz (eds), *Grundgesetz 95* (Munich, CH Beck, 2021) Art 5, marginal no 234.

[25] BVerfGE 20, 162, 174: 'As important as the "public task" thus falling to the press is, it cannot be fulfilled by organised state power. Press enterprises must be able to form themselves freely in the social sphere. They work according to private-sector principles and in private-law forms of organisation. They are in intellectual and economic competition with each other, in which public authority may not intervene as a matter of principle'.

[26] Abott J Liebling, 'The Wayward Press: Do You Belong in Journalism?' *New Yorker* (14 May 1960) 105, 109.

the leading newspaper of conservative political opinions in Germany, a board of journalists working for that specific paper.

The Federal Constitutional Court has stated that the freedom to determine, maintain, change and implement the attitude of a newspaper, which is crucial for democracy, requires that this presupposes the existence of a relatively large number of press products that are independent of the state and which compete with each other in terms of their opinions, political leaning or basic ideological attitudes, which in turn depends on the fact that the basic policy of a newspaper can be determined and implemented without being influenced.[27] Such an influence can be performed by the state, for example through public boards of control, or can also be performed by journalists working for a specific paper having different political ideas. If a newspaper wants to stand for one specific ideology, only the publisher can safeguard this direction.

7. Freedom of the Press as Protection of Content

Freedom of the press involves the dissemination of facts and opinions without any interference from the state. Concerning opinions, however, the Federal Constitutional Court gives priority to the right to free speech in the first sentence of Article 5(1) GG, in the sense that the content of the press delivering opinions is covered by free speech and not by freedom of the press.[28] The Constitutional Court also states that statements of facts are not expressions of opinion in the strict sense,[29] because they focus on the objective relationship between the utterance and reality. Unlike opinions, facts can be checked for their truthfulness. But this does not necessarily mean that factual allegation falls beyond the scope of Article 5(1)(1) from the outset. Since opinions are generally based on actual assumptions or relate to actual circumstances, they are protected by free speech insofar as they are a prerequisite for the formation of opinions.

---

[27] BVerfGE 52, 283, 295: 'Das setzt die Existenz einer relativ großen Zahl selbständiger, vom Staat unabhängiger und nach ihrer Tendenz, politischen Färbung oder weltanschaulichen Grundhaltung miteinander konkurrierender Presseerzeugnisse voraus … die ihrerseits davon abhängt, daß die Grundrichtung einer Zeitung unbeeinflußt bestimmt und verwirklicht werden kann'. ('This presupposes the existence of a relatively large number of independent press products, independent of the state and competing with each other according to their tendency, political colouring or ideological stance … which in turn depends on the fact that the basic direction of a newspaper can be determined and realised without influence'.).

[28] BVerfGE 85, 1(11): 'Freedom of the press is neither a special fundamental right for opinions disseminated in print, nor is it a repetition of freedom of expression aimed at the press'.

[29] BVerfGE 90, 241, 247: 'Factual assertions, on the other hand, are not statements of opinion in the strict sense. In contrast to these, the objective relationship between the statement and reality is in the foreground. In this respect, they are also amenable to verification as to their truthfulness. However, factual assertions do not fall outside the scope of protection of Sentence 1 of Article 5(1) GG from the outset. Since opinions are usually based on factual assumptions or take a position on factual circumstances, they are protected by the fundamental right at least to the extent that they are a prerequisite for the formation of opinions'.

Free speech covers all types of opinions and facts regardless of their importance for social discourses or even their credibility. Their specific content and quality are irrelevant.[30] Scandal sheets and tabloids are protected in the same way as the political journalism of traditional newspapers or periodicals. If the publication of opinion is likely to be harmful to others, the different constitutional values involved must be balanced. However, this balancing affects the limitations laid down in Article 5(2) GG rather than the scope of the protection.[31]

8. False Information

Factual statements can be false, and published facts can be checked for their truthfulness. The protection of false information is questionable. In principle, freedom of the press, like the Constitution as a whole, is based on the liberal model of responsible, reasonable citizens. As such, it leaves it to the individuals' own responsibility to inform themselves about the truth, possibly by consulting different sources. On top of this for journalists, it may be hard to decide if a fact is true or false. Very often the press is under pressure to produce an urgent publication without having time to check all the relevant sources. In conformity with the jurisprudence of the Supreme Court of the United States (US),[32] however, reports cross the boundary lines of protection when, at the time they are written, their authors deliberately or blatantly include untrue statements of fact or when a fact is presented in a distorted way.[33] At the level of state law, this is enshrined in Article 111(1) of the Bavarian Constitution, which states that the press has the task of reporting truthfully on events, conditions and institutions and personalities in public life in the service of democratic ideas.[34] Specifically, the right to free speech and a free press does not cover so-called 'Holocaust denial',[35] which constitutes a crime in itself under German federal criminal law.[36]

---

[30] Jarass and Pieroth (n 11) Art 5, marginal no 34.

[31] 'The Basic Rights make a difference between the areas protected, here freedom of the press and the regime of limitations. Freedom of the press as shown below finds its limitations in Article 5(2) GG naming individual and public values suitable for this limitation'.

[32] *New York Times Co v Sullivan* 376 US 254 (1964): 'The First Amendment protects the publication of all statements, even false ones, about the conduct of public officials except when statements are made with actual malice'.

[33] BVerfG, decision of 25 January 1961, 1 BvR 9/57, NJW 1961, 819, 820; Jarass and Pieroth (n 11) Art 5, marginal no 35.

[34] BVerfGE 52, 283, 295: 'The press has the task of reporting truthfully on events, conditions, institutions and personalities in public life in the service of democratic thought'.

[35] BVerfGE 90, 241, 248: 'The forbidden statement that there was no persecution of the Jews in the Third Reich is a factual claim that has been proven untrue according to countless eyewitness reports and documents, the findings of the courts in numerous criminal proceedings and the findings of historical science. On its own, therefore, a claim of this content does not enjoy the protection of freedom of expression'.

[36] Article 130(1) Federal Criminal Code (StGB): '(3) Anyone shall be punished with imprisonment of up to five years or a fine, who commits an act of the kind specified in Article 6(1) of the Code of Crimes

The press is obliged to check the truth of news and allegations that it passes on.[37] In terms of sub-constitutional law, this is expressed by the fact that case law, for example in private-law liability issues, places special demands on those working in the press. In the context of justifying interference, it places special demands on the worthiness of the protection of the concrete conduct in individual cases (due diligence appropriate to the press).[38]

9. Free Speech and Other Press-Related Activities

9.1. The Principle

Freedom of the press does not only protect the content of articles or the general political outlook of a newspaper or a periodical. In the interest of the comprehensive protection of all activities that are essentially related to the freedom of the press, auxiliary activities that are not related to such content and that are carried out in the context of the editorial production of articles, commentaries and reports, and that are indispensable for the functioning of the press, are also protected. These include preparation, the work involved and the area of affect, the collection of information, editorial implementation and the sale of the press products. The type of organisational integration of any such activity into the press business is thereby not a decisive factor in the scope of this protection.[39] As the Federal Constitutional Court stated in its *Cicero* decision: 'The areas in which freedom of the press and broadcasting are guaranteed include those prerequisites and auxiliary activities without which the media cannot adequately fulfill their function.'[40]

9.2. Disclosure of Sources

Unlike the free press clause in the First Amendment of the US Constitution,[41] Article 5(1) GG grants the right of the press not to disclose its sources.[42] In the

against International Law, committed under the rule of National Socialism, in a manner that is likely to disturb public peace, in public or in an assembly, which approves, denies or downplays them'.

[37] BVerfG, decision of 25 January 1961, 1 BvR 9/57, NJW 1961, 819, 820. Because of the special credibility placed in images, this applies in particular to deep fakes, the deceptively genuine-looking technical image manipulations.

[38] Dürig, Herzog and Scholz (n 24) Art 5, marginal no 445 f.

[39] ibid Art 5, marginal no 271 f.

[40] BVerfGE 117, 244, 259: 'The areas of guarantee of freedom of the press and broadcasting include those conditions and auxiliary activities without which the media cannot fulfil their function in an appropriate manner'.

[41] In *Branzburg v Hayes* 408 US 665 (1972) Justice White stated: 'From the beginning of the country, the press has operated without constitutional protection for press informants, and the press has flourished'.

[42] BVerfGE 117, 244, 259: 'In particular, the confidentiality of the information sources and the relationship of trust between the press or radio and the informants are protected' (*cf* BVerfGE 100, 313 [365]

Cicero decision, similarly to several of its other decisions, the Constitutional Court stated that the confidentiality of information sources and the relationship of trust between the press or broadcasting and the informants are protected. The Court considers this protection indispensable because the press cannot function without private communications, but this source of information can only flow productively, in some situations, if the informant can basically rely on the preservation of editorial secrecy.[43]

This approach is in conformity with the jurisprudence of the European Court of Human Rights (ECtHR). In its decision on *Tillack v Belgium* concerning the German periodical *Der Stern* the Court stated:

> Protection of journalistic sources is one of the cornerstones of freedom of the press. Without such protection, sources may be deterred from assisting the press in informing the public on matters of public interest. As a result, the vital public-watchdog role of the press may be undermined and the ability of the press to provide accurate and reliable information may be adversely affected. Having regard to the importance of the protection of journalistic sources for press freedom in a democratic society, such a measure cannot be compatible with Article 10 of the Convention unless it is justified by an overriding requirement in the public interest.[44]

9.3. Access to Sources

The press has a constitutionally based right of access to all sources which are open to the public.[45] These can be private or public sources. If the state is in charge of such a source which principally must be open to the public as, for example, is the case in court trials, the court is not allowed to exclude journalists from specific newspapers from the hearing by arguing that the way this newspaper reports about a specific case is likely to disturb a fair trial. In doing so the Court could use its competences to 'reward' or 'punish' press representatives at will for the way they practise their profession, control future reporting and ultimately gain influence over the appearance and content of press releases.[46]

---

with further references). 'This protection is indispensable because the press cannot do without private communications, but this source of information only flows productively if the informant can basically rely on the preservation of editorial secrecy' (*cf* BVerfGE 20, 162 [176, [187]; 36, 193 [204]]).

[43] BVerfGE 100, 313, 365.

[44] *Tillack v Belgium*, App no 20477/05, judgment of 27 November 2007.

[45] BVerfGE 50, 234, 240: 'Only the principally unhindered access to information puts the press in a position to effectively perform the role established to it in a free democracy'.

[46] BVerfGE 50, 234, 243: 'If the judge were allowed to justify the removal of a press representative from the courtroom (§ 177 GVG) with reference to the – earlier or future – reporting of the press organ he represents, he could, by means of the powers granted to him by the session police, "reward" and "punish" press representatives at will for the way they exercise their profession, control future reporting and thus ultimately gain influence on the appearance and content of press publications. This would be incompatible with Sentence 2 of Article 5(1) GG'.

It is a matter of controversy among scholars whether freedom of the press grants rights of access to sources run by the state or its subdivisions which the state wants to disclose. The Federal Administrative Court in 2015 stated that in the absence of a statutory regulation, the fundamental right to the freedom of the press gives the press a right deriving directly from the Constitution to information from federal authorities.[47] Due to this right, press representatives can request official information in a suitable form if no legitimate interests of private or public bodies are in conflict with this.[48] This right to information is still not precisely defined, however. The Federal Constitutional Court has yet to take a concrete position on such a right following directly from Article 5(1) GG, nor on the limitations of such a right.[49] To date it has mainly been left to the statutory law to grant such rights of access (paragraph 6(1) Landesmediengesetz Rheinland-Pfalz; paragraph 5 Sächsisches Mediengesetz; Article 4(1) Bayerisches Pressegesetz).

10. Freedom of the Press as an Institutional Guarantee

Generally, the basic rights under the Federal Constitution, similarly to human rights under European and international conventions, grant individual rights to protect a specific freedom against public interference. Hence, as noted above this is the object of the second sentence of Article 5(1) GG. However, basic rights can also have an objective dimension. In the case of a free press, the Federal Constitutional Court calls it the institution of a free press.[50] There are some fundamental differences between the individual rights against the state and the institutional guarantee of a free press. First, the institutional guarantee must be considered by any state regulation concerning the press no matter whether it is claimed specifically by individual journalists or press organs. It is in that sense self-executing.[51] Moreover, the state is not only obliged not to interfere, it is also obliged to protect the press by creating rules that make it possible and more effective for the press to perform.

---

[47] BVerwGE 146, 56, para 11: 'In the absence of a simple statutory regulation by the federal legislature, the fundamental right of freedom of the press confers on the press a constitutional right to information vis-a-vis federal authorities'. Recently BVerwG, judgment of 8 July 2021, BVerwG 6 A 10.20, NVwZ 2022, 248.

[48] BVerwG, judgment of 8 July 2021 – 6 A 10/20, para 2(a): 'On the basis of this constitutional right to information, members of the press may request information from the authorities in response to sufficiently specific questions, provided that the relevant information is available at the authority and that the confidentiality of the information does not conflict with the interests of public bodies or private persons that are worthy of protection'.

[49] Explicitly left open in BVerfG, decision of 8 September 2014, 1 BvR 12/14, NJW 2014, 3711, marginal no 26.

[50] 'In accordance with the systematic position of the provision and its traditional understanding, a subjective fundamental right is granted to persons and companies working in the press sector, which guarantees its bearers freedom from state interference and grants them a privileged legal position in certain contexts, but the provision has at the same time also an objective legal side. This is the guarantee of the institute of a free press'.

[51] BVerfG, judgment of 5 August 1966, 1 BvR 586/62, BVerfGE 20, 162.

As already noted, there must be statutory rules granting access to sources, the press must be protected against attacks by civilians through defamation, insult or even physical threat. The state's duty to protect must be considered, above all, with regard to the threat posed to journalists by extremist groups. In so-called 'blacklists', personal data such as the real names and addresses of numerous journalists are compiled in a publicly visible manner; in this context, there are also regular calls for violence against those concerned.[52] This is associated with a massive potential threat to those working in the press, ranging from threatening letters to acts of violence. The legislator has already acted and has presented a draft law addressing this issue, which has already been discussed in a first reading in the Bundestag. An amendment to the Criminal Code is intended to enable law enforcement authorities to take consistent action against such blacklists.[53] The development of the legislative process regarding this topic remains to be seen.

Furthermore, the institutional guarantee also contains aspects that can be 'dangerous' for the actual concept of a free press. The press, like broadcasting, plays a vital role in the functioning of democracy.[54] Democracy is not a human right driven by the protection of individual freedom, but a fundamental principle of the state. Its functioning is in the interests of the state and society in general. For broadcasting, the consequence of this role to 'serve' democracy was the creation of public broadcasters which are not part of the state but which are under a significant influence of state officials and relevant political parties. Public broadcasters cannot claim to be free in choosing their content. They are under a legal obligation to serve the specific interests of their viewers and hence of democracy. This also justifies the fact that there is a legal obligation for all people to pay a contribution of €8.4 billion[55] a year to finance their activities, which are prescribed in the relevant media law.

Broadcasters must not only be able 'to do their job' for democracy. The system must guarantee a minimum of pluralism in the sense that most of the relevant groups like parties, public and private associations, religious communities and others are represented in their programming schedule. In respect to broadcasting, the Federal Constitutional Court is convinced that mere competition between private broadcasters is not sufficient to safeguard pluralism. Only together with the public broadcasters who through the legally prescribed composition of their boards are pluralistic in themselves can the system meet all democratic needs. As shown above, the organisation of the press has gone a different way. Moreover,

---

[52] *Press Freedom Ranking 2020* (n 3) 2.

[53] Critical of this, ibid 8; BT-Drs 19/28678, 1.

[54] See para 3 Landespressegesetz BW: 'The press fulfills a public task if it procures and disseminates news in matters of public interest, comments, criticizes or otherwise participates in the formation of opinion'.

[55] Bericht der Arbeitsgemeinschaft Beitragsservice von ARD, ZDF und Deutschlandradio 2021, available at: presse.rundfunkbeitrag.de/pressreleases/beitragsservice-stellt-jahresbericht-2021-vor-stabilitaet-trotz-corona-3188462.

it has, as the Federal Constitutional Court stated, the same, or nearly the same, relevance for democracy as broadcasters.[56] Unlike the situation in broadcasting, in professional journalism the coverage of actual topics and pluralism have up to now been safeguarded by a market of different fully private competitors.

With the rise of the Internet, this market has come under more and more pressure. The press, which must finance all its costs itself, has had to dramatically change its income strategies, traditionally mainly based on the advertising of jobs, housing, holidays or cars. This market has almost completely gone over to other platforms on the Internet. Selling physical newspapers is also a shrinking market. Under the rules of the Internet, press organisations must either sell their content differently or attract advertising connected to their content. This strategy can only be successful if this content is still regarded as valuable enough to spend money on. This is the root of the problem. The biggest competitors of the newspapers, with the power to ruin them, are the public broadcasters on the one hand, and the big Internet corporations with their information and social media platforms on the other.

Public broadcasters serve the same needs as many press organs. They inform their viewers and listeners about politically and socially relevant topics from all over the world and in every region, they invest a huge amount of money in the very popular sport market,[57] and they are also active in the fields of both high and popular culture and on the topics of the 'yellow press'. They do not have to find customers to finance their offers, however. As shown above, they get billions of euros through the legal obligations of the whole population, regardless of whether somebody uses their services or not. Some call this obligation to pay a monthly fee a 'contribution of the society to democracy'.[58]

Through the big media companies people can access the same information from varied sources. The source of this information is often the big news agencies which also sell their content to newspapers or journals. While their content

---

[56] The Court sometimes mentions that moving images of broadcasting have more influence on opinion making than the written giving broadcasters the role of a 'leading' media. BVerfGE, 1 BvF 1/91, para 106: 'Television is not the only medium that provides information about events of general importance. However, it is the only medium that is able to report on an event simultaneously in image and sound. Because of the semblance of authenticity and witness it conveys, as well as its convenient availability, it has become the medium from which most of the population obtains its information'.

[57] Between 2017 and 2020, ARD (community of all regional public broadcasters in Germany) and ZDF (broadcaster founded by an interstate treaty of all states) together paid €1.163 billion for sport rights; Joachim Huber, 'KEF-Anmeldung der ARD: Beitrags-Milliarden für Fußball und Olympia' *Tagesspiegel* (18 September 2015), available at: www.tagesspiegel.de/gesellschaft/medien/kef-anmeldung-der-ard-beitrags-milliarden-fuer-fussball-und-olympia/12337734.html.

[58] See, among many others, Alexander Neubacher, 'Was hat Käpt'n Silbereisen mit Demokratie zu tun?' *Der Spiegel* (21 November 2020), available at: www.spiegel.de/politik/deutschland/rundfunkgebuehren-streit-was-hat-kaept-n-florian-silbereisen-mit-demokratie-zu-tun-a-00000000-0002-0001-0000-000174103602. (Explanation: Silbereisen is an actor in a soap opera *Dream Ship* (*Das Traumschiff*) where he plays the captain of that ship. *Der Spiegel* is a weekly journal well known for its political journalism asking in that article where the link between a soap opera and democracy can be found.)

at first sight seems to be free, in the end people pay with their personal data. The top Internet corporations, which have great market power, are gaining in importance, intervening in communication in a regulatory manner within the framework of their terms and conditions or based on legal obligations. Freedom of the press is particularly affected where the algorithms of the platforms favour the distribution of certain digital press products at the expense of others.[59] In addition, the market of opinions has diversified even more radically. On media platforms users create 'bubbles' often based on misinformation or at least non-professional ways of gathering information of dubious provenance. Misinformed and misled people develop their own 'reality', following politicians who explain the world to them in the simplest way and sometimes in a radical manner and forming radical groups attacking verbally or even physically the core values of our society.

If at the end of that process the already heavily struggling quality newspapers and journals are in real danger of disappearing, state officials could follow the same strategy as with broadcasters and 'protect' the press against the market. They could organise them on publicly financed platforms or give them other forms of contributions. As the broadcasting system shows, such a transformation would have its costs in the sense of risking political influence on the press. In the end this solely private not state-influenced and not only profit-driven professional voice based on journalistic ethics would lose its specific role in our society.

11. Persons Protected

Freedom of the press is a natural human right open to all persons, without any discrimination in relation to their citizenship. Article 19(3) GG also includes private legal entities like, for example, limited companies and other non-corporate entities within the scope of the protection of freedom of the press. It is also worth noting that the text is not restricted to German entities due to the prohibition of discrimination in Article 18 of the Treaty on European Union, which also applies to legal persons of other EU Member States.[60]

It is not only journalists in the traditional meaning but bloggers, active on media platforms, who can rely on freedom of the press if they meet with its conditions. First, the opinion or information disseminated must be directed at the public. Private communication is not covered. But nobody needs professional training to be a journalist and there is no need to work for an edited press organ. The so called 'Pressecodex', meaning the journalistic standards that are usually preserved by traditional press organs publishing in Germany, is not a mandatory law.

---

[59] For an overview, see Hauck et al (n 18).
[60] Schmidt-Bleibtreu, Hofmann and Henneke (n 7) Art 5, marginal no 1.

It is given by the 'Presserat', a registered association under private law formed by organisations founded by publishers and journalists. But each 'journalist' relying on freedom of the press must publish under his name or the name of the publisher responsible. Anonymous publications as often found on the Internet are not covered by freedom of the press.[61] This minimum obligation is necessary to make the right to publish counterstatements effective if 'facts' published are wrong. Also, if the content is harmful, private liability and criminal responsibility can only be safeguarded this way.

12. Interference and its Justifications

12.1. Definition of Interference

Generally speaking, there are two possible definitions of interference. The more formal and narrow approach covers all measures by the state or of one of its sub-divisions which have the intention of setting limitations on basic rights. In this definition, all measures that are directed against any of the protected press activities, such as censorship of content, represent interference with freedom of the press. A consensus has emerged, however, that this formal approach is too narrow. It can be easily bypassed, for example, by raising a tax on a specific newspaper that makes it financially impossible for it to be published or by imposing an obligation to be licensed when the procedure for granting the licence is handled arbitrarily. As a result, a wider and less formal approach qualifies every measure taken by the state or one of its sub-divisions as interference if it has factual consequences which prevent or obstruct the freedom of the press.[62] In the above-mentioned *Cicero* decision, the Federal Constitutional Court, taking this wider approach, stated that ordering newspaper offices to be searched represented interference in the freedom of the press because of the associated disturbance of the editorial work and the possibility of an intimidating effect.[63]

12.2. Censorship

The third sentence of Article 5(1) of the GG states that censorship is prohibited. This means only pre-censorship. There can be no prior control of press content by the state and its sub-divisions. The press must never need *ex ante* permission to

---

[61] Dürig, Herzog and Scholz (n 24) Art 5, marginal nos 220, 222.
[62] Jarass and Pieroth (n 11) Art 5, marginal no 39.
[63] BVerfG, 1 BvR 538/06, decision of 27 February 2007, para 44: 'A search in press rooms constitutes an interference with the freedom of the press because of the associated disruption of editorial work and the possibility of an intimidating effect'.

publish its content. State control of press content is only possible after publication.[64] This regulation has a long tradition in German history. In 1819, Conservative politicians[65] passed the so called 'Karlsbader Beschlüsse' as a law of the 'Deutsche Bund'[66] strictly regulating the press, including pre-censorship to suppress liberal and national movements all over Germany. In the Revolution of 1848 these regulations were lifted, and the prohibition of pre-censorship became part of the constitutions of 1849,[67] 1919[68] and of the Basic Law in 1949.

12.3. Interference Through Generally Applicable Laws

According to Article 5(2) GG, all rights mentioned above in section 1, including freedom of the press, find their limits in the provisions of generally applicable laws (*Allgemeine Gesetze*). In this way, the Basic Law grants the legislature authorisation to regulate freedom of the press by statutory law. This is not a carte blanche, however. Generally, applicable laws must fulfil certain requirements in regard to freedom of the press. First, the law is only 'generally applicable' if it is not directed against the press itself or at specific opinions disseminated by the press. The law must protect public values that are not specifically related to press activities. In the above-mentioned *Cicero* decision the criminal law on which the search of press premises was based was aimed to protect the confidentiality of classified information. This confidentiality can be breached by many activities, not necessarily only through articles in the press. This implies that the law is generally applicable.

In principle, it is also not allowed to suppress specific opinions. In particular, intellectual debates or disputes about political and social ideas should not be influenced by state interference.[69] It is conspicuous in this respect that paragraph 130(3) of the Criminal Code does not meet these requirements, as the provision is directed against a specific opinion by threatening the glorification of the Hitler regime with criminal punishment. The provision is nevertheless compatible with Article 5(2) of the Basic Law, because the Basic Law sees itself as a counter-draft to the National Socialist rule of violence and arbitrariness and an exception to the prohibition of a special law for its propagandistic approval is inherent in it.[70] In this respect, this represents a German peculiarity.

Secondly, the Federal Constitutional Court developed, for this kind of law, the doctrine of interrelationship (*Wechselwirkungslehre*). In the famous *Lüth* case, a

---

[64] BVerfGE 33, 52, 72.

[65] The most prominent of these was Klemens Metternich, who at that time was *Staatskanzler* (leading minister) of the Habsburg Monarchy.

[66] A federation of German sovereign entities founded at the Congress in Vienna in 1815 to replace the Holy German Empire.

[67] The so-called *Paulskirchenverfassung*, which never came into force.

[68] The so-called *Weimarer Reichsverfassung*, transforming Germany from a monarchy to a republic.

[69] Jarass and Pieroth (n 11) Art 5, marginal no 66 f.

[70] BVerfG, decision of 4 November 2009, 1 BvR 2150/08, BVerfGE 124, 300 with comment F Hufen, 'Die Menschenwürde' [2010] *Juristische Schulung* 559.

landmark decision from the 1950s, the Court stated that the generally applicable laws, in their restricting effect on the fundamental right, must be seen in the light of the importance of this fundamental right and must be interpreted in such a way that the particular value of this right, which in a liberal democracy is a fundamental presumption for freedom of speech in all areas, but specifically in public life, is preserved in any case.[71]

12.4. Restrictions to Protect Personal Honour

Article 5(2) of the Basic Law also allows state action to protect personal honour and protection of the young. These are public values that are based directly on the Constitution so this section thus reflects the general principle that all human rights of the Federal Constitution except human dignity (Article 1(1) GG), but including freedom of the press find their limits in conflicting constitutional laws. 'Personal honour' is an old-fashioned term for a bundle of rights deriving from human dignity in interaction with the general right to freedom laid down in Article 2(1) GG. Based on this 'fusion', the Federal Constitutional Court developed generally applicable rights that affect different spheres of the personality. The closer these rights are linked to human dignity the stronger the level of protection must be.

One good example of this is the right to own a picture. This is part of the personal rights based on human dignity and personal freedom. It is not necessarily linked with copyrights. Copyrights only come into play if, for example, a photographer takes a photograph of a person which another person or the media want to use. In this case the photographer not the person on the photograph can claim a copyright. Nevertheless, under the right to own a picture, if a press organ wishes to publish a picture, which allows the identification of a specific person, this generally requires the consent of the person affected. However, when this person is a politician or a prominent person, what the ECtHR calls 'public figures',[72] then a publication without consent may be allowed because the public interest may then prevail over the right to privacy. This is only valid if the picture is not linked to private or very private activities, where human dignity prevails. Hence, publishing

---

[71] BVerfGE 7, 198, 208 f: 'General laws, in their effect of restricting the fundamental right, must in turn be seen in the light of the significance of this fundamental right and interpreted in such a way that the special value content of this right, which in a liberal democracy must lead to a fundamental presumption in favour of freedom of speech in all areas, but especially in public life, is preserved in any event'.

[72] *Von Hannover v Germany (No 2)* App nos 40660/08 and 60641/08, judgment of 7 February 2012, para 110: 'The role or function of the person concerned and the nature of the activities that are the subject of the report and/or photo constitute another important criterion, related to the preceding one. In that connection a distinction has to be made between private individuals and persons acting in a public context, as political figures or public figures. Accordingly, whilst a private individual unknown to the public may claim particular protection of his or her right to private life, the same is not true of public figures'.

pictures showing activities in the bedroom is absolutely prohibited while also generally all kinds of pictures taken in a private house, behind closed doors, are also taboo.

12.5. Protection of the Young

The other value that Article 5(2) GG specifically mentions is the protection of the young. Like personal honour, the protection of the young is based on the Federal Constitution. It derives on the one hand from human dignity, and on the other from family rights under the first sentence of Article 6(2) GG and the obligation of the state to ensure the process of education of minors in the second sentence of Article 6(2) GG. The core of these rights is human dignity.

As the Federal Constitutional Court has stated, children and young people have a right to the development of their personality within the meaning of human dignity and the right to freely develop their personality under Article 2(1) GG. They need protection and help to develop into responsible personalities within the social community. This also applies to protecting them from sexual dangers and enabling sex education that respects personal rights. It also applies to violence specifically if violence is shown in a glamourised way. This point of view entitles the state to keep children and young people away from influences that could have an adverse effect on their attitudes towards sex and violence and thus on the development of their personality.[73] The right of parents to educate their children and the right of the state to supervise this education deriving from Article 6(2) GG share the same purposes. Parents are not allowed to educate their children in their own interests. The only legitimate goal of education is to help children to freely develop their personalities.

13. Conclusion

Freedom of the press is a fundamental right for every democratic society. An independent, solely privately owned press serves as a check on state activities, provides the public with the necessary information to enable political and social

---

[73] BVerfGE 83, 130, 139: 'The protection of children and young people also has constitutional status on the basis of Article 1(1) in conjunction with Article 2(1) GG. Children and juveniles have a right to the development of their personality within the meaning of these fundamental rights standards. They require protection and assistance in order to develop into independent personalities within the social community (*cf* BVerfGE 79, 51 [63]). This also applies in particular to their protection from sexual dangers and to enabling them to receive sex education that respects their personal rights (*cf* BVerfGE 47, 46 [72 f]). This point of view entitles the state to keep away from children and juveniles influences which could have a detrimental effect on their attitude to sex and thus on the development of their personality'.

discourses, and gives its own view on these discourses. At the same time, the press has a particularly strong influence on public opinion, often precisely because of the trust placed in it. Because of that it is not guaranteed without limits. At the same time, many old questions arise anew in view of technological progress. The progress of technology brings new opportunities but also creates problems for the survival of the concept of an independent press. The Basic Law gives the legislature the opportunity to react appropriately to this. It is obliged – wherever necessary – to make adequate and moderate use of this. Within the framework of loose state regulation, compliance with ethical standards is incumbent on the press itself; the flip side of its independence is the trust placed in it, and the responsibilities which that entails.

5

Press Freedom in Ireland: Laggard or Innovator?

DAITHÍ MAC SÍTHIGH

1. Introduction

Assessing press regulation in Ireland requires attention to a number of distinctive and potentially contradictory features. Some of the relevant factors are immediately recognisable to the English observer, given a shared legal history and the continued relevance of a range of common law doctrines, notably in tort. Ireland's written constitution includes various provisions on fundamental rights, though the material relevant to the press is not just found in a clause on the press but also in other provisions. Decisions of the European Court of Human Rights (ECtHR, Strasbourg Court) have certainly had an impact, though only in the context of Ireland's dualist approach to international agreements. And Ireland has long enjoyed both a vibrant domestic press (national and local) as well as significant imports or local versions of UK titles. Public service broadcasting arrived in line with other states for radio (1922), but relatively late by European standards for television (1962); regulated commercial radio (1989) and TV (1998) came much later again, with overspill from UK broadcasters being and continuing to be a feature in the market.[1]

Importantly, though, there are a number of recent developments that have attracted particular attention, notwithstanding the relative size of Ireland and its media markets. Both are considered in this chapter. The first is the creation of a new Press Council of Ireland (PCI) in the mid-2000s, which had a distinctive statutory basis and so has often been pointed to by reformers elsewhere as a case study. The second is the pace (and unevenness) of wider media regulatory reform in the most recent years, especially in the context of Ireland's significance in the wider

---

[1] M Walsh, 'Media and Culture in Ireland, 1960–2008' in R Bourke and I McBride (eds), *The Princeton History of Modern Ireland* (Princeton, NJ, Princeton University Press, 2016); T O'Malley, 'Readers and Readerships' in M Conboy and A Bingham (eds), *The Edinburgh History of the British and Irish Press, volume 3* (Edinburgh, Edinburgh University Press, 2020).

European Union (EU) as the location of choice for many multinational companies providing online services.

Section 2 of this chapter sets out the constitutional context for press freedom and regulation in Ireland. Section 3 explores in more detail specific regulatory mechanisms, across civil law and statutory provisions; the PCI is introduced in this section. Section 4 then considers the work of the PCI and places it in a wider context, including an assessment of how it has been received and debated beyond Ireland. Section 5 looks at emerging issues, including the work of the Future of Media Commission which reported in 2022. Section 6 concludes.

2. Constitutional Context

Constitutional provisions in respect of speech, press and media are found in the Irish Constitution, adopted in 1937 (therefore predating the Universal Declaration of Human Rights and the Convention for the Protection of Human Rights and Fundamental Freedoms (ECHR)). Other than the 2018 removal by referendum of a reference to blasphemy in criminal law,[2] the relevant provisions have not been amended since then. A characteristic feature of the Irish order in respect of speech and media is that, read in light of case law, there are two different references to these matters, although both are found in the 'rights' provisions of Article 40. The most explicit reference to the press is Article 40(6)(1)(i), which is both a provision on freedom of expression and a justification for media (including press) regulation. However, there are other constitutional contexts in which issues of expression and information can potentially be dealt with – most notably a recognition of freedom of communication as an unenumerated personal right (Article 40(3)).

These provisions are supplemented by the effect of Article 10 ECHR itself (and other relevant provisions of the Convention) in Irish law, through the interpretation of constitutional and statutory provisions in a Convention context. A small number of media-related cases in respect of Irish provisions have been heard by the Strasbourg Court, and a statutory mechanism for a domestic 'declaration of incompatibility' was introduced in 2005. Turning first to the explicit reference to freedom of expression, the text is:

> The State guarantees liberty for the exercise of the following rights, subject to public order and morality: i. The right of the citizens to express freely their convictions and opinions. The education of public opinion being, however, a matter of such grave import to the common good, the State shall endeavour to ensure that organs of public opinion,

---

[2] The 37th Amendment to the Constitution (26 October 2018) and Blasphemy (Abolition of Offences and Related Matters) Act 2019; see further DH Moore, 'The Blasphemy Referendum 2018' (2019) 34 *Irish Political Studies* 315; N Cox, 'Stephen Fry, the Meaning of Life, and the Problem with Irish Blasphemy Law' (2019) 8 *Oxford Journal of Law and Religion* 247.

such as the radio, the press, the cinema, while preserving their rightful liberty of expression, including criticism of Government policy, shall not be used to undermine public order or morality or the authority of the State. (Article 40(6)(1))

For some time, the perceived narrowness of the above positions meant that a number of decisions saw the exploration of an unenumerated 'right to communicate' emanating from the constitutional provision on defending and vindicating 'the personal rights of the citizen' (Article 40(3)). Initially, the matter was explored in a case on the state monopoly over postal services;[3] the important *Murphy* case[4] on religious advertising saw both Articles considered, including discussion at the Supreme Court of the 'different philosophical systems' from which they are derived and their distinctive roles.[5] More recently, *Kivlehan v RTÉ*,[6] one of the many cases to reach the Irish courts regarding debates, time and prominence in election and referendum coverage, saw recollection of the argument that Article 40(3) has a personal focus, whereas Article 40(6) focuses on public activities of citizens,[7] and an interesting framing of Article 40(6)(1) as a positive obligation for public service broadcasters to inform and educate – in turn utilised as a stipulation to give high protection to the 'singular and unique' editorial process found in the 'press and media'.[8]

Reform of these provisions has been proposed on a number of occasions. For instance, the Constitutional Reform Group advised in 1996 that Article 40(6)(1) be replaced by a new clause drafted along the lines of Article 10 ECHR,[9] and the Joint Committee on the Constitution concluded in 2008 that it was 'a provision which is a creature of its time whose language and structure do not sufficiently reflect the primacy which must be placed on the freedom of expression in a modern democracy'[10] – although in light of the development of case law including the influence of ECtHR decisions, it suggested that a constitutional amendment (only possible in Ireland by way of referendum) was desirable but not urgent. In the meantime, key cases such as *Mahon v Post Publications* (on confidentiality and injunctions)[11] and *Mahon v Keena* (on the protection of sources)[12] have seen the Irish courts engage in detail with Article 10 jurisprudence both as an aid to understanding the constitutional provisions and in fulfilment of the statutory

---

[3] *Paperlink v AG* [1984] ILRM 373.
[4] *Murphy v Ireland* [1999] 1 IR 12.
[5] ibid [50].
[6] *Kivlehan v RTÉ* [2016] IEHC 88.
[7] ibid [30]; see commentary in E Carolan, 'Constitutionalising Discourse: Democracy, Freedom of Expression and the Future of Press Regulation' (2014) 51 *Irish Jurist* 1.
[8] [2016] IEHC 88, [59]. On positive free speech and the combined effect of the two Irish provisions, see further E Carolan, 'Promoting Civic Discourse: A Form of Positive Free Speech under the Constitution of Ireland?' in AT Kenyon and A Scott (eds), *Positive Free Speech: Rationales, Methods and Implications* (Oxford, Hart Publishing, 2020).
[9] Constitution Review Group, Report (May 1996) 292–93.
[10] Joint Committee on the Constitution, First Report (July 2008) [5.1].
[11] *Mahon v Post Publications* [2007] IESC 15.
[12] *Mahon v Keena* [2009] IESC 64.

interpretation duties under the 2005 Act. In the *Post Publications* case, too, the Supreme Court emphasised the link between the two provisions, finding that the Constitution 'unequivocally guarantees both the right to express convictions and opinions and the right to communicate facts or information', being inseparable rights and, in the present case, not being relevant which provision provides the guarantee.[13] Eoin Carolan argues that notwithstanding the established view that Ireland is a 'freedom of expression laggard', the position is more nuanced;[14] recent developments have shown the maturing of case law working with the additional text – in some cases offering protection to expression in a way that the present-day ECtHR does not necessarily do.

3. Regulation of the Press: Private and Public Law Perspectives

3.1. Defamation and Privacy Law

As expected in light of its legal and constitutional context, and despite the equal reference to 'radio', 'press' and 'cinema' in Article 40(6)(1)(i) as noted above, Ireland does not, in common with many common law legal systems, have specific legislation in respect of the press. In terms of the body of law affecting the press, then, one turns to the usual civil causes of action (historically libel/defamation law, joined in more recent years by privacy).[15] In practice, therefore, public and academic discussion in respect of the law and press freedom in Ireland has often coalesced around matters of civil law and of defamation law in particular.

The broad parameters of defamation law in Ireland are,[16] as they are in England and Wales and across the Commonwealth, through diverging statutory change – and indeed an explicit constitutional reference to the protection and vindication of the 'good name' of citizens (Article 40(3)(2))[17] – mean that assumptions cannot always be made about the tenets of the law or indeed the relevance of leading authorities. However, it is in the case of privacy that the Irish position is even more distinctive. The cause of action equivalent to 'misuse of private information' or similar is, in Ireland, a combination of the (again, unenumerated) constitutional right of privacy under Article 40(3) and the Irish doctrine that breach

---

[13] [2007] IESC 15, [51].

[14] Carolan, 'Constitutionalising Discourse' (n 7) 2.

[15] Although it is beyond the focus of the present chapter, there are a number of authorities in Irish law in respect of the privileges of the press, of journalists, etc. See, eg, *Cornec v Morrice* [2012] 1 IR 804 (protection of sources applicable to a blogger).

[16] See, generally, N Cox and E McCullough, *Defamation Law and Practice* (Dublin, Clarus Press, 2022).

[17] See discussion in, eg, *Higgins v Irish Aviation Authority* [2022] IESC 13, [116].

of constitutional rights (in some circumstances by non-state actors) can be the subject of an action against the infringing party.

The roots of today's approach to civil actions in respect of privacy are in two separate judicial developments in the 1970s: a recognition that remedies for breach of constitutional rights are available against both the state[18] *and* against private parties (in *Meskill*);[19] and the recognition of privacy as one of the personal rights protected by Article 40.[20] These actions are by and large treated as if they were torts, and injunctions and damages are available.[21] Although a bill was introduced in 2006 with the intention of codifying and amending what had happened in the courts, it came under significant criticism (especially from the media) and was ultimately withdrawn (in favour of a focus on defamation reform and the PCI – considered further in this chapter). So for the time being, the constitutionally derived action is a key part of the legal picture for the Irish media, with significant damages being available; as in other jurisdictions, typical cases can be focused on privacy alone[22] or on both privacy and reputation (defamation) claims.[23]

3.2. Regulation of Broadcasting

Again following a similar pattern to legal systems in many parts of the Commonwealth, there is a marked difference between the regulatory context in Ireland for press and for broadcast media. Ireland was relatively late in seeing the development of regulated private and community broadcasting, with the sole public service broadcaster established initially as a radio service in the 1920s and expanding to a television service in the 1960s.[24] In reaction to, amongst other things, the (similarly late) development of highly popular unlicensed ('pirate') radio broadcasting in the 1980s,[25] the first regulatory and statutory licensing system for broadcasting was established in 1988. This was followed quickly by the licensing and launch of a range of radio services, though it was not until 1998 that the first licensed private television service was launched[26] (notwithstanding Ireland's transposition of the 1989 Television Without Frontiers Directive which

---

[18] *Byrne v Ireland* [1972] IR 241.

[19] *Meskell v CIE* [1973] IR 121.

[20] *McGee v AG* [1974] IR 284; *Kennedy v Ireland* [1987] IR 587; *Cogley v RTE* [2005] 2 ILRM 529; *Gray v Minister for Justice* [2007] IEHC 52; *Herrity v Associated Newspapers* [2008] IEHC 249.

[21] *McDonnell v Ireland* [1998] 1 IR 134; *Murray v News Group Newspapers* [2010] IEHC 248.

[22] *Herrity* (n 20).

[23] *Nolan v Sunday Newspapers* [2019] IECA 141.

[24] FJ Corcoran, *RTÉ and the Globalisation of Irish Television* (Bristol, Intellect, 2004); Walsh (n 1) 264–65.

[25] J Walsh and B Greene, 'Irish Pirate Radio 1978–1988: How Political Stasis Allowed Unlicensed Radio to Flourish and Innovate' (2020) 27 *Journal of Radio & Audio Media* 274.

[26] E Komorek, *Media Pluralism and European Law* (Alphen aan den Rijn, Wolters Kluwer, 2013) 213.

was completed by 1991); further channels arrived in 2006.[27] (In practice, however, Irish audiences have long had access to television services regulated in the United Kingdom, initially through the ability on the east coast in particular to receive over the air transmissions from the United Kingdom (including Northern Ireland) and latterly through cable, satellite and other mechanisms.)[28]

The regulator established for its first years was the Independent Radio and Television Commission (IRTC) in respect of services other than the public service broadcaster Raidió Teilifís Éireann (RTÉ). The IRTC was reborn as the Broadcasting Commission of Ireland (2001) and then as the Broadcasting Authority of Ireland (2009). The 2009 reforms brought the public service broadcasting system under the Broadcasting Authority of Ireland's (BAI) overall remit though with a significant role retained for the separate RTÉ Board. A broadcasting complaints mechanism was instigated in 1990 in respect of IRTC-regulated services (having already been in place since 1976 for RTÉ); in the 2009 changes, the Broadcasting Complaints Commission was reconstituted as a committee of the new Authority (the Compliance Committee). Broadcast advertising also falls under the BAI, with the system and its operating reflecting the various provisions of EU law from Television Without Frontiers onwards; the major rules (for example, minutes per hour) are found in legislation, with more detailed rules sitting in a code adopted under statutory authority. One distinctive provision is the former total ban on political and religious advertising (section 10(3) Radio and Television Act 1988), which was challenged before the ECtHR in *Murphy v Ireland*, which led to the narrowing of the ban through subsequent legislative change; see now section 41 of the Broadcasting Act 2009, which bans political advertising while allowing for religious advertising that is not focused on adherence to or membership of a particular faith or organisation.

The other aspect of press and media regulation in Ireland is found through the control of ownership.[29] Within competition legislation, there are specific provisions for media businesses, with a particular role prescribed for the minister responsible for media in respect of media plurality.[30] In common with many EU Member States, there has also been close scrutiny of state-financed public service broadcasting in terms of EU provisions on state aid; to date, this has only arisen in respect of the major public service broadcasters (RTÉ and the Irish language TG4), and there is no tradition of state aid or subsidy towards the press in the Irish case.[31]

---

[27] JD Jackson et al, 'The Socio-Cultural Context of Broadcasting Markets' in GF Lowe and CS Nissen (eds), *Small Among Giants: Television Broadcasting in Smaller Countries* (Göteborg, Nordicom, 2011) 99–100.

[28] E Brennan, 'Memories of Television in Ireland: Separating Media History from Nation State' in M O'Brien (ed), *Media Connections Between Britain and Ireland* (Abingdon, Routledge, 2023); T Gibbons and P Humphreys, *Audiovisual Regulation Under Pressure: Comparative Cases from North American and Europe* (Abingdon, Routledge, 2012) 168–69.

[29] Komorek (n 26) 219.

[30] Competition Act 2002, Part 3A (as amended, notably by the Competition and Consumer Protection Act 2014).

[31] Case E 4/2005 (ex NN 99/1999); see further B Brevine, *Public Service Broadcasting Online: A Comparative European Policy Study of PSB 2.0* (London, Palgrave, 2013) 111–12.

3.3. Press Council of Ireland

The current Press Council owes its existence, in large part, to the ups and downs of libel reform efforts over a prolonged period. The idea is traced back to the 1970s (with influence from the (UK and Ireland-wide) National Union of Journalists and other UK developments of the period), and to intermittent observation of models in other jurisdictions (most notably Sweden). Meanwhile, libel tells a tale of the piling up of unimplemented reports: the 1991 Law Reform Commission Report; the 1996 'Finlay Commission' on the newspaper industry; and finally the Legal Advisory Group on Defamation which reported in 2003.[32] The 1996 Report touched on the idea of an ombudsman or alternative complaints mechanism, while the 2003 Report favoured (in the context of broad proposals for libel reform, including many aspects that would lessen the burden on defendants) a statutory press council with mandatory membership.

The interconnectedness of the agendas is well encapsulated by a commitment in the 2002 programme for government (coalition agreement), which included on the policy and legislative agenda three combined objectives: libel reform informed by comparative analysis, but 'in the context of a statutory press council and improved privacy laws'. Indeed, even the above-mentioned abandonment of privacy law reform was linked to the need to ensure progress on the remaining components of the agenda. The result, as is well known and as highlighted in the conclusion of this volume, is a statutory context for a press council. Two aspects of the eventual result of libel reform efforts – the Defamation Act 2009 – bring this about. The first is the ability of a minister to recognise the existence of a press council, where it meets a set of requirements in respect of its functions and constitution (Schedule 2 of the Act). For instance, designation is only possible if the body has a lay majority and provides an ombudsman service. The second is a reference to said council in the new statutory defence (section 26) in respect of (*Reynolds*-like) fair and reasonable publication.[33] One of the points that a court can take into account, where the defence is in play, is the extent to which the defendant had adhered to the code and determinations of the Press Council (if it is a member) or met equivalent standards (if it is not). However, there are no other statutory rights or privileges associated with membership of the Council.

Many observers point to the creation of the PCI, and its recognition under the terms of the statute, as a 'quid pro quo' or compromise. Eva Nagle, for instance, describes it as 'self regulation in return for libel reform', and echoes the comment of the first Ombudsman that the result is that journalists can be 'more critical

---

[32] S Dunne, 'Policing the Press: The Institutionalisation of Independent Press Regulation in a Liberal/North Atlantic Media System' (PhD thesis, Dublin City University, 2017); Inquiry into the Culture, Practices and Ethics of the Press (2012) HC 779, 1708 (hereinafter: Leveson Report).

[33] Not necessarily a faithful representation of the Reynolds doctrine (in original or evolved form) but a specific set of statutory criteria, see, eg, AT Kenyon, 'Protecting Speech in Defamation Law: Beyond Reynolds-Style Defences' (2014) 6 *Journal of Media Law* 21; N Cox, 'The Future of the *Reynolds* Defence in Irish Defamation Law Following the Defamation Act 2009' (2014) 51 *Irish Jurist* 28.

without being malicious'.[34] Marie McGonagle – whose own earlier academic work informed the design of the Council – makes a similar argument.[35] The degree to which a fully statutory council was a prospect is also highlighted – John O'Dowd emphasising that change would not have come about were it not for the threat[36] – with the result being a 'middle way' between the status quo and statutory regulation;[37] Carolan characterises the statutory mechanism eventually adopted as an 'incentivist approach' to press regulation.[38]

It is also significant here – and not apparent from the statutory text – that the new Council was established through careful choreography – with close contact between the government and its industry proponents at an early stage.[39] Indeed, its structure (put together by the industry through its Press Industry Steering Committee) can be traced to 2004 ideas and a 2006 draft; crucially, it was fully operational (without statutory recognition) by 2007, with the statutory change being introduced for parliamentary consideration in 2006 but not enacted until 2009 (and the actual recognition of the Council coming in a 2010 statutory instrument).[40] Moreover, this meant that the initial activity of the Council formed part of the parliamentary consideration of the bill and its recognition provisions (though as it transpired no actual changes to these aspects of the proposed legislation were made between 2006 and 2009). Ireland therefore continues to have a plurality of regulatory models across the media. In particular, the Press Council/Ombudsman does not deal with broadcasting, and the statutory broadcasting complaints mechanisms do not deal with print or online media.

4. Exploring Regulation

4.1. Duties and Responsibilities

Specific legal duties in respect of the broadcast media are set out in detail in the broadcasting legislation. For instance, the Broadcasting Act 2009 sets out the statutory duties of licence holders in respect of matters including objectivity and impartiality in news, the amount of time devoted to news and current affairs on radio services, and the protection of privacy. This is further taken up through the licensing process – for instance, a station licensed as a local service may have as

---

[34] E Nagle, 'Keeping Its Own Counsel: The Irish Press Council, Self-Regulation and Media Freedom' (2009) 20 *Entertainment Law Review* 93, 95.

[35] M McGonagle and A Brody, 'The Irish Defamation Act 2009 – Too Little, Too Late?' (2010) 15 *Communications Law* 43, 47.

[36] J O'Dowd, 'Ireland's New Defamation Act' (2009) 2 *Journal of Media Law* 173, 190.

[37] Dunne (n 32) 97.

[38] Carolan, 'Constitutionalising Discourse' (n 7) 23.

[39] P Cavaliere, 'From Journalistic Ethics to Fact-Checking Practices: Defining the Standards of Content Governance in the Fight Against Disinformation' (2020) 12 *Journal of Media Law* 133, 149.

[40] SI 2010/63.

a condition of the licence certain commitments to local programming. Moreover, the BAI has under this Act a statutory obligation to adopt a broadcasting code, compliance with which is therefore an obligation of all licence holders. While much of the content of such a code is quite similar to that in the United Kingdom and other jurisdictions, one point of departure is that Ireland, in implementing the Audiovisual Media Services Directive,[41] adopted a specific statutory provision in respect of the 'right of reply' (Broadcasting Act 2009, section 49) applicable to broadcast media, though the protection does not appear to have attracted anything other than occasional academic attention and no judicial treatment.

One might also conceive of aspects of the press regulatory system as being the implementation of (non-statutory) duties, though this is limited in scope. There is no attention in the system, for instance, to impartiality, or the highlighting of local stories. On the other hand, from time to time, the Ombudsman issues 'advisory notices' (a number of times each year) in respect of specific issues, such as accuracy in Covid-19 reporting, and the privacy of individuals arising out of (for example, major media stories concerning institutions). It also took part in the most recent consultation process on the reform of defamation law, offering some criticism of the cost of proceedings and the level of damages, while also proposing that the existing statutory provisions in respect of membership of the PCI (discussed above) be 'amended and strengthened to encourage all publications to join the Press Council.'[42]

4.2. The Work of the Press Ombudsman and Council

In a typical year,[43] the Ombudsman receives about 300 complaints; this has not changed all that much over a decade and a half of activity.[44] Where there are peaks above this, it tends to be as a result of multiple complaints regarding the same article (sometimes as a result of viral or coordinated activity, which has no impact on the handling of the complaint). Of those complaints, around 30 become the subject of a full decision, with around 10–15 proceeding (on appeal) to the Council itself; again, these proportions have been fairly stable over the years. The greatest number of complaints arise under Principle 1 of the Code (truth and accuracy). Cases not further examined are usually those where a complainant does not wish to proceed further, or the matter is out of the remit or scope of the Ombudsman

---

[41] Directive 2010/13/EU of the European Parliament and of the Council of 10 March 2010 on the coordination of certain provisions laid down by law, regulation or administrative action in Member States concerning the provision of audiovisual media services [2010] OJ L95/1.

[42] Press Council of Ireland, Annual Report 2017; see further the discussion of the 2022 review, below.

[43] The analysis in this and the following paragraph is the author's assessment of the last five annual reports of the PCI (up to the 2021 report, published in June 2022); these reports are available at: www.presscouncil.ie.

[44] There were 2,000 complaints over the first five years with up to 15% fully examined: Dunne (n 32) 127.

(for example, concerning a non-member organisation or a matter not addressed in the Code).

The system costs about €400,000 a year to run, and is fully funded by its industry membership. Those members are primarily drawn from the news print media – 16 national newspapers, around 55 local or regional newspapers and 12 student newspapers. Also participating as members are a falling number of periodicals or magazines (now 15) and a growing number of online-only news sites (now 18). By statute, a number of publishers are entitled to membership.[45] However, this does not prevent the recognised Council from taking a broader approach; indeed, its own memorandum of association refers to material 'circulated in the State by way of hard copy or internet distribution'.

The current Ombudsman (since October 2022), Susan McKay, is the third holder of the office since 2007. As well as the formal assessment of complaints, conciliation and mediation services are also offered. The Code, on the other hand, is reviewed by an industry committee and revised by said committee and the Council. It has indeed been amended from time to time, such as with the creation of a new principle in respect of the reporting of suicide, formerly an aspect of Principle 5, but now a new Principle 10 in its own right.

4.3. Impact of the Irish Model

The model adopted in Ireland in response to the particular circumstances of defamation and privacy reform has, perhaps surprisingly, attracted broader attention. One close observer refers to it as the 'first of its kind in the North Atlantic Liberal system',[46] and so its reception in the neighbouring jurisdictions of the United Kingdom is of particular interest. In the 'Leveson Inquiry', it was frequently pointed to as an illustration of how industry-led or industry-involved regulation of standards could function within a statutory context. For instance, the then Ombudsman gave evidence,[47] and it was one of the models discussed in Lara Fielden's influential evidence; she described the model as a departure from the press council mode, 'offer(ing) substantial benefits and therefore incentives, to members' through explicit statutory recognition.[48] Unsurprisingly, then, in

---

[45] Defamation Act 2009, Sch 2, clause 4 ('The owner of any periodical in circulation in the State or part of the State shall be entitled to be a member of the Press Council'); 'periodical' in turn defined as 'any newspaper, magazine, journal or other publication that is printed, published or issued, or that circulates, in the State at regular or substantially regular intervals and includes any version thereof published on the internet or by other electronic means' (s 2).

[46] Dunne (n 32) 71, drawing upon the models of media systems set out by Daniel C Hallin and Paolo Mancini.

[47] Leveson Report (n 32) 1670; see further J Heawood, 'Independent and effective? The post-Leveson framework for press regulation' (2015) 7 *Journal of Media Law* 130.

[48] L Fielden, *Regulating for Trust in Journalism: Standards Regulation in the Age of Blended Media* (Oxford, Reuters Institute for the Study of Journalism, 2011).

Leveson's analysis of 'regulatory models for the future' Ireland on its own forms one of three categories (the others being 'Australia/New Zealand' and 'Europe and beyond').[49] In turn, the first introduction of and the first substantive parliamentary debate on the report saw multiple government and opposition speakers highlight the Irish approach and indeed emphasise to a great extent the happy compliance of UK-owned newspapers with it,[50] and the subsequent consideration of possible legislative change and associated Royal Charter in respect of England saw further references as well as engagement with the PCI itself.[51]

In terms of the expanded understanding of regulatory models that goes beyond a dichotomy of self-regulation and state control, it also fits well into the 'co-regulatory' category that was popular in the literature of the time (though few referred to it as such in the contemporaneous debate in Ireland).[52] One must also note a number of particular aspects of the Irish approach to media regulation that may have affected the choice of model, such as the long-standing absence of an alternative remedy in respect of reputational issues,[53] and the way in which the Broadcasting Complaints Commission had evolved.[54]

Yet in parallel with this attention and attributed influence is some doubt about what values and mechanisms the Irish model is actually a cipher for. Even in the earlier days, O'Dowd rightly pointed out that there was very little relationship between, on the one hand, the caseload that the Ombudsman and Council was facing, and on the other the type of situation that would by any stretch lead to a *Reynolds* defence.[55] Similarly, Paul Wragg responds to Fielden's categorisation of the Irish model by highlighting the risk of overstating the 'incentive' and the lack of discernible impact of the particular lever utilised.[56] On these bases (and noting that current statistics bear out O'Dowd's predictions and Wragg's later analysis), while the coupling of *Reynolds* defences against potential liability and membership of a statute-backed ombudsman system might appear logical, it is harder to make assumptions about behavioural responses or the extent to which other jurisdictions with a version of *Reynolds* could achieve similar results by following the same logic. (Indeed, the post-Leveson attempt in England and Wales to legislate used as the carrot (or stick) not *Reynolds* but the availability of exemplary damages.)[57]

---

[49] Leveson Report (n 32) 1708–33.

[50] Hansard HC Deb vol 554 col 446 ff (29 November 2012); Hansard HC Deb vol 554 col 594 ff (3 December 2012).

[51] Hansard HC Deb vol 558 col 867 (13 February 2013); Hansard HC Deb vol 560 col 632 ff (18 March 2013).

[52] See, eg, CT Marsden, *Internet Co-Regulation: European Law, Regulatory Governance and Legitimacy in Cyberspace* (Cambridge, Cambridge University Press, 2011).

[53] McGonagle and Brody (n 35) 46.

[54] O'Dowd (n 36) 178.

[55] ibid 181.

[56] P Wragg, *A Free and Regulated Press: Defending Coercive Independent Press Regulation* (Oxford, Hart Publishing, 2020) 58.

[57] Enterprise and Regulatory Reform Act 2013, s 96; Crime and Courts Act 2013, ss 34–42.

5. Recent Developments

Media regulation is undergoing a certain amount of change in Ireland at the time of writing, though the recent developments are in respect of areas other than the PCI. The new regulatory body, Coimisiún na Meáin (which translates as 'Media Commission') is in the process of being established, as a new multi-member commission with specific commissioners for online safety, broadcasting and so forth; the 2022 legislation replacing the BAI with the new body, which became law in December 2022,[58] also serves as the completion of Ireland's implementation of the 2018 amendments to the Audiovisual Media Services Directive. In this context, it addresses a range of issues including video-on-demand services and social media, albeit in many cases as a parallel track rather than duplicating the provisions in respect of radio and television. The PCI system is therefore likely to continue as a discrete, press-focused regulatory system albeit with the prospect of some overlap between a plurality of regulatory systems as media services continue to evolve. On the other hand, the new Commission will have a range of activities in respect of newly defined 'communications services' which include newspapers and periodicals as one of four types (alongside broadcasting, on-demand and certain online services). For instance, it will have the power to promote high quality news and current affairs content, to promote Irish-language content and to carry out research, across all services.[59]

The separate Future of Media Commission, an independent body (including one member of the PCI as one of its members) established as a result of a commitment in the current Coalition programme for government, reported in mid-2022 (that is, after the media reform legislation was introduced in the legislature, but shortly before it completed its passage).[60] Its main discussions of the print news media are in the context of circulation, financial viability, VAT status, trust and market change. In its discussion of regulation, it summarises the PCI system though makes no particular comment or recommendation on it (apart from a discussion of desirability of defamation reform where it 'strongly endorses the view of the Press Council on the matter').[61] On the other hand, it advocates for 'platform-neutral' definitions of public service media and public service content,[62] and proposes further protections for the independence of the new Media Commission, and its monitoring of the public service broadcasters. It also contemplates a situation where public funding of public service content

---

[58] Online Safety and Media Regulation Act 2022.

[59] ibid, s 7(3); s 7(5). Note that the previous Act did refer to 'communications media' including newspapers but only in the context of particular provisions in respect of cross-ownership: Broadcasting Act 2009, s 2, s 66, s 137.

[60] Report of the Future of Media Commission (July 2022), available at: www.gov.ie/en/campaigns/54a35-the-future-of-media-commission.

[61] ibid 249.

[62] ibid 247–52.

would be available in respect of print publications and of news content (neither having been possible to date under the 2009 provisions).[63] Other proposed state interventions – a Local Democracy Reporting Scheme, a News Reporting Scheme and Courts Reporting Schemes – would similarly be open to all. It recommends tax and charity law changes that would be financially advantageous for newspapers and other media organisations.[64] Interestingly, one suggestion made by the owners of a major national newspaper was that only PCI members should be able to quality for a new VAT exemption if adopted;[65] a similar provision is floated by the Commission in respect of the three above-mentioned reporting schemes, through what it refers to as 'conditionality'.[66]

Meanwhile, the position in respect of civil liability is now characterised by a number of calls for reform, with the 2009 changes in defamation law (which in part reflect the currents and debates of the early 2000s) now nearly a decade and a half in the rear-view mirror. Key actors, especially in the press, now argue that the Irish legislation requires significant revision, in respect of matters such as juries (still used in Ireland), a serious harm threshold (as adopted in England and Wales) and social media.[67] Industry representatives describe the current position as 'among the most restrictive in Europe and throughout the English-speaking world'.[68] A review was published by the government in early 2022,[69] following a consultation process that ran over a number of years. This review saw a range of submissions regarding the future role of the PCI, explained and to some extent evaluated in the report, including proposals that use of or failure to use the ombudsman mechanism be a factor in any subsequent proceedings, and a potential link between PCI membership and the determination of damages in defamation proceedings.[70] Draft legislation has not yet emerged, though it is included in the government's legislative plan and is intended to be published in outline form in early 2023.[71]

As noted above, the PCI has itself been a vocal advocate for change, reflecting its close connection with the industry, but also the distinctive relationship between dispute resolution schemes, on the one hand, and the reform (or lack thereof) of the more established mechanisms on the other. Indeed, the wide-ranging and

---

[63] ibid 168 ff.

[64] ibid 176.

[65] ibid 153.

[66] ibid 170–73.

[67] See, eg, 'The *Irish Times* View on Ireland's defamation Laws: Inching Towards Essential Reform' *Irish Times* (2 March 2022), available at: www.irishtimes.com/opinion/editorial/the-irish-times-view-on-ireland-s-defamation-laws-inching-towards-essential-reform-1.4815683.

[68] See: newsbrandsireland.ie/policy-issues/defamation.

[69] Department of Justice, Report of the Review of the Defamation Act 2009 (1 March 2022), available at: www.gov.ie/en/publication/4478f-report-of-the-review-of-the-defamation-act-2009; see further Dáil Debates, vol 1021, no 7 (11 May 2022).

[70] Report of the Review of the Defamation Act 2009, ibid 184–85.

[71] Department of Tourism, Culture, Arts, Gaeltacht, Sports and Media, 'Future of Media: Implementation Strategy and Action Plan' (18 January 2023), available at: www.gov.ie/en/publication/e2cbb-tuarascail-an-choimisiuin-um-thodhchai-na-mean-straiteis-feidhmithe-agus-plean-gniomhaithe, 48.

prospective work of the Future of Media Commission, in this regard, adopted and endorsed the PCI's approach and in doing so situated libel reform as one of the facets of the media regulatory landscape for Ireland.

One should also note that Ireland has not returned to the unfinished business of the 2000s in respect of civil actions in privacy. It is true that there has been some judicial development of the doctrine since then, and that the PCI itself has a broad mandate that includes some of the matters at the heart of this action and similar actions elsewhere (see, for example, Clause 5 of its Code). On the other hand, the volume of case law and doctrinal innovation seen in England and Wales and in a number of Commonwealth jurisdictions, in respect of breach of confidence or its equivalents,[72] has yet to be seen. Ireland has also not benefited from the type of systematic review seen in, for instance, New Zealand; this is significant in terms of pressure for legislative change but also for how it could affect the evolution of the constitutional and common law authorities (again as seen in New Zealand itself, where later courts have drawn upon the volume of Law Commission work).[73]

6. Conclusion

The story of press regulation in Ireland, and in particular the statutory dimension to such, can be seen as falling into three eras. The first, broadly sitting within the first decade of the twenty-first century, was almost entirely a domestic one, with the ebb and flow of proposals for self-regulation, statutory regulation, privacy law reform and more, culminating in the particular arrangements reflected in the Defamation Act 2009 and in the establishment and early activity of the Ombudsman and Council. Here, the emphasis was on trade-offs and on seeking to complete a long-promised review of libel law. The second, in the subsequent decade, saw relatively little by way of domestic law reform efforts, but the settling into regular business for the Ombudsman and Council, coupled with a substantial increase in international attention to the model, especially in the context of the Leveson Inquiry in the United Kingdom. In this period, the idea of the statutory dimension to the Irish settlement was the focus, rather than the day-to-day work of the Ombudsman or indeed the fuller picture of why the system emerged in the way that it did. The third, occupying the years leading up to the publication of this volume, has seen renewed interest in Ireland in a number of key questions, including libel reform itself, the plurality of regulatory models that might be relevant in today's media landscape, and – strikingly – a range of new suggestions for incentivising membership of the Council, ranging from eligibility for subsidies to VAT treatment to liability (including quantum of damages) in defamation law.

---

[72] See, eg, TDC Bennett and D Mac Síthigh (eds), *The Campbell Legacy: Reflections on the Tort of Misuse of Private Information* (Abingdon, Routledge, 2018).

[73] NA Moreham, 'A Conceptual Framework for the New Zealand Tort of Intrusion' (2016) 47 *Victoria University of Wellington Law Review* 283.

Time will tell whether any of these suggestions are taken up, or indeed whether the level of interest in the Irish model found in the 2010s leads to further scrutiny of these later innovations. The new links that are being drawn between press regulation and a broad media and information policy agenda (most notably in the work of the Future of Media Commission), rather than positioning press regulation as the counterpart of libel and privacy reform, certainly presents a fresh set of questions. These questions recall some of the more unusual constitutional debates around communication and expression, around public and institutional speech, and on the 'singular and unique' role of the media in Irish democracy and discourse. These are not uniquely Irish problems by any means, but the degree to which the Irish 'model' has already blended a number of intellectual and regulatory traditions – in a state with close (legal, cultural and linguistic) links to its immediate neighbour in the United Kingdom tempered by its firm identity as an EU Member State (and domicile of choice for non-EU multinational tech companies), in seeing tort, statutory and constitutional aspects of media freedom and regulation – means that the potential experimentation of the next few years ought to be watched closely.

6

Freedom of the Press in Italy

PIETRO DUNN AND ORESTE POLLICINO*

1. Introduction

This chapter provides an overview of the legal framework in relation to freedom of the press within the Italian Republic, a framework that is directly the result of the history of the country and, in particular, of the tragic experience of the Fascist era.[1] Freedom of the press was first recognised in Italy in 1848, with the adoption of the Albertine Statute under the reign of Charles Albert as the Constitution of the Kingdom of Sardinia and, subsequently, of the Kingdom of Italy (from 1861). Article 28 of the Statute expressly stipulated that the press should be free from state intervention, although it required the law to establish the rules to avoid any abuse of such a right. This was done initially through the adoption of Royal Decree No 695/1848, the so-called Edict on the Press, imposing both administrative obligations and criminal penalties for the commission of offences by the press. Despite the Edict's inherent goal of respecting the Albertine Statute's spirit, with its aim of fully guaranteeing freedom of the press, subsequent legislative acts and a restrictive interpretive approach soon led to a restriction of the liberties enshrined within Article 28. This partly changed at the beginning of the twentieth century, with the enactment of a liberal reform under the 'Giolittian age'.[2] However, this liberal phase was short lived, as the outbreak of the First World War caused the regulation of the press to once again take a restrictive turn, with the reintroduction of highly illiberal measures (including extensive powers of censorship).[3]

---

* Pietro Dunn is the author of sections 4, 6, 7 and 8. Oreste Pollicino is the author of sections 1, 2, 3 and 5.

[1] For an outline of the history of freedom of the press in Italy, see U De Siervo, 'Stampa' (1990) XLIII *Enciclopedia del Diritto* 577; P Caretti and A Cardone, *Diritto dell'informazione e della comunicazione nell'era della convergenza* (Bologna, Il Mulino, 2019); R Zaccaria, A Valastro and E Albanesi, *Diritto dell'informazione e della comunicazione*, 11th edn (Padova, Cedam, 2021).

[2] Law No 278/1906.

[3] See Caretti and Cardone (n 1) 38–39.

The subsequent advent of Fascism in 1922 greatly accelerated the process of moving towards a limited (or rather, non-existent) protection of the freedom of the press. Benito Mussolini was aware of the deep interconnection between communication and politics and was thus determined to make the press a tool for the purposes of promoting his regime's propaganda: under totalitarian rule, therefore, the press soon became an instrument for further empowering the central authorities. This was made possible also by the flexible nature of the Albertine Statute – the latter, in fact, was not hierarchically superior to primary-level law, nor did it foresee a system of constitutional review aimed at verifying the consistency of the law with its principles.

First, Fascist law intervened to modify the rules concerning access to the journalistic profession. With this aim, in 1928, the Order and the Register of Journalists was established;[4] in order to be enrolled within it, among other criteria, journalists ultimately had to align with the regime's political agenda. Second, newspapers and periodicals had to be 'recognised' (that is, authorised) by the local administrative authority (*prefetto*), which could revoke such recognition at any moment. Third, the criminal law regime concerning the press was greatly revised, including through the introduction of the new Criminal Code of 1930 (the so-called 'Rocco Code'):[5] on the one hand, the new position of responsible director (*direttore responsabile*, replacing the previous *gerente responsabile*) was created, making this individual personally accountable for any offence committed through the publication of the press; on the other hand, the Rocco Code significantly increased the level of penalties levied for the commission of press-related offences, while punishing an extremely wide array of thought crimes.[6] Fourth, a reform of the legal regime on the protection of public order introduced a complex system of police licences limiting the scope of action of freedom of expression while transforming the instrument of the seizure of printed works and newspapers into a preventive measure not requiring any reasoned order by the judiciary.[7] Fifth, the Fascist regime introduced economic measures and created dedicated administrative bodies aimed at promoting and aiding the dissemination of information;[8] however, any financial help was reserved only for those newspapers that actively promoted fascist interests and propaganda.[9]

---

[4] See Law No 2307/1925 and the subsequent Royal Decree No 384/1928.

[5] Royal Decree No 1398/1930.

[6] eg, contempt of the state religion (ie, the Catholic religion) and of permitted religions, as well as contempt of the Crown, of the Government, of the Great Council of Fascism, of the Parliament, of Police Forces and of the Judiciary. Incitement to commit offences against the public order, as well as apology of such offences, were also criminalised.

[7] See, most notably, the Consolidated Law on public security of 1926 (Royal Decree No 1848/1926) and the subsequent one of 1931 (Royal Decree No 773/1931).

[8] See Caretti and Cardone (n 1) 45–46.

[9] With regard to freedom of the press under Fascism, see also PV Cannistraro, *La fabbrica del consenso: fascismo e mass media* (Rome, Laterza, 1975); N Tranfaglia, P Murialdi and M Legnani, *La stampa italiana nell'età fascista* (Rome, Laterza, 1980).

As will emerge in the following sections, the legacy of the liberal monarchy era and, especially, of Fascism has deeply influenced and impacted the subsequent development of freedom of the press in Italy. Most notably, the new republican Constitution represents in many ways a direct response and a reaction to the totalitarian experience. Section 2 of this chapter analyses precisely how the end of the Second World War, and the consequent creation of the Italian Republic, represented a turning point for the development of fundamental rights and liberties on the peninsula, including freedom of the press. Section 3 focuses on a fundamental institution that complements the general legal framework on the journalistic profession, that is, the reformed Order (and Registry) of Journalists. Section 4 and section 5 address some of the main privileges and rights, as well as the duties and responsibilities, that are inherently connected to the exercise of such a freedom, underscoring the main issues and challenges in the contemporary framework. Most notably, as described in section 6, significant challenges have arisen connected to the applicability of those privileges, rights, duties and responsibilities to the digital landscape. Finally, section 7 briefly explores some of the main measures adopted by the Italian authorities with respect to the promotion of diversity and pluralism, notably, on the one hand, the introduction of anti-trust regulation and, on the other, the deployment of economic and financial assistance aimed at sustaining, in particular, smaller news outlets.

2. Freedom of the Press under the Italian Republic: The Constitutional and Legal Framework

In the aftermath of the Second World War, after the general referendum of 2 June 1946 on the institutional regime of the country, Italy transitioned from a monarchy to a republic. Two years later, in 1948, the new Republican Constitution was finally enacted. The text of the Constitution clearly bears the marks of the tragic Fascist experience, and represents in many ways a reaction to the totalitarian regime. Thus, for instance, unlike the Albertine Statute, the flexible model was abandoned in favour of a rigid structure, pursuant to which the Constitution's provisions were to be hierarchically superior to primary-level law while a system of constitutional review was established, with a view to constraining the powers of political actors.[10] Within this new framework, Article 21 introduced a whole new set of guarantees protecting both freedom of expression and freedom of the press which had been deeply affected and limited in the previous 20 years.

---

[10] Art 134 of the Italian Constitution recognises the Constitutional Court's power to decide about the constitutional legitimacy of laws which, if found unconstitutional, cease to have any effect from the day subsequent to the publication of the decision (Art 136). The text of the Constitution may be modified but only through the specific and complex procedure described in Art 138 (additionally, Art 139 specifies that the republican regime cannot be modified).

The provision, most notably, recognises generally the right of all individuals to 'freely express their thoughts in speech, writing, or any other form of communication'. Additionally, it introduced a series of particular rules specifically protecting freedom of the press.

Under Fascist rule, as mentioned above, newspapers had been subject to strict rules allowing for preventive censorship by the government, as well as for the indiscriminate preventive seizure of printed works.[11] Article 21(2) of the new Constitution thus intervenes to consistently limit the powers of the executive and administrative powers with regard to these aspects. On the one hand, the second paragraph explicitly states that no preliminary authorisation should be required of the press, nor should censorship of journalistic activity be permitted. On the other hand, the Constitution provides for substantive and procedural rules identifying the limits and constraints on the governmental deployment of the measure of the seizure of the press. Most notably, the third paragraph of Article 21 established two obligatory conditions, the first relating to the principle of rule of law, and the second relating to the due process of law: first, the presence of a pre-existing law on the press identifying the criminal offences which may justify such an intervention of the public power (*riserva di legge*); second, the need for a preventive order by the judicial authority clearly stating the reasons for the adoption of the measure (*riserva di giurisdizione*). These principles are, in fact, recurrent guarantees within the Italian Constitution, aimed at protecting a wide array of individual rights from public interference (notably, from the executive power).[12]

Article 21 also clarifies some important points with respect to the requirements of '*riserva di legge*' and '*riserva di giurisdizione*'. On the one hand, with respect to the former, the Constitution leaves quite an ample margin of discretion to the lawmaker in the determination of punishable criminal offences, although Article 21(6) explicitly requires that 'publications, performances and other exhibits offensive to public morality' be prohibited by law. This notion of 'public morality' has been for many years at the centre of legal debate, but today it is generally agreed that the expression should be interpreted in a restrictive way, in the sense that it refers exclusively to the respect for sexual decency.[13] On the other hand, as regards the '*riserva di giurisdizione*', the fourth paragraph of Article 21 allows the police to seize press publications without a prior judicial order only in cases of absolute urgency where the timely intervention of the judiciary is not possible. Moreover, within 24 hours, the police are obliged to refer the matter to the judicial authority to require the validation of the measure; if such a validation does not

---

[11] See above, section 1.

[12] On these notions, see R Balduzzi and F Sorrentino, 'Riserva di legge' (1989) XL *Enciclopedia del Diritto* 1207; F Battaglia, 'Libertà di manifestazione del pensiero' (1974) XXIV *Enciclopedia del Diritto* 424, 446–47.

[13] See Italian Constitutional Court, No 9/1965, No 49/1971. On this topic, see A Pace and M Manetti, *Rapporti civili. La libertà di manifestazione del proprio pensiero. Art 21 Costituzione* (Bologna, Zanichelli, 2006) 204 ff.

take place, within the subsequent 24 hours, the measure is revoked and considered null and void.

In summary, Article 21 establishes that it is up to the law to foresee the limitations and duties that are inherently connected to the exercise of the freedom of the press (including, for example, the duty to disclose the financial sources of periodical publications).[14] The constitutional framework thus needs to be complemented by that of primary-level law. In this respect, Law No 47/1948, the so-called 'Law on the Press', represents the most relevant piece of legislation. The law intervened by revising some important rules concerning the press, including, notably, the definition of the information that must be provided about printed materials (Article 2);[15] the role, function and duties of the responsible director (Article 3) and of the owner (Article 4) of a newspaper or other periodical printed publication; and the rules concerning the registration of newspapers and other periodical printed publications (Article 5). With respect to the latter point, it is important to highlight the shift from the need for an administrative preventive authorisation from the prefect to an obligation to register before the local judicial authority: the Italian Constitutional Court clarified that, in this respect, the judicial authority only retains the power to verify the existence and validity of the documents required for the purposes of registration. In this way, the Constitutional Court was able to respond to the doubts concerning the constitutional legitimacy of the law on the press by denying that judges had any discretion in deciding on the merits of the application for registration.[16]

On the subject of criminal offences committed via the press and printed works, the 1930 Criminal Code is still the most relevant legislative source. Indeed, the 1948 Law on the Press did not initiate a systemic revision of the criminal regime of the press but simply introduced some complementary provisions. Article 57 of the Criminal Code, most importantly, establishes that the responsible director or vice-director is subject to criminal liability if he or she negligently fails to exercise his or her duty of control over the contents published (*culpa in vigilando*). In this respect, Article 11 of the Law on the Press establishes at the same time that civil liability for the damages resulting from such offences is shared by the author and the responsible director or vice-director, along with the owner and editor of the printed material.

3. The Order and Registry of Journalists

Another fundamental piece of legislation is Law No 69/1963, concerning the regulation of the Order and of the Registry of Journalists. In fact, as mentioned above,

---

[14] Italian Constitution, Art 21(5).

[15] Printed material must indicate the place and year of publication, the name and domicile of the printer and, where existent, of the editor; periodical newspapers also have to indicate the name of their owner and of the responsible director or vice-director.

[16] Italian Constitutional Court, No 31/1957. See Caretti and Cardone (n 1) 50.

both the Order and the Registry had already been established under Fascism, allegedly as a response to a 'long-standing desire' on the part of press professionals to create a body governing and protecting its professional standards and values while, in practice, serving as a tool to further filter out 'undesirable' voices that were at odds with the totalitarian regime. The new republican law, however, significantly revised the legal framework in this respect.

Currently, it is up to the Order of Journalists, composed of regional and inter-regional councils (Article 3), along with a national body, the National Council (Article 16), established within the Ministry of Justice, to keep the records for the Registry. In order to be enrolled, journalists must comply with a range of positive and negative requirements, including the absence of any prohibition from the exercise of a public function as a result of a criminal conviction (Article 31). The regional and inter-regional councils are vested with the responsibility for deciding on admission to and erasure from the Registry, although any decision may be challenged before the judiciary (Article 63).[17]

An important distinction established by Law No 69/1963 is that between professional journalists, who, as suggested by their title, operate as reporters on a continuative and exclusive basis, and publicist journalists, who work occasionally with the press as freelancers (Article 1). Persons may be enrolled in the Registry as professional journalists if they are over 21 years of age; if they have been previously enrolled as trainees and worked as such for at least 18 months; and if they have sat and passed an exam before a commission composed of five journalists and two magistrates (Articles 29 and following). Enrolment in the Registry as publicists, conversely, is not subject to the previous completion of a traineeship and to the passing of a professional exam but is conditional upon demonstrating continuous (although occasional) experience of at least two years of paid publications (Article 35). As will be underscored below, such a distinction is especially important with respect to the ability of journalists to enjoy specific rights, such as that of maintaining the secrecy of their sources.

Apart from the keeping of the Registry, the Order of Journalists is also vested with disciplinary powers over the individuals enrolled therein. It should also be noted that, pursuant to Article 48, journalists whose conduct is not consistent with the decorum and dignity typical of the profession, or whose actions may compromise the reputation or the dignity of the Order itself, may be subjected to disciplinary proceedings which can result in a variety of progressively severe punishments identified by Article 51, escalating from 'warning' through to 'official reprimand', 'suspension from the exercise of the journalistic profession for a time period of two months to one year' up to the gravest measure, that of deletion from the Registry.

---

[17] In such cases, the court is complemented with journalists who are required to assist the judges in their decision. See Art 27 of Legislative Decree No 150/2011.

The republican regulation involving the Order and Registry, if compared with the previous system established under Fascist rule, is characterised by the disappearance of any prerequisite based on political, rather than professional, criteria. Whereas the system envisaged by the lawmaker of the 1920s represented, in practice, a tool to further the dissemination of Fascist propaganda, Law No 69/1963 does, in fact, aim at guaranteeing a higher quality of information. However, doubts and concerns about the constitutional validity of the new rules still emerged in the following years. In a 1968 judgment, the Constitutional Court rejected such doubts.[18] Most notably, the judges asserted that the existence of a registry does not impede, per se, the occasional use of the press as a means for the exercise of one's freedom of expression: the requirement to enrol in the Registry, in fact, is obligatory solely in order to work as a professional journalist in a continuous and exclusive manner. At the same time, the Court evaluated whether Law No 69/1963, which does in practice impose some hurdles and conditions on access to the profession, is compatible with the Italian constitutional framework and whether the measures envisaged by it are proportionate or not.

As regards the constitutional basis of the Act, the Constitutional Court found that the creation of an Order and Registry of Journalists was inherently motivated by the aspiration to protect the independence of the professional activity of journalists, not only from the interference of public institutions but also from the influence of economic powers (notably, the owners and editors of newspapers). In other words, by creating an independent body to set the standards and rules governing the professional duties of journalists, the lawmaker's aspiration was to avoid the risk of external, unwarranted pressures bringing down the quality of the Italian press – a goal which, in the opinion of the Court, is perfectly aligned and coherent with the content of Article 21 of the Constitution. Besides, such an aspiration is also the basis of the law's regulation of the disciplinary powers of the Order. At the same time, with respect to the proportionality of the measures adopted, the Court underscored that for the purposes of the journalists' enrolment in the Registry, the evaluation carried out by the Order is only oriented towards the assessment of the candidate's technical and basic knowledge concerning the exercise of the journalistic profession and does not take into account their personal ideologies and opinions. Moreover, the Court considered that the procedural safeguards[19] of the Order are satisfactory and represent an additional guarantee ensuring the respect for Article 21.

The conclusions of the Court, which were, in fact, reiterated in the following years,[20] have not been able, however, to fully convince the entirety of Italian legal scholarship: in particular, some commentators believe that the risk of a

---

[18] Italian Constitutional Court, No 11/1968.

[19] eg, the duty of the Order to state the reasons of any negative decision, as well as the possibility for journalists to challenge any disciplinary decisions.

[20] See, among others, Italian Constitutional Court, No 80/1968, No 113/1974 and No 114/1974.

distorted use of power by the Order may still be possible and thus represents a threat to freedom of the press.[21] Another source of concern as to the constitutional legitimacy of Law No 69/1963 lies in the distinction between professionals and publicists, a distinction which does not seem to reflect the contemporary job market in the field of the press, and which entails some important differences as to the legal regime and rights provided to journalists,[22] most notably, as will be underscored in the following section, the right to secrecy as regards sources of information.

4. The Rights of Journalists: A Selection of Open Issues

As 'watchdogs of democracy',[23] journalists enjoy certain rights and privileges that are essential for the proper conduct of their professional activity. In fact, Article 2 of Law No 69/1963 clearly defines the right of journalists to inform and criticise as 'irrepressible', albeit within the limitations and obligations provided by the law;[24] besides, as described above, Article 21 of the Constitution also accords freedom of the press a special value. Nonetheless, Italian law still includes some problematic aspects and issues in this regard.

One of the most relevant sets of issues concerns the right of journalists to secrecy with respect to their sources of information. Article 2 of the law establishing the Order of Journalists not only provides for such a right but actually states that maintaining such secrecy represents a duty of journalists and editors whenever this is required by the relationship of mutual trust they entertain with the source herself.[25] For many years, however, such a right or duty was in open contrast to the Code of Criminal Procedure of 1930,[26] which did not recognise the possibility for journalists to refuse to disclose their sources during a criminal trial. In fact, Article 351 of the Code did contain a provision concerning the possibility of exempting certain professional categories from the duty of testifying in court,

---

[21] See, among others, S Fois, 'Giornalisti (ordine dei)' (1969) XVIII *Enciclopedia del Diritto* 707; P Barile, 'Vecchi e nuovi motivi di incostituzionalità dell'Ordine dei Giornalisti' (1989) 1 *I problemi dell'informazione* 7; De Siervo (n 1); MC Grisolia, 'Libertà di informazione e ordine dei giornalisti alla luce della riforma degli ordinamenti professionali' (2012) 4 *Rivista AIC* 1.

[22] As highlighted by M Cuniberti, 'La professione del giornalista' in GE Vigevani et al (eds), *Diritto dell'informazione e dei media*, 2nd edn (Torino, Giappichelli, 2022) 169, many publicists work, in fact, as professionals: as a matter of fact, obtaining a working position as a trainee journalist is rather difficult, so that many aspiring journalists end up enrolling as publicists rather than professionals.

[23] The famous metaphor of journalists as watchdogs of democracy, typical of the case law of the European Court of Human Rights (see, eg, *Jersild v Denmark* Series A no 298 (1994)), has been in fact adopted by the Italian Constitutional Court itself. See Italian Constitutional Court, No 150/2021.

[24] In this respect, see section 5 below.

[25] 'Giornalisti e editori sono tenuti a rispettare il segreto professionale sulla fonte delle notizie, quando ciò sia richiesto dal carattere fiduciario di esse'. See Cuniberti (n 22) 290.

[26] Royal Decree No 1399/1930.

however, the list only included the religious ministers of the Catholic religion and of the other religions admitted by the law, as well as the professionals of the law and those who worked within the healthcare system.[27] The situation only changed in 1988 when the new Code of Criminal Procedure was enacted.[28] Article 200(3) of the current Code states that registered professional journalists are allowed to refuse to disclose the names of the sources from whom they have received information and with whom they entertain a relationship of mutual trust as established by Article 2 of Law No 69/1963. Nonetheless, the provision also establishes that if such information as provided to the journalist constitutes essential proof for the trial and if the truthfulness of such information cannot be proved without identifying its source, the judicial authority may order the disclosure of the identity of the source: an exception which, evidently, significantly reduces the effectiveness of the journalists' right to secrecy.

Furthermore, the guarantee set out in Article 200 of the Code of Criminal Procedure involves some important limits, both objective and subjective. In terms of its objective scope, the provision only applies to the name of the source of information. Therefore, journalists may still be obliged to disclose to the judiciary the substance of what they have learnt. Additionally, the question soon emerged with respect to the applicability of the rule also to those cases where the judiciary may avail itself of indirect means of identifying the source of information, for instance, through the seizure of notebooks, USB memory or digital devices of journalists and people working with them, as well as through the resort to wiretapping. In this respect, the Italian Supreme Court (Court of Cassation), in line with the approach of the European Court of Human Rights (ECtHR, Strasbourg Court),[29] denied, for instance, that the institute of seizure could be abused to circumvent the guarantees set by Article 200, arguing that an order adequately justified by the judge is necessary in order to enforce such a measure on journalists' goods.[30] Conversely, the Court has not yet intervened to extend such an interpretation to the practice of wiretapping and to the collection and analysis of journalists' Internet traffic data.[31]

---

[27] The Italian Constitutional Court held that the provision was not unconstitutional, although it admitted that the balance established by the 1930 Code was not fully satisfactory, thus inviting the Parliament to intervene. See Italian Constitutional Court, No 1/1981; G Conso, 'Il segreto giornalistico dopo la sentenza della Corte Costituzionale' (1981) 1 *Giurisprudenza costituzionale* 18.

[28] Decree of the President of the Republic No 447/1988.

[29] On the objective scope of the right or duty to journalistic secrecy see, eg, *Roemen and Schmit v Luxembourg* Reports of Judgments and Decisions 2003-IV (2003); *Sanoma Uitgevers BV v the Netherlands*, App no 38224/03, judgment of 14 September 2010; *Sedletska v Ukraine*, App no 42634/18, judgment of 1 April 2021. On these decisions, see I Høedt-Rasmussen and D Voorhoof, 'The Confidentiality of the Lawyer–Client Relationship Under Pressure? *Roemen and Schmit v Luxembourg*' (2003) Special Issue *European Human Rights Law Review* 147; D Voorhoof, 'Extra Procedural Safeguards for Protection of Journalistic Sources: *Sanoma Uitgevers BV v the Netherlands*' (2010) *Strasbourg Observers*, available at: www.strasbourgobservers.com/2010/09/16/extra-procedural-safeguards-for-protection-of-journalistic-sources-sanoma-uitgevers-b-v-v-the-netherlands/; D Voorhoof, 'European Court of Human Rights: *Sedletska v Ukraine*' (2021) 5 *IRIS* 1.

[30] Cass Pen, VI s, No 31735/2014; Cass Pen, VI s, No 24617/2015.

[31] See Cuniberti (n 22) 299.

As regards its subjective scope, Article 200(3) only applies to those journalists who are enrolled as 'professionals' on the Registry of Journalists, thus leaving out both trainee journalists and publicists. Indeed, in the original intentions of Law No 69/1963 trainees should always be assisted by a professional journalist who, therefore, should personally deal with the more sensitive sources of information; at the same time, the lawmaker did not envisage that publicists, being occasional freelancers, would dedicate themselves to investigative journalism. However, these expectations have repeatedly clashed with reality; most notably, it is more and more frequent that journalists registered as publicists take on important investigative enquiries and thus require the protection of their right to professional secrecy.[32] Additionally, the reference by the provision to professionalism also clearly excludes from the right to secrecy any individual engaging in forms of 'citizen journalism'.[33] Because the importance of citizen journalism has arguably grown exponentially in the last few decades, partly as a result of the spread of the Internet, the appropriateness of its complete exclusion from the scope of action of the provision may well be called into question.

The subjective limitations of Article 200 thus raise significant questions with respect to the conformity of Italian law with freedom of expression and freedom of the press, especially within the framework of the Council of Europe and of the Convention for the Protection of Human Rights and Fundamental Freedoms (ECHR).[34] Indeed, as emphasised by the Committee of Ministers of the Council of Europe, the notion of journalist, and thus the subjective scope of the right to secrecy, should refer to 'any natural or legal person who is regularly or professionally engaged in the collection and dissemination of information to the public via any means of mass communication',[35] so that granting a journalist recognition as a 'professional' – or not – should not constitute a limit to the applicability of said guarantees. The question concerning the consistency of Italian law with the framework of the Council of Europe and with the ECHR is, furthermore, of paramount importance, since, pursuant to Article 117 of the Italian Constitution, primary-level law must be compliant with the ECHR system itself.[36] Moreover, the different

---

[32] See above (n 22).

[33] The term 'citizen journalism' is still rather debated at scholarly level. In the context of the present contribution, the term is used as comprising a wide range of cases where news and information are produced by individuals who do not work as journalists, either autonomously or by cooperating occasionally with news outlets (eg, user-generated content). See M Wall, 'Citizen Journalism. A retrospective on what we know, and agenda for what we don't' (2015) 6 *Digital Journalism* 797. However, *cf* JY Abbott, 'Tensions in the scholarship on participatory journalism and citizen journalism' (2017) 41(3–4) *Annals of the International Communication Association* 278, 286, defining citizen journalism narrowly, 'as news produced by people untrained in journalism without the help of professional journalists'.

[34] See, most notably, *Goodwin v the United Kingdom* Reports of Judgments and Decisions 1996-II (1996).

[35] Appendix to Recommendation No R (2000) 7 of the Committee of Ministers to Member States on the right of journalists not to disclose their sources of information.

[36] Italian Constitutional Court, No 348/2007, No 349/2007. See, among others, D Tega, 'Le sentenze della Corte costituzionale nn 348 e 349 del 2007: la CEDU da fonte ordinaria a fonte "sub-costituzionale" del diritto' (2018) 1 *Quaderni costituzionali* 133.

treatment of trainees and, especially, publicists, as opposed to professional journalists, further amplifies the above-mentioned concerns relating to the constitutional legitimacy of the rules governing the Order and Registry of Journalists.[37]

Another problematic area with respect to the sphere of rights and privileges of journalists within Italian law is represented by the relationship between journalists and their employers.[38] Most notably, this issue may arise with respect to the independence and autonomy of journalists in the expression of their thoughts and opinions – the freedom of expression of the journalist and their right to inform the public may in some cases collide with the specific interests of the newspaper they work for, and/or be at odds with its editorial line. On this point, the law does not set any relevant guarantees aimed at protecting the independence of the individual journalist. The only forms of such protection have in fact come from the national collective agreements between the journalistic unions and the representatives of journalistic enterprises. Those agreements introduced specific (so-called 'conscience') clauses pursuant to which a journalist may decide to submit their resignation at any time (and without any impact as to their severance pay) whenever they enter into conflict with their employer's editorial line or ideology.[39] Although such a measure represents a fundamental tool for guaranteeing the independence of journalists under labour law, a more protective approach may ultimately be desirable in order to reduce the power gap between the two parties.[40]

Finally, a third category of problems is posed by the set of rules concerning the protection, including through criminal law,[41] of national secrets. Indeed, on this point, the Italian lawmaker has proven to be rather unwilling to intervene. One of its limited interventions, in this respect, was made through Law No 801/1977 which restricted the scope of criminal prosecution for the publication of national secrets only to cases where secrecy is necessary for national security.[42] At the same time, however, a range of provisions from the Criminal Code and Criminal Procedure Code addresses the protection of secrets with regard to criminal investigation and prosecution, still limiting quite broadly the possibility for journalists to gain access and share information. In relation to these provisions, some authors believe that the current legal regime of public secrecy, because of the incapability of the Italian lawmaker to put in place an organic reform of the relevant rules, is not fully respectful of the principle of proportionality and does not, therefore, enforce an appreciable balance between the interests of the state and freedom of the press.[43]

---

[37] See section 3 above.

[38] On this topic, see Grisolia (n 21) 12 ff.

[39] See, in particular, Art 32 of Contratto nazionale di lavoro giornalistico commentato (National Collective Agreement on Journalistic Work, CCNLG).

[40] See Caretti and Cardone (n 1) 65–66.

[41] See, most notably, Arts 256 and 261 of the Criminal Code.

[42] Pursuant to Art 39 of Law No 124/2007, 'national security' includes the protection of the integrity of the Republic, also with respect to international agreements, of its constitutional institutions and of its international independence.

[43] Caretti and Cardone (n 1) 66.

5. Duties and Responsibilities of the Press

While recognising the fundamental role played by the press in the smooth functioning of democracy, at the same time the law sets the boundaries both of the exercise of journalists' freedom of expression and of their right to inform and express criticisms. It is evident that such limitations, given the constitutional requirement that laws have to comply with the ECHR, must be aligned with the case law of the Strasbourg Court itself.[44]

In this respect, the most relevant limitation to freedom of the press is represented by the set of criminal law provisions punishing, often with particularly high penalties, a range of offences committed via the press. It is important to emphasise once again in this regard that Article 57 of the Criminal Code considers the responsible director or vice-director of a newspaper criminally liable for any offence committed by a publication if she or he negligently fails to exercise the necessary control over the content published. In such cases, however, the penalty may be diminished by up to a third of the penalty imposed on the author of the incriminated publication. A significant issue concerned the possibility of applying Article 57 to online press publications, provided that the notion of 'press', expressly mentioned within the provision, does not explicitly cover its digital counterpart;[45] additionally, because a central tenet of Italian criminal law is the prohibition of analogical interpretation *in malam partem*, such an extension of the scope of action of the provision was debated several times in the legal academic literature. Eventually, however, the Court of Cassation concluded that Article 57 is, in fact, also applicable to online press publications.[46]

Among other offences, the crime of defamation has possibly been the most discussed topic within scholarly and judicial debate,[47] especially because of the high risk of prosecution that journalists face for the alleged publication of libellous material. Article 595 of the Criminal Code defines 'defamation' as the act of offending, by communicating with a wider audience, another person's

---

[44] See above (n 36).

[45] See section 6 below.

[46] Cass Pen, su No 31022/2015; Cass Pen, V s No 1275/2018. See L Armerio, 'La responsabilità ex art 57 cp del direttore di testate telematiche: tra estensione interpretativa ed analogia *in malam partem*' (2019) 2 *Rivista di diritto dei media* 283; RE Mauri, 'Applicabile l'art 57 cp al direttore del quotidiano online: un revirement giurisprudenziale della cassazione, di problematica compatibilità con il divieto di analogia' (*Diritto Penale Contemporaneo*, 2019), available at: www.archiviodpc.dirittopenaleuomo.org/d/6501-applicabile-lart-57-cp-al-direttore-del-quotidiano-online-un-revirement-giurisprudenziale-della-cas. Conversely, with respect to the criminal liability of the managers of an online website with respect to third-party content, Cass, V s No 7220/2021 concluded that Art 57 is not applicable, although, if there are elements suggesting an involvement of the manager in the publication, then the manager may be convicted as an accessory in the crime of aggravated defamation. See S Vimercati, 'La responsabilità del gestore del sito per i contenuti pubblicati da soggetti terzi' (2021) 2 *Rivista di diritto dei media* 247.

[47] On the crime of defamation within the Italian legal system, see F Antolisei, *Manuale di diritto penale. Parte speciale – 1*, 17th edn, ed A Rossi (Giuffrè, Milan, 2022) 270–76.

(or other people's) reputation.[48] The offence is generally punished either with imprisonment, for a period ranging from 15 days to one year, or with a fine, although the penalty shall be higher if the offence is committed by attributing to the defamed person a specific action or conduct, so that in such cases imprisonment may rise to up to two years (although an alternative pecuniary fine may be imposed); similarly, if the defamation takes place via the press, the penalty will be either imprisonment for a period stretching from six months to three years or, once again as an alternative, the payment of a fine. Article 13 of Law No 48/1947 foresaw an additional increase in the penalty, namely imprisonment from one to six years, if the defamation, spread via the press, consisted in attributing to the defamed person a specific conduct. In such cases, however, a custodial sentence was not simply an option but was mandatory.

Besides, pursuant to Article 597 of the Criminal Code, a person may only be prosecuted and punished for the crime of defamation upon being sued by the victim, therefore, the judicial authorities may not intervene if no complaint has been raised by the person targeted by the publication. In this respect, victims of defamation enjoy a rather ample measure of discretion as to the legal avenue they may take. On the one hand, they may decide to bring criminal action against the alleged offender. In such cases, it will be up to the criminal judge to decide with respect to both criminal and civil liability.[49] On the other hand, victims may decide to bring only a civil action to require compensation for the pecuniary and non-pecuniary damages suffered, based on Article 2043 of the Italian Civil Code. Indeed, the provision, which represents the basis of Italian tort law, explicitly requires that 'any intentional or negligent act causing an unjustified injury to another obliges the person who has committed the act to pay damages'. As stated by the Court of Cassation, in the case of defamation, the obligation to compensate damages is the result of the unlawful breach of another person's fundamental personality rights, such as the right to dignity, to personal image and to reputation, as protected by Articles 2 and 3 of the Constitution itself.[50]

The legal regime for the crime of defamation described above represented, potentially, a serious hurdle to the enjoyment by journalists of their constitutional prerogatives. In recognition of such a risk, the Italian judiciary has striven to strike an appropriate balance between the need to protect individuals' right

---

[48] A specific requirement, which pursuant to Italian law distinguishes defamation from the de-criminalised conduct of insulting, is that the defamed person must be absent and, in any case, incapable of perceiving the assault on their reputation. Art 594 of the Criminal Code, prohibiting the act of insulting, was, in fact, repealed by Legislative Decree No 7/2016; however, today, such conduct may still be subjected to civil pecuniary penalties, as well as to the compensation of the damages inflicted on the person (or people) insulted.

[49] As highlighted by the Court of Cassation, criminal liability always entails also civil liability, leading to the obligation of compensation for damages; conversely, there may be cases where a person is a liable for tort on civil grounds and not punishable, however, on criminal grounds. See Cass Civ, I s No 5259/1984.

[50] Cass Civ, su No 26972/2008.

to dignity and reputation and the need to ensure the respect for freedom of the press. The judiciary thus developed an extensive body of case law which, based on Article 51 of the Criminal Code, aimed at fully protecting the rights of journalists. Pursuant to Article 51, when a person commits an action which amounts to a criminal offence, the fact that the action was committed as a result of the exercise of a personal right may represent a cause for justification. When applied to the case at hand, such a provision entails that the publication of a certain text which may represent, theoretically, a form of defamation, may not in fact constitute a crime if that publication represents a manifestation of the freedom of the press.

The Italian judiciary, nonetheless, identified criteria which journalists must comply with in order for their freedom to impart information to overcome the reputational interests of the person targeted by the publication. Within its case law, the Court of Cassation has indeed repeatedly underlined the main tenets governing the operationalisation of such a balancing of rights. In this respect, the so-called 'catalogue decision' (*sentenza decalogo*) of 1984[51] represents one of the most historic judgments of the Court of Cassation. Addressing a request for compensation for the damages suffered by a financial company whose investment funds had been criticised rather harshly by a newspaper, the decision formalised and clarified the three conditions that the exercise of freedom of the press must respect in order to avoid criminal and/or civil liability for defamation. First, the published information must be relevant to the public and have a social function. Second, the publication must be truthful, although truthfulness does not entail the duty that those statements actually correspond to reality. Truthfulness may also be simply putative. In such cases, however, the inconsistencies of the journalists' allegations with reality must not be the consequence of negligence. In other words, for the criterion of truthfulness to be complied with, it is necessary that the author has done diligent and appropriate preliminary research. At the same time, the Court of Cassation also clarified that journalists must not omit any significant part or element of the truth, since truthfulness is incompatible at its core with the activity of cherry-picking. Third, the exposition of facts must be civilised, meaning that journalists must express themselves in a manner that is not over-exaggerated and that is oriented towards the purposes of objectivity (*continenza formale*).

Clearly, the limits of social interest, truthfulness and '*continenza formale*' apply first and foremost to the right of the press to report (factual) news. As these apply to the right of criticism, which may consist of the simple expression of personal views and opinions of the journalist, those criteria are nonetheless still applicable, although their role in the evaluation of the defamatory status of the allegations may vary. Thus, for instance, the requirement of truthfulness is much less stringent in such cases precisely because there is no narration of factual events: as recently highlighted by the Court of Cassation, the truthfulness criterion, with respect to

---

[51] Cass Civ, I s No 5259/1984. See, among others, F Petrangeli, 'Cronaca e critica (diritto di)' (2001) Agg V *Enciclopedia del diritto* 303; LG Sciannella, 'Il diritto di cronaca' in G Avanzini, G Matucci and L Musselli, *Informazione e media nell'era digitale* (Milano, Giuffrè, 2019).

the right of criticism, is necessarily feebler, since criticism, being of its nature the expression of a merely subjective opinion, naturally entails an inherently speculative character.[52] This does not mean, however, that the expression of any thought or opinion may be acceptable, since criticism, too, should be founded on grounds that adhere to some extent to reality.[53] Additionally, the weakening of the importance of truthfulness in the context of the right of criticism is counterbalanced by the need to guarantee, in any case, the respect for the requirement of '*continenza formale*':[54] thus, the Court of Cassation has stressed that criticism cannot turn into uncontrolled verbal aggression towards the criticised person (or people), nor into the use of terms that are seriously insulting or unnecessarily humiliating.[55]

The Italian legal framework on defamation has nonetheless encountered some very strong criticisms of its consistency with freedom of the press. Most notably, the system of criminal penalties provided by the Criminal Code and by the law on the press was at the centre of the 2019 ECtHR decision in *Sallusti v Italy*.[56] In this case, an Italian journalist, the director of *Libero*, had been sentenced to 14 months' imprisonment after an anonymous article was published on the newspaper's front page denouncing the case of a 13-year-old girl who had supposedly been obliged to have an abortion by her parents and by the tutelary judge. The article described the parents, judge and gynaecologist as murderers deserving death. The ECtHR did not find against the conviction of Alessandro Sallusti, highlighting that the honour and right to privacy of the tutelary judge (who had pressed charges against *Libero*), as well as those of the parents and of the gynaecologist, had indeed been tarnished and violated. Nonetheless, the Court stated that it considered the imposition of a custodial sentence for a media-related offence compatible with freedom of the press only in exceptional circumstances and that, in the case at hand, there was no justification for the adoption of such a measure. According to the ECtHR, as a matter of fact, sentencing journalists to prison terms would inevitably translate into excessive and unwarranted chilling effects. In 2021, in line with the approach of the ECtHR, the Italian Constitutional Court also intervened in the matter of

---

[52] Cass Pen, V s No 4938/2010. See also, more recently, Cass Pen, V s No 31263/2020.

[53] Think, eg, of a case where a journalist described a politician as a '*mafioso*' or as a Fascist without there being any indication whatsoever of that person's affiliation to mafia or to Fascism. See Cass Pen, V s No 39047/2019.

[54] In fact, the requirement of '*continenza formale*', especially with respect to the right to criticism, has caused the concerns of a variety of scholars, who have highlighted how such a condition may ultimately impair the full enjoyment of such a right. See, among others, L Paladin, 'Libertà di pensiero e libertà di informazione: le problematiche attuali' (1987) 1 *Quaderni costituzionali* 5; GE Vigevani, 'L'informazione e i suoi limiti: il diritto di cronaca' in GE Vigevani et al (eds), *Diritto dell'informazione e dei media*, 2nd edn (Torino, Giappichelli, 2022) 42.

[55] Cass Pen, V s No 29730/2010.

[56] *Sallusti v Italy*, App no 22350/13, judgment of 7 March 2019. See, among others, S Turchetti, 'Diffamazione, pena detentiva, caso Sallusti: ancora una condanna all'Italia da parte della Corte EDU' (*Diritto Penale Contemporaneo*, 2019), available at: www.archiviodpc.dirittopenaleuomo.org/d/6566-diffamazione-pena-detentiva-caso-sallusti-ancora-una-condanna-allitalia-da-parte-della-corte-edu.

the criminal law regime for defamation via the press by declaring Article 13 of Law No 47/1948 unconstitutional and, therefore, declaring it void.[57] Most notably, although not excluding the possibility that in some cases it may be necessary to resort to custodial measures as a response to particularly serious cases of defamation, the Court held that the structure of the provision was not in conformity with Article 21 of the Constitution because it actually obliged the judge to impose the penalty of imprisonment whenever defamation via the press consisted in the attribution of a fact or conduct, and thus not allowing for the adoption of a less onerous measure.[58]

Moving on to offences committed by the press besides defamation, Law No 47/1948 also sets some additional provisions concerning the nature of the contents that may be published, with a view to protecting specific interests which may potentially collide with an unbridled regime of freedom of the press. Thus, for instance, Article 14 sets some additional rules for the protection of minors, prohibiting, under the threat of criminal prosecution, any publication intended for children and/or teenagers that may offend their moral sentiments or incite them to corruption, to the commission of crimes, or to suicide, while Article 15 proscribes under criminal law the publication of printed material showing or describing real-life or imaginary events in an excessively gruesome or disturbing manner.

Such provisions are ultimately connected to the underlying principle that the press should in all cases fully respect the dignity of all natural persons. This underlying principle also emerges from a wide range of other provisions and norms set by the law. Thus, Article 8 of Law No 47/1948 explicitly requires that any person whose images have been published in a newspaper, or to whom specific actions, opinions or words have been attributed, may demand that the newspaper publishes, free of charge, any rectification or reply at the request of the interested person. Such a request may be made whenever the latter believes that the newspaper's allegations are false or that their right to dignity has been infringed. Besides, the Court of Cassation has clarified that the right to rectification provided by Article 8 does not exhaust the related right to compensation for damages caused by the offence to the victim's dignity.[59]

Additionally, newspapers and journalists are subject to specific duties and obligations aimed at guaranteeing the full protection of the rights to privacy and data protection[60] of the people they mention in their work or whose data is, in any form, processed for the purposes of journalistic activities; however, these rules are the

---

[57] Italian Constitutional Court, No 150/2021. See C Magnani, 'La Corte costituzionale rivede la detenzione per la diffamazione tramite i media. Prime note sulla sentenza n 150 del 2021' (2021) 5 *Osservatorio AIC* 171.

[58] Conversely, Art 595 of the Criminal Code was considered by the Court constitutionally legitimate, provided that it was interpreted as merely giving the opportunity to judges to resort to the custodial measure, without, however, obliging them to do so.

[59] Cass Civ, III s No 1152/2021. See, on this point, S Peron, 'La finalità riparatoria dell'istituto della rettifica ex art 8 L. 47/1948' (2021) 1 *Rivista di Diritto dei Media* 325.

[60] See C Melzi d'Eril, 'Privacy e attività giornalistica' in GE Vigevani et al (eds), *Diritto dell'informazione e dei media*, 2nd edn (Torino, Giappichelli, 2022).

result of the combination of both national law and European Union (EU) law, with an increasing role accorded to the latter, especially in the wake of the General Data Protection Regulation (GDPR).[61] Within the Italian legal framework, the right to privacy, since it is not enshrined within the Civil Code, was first recognised through judicial interpretation by the Court of Cassation in the 1975 *Soraya* judgment,[62] where the Court concluded that the constitutional protection of privacy should be derived from Article 2 of the Constitution, *de juncto* with a range of other provisions protecting various aspects of the personal lives of individuals (for example, Article 15 on the right to secrecy in personal communications). However, the Italian lawmaker did not intervene to introduce specific legislation protecting the right to privacy until the turn of the millennium when it eventually had to comply with EU law; currently, the Italian legal framework on privacy and data protection is contained and codified within the so-called 'Privacy Code' of 2003.[63]

The constitutional and legal recognition of privacy as a personal right has made it possible to bring before the judicial authority actions for the civil compensation of privacy-related damages pursuant to the Civil Code's general rules on tort liability (Articles 2043 and following). In criminal law, Articles 167 and following of the Privacy Code contain the main relevant provisions, providing, for instance, for the criminalisation of the unlawful processing of personal data, as well as of the unlawful publication or dissemination of, and the fraudulent acquisition of, personal data. Nonetheless, specific rules (Articles 136 and following) are provided with respect to journalistic activity, with a view to balancing privacy with the protection of freedom of the press; most notably, journalists may process the personal data mentioned within Articles 9 and 10 of the GDPR without the consent of the data subjects involved (Article 137) if they comply with the relevant codes of conduct adopted and enforced by the Order of Journalists together with the Italian Data Protection Authority.[64]

An important role in the definition of the duties and responsibilities of journalists has been played precisely by the adoption of such self-regulatory codes of conduct, setting the rules on the duties and ethics of the journalistic profession. Originally, these rules were contained in a variety of documents, however, in 2016, the Order of Journalists decided to codify them within a single, consolidated text of the duties of the journalist (*testo unico dei doveri del giornalista*). The consolidated text (revised in 2019) recognises journalists' freedom of information and of criticism (Article 1) while also establishing the ethical principles which should

---

[61] Regulation (EU) 2016/679 of the European Parliament and of the Council of 27 April 2016 on the protection of natural persons with regard to the processing of personal data and on the free movement of such data, and repealing Directive 95/46/EC (General Data Protection Regulation) [2016] OJ L 119/1.

[62] Cass Civ, s I No 2129/1975.

[63] Legislative Decree No 196/2003.

[64] See Garante per la Protezione dei Dati Personali, Order No 491/2018 [doc web No 9067692], Deontological rules on the processing of personal data in the exercise of journalistic activities published pursuant to Art 20(4) of Legislative Decree of 10 August 2018, No 101 – 29 November 2018.

guide their activities and work, such as the respect for the fundamental rights of other people (Article 2), including the right to personal identity and the right to be forgotten (Article 3) as well as to the protection of personal data (Article 4). Specific rules also aim to protect minors (Article 5) and people in conditions of frailty (Article 6), as well as to avoid discrimination based on gender (Article 5-bis) and on being a foreigner (Article 7). Additional provisions concern the reporting of news concerning judicial proceedings (Article 8); the duty of rectification[65] and that of respecting the sources of information (Article 9); advertising and the use of surveys (Article 10); and the dissemination of economic (Article 11) and sports-related (Article 12) information. Pursuant to Article 15, which explicitly refers to Law No 69/1963, it is up to the Order of Journalists to monitor the respect for and enforce the consolidated text; most notably, failure to comply with the rules set therein may lead to the adoption by the Order of the disciplinary measures identified within Article 51 of Law No 69/1963.[66]

6. Online Press and Constitutional Guarantees

Another important subject of debate concerns the actual scope of protection of freedom of the press. Most notably, questions have arisen with respect to the possibility of applying the guarantees and rules provided by the law also to the digital landscape. Article 1 of Law No 47/1948, for example, offers a definition of the press which is rather outdated since it refers explicitly to the use of typographic (or other mechanic or physical-chemical) means of production of material destined for publication.

With a view to overcoming the technical gap between the legal framework and reality, Law No 62/2001, setting new rules concerning the publishing industry, introduced the notion of 'editorial product' which includes any electronic product destined for publication (Article 1). Additionally, the provision was updated by Law No 198/2016 which explicitly added online newspapers to the scope of application of editorial products: online newspapers, as clarified by Law No 198/2016, are characterised by the feature of publishing their content mainly via the Internet. According to these pieces of legislation, editorial products (and, therefore, also online newspapers) are subject, most notably, to the provisions of Articles 2 and 5 of the law on the press concerning, respectively, the duty to indicate on the printed document specific information (for example, the place and time of printing, the name of the printer, editor and owner, etc) and the obligation of registration before the local tribunal.[67] Laws No 62/2001 and No 198/2016, however, have not solved in a definitive way the question of whether the press online should be subject to the

---

[65] See above.

[66] See section 3 above.

[67] See section 2 above. The current Art 1(3-bis) clarifies that online newspapers, just like traditional ones published on paper, must be registered before the local tribunal and must be governed by a director who is enrolled, either as a professional or as a publicist, within the Registry of Journalists.

exact same legal regime as the offline press in all its aspects. The question is quite a tricky one, as in the age of convergence the Internet seems to be more and more a preferred channel for delivering content and information.

In particular, the applicability of the guarantees set within Article 21 of the Constitution, that is, the requirements of '*riserva di legge*' and '*riserva di giurisdizione*' when it comes to the enforcement of the seizure of press products,[68] has been at the centre of notable case law. Moving on from the wording of Article 21, one option is to consider that the above-mentioned guarantees should apply to any form of exercise of freedom of the press, regardless of the specific technical medium; thus, the reference to traditional paper press should be intended as a mere historical legacy, whereas the protective provisions enshrined by the Constitution should apply to the essence of the freedom as such. This would also be in line with Article 21(1), which expressly states that freedom of expression is equally protected irrespective of the means used. Indeed, the Court of Cassation, in 2015, held precisely that operators in the field of professional journalism should enjoy the guarantees set by the Constitution also when using the Internet as a means to disseminate information. Therefore, the Constitution generally subjects the seizure of a journalistic website to the requirements of '*riserva di legge*' and '*riserva di giurisdizione*' as the type of activity conducted by an online newspaper is ontologically and functionally identical to that of an offline newspaper.[69]

Although the Court's decision has been welcomed because of its openness towards the expansion of freedom of the press also to online newspapers, some scholars believe that the judgment also represents a missed opportunity. The Supreme Court provided, in this respect, an evolutive interpretation of the scope of application of Article 21, clarifying that the specific medium does not make any difference. However, the Court of Cassation has not been able to go further and expand the Constitution's safeguards to a whole range of websites and portals, such as blogs and news forums, which although not being formally registered pursuant to Laws No 47/1948 and No 62/2001, still represent important sources of information for the public and are a means to enjoy freedom of expression in the context of the digital age. Most notably, actors working in the context of 'citizen journalism' are not at all protected under constitutional law. Because, today, the Internet can work as a medium to deliver audiovisual content or news even without being encapsulated within the traditional notion of the 'press' or

---

[68] See section 2 above.

[69] Cass Pen su No 31022/2015. On this decision, see, among others, M Bassini, *Internet e libertà di espressione. Prospettive costituzionali e sovranazionali* (Rome, Aracne, 2019); P Caretti, 'La Cassazione pone, meritoriamente, alcuni punti fermi in tema di regolazione dell'informazione via internet' (2015) 4 *Quaderni costituzionali* 1013; G Corrias Lucente, 'Le testate telematiche registrate sono sottratte al sequestro preventivo. Qualche dubbio sulla "giurisprudenza legislativa"' (2015) 6 *Diritto dell'informatica* 1041; A Pulvirenti, 'Sequestro e Internet: dalle Sezioni Unite una soluzione equilibrata ma "creativa"' (2015) 6 *Processo Penale e Giustizia* 78; L Paoloni, 'Le Sezioni Unite si pronunciano per l'applicabilità alle testate telematiche delle garanzie costituzionali sul sequestro della stampa: ubi commoda, ibi et incommoda?' (2015) 10 *Cassazione penale* 3454; S Lorusso, 'Un'innovativa pronuncia in tema di sequestro preventivo di testata giornalistica on line' (2015) 8–9 *Giurisprudenza italiana* 2003.

of the 'media', some commentators have argued that a further expansion of the concept of freedom of expression would be paramount for the deployment of the full informative potential of the Internet.[70]

7. Fostering Media Pluralism: The Rules against Concentration and on Economic Aid to the Press

A range of legal and administrative measures are foreseen within the Italian landscape with a view to protecting and fostering media pluralism and an informational landscape that is appropriate and adequate to the needs of the population and of democracy. These measures pertain to two macro areas: on the one hand, the rules aimed at reducing the concentration of press outlets and at protecting competition in the press market; on the other hand, the provision of economic aid to help its expansion and avoid the suffocation of smaller journalistic enterprises.[71]

As regards the first body of rules, the goal of the Italian lawmaker has been to guarantee a balance between freedom of expression, both in its active and passive dimension (Article 21 of the Constitution),[72] and the freedom to conduct business (Article 41). For this reason, the law establishes a system of thresholds to limit the power over the market of those actors that are in an economically 'dominant position'. The notion of such a dominant position is defined by Article 3 of Law No 67/1987 and is based on the percentage of newspapers owned, edited or in any way controlled by a single natural or legal person over the total amount of newspapers published at the national or local level.[73] The thresholds thus identified must not be exceeded. In this way, the law aims to pursue what the Constitutional Court has defined over the years as 'external pluralism',[74] that is, the coexistence of a plurality of different editorial and journalistic enterprises, capable of ensuring that citizens are able to receive information from a variety of different sources.

---

[70] See Bassini (n 69) 278.

[71] On this topic, see V Pampanin, 'Tutela del pluralismo informativo e regolazione economica del mercato convergenete della comunicazione' in G Avanzini and G Matucci, *Libertà, pluralismo e trasparenza* (Naples, Editoriale Scientifica, 2016); V Pampanin, 'Strumenti di regolazione a garanzia del mercato pluralistico dell'informazione *online*' in G Avanzini, G Matucci and L Musselli, *Informazione e media nell'èra digitale* (Milano, Giuffrè, 2019).

[72] On the passive dimension of freedom of expression, see O Pollicino, 'Fake News, Internet and Metaphors (to be handled carefully)' (2017) 1 *Rivista di diritto dei media* 23; G Pitruzzella and O Pollicino, *Disinformation and Hate Speech. A European Constitutional Perspective* (Milan, Bocconi University Press, 2020) 59.

[73] Most notably, the expression identifies those subjects who are the editors of or, in any case, who control those companies publishing newspapers for at least 20% of the press market in Italy for the reference year; at the same time, a subject may be considered to be in a dominant position if they are the editors or control companies publishing newspapers for at least 50% of the press market within one of four inter-regional areas (North-West; North-East, Centre and South) for the reference year; or those subjects who are the editors of or, in any case, who control those companies publishing newspapers for at least 30% of the press market in Italy for the previous year.

[74] See, eg, Italian Constitutional Court, No 826/1988.

To ensure the respect for this system of thresholds, the law sets out a range of transparency duties and obligations,[75] the violation of which, including through the presentation of false information, may result in criminal liability.[76] Additionally, the enforcement of anti-trust rules is devolved to a dedicated independent authority whose powers and nature have been subjected to a series of progressive reforms and which is, today, represented by the Department for Information and the Press, which is part of the Presidency of the Council of Ministers.[77] Finally, as concerns penalties for exceeding the above-mentioned thresholds, Article 3(4) of Law No 67/1987 rules that the contracts and agreements that have led to the overconcentration of editorial products under the umbrella of a single subject in violation of the law may be declared void by the judiciary; moreover, subjects that are recognised as being in a dominant position are not eligible for state financial aid, and the provision of any previous aid is to be suspended or cancelled.

Clearly then, as already anticipated, the Italian government deploys economic measures that are meant to uphold the market of the press and the survival of a plurality of sources of information.[78] Forms of financial aid also existed under the Fascist regime, with the protectionist goal of promoting the national market as well as with the aim of further promoting the government's propaganda. However, under the republican framework the purpose is much different and is, instead, in line with the passive dimension of freedom of expression as protected by Article 21 of the Constitution, and with the goal of promoting external pluralism. Initially, the state intervened through the granting of forms of direct contributions.[79] Subsequent Acts introduced further financial tools, such as the granting of additional funds to periodical publications characterised by an 'elevated cultural value'.[80] However, these kinds of direct contributions were progressively substituted by forms of indirect financing. First, public intervention moved in the direction of fostering the offering of favourable credit terms for newspapers' loans. These measures, first introduced by Law No 1063/1971, were progressively implemented and increased to guarantee the possibility for the press to easily gain access to liquid finances. Second, Law No 416/1981 introduced

---

[75] eg, newspapers must be enrolled within the Registry of Communication Operators, established by Art 1 of Law No 249/1997, indicate every year their financial reports and communicate any transfer of shares exceeding the 10% of the total. Additionally, those companies that control and administer a plurality of newspapers must provide a combined financial report that includes all the controlled newspapers.

[76] See Art 1 of Law No 249/1997.

[77] See Law No 400/1988 and the Decree of the President of the Council of Ministers of 1 October 2002. See, moreover, the Decree of the Undersecretary of State for Information and the Press of 26 May 2016, containing new rules concerning the organisation of the authority.

[78] On this topic, see MR Allegri, 'Il finanziamento pubblico all'editoria e particolarmente ai giornali di partito prima e dopo la riforma del 2012' (2012) 3 *Rivista AIC* 1.

[79] See, eg, Law No 1063/1971.

[80] Law No 416/1981.

favourable terms and conditions for newspapers with respect to the provision of a range of services (for example, telephone and telegraph lines, post and transport), as well as favourable tax regimes.[81]

Italian law has thus adopted an economic and financial approach to the regulation of the market of the press aimed specifically at guaranteeing as far as possible the diversity of the media and, therefore, at protecting the interests of the population, with respect to its freedom to receive pluralistic information, and the related constitutional goal of ensuring a well-functioning democratic process. This is done, on the one hand, via the implementation of measures designed to ensure competition within the press market and, on the other, via the deployment of financial aid meant to help the survival of a wider variety of journalistic sources.

8. Conclusions

The current legal framework governing the freedom of the press in Italy is deeply connected with the country's history and, in particular, represents in great part a reaction to the totalitarian experience of the Fascist regime. In this sense, the text of the Constitution, and most notably of its Article 21, contains several fundamental principles and guarantees aimed at ensuring the protection of this important freedom, which is considered, in line with the wider European landscape, an essential tool for the wellbeing of democracy. This approach, moreover, is reflected in the case law both of the Constitutional Court and of the Court of Cassation, bodies which have repeatedly intervened to clarify and define the content, as well as the boundaries, of freedom of the press. Additionally, the Italian authorities have adopted a number of measures that are specifically meant to ensure that the population is provided with sufficiently diverse and pluralistic content, both through the adoption of dedicated anti-trust regulations and through the deployment of economic and financial aid aimed at guaranteeing the survival of minor newspapers and editorial products.

At the same time, the regulation of freedom of the press in Italy still faces some important challenges and issues. For instance, the current regime concerning professional secrecy of journalistic sources seems to be deserving of a careful revision, especially with a view to ensuring that the relevant guarantees are extended to publicists and not limited only to professional journalists. Other areas which should be addressed by the law include the regulation of the relationship between individual journalists and their employers, as well

---

[81] With respect to subsequent developments in the regulation of indirect contributions see, eg, Law No 662/1996 and Law No 52/2001. More recently, Law No 198/2016 foresaw the establishment of a Fund for Pluralism and Innovation of Information, whereas Legislative Decree No 70/2017 redefined the range of subjects that are eligible for those contributions. On this topic, see Caretti and Cardone (n 1) 73–85.

as the regime concerning national and judicial secrets. Additionally, another aspect which has been increasingly debated in recent years concerns the criminal treatment of the offence of defamation: as highlighted by the ECtHR, and as implicitly highlighted by the Italian Constitutional Court, the imposition of custodial penalties should be limited as much as possible, thus, a revision of Article 595 of the Criminal Code may be essential in order to further constrain the possibility of imposing such punishments on journalists. Finally, in the context of the developing digital landscape it will arguably be necessary for the Italian lawmaker to intervene to clarify the exact scope of application of the laws concerning the press with respect to the online environment. Most notably, the situation of 'atypical' forms of the press should be addressed with a view to building a legislative framework capable of ensuring that the full informative potential of the Internet is deployed.

7

Freedom of the Press and Press Regulation in Poland

JOANNA KULESZA

1. Introduction

Contemporary Polish media law dates back to the 1918 revival of the independent Republic of Poland following the Treaty of Brest-Litovsk, which dealt with Russia's withdrawal from the First World War. The Polish Republic inherited three legal systems, two of Austrian/Prussian origin and one of Russian. The reason for this was that for 123 years there was no Polish state. In 1795, as a result of the Third Partition, the Polish–Lithuanian Commonwealth was divided between three occupying powers: Prussia, the Habsburg monarchy and the Russian Empire. The occupying powers acted vigorously to ensure that Polish culture, language and normative standards were eradicated from their new territories. This process involved not only mandatory language training for all their new subjects but also the extension of national laws including those relevant to the media in what used to be the Commonwealth territories. When Poland regained its national independence in 1918, one of the biggest challenges facing it was to introduce a comprehensive legal system that would allow the unification of components originating from three different states. Given that the majority of the new Polish state came from under Germanic (Imperial German and Austro-Hungarian) rule, the legal framework inherited in these regions of the country was given precedence in the law-making work preparing the state for independence. This was also the case for press law regulations, since while the statutory committee of the Parliament was founded early on, in 1919, it did not succeed in producing any draft laws until late 1938. This was primarily due to the lack of a consensus on the required limits of free expression in the new republic, which was torn by political conflict and turmoil.

It was only in 1938 that the authoritarian President of the Republic proposed a decree on the press law. Little did he know that this would be the only legal act regulating Polish media law up until the late twentieth century. The 1938 press law decree was based on a German approach to media regulation and foresaw the introduction of measures such as a duty to register all periodicals and a higher standard of diligence required from media professionals. Editors-in-chief could be held liable for a crime committed by the publication of a commissioned piece even if they held no fault of their own but rather failed to show due care in preventing such a crime from being committed. Practice in implementing the new Polish Press Law Act was scarce, however, since less than a year later the Second World War broke out.

After the war, Poland was in the sphere of Soviet influence and the political agenda of the Communist Party meant that there was little to no media freedom. For this reason, there were no direct attempts to introduce a dedicated legal framework that would protect the interests of journalists and give them a code of law that would support their professional interests. It was only in 1984 that the first post-war Press Law Act was introduced, as a symbolic gesture on the part of the Communist Party to appease the people after martial law was introduced to curb the mass protests led by the Solidarity movement (Solidarność) in the early 1980s. With the lifting of martial law in 1984, a new, comprehensive Press Law Act was introduced. The government claimed it as its own, yet the text that was eventually published largely relied on a civil society draft law proposal made by academics and journalists in the early 1980s as part of their protest-driven demands. The 1984 Press Law Act envisaged a solid framework allowing journalists to practise journalistic secrecy and protecting them from direct attacks. Although far from perfect, it is this law that has served as the basis for all media law regulation in Poland until today.

While after the political shift in the early 1990s, numerous plans have been made to revoke the 1984 act and replace it with a regulation that would be more modern and better suited to attend to the challenges of today, no political consensus could be found to implement them. The 1984 Press Law Act was, however, revised and complemented by the introduction of the 1992 Broadcasting Act on Radio and Television, which was later significantly amended in 2011 following the adoption of the European Union's (EU) Audiovisual Media Services Directive (AVMSD).[1] With Poland joining the EU in 2004, all that body's media law-related regulations, including those covering intermediary liability, have been duly implemented. Together with civil and criminal law provisions such as those on defamation or the protection of personal rights, including privacy and reputation, they constitute a comprehensive normative framework for Polish media law.

---

[1] Directive (EU) 2018/1808 of the European Parliament and of the Council of 14 November 2018 amending Directive 2010/13/EU on the coordination of certain provisions laid down by law, regulation or administrative action in Member States concerning the provision of audiovisual media services (Audiovisual Media Services Directive) in view of changing market realities [2018] OJ L303/69.

2. Theory of Press Freedom

The Polish approach to the freedom of the press reflects the pan-European consensus expressed in Article 10 of the Convention for the Protection of Human Rights and Fundamental Freedoms (European Convention on Human Rights, ECHR) and Article 11 of the Charter of Fundamental Rights of the European Union. Free speech is seen as a non-absolute right, to be exercised within specific boundaries, clearly defined by law. Press freedom is rooted in the understanding that everyone has the right to hold opinions and to receive and impart information and ideas without interference by the public authorities and regardless of frontiers. Freedom of the press is explicitly named as a constitutional principle with a firm place in the first Chapter of the Polish Constitution, Article 14 of which states that the Republic of Poland ensures freedom of the press and other means of social communication.

This normative principle, established in Chapter I of the Constitution as a guiding legislative principle, is specified and complemented by the recognition of the free press as the cornerstone of democracy, which was reflected in Article 54. According to its provisions, 'freedom to express opinions, to acquire and to disseminate information shall be ensured to everyone' whereas the press is considered to be a particularly significant beneficiary of this right with specific protections granted in the dedicated Press Law Act. This provision also includes a prohibition of preventive censorship of the means of social communication and the licensing of the press, while allowing for statutes to require the receipt of a permit for the operation of a radio or television station, in accordance with necessary technical constraints. While Article 54 does not explicitly refer to freedom of speech (as 'freedom of expression' incorporates all types of expression, 'speech' included), this phrasing does appear in Article 213 of the Constitution, which establishes the National Council of Radio Broadcasting and Television as a guardian of 'freedom of speech', the right to information and the public interest regarding radio broadcasting and television.[2] Together, these provisions are considered the fundamental normative framework for media regulation in Poland.

3. Constitutional Press Freedom

As noted above, freedom of speech is considered the cornerstone of press and media freedom, with the two being perceived as complementary rights. The Constitution provides explicit protection for both, while the Press Law Act

---

[2] M Florczak-Wątor, 'Article 54' in P Tuleja (ed), *Konstytucja Rzeczypospolitej Polskiej. Komentarz*, 2nd edn (Warsaw, LEX/el, 2021).

establishes a more detailed legal framework offering specific protection and privileges to journalists as compared to the general public. The notions of a press, press materials and journalists, although legally defined, as explained herein below, remain ambiguous and subject to judicial interpretations.

The reading of Article 54 of the Polish Constitution is in line with that of Article 10 of the ECHR and Article 11 of the Charter of Fundamental Rights of the European Union. Polish jurisprudence understands 'expression' as an activity whereby one's views and beliefs are shared in any form available, going beyond merely verbal communication. It encompasses artistic expression, scientific works and commercial communications. 'Statement' is understood to be an observation about facts as well as an expression that contains their evaluation. These guarantees are to be applied regardless of frontiers and the medium through which they are being exercised. As reiterated by the Constitutional Tribunal in its judgment of 5 May 2004, in the Polish Constitution the principle of freedom of expression consists of three separate, but related and interdependent, freedoms of the individual.

These include the freedom to express views, the freedom to obtain information and the freedom to disseminate information. The Tribunal shared the view expressed in the doctrine that the term 'view', used in the Constitution should be understood as broadly as possible, not only as expressing personal judgements on facts and phenomena in all manifestations of life but also including opinions, assumptions and forecasts, and in particular informing about facts, both real and presumed.[3] Moreover, this provision ensures that media freedom is also understood as containing three fundamental components which include the freedom to establish media, that is, to set up media companies, the freedom to perform activities through public communications, and the freedom to decide upon the ownership structure of mass media outlets.[4] Freedom of the press should, therefore, be understood as complementary to freedom of expression.[5]

The Constitutional Tribunal has confirmed that freedom of expression is 'one of the foundations of a democratic society, (and) a condition for its development and self-fulfilment'. As such, it 'must not be limited to information and views that are favourably received or perceived as harmless or indifferent'.[6] The role of journalists is to disseminate information and ideas about matters of public interest and importance, and this right is closely related to the right to an opinion. Under Article 31(3) of the Polish Constitution, freedom of expression may be subject to restrictions, with the most elementary condition for restricting this freedom comprising the requirement of statutory regulation, while recognising the need to ensure the precision of the provisions introduced in the laws. When considered as

---

[3] See P Sarnecki, 'Note 5 to Article 54' in L Garlicki (ed), *Commentary to the Constitution of the Republic of Poland* (Warsaw, 2003).

[4] Judgment of the Constitutional Tribunal of 9 November 2010, K 13/07, OTK-A 2010, No 9, item 98.

[5] Judgment of the Constitutional Tribunal of 12 May 2008, SK 43/05, OTK-A 2008, No 4, item 57.

[6] Judgment of the Constitutional Tribunal of 23 March 2006, K 4/06, OTK-A 2006, No 3, item 32.

an individual right, freedom of expression protects the intellectual improvement of an individual, the development of their individuality, and the pursuit of self-fulfilment. In the complementary collective understanding of free expression, it is a necessary precondition for the functioning of democracy, as it enables public debate, the articulation of one's needs, and checks and balances on the performance of state authority.[7] It is these two dimensions of freedom of speech that result in its 'mixed' nature, one that combines personal freedom as a component of private life with political freedom exercised in public life.[8]

4. Press Regulation

The collection of legislation usually referred to as media law is a set of legal norms directly relating to the media and regulating their functioning.[9] Delimiting this particular area of regulation can prove challenging given its broad and quickly expanding nature. Media law thus covers a significant number of provisions of civil, criminal and administrative law. Key regulations of the media are included in the Press Law Act[10] and the Broadcasting Act on Radio and Television which reiterate and specify the constitutional principles discussed above. These are to be read together with the Civil Code, Penal Code and several administrative law acts to include, for example, the Law on Access to Public Information[11] and the Law on the Protection of Classified Information.[12] All of these provisions should be read in the context of Articles 14, 54 and 213–15 of the Polish Constitution, discussed above.

The 1984 Press Law Act explicitly reinstates the constitutional freedom of expression clause, stating that under the Constitution of the Republic of Poland, 'the press enjoys the freedom of expression and implements the right of citizens to reliable information, transparency in public life, and social control and criticism'. While the notions of 'reliable information', 'public life' and its 'transparency' as well as 'social control and criticism' might seem ambiguous or outdated, they have been well defined in the doctrine and through the application of press law and are also based on complementary legal provisions such as those of the Act on Access to Public Information 2001, which help to define the 'transparency of public life' as well as the 'reliability' of information deriving from the criminal and

---

[7] See judgment of the Constitutional Tribunal of 11 October 2006, P 3/06, OTK-A 2006, No 9, item 121.

[8] Decision of the Constitutional Tribunal of 4 October 2011, K 9/11, OTK-A 2011, No 8, item 85.

[9] M Zaremba, 'Article 1' in K Drozdowicz, M Łoszewska-Ołowska and M Zaremba, *Prawo prasowe: Komentarz* (Warsaw, Wolters Kluwer, 2018).

[10] Act of 26 January 1984, Press Law (*Journal of Laws* of 1984, item 24, as amended).

[11] Act of 6 September 2001 on Access to Public Information (*Journal of Laws* of 2022, item 902).

[12] Act of 29 December 1992 on Radio and Television (*Journal of Laws* of 2017, item 1414).

civil law provisions on libel. Reliable information is considered to be a cornerstone for assessing the due diligence of the press and its agents. The Press Law Act refers to it specifically in Article 6, which calls for the press to 'truthfully present' the circumstances and events it covers. Journalists, as defined in Article 7, are required to act with due professional care in the performance of their duties.[13]

While the Polish legal system does not demand the search for objective truth as it is considered unobtainable, the pursuit of a subjective truth by an individual acting as a journalist can be subject to a court proceeding based on a standard of due professional care. Such a standard will be applied by a court with due regard to the specific circumstances of each case, although as a general rule it excludes any form of exaggeration, presenting only a selection of facts or opinions about the given circumstances or events, and the excessive expression of personal emotions or bias. If, in the performance of their professional activity, a journalist puts forward a hypothesis about an event or occurrence they are reporting on, which they are entitled to do, such a hypothesis must be identified in the publication and be distinguished from the report on the facts. A journalist who fails to show due professional care in the performance of their duties can be considered as having failed to perform their professional duties and can, as such, be subject to prosecution for crimes of omission or for failure to perform their labour law duties.

These principles are to be applied to all journalists, regardless of the form or medium in which they pursue their activity. These obligations are implied by the phrasing of Article 12 of the Polish Press Law Act 1984, which obliges a journalist to 'exercise particular diligence and precision when collecting and using press material, especially to check compliance with the truth and reference the source'. This obligation is complemented by the legal duty to protect journalistic sources, as laid down in Article 12(1) which states that a journalist must 'protect personal interests and interests of informants acting in good faith and of other individuals entrusting information to them'. Journalists are therefore under a legal obligation to refrain from sharing any details about an individual who had entrusted them with evidence, including if they are called as a witness in a court of law. According to Article 180 of the Polish Code of Criminal Procedure, individuals who are obliged to keep secrets relating to the performance of a profession or function may refuse to testify as to the circumstances to which this obligation extends unless the court or the prosecutor for the benefit of the administration of justice dismisses these persons from the obligation of secrecy, unless specific laws provide otherwise.

Such individuals, including journalists, who are obliged to keep journalistic secrets, may be questioned as to the facts covered by these secrets only if it is necessary for the good of the administration of justice, and the circumstance cannot be established based on any other evidence. The journalist's exemption

---

[13] The Polish press law regards a journalist as a person who edits, creates or prepares press materials, is in an employment relationship with the editorial office or carries out such activities for and under the authority of the editorial office. Further definitions are discussed herein below.

from the obligation to maintain confidentiality may not apply to data enabling the identification of the author of the press material, a letter to the editor, or other material of this nature, nor to the identification of persons providing information published or submitted for publication if those persons stipulated that such data should not be disclosed. These provisions put all journalists in a position to make case-specific choices on information they believe they can share in a particular context. Failing to keep the information confidential may result in them being held criminally liable for the breach of professional secrecy under Article 266 of the Polish Penal Code.[14]

The notion of 'particular' due care has been well defined by jurisprudence and judicial practice. Journalists are expected to act with 'exceptional, special, extraordinary diligence', and therefore greater than that normally expected in everyday activities or from non-journalists.[15] The practical question is whether a false allegation published by the press must be subject to civil liability or criminal prosecution, according to Article 24(1) of the Polish Civil Code or Article 212(2) of the Polish Penal Code, respectively, when the journalist exercised particular care and diligence in collecting and using press materials.

The Supreme Court noted that it is indeed the level of care that a journalist has shown in the preparation of a publication that is conclusive for determining their liability for harm caused by statements that have proven to be false. If a journalist acts with due care in collecting and publishing material, they are not to be held liable or responsible for such harm. If, however, they have acted with a degree of care that falls below the threshold usually expected from a professional in given circumstances, they might be subject to litigation. The Polish Supreme Court has confirmed that to avoid liability for infringement of personal rights the journalist must prove the truthfulness of the allegation.[16]

The obligation to show 'particular' due care is complemented by the legal protection of transparency of public life expressed in Article 61 of the Polish Constitution. It grants everyone the right to 'obtain information on the activities of organs of public authority as well as persons discharging public functions'. This includes the right to obtain information on the activities of self-governing economic or professional organs and other persons or organisational units relating to the field in which they perform the duties of public authorities and manage communal assets or property of the State Treasury. It includes the right to access

---

[14] Under Art 266 of the Polish Penal Code anyone who, contrary to the obligation upon them, discloses or uses information which they became acquainted with in connection with their function, work, public, social, economic or scientific activity, are subject to a fine, the penalty of restriction of liberty or imprisonment up to two years.

[15] E Ferenc-Szydełko, 'Article 12' in K Drozdowicz, M Łoszewska-Ołowska and M Zaremba, *Prawo prasowe: Komentarz* (Warsaw, Wolters Kluwer, 2018).

[16] Supreme Court of 22 December 1997, II CKN 546/97 181; of 23 June 2004, V CK 538/03 182; of 29 March 2012, I CSK 370/11 183; and of 2 December 2010, I CSK 11/10 184.

documents and to 'enter meetings of collective bodies of public authority elected in general elections, with the possibility of recording sound and image'.

While the Law on Access to Public Information fails to define 'public life' and provides only for a negative definition of 'public information' understood as 'any information on public matters' the access to which has not been prohibited by other provisions of law, it does include a broad, open catalogue of categories of information, public bodies and other entities providing public services which define the scope of 'public life' in Article 4.[17]

These provisions are fundamental to ensuring that media have access to information, with public authorities directly obliged to provide the information in question without undue delay. This obligation is complemented by Article 2 of the Polish Press Law Act, which requires all state bodies to create the necessary conditions for the press to execute its functions and tasks. The state is obliged to ensure the conditions to enable the editorial offices of newspapers and magazines to exercise their statutory functions while ensuring the diversity of programmes, subjects and opinions. Investigative journalism is key to achieving these aims.

In parallel, the notions of 'control' and 'social criticism' on the part of the press are directly dependent on its ability to publicly disclose matters of public life. Both of these terms refer directly to the need to ensure transparency in public life and the 'journalistic right to negative evaluation' or 'journalistic right to exaggerate', while at the same time acting with journalistic due care.[18] The right of journalists to criticism is detailed in Article 41 of the Polish Press Law, which obliges the press to publish 'reliable, compliant with the principles of social coexistence, negative assessments of scientific or artistic works or other creative, professional or public activity serves the purpose of carrying out the tasks specified in Article 1', such as public service and keeping the society informed. This right to exercise journalistic criticism is protected by law. Legitimate criticism involves respect for the reader and complying with ethical norms aimed at improving the undesired state of affairs which is the subject of the press publication.

The Supreme Court observed that 'criticism generally consists in communicating by the sender of the criticism the assessment of his action or omission based on the juxtaposition and confrontation (analysis) of factual circumstances with the adopted assumptions'.[19] It can be directed towards people and to their

---

[17] According to Art 4 of the Act on Access to Public Information 2001, entities obliged to provide public information include, in particular, public authorities, economic and professional self-government bodies, entities representing the State Treasury in accordance with separate regulations, entities representing state legal persons or legal persons of local government and entities representing other state organisational units or organisational units of local government and entities representing other persons or organisational units that perform public tasks or have public property, and legal persons in which the State Treasury, local government units or economic or professional self-government have a dominant position within the meaning of the provisions on competition and consumer protection.

[18] Polish Press Law Act, Art 12.

[19] Supreme Court of 17 December 1965, VI KO 14/59.

actions, conduct and behaviour, as well as certain states of affairs. Criticism may be based on one's own observations and findings of facts, as well as on observations and findings made by third parties, to which the critic refers while recognising their credibility and truthfulness. Taking into account the structure of the critical statement, three elements of a legally protected right to criticism can be distinguished: it must include a descriptive statement relating to facts, complemented by an assessment and generalisation of these facts, followed by an expression of statements, judgements and generalisations.

5. Press and Media Freedom

According to Article 7(2) of the Polish Press Law Act, the press has been defined as 'periodical publications that do not form a single and complete whole, are published at least once a year and bear a constant title or a name, a number and a date'. This definition covers in particular 'daily newspapers and periodicals, news agencies bulletins, constant telex messages, radio and television broadcasts'. Moreover, the press is also to be understood as 'all existing and emerging in the course of technological advancement means of mass media, including broadcasting stations and television and radio broadcasting systems installed in facilities that distribute periodically publications via print, image, sound or any other broadcasting means'. It is this second part of the definition that has led to the interpretation, confirmed by the Supreme Court, that all periodical publications, whether published by print or electronically, are covered by the press law with all the ensuing rights and obligations.[20]

The Press Law defines journals (*dzienniki*) and periodicals (*czasopisma*) in Article 7(2)(2) and 7(2)(3) as 'a periodic print (*sic*) or a transmission of sound or sound and vision of general information, appearing no less than once a week' (item 2), while 'a periodical is a periodic print (*sic*) appearing no more than once a week and no less than once a year; the regulation may also apply appropriately to transmissions of sound or sound and vision other than described in Paragraph 2'. Article 20 requires the registration of journals and periodicals but not of the press as such. Registration should be done at a district court where the publisher has their registered office. A registration application, as mentioned in section 1of the Press Law, must include the title of the daily newspaper or periodical in question together with the seat and an exact address of its editorial office, the particulars of the editor-in-chief, the specification, seat and exact address of the publisher, and the daily newspaper's or the periodical's frequency of publishing. A registrar court

---

[20] See J Kulesza, 'Which Legal Standards Should Apply to Web-logs?' (2009) 13(3) *Lex Electronica*, available at: www.lex-electronica.org/docs/articles_221.pdf, discussing Supreme Court Resolution of 15 December 2010, III KK 250/10.

issues the decision to register a daily newspaper of a periodical only upon a motion being passed. A daily newspaper or a periodical can be published if a registrar body fails to decide upon the application for the registration within 30 days from the day of the submission of the application for registration.

Failing to meet this obligation may result in a fine or a criminal sentence of up to 12 months of public service, according to Article 45 of the Act. According to the current reading of the Act, dailies and periodicals can also both be published as 'electronic print' and as such are to be registered no later than when the first number has been published. If the court does not object to the request for registration within 30 days of its submission, the publisher is deemed to have duly registered the daily or periodical and is free to continue with further publications. An objection from the court to a request for registration may result from a failure to meet a formal requirement or a request to register a press title that has already been submitted. Polish press law also provides a definition of a journalist, as anyone preparing, producing, or publishing a press material, where press material is defined broadly to include any informative, journalistic, documentary, or other text or image already published or provided to the publisher and intended for publication in press, irrespective of the means of transmission, type, form, destination or authorship of the material.

With these broad definitions of the press and of journalists, all press law provisions are to be applied to anyone who regularly publishes any kind of content, whether in print or online, where a 'publication' is to be interpreted as making content available to the general public and the prerequisite of 'regularity', in the context of Article 7(2)1 means appearing at least once a year. Concerning electronic publications, an update of a substantial part of the material can be considered as meeting the criterion of a new issue being published. Any content the access to which is limited, even if only by the need to formally register to join a social media closed group, would not be considered as meeting the criterion of a publication.

According to Article 25(4), the editor-in-chief bears the responsibility for the content of the material prepared by the editorial team and the organisational and financial issues of the company within the framework set up in the articles of association or relevant regulations. The editor-in-chief is also responsible for safeguarding the linguistic correctness of press materials and counteracting their vulgarisation. With respect to online publications, the role of a journalist, editor and editor-in-chief may be held by the same individual, making them solely responsible for all the activities of the outlet. The principles of press responsibility are framed in Articles 37 and 38, which indicate that the responsibility for harm caused by rights injured due to the publishing of a press material is set according to the general rules of the law unless stated differently in the press law act itself. Civil liability for damage caused by publishing a press material is to be borne by the author, editor or any other person who had caused that press material to be published, including the responsibility of the publisher. They shall all bear joint material responsibility, meaning that anyone who falls victim to an infringement caused by a press publication is free to choose to whom they wish to direct their claim: whether the author, editor or publisher.

The Press Law Act establishes the fundamental framework for all media regulation in Poland. The *lex specialis* on audiovisual services is the 1992 Broadcasting Act. Although the name of the Act refers to radio and television, the key term defining the scope of regulation is that of a 'media service' as derived from the AVMSD. Respectively, Article 4 of the Polish Broadcasting Act defines a 'media service' as a service in the form of a programme service or an on-demand audiovisual media service, which falls under the editorial responsibility of its provider and the principal purpose of which is the provision of programmes to inform, entertain or educate the general public by telecommunications networks. Moreover, the commercial communication shall also take the form of a media service. Media services are to be distinguished from 'on-demand audiovisual media services' which are media services provided within the context of business operations carried out for this purpose, consisting of the provision of audiovisual programmes to the general public from a catalogue of programmes created by the service provider and by linear media services, which do not meet the criteria of allowing the active selection of a programme, that is, they are not interactive. The Broadcasting Act applies to 'broadcasters' whose activity consists of producing and organising programme services and which is to be carried out in the form of editorial activity as defined in the press law.

Article 2 states that the right to transmit radio and television programme services can be granted to public broadcasting organisations as well as to natural persons, legal persons and partnerships that have received a broadcasting licence or, in the case of television programme services transmitted exclusively in information and communications technology systems, those that have been entered in the register of such programme services. The number of public broadcasters is limited and they are named directly in the Broadcasting Act. Private broadcasters must apply to the National Council of Radio Broadcasting and Television for a broadcasting licence, replying to a call for proposals issued when a need to expand the scope of programmes offered has been identified. A private licence is offered for a fee set by the National Council of Radio Broadcasting and Television. Another category is that of social broadcasters (*nadawcy społeczni*), defined in Article 4 as broadcasters whose programmes cumulatively: promote educational and charitable activities, respect the Christian system of values, while taking into consideration universal principles of ethics as the basis for their decisions, and which aim to strengthen the national identity and which do not broadcast commercial communications or charge for broadcasting, distributing or receiving their programmes. This status is awarded by the National Council of Radio Broadcasting and Television based on a licence, although, the licensing fee is waived. Should a social broadcaster fail to meet the specific criteria set for them in the Broadcasting Act, they might be held liable for paying the licensing fee in full by the Council.

The provisions of the Act do not apply to programme services transmitted or retransmitted solely for reception within a single building, programme services transmitted or retransmitted in a system where transmitting and receiving equipment belongs to the same person who is engaged in a business activity or other registered public activity, and where the content of the programme service is limited to matters relating to that activity and is addressed either to employees or to another particular group of people connected to the broadcaster.

According to Articles 213 and 214 of the Polish Constitution, the National Council of Radio Broadcasting and Television safeguards freedom of speech, the right to information and public interests with regard to radio broadcasting and television. It is authorised to issue regulations and, in individual cases, adopt resolutions. Members of the Council are appointed by the Sejm, the Senate and the President of the Republic, and a member of the Council may not be a member of a political party, a trade union, or perform public activities incompatible with the dignity of their function, to ensure their neutrality from political or other influence. Article 5 of the Polish Broadcasting Act declares that the Council constitutes the state authority competent in all matters of radio and television broadcasting. In particular, it has been constituted as the guardian of freedom of speech in the area of radio and television broadcasting, aiming to protect the independence of media service providers and the interests of the public, as well as to ensure the open and pluralistic nature of radio and television broadcasting. The tasks of the National Council include but are not limited to drawing up, in agreement with the Prime Minister, the details of state policy in respect of radio and television broadcasting, determining the terms for conducting activities by media service providers, and making decisions concerning broadcasting licences to transmit programme services and the entry into the register of programme services.

It is also authorised to grant the status of a social broadcaster or to revoke such a status, on terms laid down in the Broadcasting Act. It is, moreover, authorised to supervise all activity by media service providers within its jurisdiction, to support research into the content and audience of radio and television programme services, and to monitor the market of on-demand audiovisual media services to identify providers of on-demand audiovisual media services and evaluate their compliance with obligations arising under the Act. It is also competent to determine fees for the award of broadcasting licences and for registration and to act as a consultative body in drafting legal instruments and international agreements relating to radio and television broadcasting or on-demand audiovisual media services. The Council consists of five members, two of whom are appointed by the lower chamber of the Parliament (the Sejm), one by the higher chamber (the Senate), and two directly by the President from amongst persons with a distinguished record of knowledge and experience in public media.

The Chairman of the Council is elected by the National Council from amongst its members. The term of office of the members of the Council is six years from the day of appointment of the last member. The body which appointed a member of the Council has the authority to dismiss members in a clearly defined number of cases. These include situations where such a person has resigned, has become permanently unable to discharge his duties for reasons of ill health, has been convicted of a deliberate criminal offence by a valid judgment or has submitted an untruthful statement on their cooperation with the former Communist state secret service, as confirmed by a final and valid decision of the court, or has committed a breach of the provisions of the Broadcasting Act confirmed by the decision of the State Tribunal.[21]

According to Article 12, by the end of March each year, the National Council is obliged to submit to the Sejm, the Senate and the President an annual report on its activities during the preceding year, as well as to provide information concerning key issues in radio and television broadcasting. By way of resolutions, the Sejm and the Senate are to accept or reject the report. A resolution concerning the acceptance of the report may contain remarks and reservations. In case of rejection of the report by both the Sejm and the Senate, the term of office of all the members of the National Council shall expire within 14 days from the date of the last resolution to this effect, subject to approval by the President – the term of office will not expire unless approved in this way by the President of the Republic of Poland.

The restricted number of public broadcasters named in the Broadcasting Act includes public radio and television broadcasting organisations, operating exclusively in the form of a sole-proprietor joint stock company of the State Treasury. Their exclusive role is to carry out their 'public mission' by providing, on terms laid down in the Act, the entire society and its groups with diversified programme services and other services in the area of information, journalism, culture, entertainment, education and sport which shall be pluralistic, impartial, well balanced, independent and innovative, characterised by high quality and integrity of broadcast. The provision of Article 21 thus contains the statutory definition of the public mission to be carried out by public radio and television broadcasting. Article 21(1)(a) specifies this obligation and indicates the main tasks of public radio and television when implementing the public mission, with Article 21(a) and 21(c) complementing this duty with an obligation to a duty charter and financial and programme plans, to be presented to the Broadcasting Council. This general definition of the public mission of public broadcasters was introduced in 2004 and resulted from the adjustments made to the national law to meet the requirements of EU common market rules.

Article 33 of the Broadcasting Act stipulates that the transmission of programme services other than those of public radio and television broadcasters requires a licence to broadcast. However, the transmission of television programme services exclusively via information and communications technology systems does not require a licence, unless the programme service is to be retransmitted by terrestrial diffusion, or on satellite or cable networks. Broadcasting licences are awarded by the Chairman of the National Council. The Chairman takes decisions as regards broadcasting licences based on a resolution of the National Council.

---

[21] Polish Act on Radio and Television, Art 7.

The decision on this issue shall be final. Broadcasting licences may be awarded to natural persons of Polish nationality who permanently reside in the territory of the Republic of Poland as well as legal persons or partnerships having their seat in the territory of the Republic of Poland.

The operation of all broadcasters follows the press law rules on editorial organisation and responsibility. Article 13 of the Broadcasting Act reaffirms that all broadcasters enjoy full independence in determining the content of their programme services and are responsible for its content. Limitations to content allowed by the Act are introduced in Article 18, although it is ambiguous in scope and its wording is subject to criticism.[22] Broadcasters must ensure that, regardless of the mode of transmission, they prevent the publication of broadcasts that 'encourage actions contrary to law and Poland's raison d'Etat' or 'propagate attitudes and beliefs contrary to the moral values and social interest'. In particular, they may not include content inciting hatred or discriminating on grounds of race, disability, sex, religion or nationality. This last provision is in line with Article 256 of the Polish Penal Code which prohibits hate speech and Article 23 of the Civil Code, which protects individual personal rights. Moreover, all broadcasters in Poland must ensure that their programmes or other broadcasts 'respect the religious beliefs of the public and especially the Christian system of values'.

This provision has been subject to Constitutional Tribunal review and found to be in line with Article 53 of the Constitution ensuring the equality of all religious beliefs. This provision was the subject of the interpretation of the Constitutional Tribunal in case W 3/93 which concluded with the adoption of a resolution on 2 March 1994. In its justification, the Constitutional Tribunal stated that the provision of Article 18(2), setting out one of the limits to freedom of speech, should be interpreted as a prohibition of violating religious feelings. The content of this prohibition corresponds to the scope of protection of personal rights laid down in Article 23 of the Civil Code and the prohibition of offending religious feelings set out in Article 198 of the Criminal Code. Moreover, the Constitutional Tribunal stated that

> the linguistic interpretation of Article 18(2) leads to the conclusion that the phrase 'and especially respect the Christian system of values' used in this footnote is an exemplary enumeration, justified by the deep rooting of these values in the tradition and culture of Polish society, regardless of a person's attitude to religion.[23]

This was also the intention of the legislator mentioned by the Senator-Rapporteur who discussed the Senate's proposals for the bill at the Senate session on 29 December 1992. In the opinion of the Constitutional Tribunal, a radio or television broadcast which is inconsistent with the Christian system of values

---

[22] D Ossowska-Salamonowicz, 'Article 18' in A Niewęgłowski (ed), *Ustawa o radiofonii i telewizji: Komentarz* (Warsaw, Wolters Kluwer, 2021).

[23] Judgment of the Constitutional Tribunal of 7 June 1994, K 17/93, OTK 1994, No 11.

only violates Article 18(2), when it also offends the religious feelings of the audi-ence. Disrespect for these feelings may also be found to have been shown by a programme that is inconsistent with another system of values, as long as it offends the religious feelings of the audience, regardless of their religion.[24]

Programmes or other broadcasts may not encourage conduct that is prejudicial to health, safety or the natural environment. The transmission of programmes or other broadcasts threatening the physical, mental or moral development of minors, in particular those containing pornography or exhibiting gratuitous violence is prohibited. Programmes or other broadcasts containing scenes or content which may have an adverse impact upon the health or physical, mental or moral develop-ment of minors, other than those referred to in paragraph 4, may be transmitted only between 11 pm and 6 am. In this respect, all broadcasters are obliged to prop-erly identify programmes or other broadcasts by way of displaying an appropriate graphic symbol throughout their duration in the television programme service or by way of an oral announcement informing of the hazards arising out of their transmission on the radio.

6. Press Freedom and Platform Regulation

The liability of providers of electronically supplied services is a well-regulated issue in EU law, notably through the Directive on electronic commerce, which has been in force for more than two decades. Its basic assumption is that service providers are not responsible for the content which they allow their consumers to access. *Mere conduit* is a fundamental principle of the European approach to content control. It has also been included in the Digital Services Act (DSA)[25] in a form very similar to that known from Article 12 of the Directive on Electronic Commerce[26] and its implementation into national law.

In this regard, Chapter 3 of the Polish Act on the Provision of Electronic Services excludes the liability of the service provider for the provision of elec-tronic services.[27] Article 12 of the Act stipulates that a service provider who provides services involving the transmission in a telecommunications network of data transmitted by the recipient of the service, or the provision of access to a telecommunications network shall not be liable for the content of such data if they are not the initiator of the data transfer, do not select the recipient of the data transfer, select or modify the information contained in the transfer. This

---

[24] ibid.

[25] Proposal for a Regulation of the European Parliament and of the Council on a Single Market for Digital Services (Digital Services Act) and amending Directive 2000/31/EC, COM/2020/825 final.

[26] Directive 2000/31/EC of the European Parliament and of the Council of 8 June 2000 on certain legal aspects of information society services, in particular electronic commerce, in the Internal Market (Directive on electronic commerce) [2000] OJ L178/1.

[27] Act of 18 July 2002 on the Provision of Electronic Services, Journal of Laws of 2002 No 144, item 1204, as amended.

disclaimer also covers the automatic and short-term intermediate storage of the transmitted data, if this is done solely to carry out the transmission and the data are not stored longer than is normally necessary for the transmission. According to Article 13 of the Act, the exclusion also applies to service providers providing caching services, that is, those who, by transmitting data and providing automatic and short-term intermediate storage of such data, do so to accelerate the re-accessing of those data at the request of another entity, provided that they meet the conditions described above.

The most important of the provisions implementing this principle are contained in Article 14 of the Polish Act on Electronic Services, which introduces a variation of the notice and take-down mechanism, sometimes referred to as notice and (take) action.[28] According to the provisions of this Article of the act, the liability of hosting service providers is excluded if they are not aware of the unlawful nature of the data or related activities when providing 'ICT system resources to store data by the recipient of the service' and, upon receiving an official notification or obtaining reliable information about the unlawful nature of the data or related activities, they immediately prevent access to these data.[29] This provision is supplemented by Article 15 of the Act, which emphasises the lack of a general obligation to monitor data, an obligation which has been perceived in the EU since the beginning of its regulatory work as a potential threat to freedom of expression.[30]

Similar approaches can be found in the draft Articles 3–5 of the DSA, although formally, under Article 71, the relevant provisions of the Directive will cease to apply. However, Article 71(2) of the DSA provides that any existing reference to the Directive and the national provisions implementing it, including the Polish Act on the Provision of Electronic Services, are to be treated as direct references to the DSA. Articles 3–5 of the DSA will be supplemented by additional provisions concerning, for example, platforms or disinformation, requiring their operators to exercise due diligence in preventing violations of the legally protected interests of users.

In addition to the usual exemptions relating to transmission, caching and hosting known from the e-Commerce Directive, the DSA introduces the possibility of also exempting service providers from liability for transmitted content relating to offering access to local networks and the operation of critical Internet resources, such as the domain name system or keeping registers of top-level domain names. It should be noted that while the DSA's objective is to extend the same legal rules to as many information society service providers as possible, both the wide range of

---

[28] M Husovec et al, *Notice and Action* (2020), available at: www.greens-efa.eu/mycontentmyrights/notice-and-action.

[29] Despite several attempts, there have been no detailed, binding interpretations or guidelines issued to help internet service providers identify either 'official notification' or 'reliable information'. They make these decisions themselves, based on the individual circumstances of the case.

[30] Husovec (n 28).

inclusions and the unclear relationship between the DSA and, for example, media law, including, above all, the definition of an audiovisual media service and the editorial responsibility of its provider under the AVMSD, may be unsatisfactory.[31]

Without carrying out a detailed analysis of the above Articles and the interpretative and practical problems resulting from their content, it should be noted that since their adoption two decades ago they have been the subject of fervent and justified criticism for being unclear and for imposing on service providers a disproportionate burden of immediately deciding on the legality or illegality of the content to which they allow access.

Moreover, such decisions are often tantamount to an immediately enforceable decision taken by a single-instance, one-man quasi-court, such as an employee of the service provider acting as a moderator or examining a report regarding potentially illegal content, and therefore they directly affected the shape of individual rights. They may restrict freedom of expression (if access to the indicated content was 'immediately prevented') or deprive individuals of the opportunity to effectively assert the protection of their rights (if the entry or image is not considered by the service provider to be blocked or, in practice, removed). The biggest doubts, however, were raised not so much by the mechanism used by private individuals to protect their rights or other legally protected interests but by the particular type of cooperation that arose in the application of these provisions between organisations protecting copyright, often on behalf of foreign corporations and service providers operating in Europe. Service providers have often put in place mechanisms on their own to detect potential infringements of intellectual property rights by specific groups of operators, contributing to the discussion of the undesirable chilling effect that the legislation has produced in European practice.

Service providers, defending themselves against possible financial liability for damage caused to copyright holders that could be harmed by the distribution of certain digitised materials, have often independently and hastily decided to prevent access to them, without analysing the provisions introducing exceptions to protection, such as fair use or the specificity of the genre of creativity. Consequently, the practice of applying the Directive has often been described as encouraging lobbying by large media content providers, either from Europe or the United States.[32]

---

[31] Directive 2010/13/EU of the European Parliament and of the Council of 10 March 2010 on the coordination of certain provisions laid down by law, regulation or administrative action in Member States concerning the provision of audiovisual media services (Audiovisual Media Services Directive) (Text with EEA relevance) [2010] OJ L95/1. See also para 22, DSA and RIPE NCC, RIPE NCC Feedback on the Commission Adoption of the Digital Services Act, Amsterdam 2021, available at: www.ripe.net/participate/internet-governance/multi-stakeholder-engagement/ripe-ncc-response-to-dsa-commission-adoption.pdf.

[32] *cf* Art 17 of the Directive on Copyright and Related Rights in the Digital Single Market and amendments to Directives 96/9/EC and 2001/29/EC and the complaint Polish before the CJEU: Poland v Parliament and Council, Case C-401/19. See also, SF Schwemer and J Schovsbo, 'What is Left of User Rights? Algorithmic Copyright Enforcement and Free Speech in the Light of the Article 17 Regime' in P Torremans (ed), *Intellectual Property Law and Human Rights* (Alphen aan den Rijn, Wolters Kluwer, 2020).

This interesting aspect of the intermediary liability regime and its implementation shows that some online rights may indeed be effectively and diligently protected by service providers, granted there are sufficient incentives in place, including a pending liability. In the case of the protection of intellectual property rights these result in individual business risk assessments that prevent any potential individual harm to copyright holders.

Criticism of the principle of mere conduit in European law has focused on excessive, quasi-judicial power, which is transferred to private entities under the provisions of the e-Commerce Directive. Individuals have often been deprived of a genuine opportunity to appeal against such a decision because it is technically impossible to establish the identity of the actual infringer of their legally protected interests or, as a last resort, the difficulty of attributing to it the perpetrator of the infringement.

Moreover, in 2021, an amendment to the Broadcasting Act was introduced which explicitly concerns social media platforms. Article 1(a) refers to providers of media services and video-sharing platforms covered by the Act. The Polish Broadcasting Act applies to media service providers and video-sharing platforms established in the territory of the Republic of Poland, whereas a media service provider is deemed to be established in the territory of the Republic of Poland if it is based in the Republic of Poland and decisions made regularly in the exercise of editorial responsibility which relate to the day-to-day operation of the media service are made in the territory of the Republic of Poland. It will also be covered by Polish jurisdiction if a significant proportion of the people employed to conduct programme activities based on an employment relationship or a civil law contract operate in the territory of the Republic of Poland, and editorial decisions regarding the media service are made in another Member State of the EU.

Alternatively, the Polish Broadcasting Council will be competent when a significant proportion of the people employed to conduct programme activities based on an employment relationship or a civil law contract operate both in the territory of the Republic of Poland and in another Member State of the EU. This flexible criterion also includes those service providers which make editorial decisions in the territory of the Republic of Poland. It also applies to providers who employ a significant proportion of the people to conduct programme-related activities on the basis of an employment relationship or a civil law contract operate in the territory of the Republic of Poland. The clause also applies to media service providers based in another Member State of the EU. It covers complementarily those who started providing media services in the territory of the Republic of Poland or under the law of the Republic of Poland and maintain stable and effective economic ties with the Republic of Poland. The provision ceases to apply when the seat of the media service provider is located in another Member State of the EU and their editorial decisions regarding the media service are made in that State, or when a significant proportion of the persons employed under an employment relationship or a civil law contract to provide a media service operate in another Member State of the EU, in which the media service provider has its seat. When editorial decisions regarding the media service are made in the territory of another Member State of the EU these provisions are also to be applied. While all these criteria are directly derived from the AVMSD and have been implemented to ensure compliance with EU law, they do, however, grant Polish authorities a flexible legal background for exercising their jurisdiction.

Poland in 2022 possesses a comprehensive framework for media regulation, including social media and online platforms. This extensive normative landscape is comprised of the constitutional safeguard of freedom of expression, a dedicated press law act, and a dedicated broadcasting act amended to meet the AVMSD standard. Intermediary liability is covered by the Act on Electronic Services, implementing the e-Commerce Directive, which is also about to be amended to meet the requirements of the DSA. Poland is a strong supporter of the enhanced liability mechanisms for large platforms introduced in the DSA Package. It is developing its law to allow for local control over international service providers. The Polish Ministry of Justice recently (in January 2021) presented a draft law on freedom of speech in social media.[33] The project aims to force, for example, Facebook administrators not to remove content that they consider inconsistent with the terms of use of the website, but which, in the opinion of a possibly appointed Freedom of Speech Council, would be compliant with Polish law.

In cases where the social media operator and the Council disagreed on their perceptions of what speech is allowed online, the latter would be in a position to punish the former with a fine of up to 50 million Złoty (€12 million). This proposal and its motivation illustrate well the disputed division of powers between the state and the private service provider to set the boundaries of freedom of expression and the right to be fairly informed in the age of social media.[34] Any such laws, however, will only be effective in a healthy democracy based on the rule of law. In states where the rule of law is under threat, any extensive regulation of free speech and media will result in a departure from democracy in the direction of an authoritarian state, a situation which Poland had a long history with until not long ago. Hopefully, the lessons learnt from this historical experience will keep it on the path of democracy and the rule of law rather than that of censorship and discrimination.

7. Conclusions

Transnational social media companies are increasingly being regulated by all of the EU's Member States. Both Poland and the EU have adopted the revised notice

---

[33] Protection of the freedom of speech of users of social networking sites, 7 January 2022, available at: www.gov.pl/web/sprawiedliwosc/ochrona-wolnosci-slowa-uzytkownikow-serwisow-spolecznosciowych2.

[34] See: bip.brpo.gov.pl/pl/content/rpo-ms-uwagi-projekt-wolnosci-slowa-internet.

and take action framework described above. However, as has been noted they appear to have different perceptions of questions of state sovereignty and of the boundaries of national authority online. This is particularly interesting when analysing the approaches found in post-Soviet bloc states. In the past, Poland has practised media control, as have all post-Soviet states. However, such practices are a part of a history that it was keen to forget after 1989. The democratic values of free speech and the rule of law have served as the foundation for Poland's contemporary media system. The EU's fundamental rights regime for civil societies with free and open media is also based on these paradigms. Yet, as countries in Central and Eastern Europe such as Poland have struggled with the rule of law since the late 2010s, the issue of proper media control has become a hot topic of discussion.

Since 2016, the Polish government has put in place legislative and administrative mechanisms that firmly connect public media to the ruling party. This was accomplished both through legislative action and in the selection of who would be in charge of the Polish public media. This stance is also reflected in the Polish reading of the DSA. Poland anticipates that the new intermediary regime will ensure that the law is applied in a way that reflects its particular interpretation of freedom of expression and safeguards traditional values, including those relating to religion. While this is an intriguing approach, it is very different from the initial stance that the EU established for free media. On the one hand, there is an efficient system of intermediary liability that allows online actors to express themselves freely. On the other, however, post-Soviet nations like Poland are returning to a rigorous stance on media freedom.

The lessons learnt from this process might include the need to balance the national approach to intermediary liability, taking into account both the values enshrined in the Universal Declaration of Human Rights and experiences from the post-Soviet past, which may have an impact on how these universal principles are understood and applied locally. Moreover, the DSA has a transnational universal effect on freedom of speech outside the EU too, much like the General Data Protection Regulation, which revolutionised the protection of privacy and personal information worldwide; because the EU, as with the General Data Protection Regulation, will be requiring all global actors to conform, this might therefore also be of interest to non-European actors. Currently, the DSA emphasises the inherent universality of freedom of expression. It will therefore be necessary for intermediary service providers to do the same, which will prevent their platforms from being used for hate speech, discrimination or terrorist practices, and ensure that the rule of law, democratic principles and freedom of the press are the cornerstones of the transnational regulation that the EU imposes.

8

The Legal Death of Media
Freedom in Russia

ANDREI RICHTER

1. Introduction

For 30 years I have studied Russian mass media from the angle of their regulation, publishing some 50 papers and books on the topic. Today is the time to sum up what has happened with media freedom in the country under Boris Yeltsin and Vladimir Putin, how after its bright rise in the early 1990s, this freedom was slowly put under undue and non-proportional restrictions only to be finally strangled in 2022. It was largely a downward process, with a couple of hopeful come-backs, but with hindsight, the question is if it was part of a plan, a plan to give the appearance of democracy and liberal ideas so as to strengthen the autocratic rule of Putin.

This chapter will look at the avenues along which the legal guarantees of media freedom were undermined, how it happened, what were the pretexts and, in a way, what were 'cover operations' to make it look to the general public as less dangerous for free speech than it actually was. It will suggest certain phases of this assault on independent media and refer to the media model, established as a result of these actions.

I fully understand that the law only reflects the media policy, while the policy is also embodied in other elements enabling or destroying conditions for media freedom. The economic policy of the Russian government, the state of the advertising market, freedom of business activity, media literacy and attempts to influence (or rather, poison) the public mood regarding the values of free media and democracy, the level of self-regulation and accountability of the media, Russia's international relations, state of journalism education have all played a role in the process that has led to the end of media freedom. Speaking of media freedom in Russia, we should not forget about numerous assassinations and other terrible attacks on journalists and their effect on self-censorship. These aspects of media freedom in Russia have been analysed from a variety of viewpoints and methodologies,[1] and the results point to similar negative trends.

Now, as we witnessed what is happening in 2022, these elements, their causes and effects, also need to be soberly reassessed. Still, at least in the case of post-Soviet Russia, media law serves as a fair enough indicator for media policy and media freedom. It is the legislation that gives away the Kremlin's intentions and provides their permanent record, even when the authorities put a fog over what they want to accomplish, while other controls may be more difficult to track. It is in the law that the aspirations of the enemies of free speech in Russia have become most visibly embodied, at least to me.

2. Literature Review

Freedom of the media is essential in a society to ensure freedom of expression and the enjoyment of other human rights. Therefore, it 'constitutes one of the cornerstones of a democratic society',[2] by serving as its watchdog, mediator between the state and society and/or 'fourth estate', while 'democracy thrives on freedom of expression'.[3] Such statements are not new, and are the fruits of reflections by many scholars,[4] including the editors of this book (see their Introduction).

Grading and properly labelling media freedom is a complicated research task. Some even argue that results from different studies are uncertain because media freedom is in itself an uncertain concept. Media freedom is understood differently around the world, while its measurement has been mainly by indexing.[5] In my view, freedom of the media is a universal concept, which implies that with the technical facilities to do so, individuals can circulate their thoughts and opinions among a number of people that is sufficiently large to satisfy their desire to take part in public dialogue, have a say on matters of public interest and make autonomous decisions about their life and work. It also means that individuals can circulate and obtain information on current affairs without hindrance.

---

[1] A Kachkaeva, I Kiriya and G Libergal, *Television in the Russian Federation: Organisational Structure, Programme Production and Audience*, eds M Aslamazyan and G McCormack (Strasbourg, European Audiovisual Observatory, 2006); A Pankin et al, *Mapping Digital Media: Russia*, eds M Dragomir, M Thompson and R Ruduša (London, Open Society Foundations, 2011).

[2] United Nations Human Rights Committee, General Comment, No 34, 2011 [13].

[3] *NIT SRL v the Republic of Moldova*, App no 28470/12, judgment of 5 April 2022 [GC].

[4] E Barendt (ed), *Freedom of the Press* (New York, Routledge, 2009); D Tambini, *Media Freedom* (Cambridge, Polity Press, 2021).

[5] ME Price, S Abbott and L Morgan (eds), *Measures of Press Freedom and Media Contributions to Development: Evaluating the Evaluators* (New York, Peter Lang, 2011).

Journalists and human rights activists often note rankings to assess the extent to which a free press exists in Russia compared with the rest of the world. Reporters Without Frontiers registers a downfall of Russia's position from 121st to 155th place out of 180 countries since it started ranking in 2002,[6] while Freedom House in its latest freedom of the press review (in 2017) pointed to Russia's 174th position out of 199 countries and territories, and has been rating it 'not free' in its global reviews on the state of democracy and freedom of the Internet ever since.[7] In particular, the latest report specifically points to laws being 'used to harass media outlets, curtailing their access to funding and forcing many to cease operations in Russia'.[8]

A uniform opinion of the scholars confirms that the current state of media freedom in Russia is a shambles and stands in contrast to its recent past.[9] Over the past two decades, they have pointed to particular media laws and policy developments, testifying to a general decline in freedoms once afforded Russian media by *glasnost* and initial media reforms.[10] Having thoroughly studied media legislation, Camille Jackson, for example, observed that 'there is an obvious upward trend from the early 1990s, indicating that, overall, Russian media legislation has become more restrictive over time, and, by extension, the Russian government's attitude toward media has become one of keeping a tight rein on its development'.[11] Elena Sherstoboeva comes to the conclusion that international standards 'have had an almost superficial impact' on Russian media regulation while 'non-compliance has increased since 2014'.[12]

It was not designed like this in the beginning. The launch in 1987/88 of *glasnost*, or a policy of openness, granted the then Soviet media significant freedom to argue political ideas, to reassess the modern history and standards of living in the West and, most importantly, to question the authorities. The new policy required some sort of a legal protection from the draconian bans, vague instructions and Communist directives of the past.[13] In other words, '*glasnost*

---

[6] World Press Freedom Index, available at: rsf.org/en/index.

[7] Freedom of the Press 2017, available at: freedomhouse.org/sites/default/files/2020-02/FOTP_2017_booklet_FINAL_April28_1.pdf.

[8] Freedom of the World 2022, available at: freedomhouse.org/country/russia/freedom-world/2022.

[9] C Jackson, 'Legislation as an Indicator of Free Press in Russia' (2016) 63(5–6) *Problems of Post-Communism* 354; R Simon, 'Media, Myth and Reality in Russia's State-Managed Democracy' (2004) 57 *Parliamentary Affairs* 169; C Marsh and P Froese, 'The State of Freedom in Russia: A Regional Analysis of Freedom of Religion, Media and Markets' (2004) 32 *Religion, State and Society* 137; K Lehtisaari, 'Formation of Media Policy in Russia: The Case of the Iarovaia Law' in M Wijermars and K Lehtisaari (eds), *Freedom of Expression in Russia's New Mediasphere* (Abingdon, Routledge, 2020).

[10] Jackson (n 9); D Skillen, Freedom of Speech in Russia: Politics and Media from Gorbachev to Putin (Abingdon, Routledge, 2017); O Koltsova, News Media and Power in Russia (New York, Routledge, 2006).

[11] Jackson (n 9) 356.

[12] E Sherstoboeva, 'Audiovisual Regulation in Russia in the Context of Council of Europe Standards' (2019) 44 *Review of Central and East European Law* 403.

[13] B McNair, *Glasnost, Perestroika, and the Soviet Media* (New York, Routledge, 1991); F Ellis, *From Glasnost to the Internet* (New York, St Martin's, 1999).

crystallised demands for the adoption of a press statute to legitimise the new status quo'.[14]

The biggest breakthrough here came with the adoption, in 1990, of the Union of Soviet Socialist Republics' (USSR) first ever Statute on the Press and Other Mass Media, and early in Yeltsin's presidency – the Russian Federation's Statute on the Mass Media (1991). The media freedom was further supported by other legal guarantees, including the 1993 Constitution, as well as numerous decrees of the President and local Acts. In addition, those times were marked by a lively discussion on the forthcoming laws on *glasnost*, that would both make the authorities transparent and accountable to the independent press, and on broadcasting, where the state will cease to control key channels.

Over time, however, harsh media restrictions appeared to have become the new normal. It has led to an international diagnosis, made in May 2022 by the quartet of intergovernmental monitors mandated to observe the state of freedom of expression and freedom of the media in the world:

> We are alarmed at the further tightening of censorship and repression of dissent and pluralist sources of information and opinion in the Russian Federation, including the blocking of social media platforms and news websites, disruption of services from foreign content and service providers, massive labeling of independent journalists and media as 'foreign agents', introduction of criminal liability and imprisonment of up to fifteen years for spreading so-called 'fake' information about the war in Ukraine or questioning Russian military action in Ukraine or simply standing for peace or even mentioning the word 'war'. We deplore the systematic crackdown on political opponents, independent journalists and the media, human rights activists, protesters and many others opposing the Russian government's actions.[15]

So far, this censorship is informal and none of the journalists is serving a lengthy prison term, but the diagnosis is clear: systematic symptoms of repression point to the agony if not the death of media freedom.

When this study dissects the changes in Russia's media legislation over the time period from 1990 to 2022, and explores its changes in key areas that enabled the Kremlin establish full control over once free speech, it is based on my previous analytical work, as well as major published reviews. Some of the insight knowledge on the mass media statutes has been provided by Mikhail Fedotov, Yuri Baturin and Vladimir Entin, three academics who drafted and to an extent were in charge of implementing the media statutes in the 1990s. A very multidimensional commentary on Russian media legislation to date has been provided by Monroe E Price and Peter Krug, particularly through the *Post-Soviet Media Law*

---

[14] E Sherstoboeva, 'The Evolution of a Russian Concept of Free Speech' in M Price and N Stremlau, *Speech and Society in Turbulent Times: Freedom of Expression in Comparative Perspective* (Cambridge, Cambridge University Press, 2017) 219.

[15] Joint Statement on the Invasion of Ukraine and the Importance of Freedom of Expression and Information, 2 May 2022, available at: www.osce.org/representative-on-freedom-of-media/517107.

and Policy Newsletter (1993–99),[16] but also in articles and edited books, including *Russian Media Law and Policy in the Yeltsin Decade*.[17] While all these authors have contributed significant insight into media legislation, their academic focus was mostly on the 1990s.

Daphne Skillen provided a thorough modern overview of the underlying factors and events, including legal ones, influencing Russian media freedom that resulted in its 'gradual but relentless erosion' leading to the situation where the mainstream outlets are no more than 'Kremlin mouthpieces' and the television channels in particular are 'instruments of war and hate'.[18] Only a few of the independent public interest media – *Ekho Moskvy, Novaya Gazeta* and *Dozhd* – remained by then in Russia, she notes, 'and even they may be working on borrowed time'.[19] All three outlets will indeed fold in 2022 following the prediction of the book that the enemies of media freedom have 'plunged Russia into its darkest period',[20] although in 2017 the degree of darkness was not yet clear to many others.

3. Main Avenues for Media Freedom Oppression

3.1. Criminalisation of Speech

Criminalisation of critical speech in Russia has generally been considered an element of the oppressive tsarist or Soviet machine. With the new democratic political approaches and *glasnost* as the new foundations of the country, the late Soviet Communist regime first abandoned and then abolished (in 1989) the two Articles in the Criminal Code that punished 'anti-Soviet agitation and propaganda'[21] and 'systematic dissemination in oral form of deliberately false fabrications discrediting the Soviet state and the social system, as well as the production or distribution in written, printed or other form of works of the same content'.[22] Both Articles spoke of fabrications or deliberately false content, while the official commentary explained that 'the perpetrator reports such facts,

---

[16] See its archive at: web.archive.org/web/20110211151350/http://www.vii.org/monroe.

[17] ME Price, A Richter and PK Yu (eds), *Russian Media Law and Policy in the Yeltsin Decade: Essays and Documents* (The Hague, Kluwer Law International, 2002).

[18] Skillen (n 10) 1.

[19] ibid 345.

[20] ibid 316.

[21] Art 70 of the Russian Criminal Code qualified it as '[a]gitation or propaganda carried out with the aim of undermining or weakening Soviet power or committing certain especially dangerous state crimes, dissemination for the same purposes of slanderous fabrications discrediting the Soviet state and social system, as well as distribution or production or storage of literature of the same content for the same purposes'.

[22] Art 190-bis of the Russian Criminal Code.

information that did not take place in life at all, or sets out individual phenomena in a clearly distorted tendentious form'.[23] Their oblivion was not for long, as between 2021 and 2022 they would make a triumphal comeback under a different pretext and name.

In 1996 when the new Russian Criminal Code was adopted, it still kept penalties for 'slander' and 'insult', as well as 'insult of public officials'. Their practical use was rare and the post-Communist tendency remained to deny criminalising political expression, in line with the 1993 Constitution. 'However, since Vladimir Putin came to power in 2000, the principled position of Russian criminal law has gradually become blurred', notes Gleb Bogush.[24] He lists the numerous cases of expanding the Criminal Code in relation to 'speech crimes'.

The major instrument for restrictions of political speech in the media initially became the 2002 Federal Statute on Countering Extremist Activity, as defying its provisions led to both criminal liability and the closure of the media outlet where extremist content appeared.[25] Originally, the Statute defined extremism by listing acts already classified as offences under the Criminal Code. But it added some new attributes, mostly by linking them to violence or calls to violence. As part of extremism, the Statute included 'planning, organising, preparing and committing acts directed at the violent … breach of the Russian Federation's territorial integrity; seizure or usurpation of power; creation of illegal armed formations; perpetration of terrorist activities' and so on. Then, in 2004, the link to violence was dropped from the definition, tremendously expanding its meaning.

Synchronously, the Criminal Code's Article on 'public calls to violent change of the constitutional order' was extended to numerous sorts of 'extremism', violent and then non-violent (for instance, non-violent separatism), such as pointing to public officials as those guilty of extremism. An Article on advocacy of ethnic or religious hatred that constitutes incitement to discrimination or violence, was added with a ban on enmity towards 'social groups', which soon the case law explained as groups of 'public officials', 'law-enforcement agencies' and other vague formations that served the state – thus providing an additional protection of the strong against the weak.

Another 'pet' instrument to stop free speech was an originally 'innocent' Federal Statute 'On Protection of Children from Information Harmful to Their Health and Development', which entered into force in 2012. The statute lists certain categories of information that may indeed present harm to children if they

---

[23] See: memorial.krsk.ru/DOKUMENT/USSR/601027.htm.
[24] G Bogush, 'Criminalisation of Free Speech in Russia' (2017) 69(8) *Europe–Asia Studies* 1242, 1244.
[25] A Richter, 'One Step Beyond Hate Speech: Post-Soviet Regulation of "Extremist" and "Terrorist" Speech in the Media' in M Herz and P Molnar (eds), *The Content and Context of Hate Speech: Rethinking Regulation and Responses* (Cambridge, Cambridge University Press, 2012) 294.

see it on the Internet. But to implement the law, amendments were made in other acts that allowed the authorities to blacklist information, access to which they may block online 'for the sake of children'. Today the ban encompasses 'any other information, dissemination of which is found by courts as violating the law of the Russian Federation'. Thus 'protection of children' from online pornography and child molesters turned into widespread bans and blocking of anything that violates any provision of any Russian law.

Following the *Pussy Riot* criminal case, the Article on 'violation of the right to freedom of conscience' was amended to add 'public disrespect aimed to offend religious feelings commissioned in places designated for religious services, religious rites and ceremonies' punishable by imprisonment for up to one year. The omnipresent Article 354 of the Criminal Code that bans 'public calls to a war of aggression', that, alas, does not work in practice, was added with Article 354(1) against 'rehabilitation of Nazism', which today also bans 'public dissemination of deliberately false information on the activity of the USSR during the Second World War', no matter whether they disturb public peace or not. This norm presupposes the existence of a well-established dogma on the 'activity of the USSR during the Second World War', which apparently denies the Soviet aggression on Poland and Finland, as well as the annexation and occupation of the three Baltic states and the territories, which later became Moldavia, the Karelo-Finnish Republic and 'Western Belorussia and Western Ukraine'.[26]

We find the method that has been used in regard to criminal penalties quite simple: the authorities would pick a clear-cut existing and generally acceptable by the public type of 'locomotive' in the law and then add numerous disfigured carriages. In addition, the added provisions would typically allow for stricter sanctions when committing these offences in the media or on the Internet.

Although during Dmitry Medvedev's presidency (2008–12), there was a positive tendency towards certain liberalisation of criminal law through abolishment of criminal insult and slander (in 2011), with the victorious comeback of Putin, slander was quickly reinstalled in the Criminal Code. Therefore, Bogush rightfully points out that, overall, these developments 'clearly demonstrate the policy of the Russian state aimed at strengthening its control over public discussion and the dissemination of ideas and information by criminalising expressions of opinion it finds undesirable'.[27]

3.2. Emergence of the Super Watchdog in the Media Sector

The collapse of censorship with the entry into force of the USSR Statute on the Press and Other Mass Media in 1990 led to a slow collapse of its key

---

[26] Bogush (n 24) 1251.
[27] ibid 1254.

institution – Glavlit (Main Directorate for the Protection of State Secrets in the Press under the Council of Ministers of the USSR) together with numerous regional branches. In October 1991 they were replaced (often keeping the staff) with the generally meaningless State Inspections on Protection of Freedom of the Press and Mass Media (under the Minister of Press and Mass Information), which were eventually abandoned two years later (together with the Ministry itself). They gave way (until 2005) to the Federal Service on Television and Radio Broadcasting and the State Committee on the Press.

The regulatory bodies under various names have always been part of the government structures of modern Russia. Initially they mostly dealt with mandatory registration of all – print and broadcast – media, as prescribed by the Statute on Mass Media (Article 8). Any application for registration has been subject to consideration by the regulator. With time, the practice of registration was gradually tightening, and, in at least in one case, *Dzhavadov v Russia*, the European Court of Human Rights even found the use of registration 'formalities' by the regulator as 'not prescribed by law'.[28]

Since 2008, the registration and licensing of media outlets in Russia is done by the Federal Service for Supervision of Communications, Information Technology and Mass Media (Roskomnadzor). Since about that time its powers, staff and influence have increased greatly thus making it the super watchdog in the field, although formally it still operates under the authority of the Ministry of Communications. Roskomnadzor today is not just the registration and licensing body; its key function is to monitor media content and ensure there are no violations of media law by registered news outlets and licensed broadcasters, including registered online media. In 2021, Roskomnadzor received a statuary basis in the Statute on the Mass Media as the body of 'state control and oversight' of the media.

3.3. Politicisation of the Broadcast Regulation

The practice of the post-Communist regulation of broadcast media in Russia began in 1990, when President Mikhail Gorbachev issued a decree 'On Democratisation and Development of Television and Radio Broadcasting in the USSR'. It gave the Councils of People's Deputies (or Soviets) at all levels, as well as public organisations, the right to set up television and radio facilities and studios, and formulated the need for proper legislation on television and radio. This decree and the governmental resolution that followed it provided the legal basis for the country's first non-state television and radio programmes.[29]

---

[28] *Dzhavadov v Russia*, App no 30160/04, judgment of 27 September 2007, [40].
[29] *The Regulatory Framework for Audiovisual Media Services in Russia* (Strasbourg, EAO, 2010) 9.

The initial wording of the 1991 Statute on the Mass Media (Article 30), envisioned the establishment of the Federal Commission on Television and Radio Broadcasting by a separate broadcasting statute. In a way, this norm kept the broadcast regulator outside the government's structure as determined by the President and thus gave hope to its independence from the executive.[30] In the absence of a specific statute on broadcasting – and several failures to have it adopted and/or enforced by the President,[31] all regulation was promulgated by the executive through politically motivated decrees and resolutions. It was through the 1991 decree of the President that Radio Free Europe/Radio Liberty was to be provided with both a Moscow bureau and radio frequencies (the decree was annulled in 2002).[32] It was through the 1993 and 1996 decrees of the President that commercial NTV, then belonging to the Most financial group, got the frequencies of the fourth national educational channel.[33] The tradition has since been established to have chief executive officers of all national broadcasters appointed and dismissed by decree of the President.

While in the beginning the decrees and resolutions were presented as 'transitional' until the broadcasting law is adopted (as, for example, the 1994 licensing regulations), further on the 'incoming' law was less and less on the national agenda.[34] Its latest draft, adopted in 1997 in the first reading, prescribed the broadcast media authority to be 'a specifically entrusted body of regulation and control by the public'. Its members, including four from the Parliament, two from the President and two from the government, were to respond to particular competences and criteria. The draft was formally abandoned weeks after Putin became the elected President.[35]

In the 1990s, governmental bodies were issuing television and radio licences on a first come, first served basis, keeping a public Commission on Television and Radio (chaired by journalism professor Yassen Zassoursky) as an advisory body in the rare situations of conflict or competition. There was no formal and explained licensing policy nor clear criteria for picking the licence-holders.[36] This advisory

---

[30] S Sheverdyaev, *О необходимости реформирования регулирующих органов в сфере телерадиовещания в России. Перспективы лицензирования телерадиовещания в России* (Moscow, Institut Problem Informacionnogo Prava, 2004) 335.

[31] S Aksartova et al, *Television in the Russian Federation: Organisational Structure, Programme Production and Audience. A Report for the European Audiovisual Observatory* (Strasbourg, EAO, 2003) 10–11.

[32] See: pravo.gov.ru/proxy/ips/?docbody=&firstDoc=1&lastDoc=1&nd=102012375.

[33] S Kolesnik, 'Controlling Content on Television in Russia' in M Price, A Richter and PK Yu (eds), *Russian Media Law and Policy in the Yeltsin Decade: Essays and Documents* (The Hague, Kluwer Law International, 2002) 189; Указ Президента РФ от 20 сентября 1996 г N 1386 'О стабилизации деятельности и улучшении качества вещания Всероссийской государственной телевизионной и радиовещательной компании и телекомпании НТВ', available at: base.garant.ru/136217.

[34] Sheverdyaev (n 30) 25–26.

[35] ibid 335–36.

[36] A Richter, 'A Post-Soviet Perspective on Licensing Television and Radio' (2007) 9 *IRIS* 5.

commission rarely met and was abandoned in 1999 with the establishment of the Ministry for Affairs of the Press, Television and Radio Broadcasting, and Mass Communications (MPTR). A new regulator, the Federal Competition Commission on Television and Radio Broadcasting (FKK), replaced it, now directly under the Ministry's authority.

The FKK – which still exists today – consists of nine members, all of whom, including the chair, are appointed by an order of the relevant minister. While in its early years the composition of the FKK pointed to at least some level of its independence with some – though always a minority – of its members being known media critics and arts figures, today all nine represent governmental bodies and pro-governmental parties, unions and institutions. The FKK is under the relevant Ministry – whatever name it might hold at the time,[37] which provides the Commission with the necessary technical, financial and administrative support (and, currently, guidance). There has never been an explanation for the terms, selection or duration of service for its members.[38] This legal vagueness and these gaps quickly led to the FKK becoming another bureaucratic and instrumental tool of the authorities.

For a long time the provisions of the 1991 Statute On the Mass Media remained the only solid foundation for regulating broadcasting. As the idea was to have a separate statute on broadcasting, they were of a very limited scope and problematic with regard to implementation. To avoid collision with governmental discretion, first, the few key provisions on broadcasting in the Statute were abolished or made even less precise in 2004 to allow for a 'temporary' use of governmental instruments of licensing. Then, in 2011, a set of subsections was added to the relevant Article of the Statute that indeed somewhat detailed licensing of broadcasting online and offline, through entrusting the government with complete jurisdiction over the matter: from setting the procedures and fees to issuing licences.

At the same time, Roskomnadzor, which then formally became the licensing body, obtained, through these amendments, authority to issue a written prescript to any broadcaster for any violation of the law as well as to suspend its activity for up to three months or to call the court with a demand to revoke the licence. The same additions allowed the President of the Russian Federation to approve the list of must-carry channels on all platforms without any competition. Interestingly enough, the President had already usurped this power in 2009, when – through a decree On National Mandatory Free Television Channels and Radio Stations – he named a particular set of channels for digital television multiplexes for an unspecified time with unspecified criteria or programme obligations. The government of the Russian Federation was instructed by the decree to provide these television channels with all necessary formal licences and to subsidise their dissemination all

---

[37] Currently its name is the Ministry of Digital Development, Communications and Mass Communications of the Russian Federation, or using the Russian abbreviation of its name: Mintsifry ('Ministry of a digit').

[38] Pankin et al (n 1) 84.

over the country. The decree was formally based on the suggestions of an ad hoc governmental commission, but was amended several times after the disbanding of the commission and, again, ignoring all existing licensing procedures. These legal changes have de facto sidelined the FKK to decision-making on minor local radio permits.[39]

3.4. Professional Associations of Journalists and Decline in Self-Regulation

The major national association of media professionals, the Union of Journalists of Russia (RUJ), has recently experienced huge transformation. During almost all of the period under review here, the RUJ was chaired by Vsevolod Bogdanov (1992–2017) with Igor Yakovenko serving as its Secretary-General (1998–2008, then this position was abolished). The policy of the RUJ leadership was then to advance professional interests while remaining in ambivalent relations with the authorities. It developed elements of a professional self-regulation system by establishing the Grand Jury – a body of the RUJ, and by partnering with the independent Public Collegium on Press Complaints.[40] It was active in international fora, spoke in defence of detained and harassed Russian journalists and called for an end to impunity of attacks against them.

The first sign of incoming policy changes in relation to the RUJ was establishing, in 2001, a 'parallel association', the Media Union. This new carefree organisation with an agenda of travel and entertainment for its activists was from the first days strongly backed by the authorities.[41] After years of tug-of-war with the RUJ as to which one is bigger and better in the sense of membership, modernity, international reputation and rank-and-file support of media workers, the Media Union failed to gain expected prominence.

Then the pressure on the RUJ intensified through back doors. This was marked by an abrupt expulsion from the organisation, in 2012, of the Center of Journalists in Extreme Situations, its main affiliate to monitor violations of the rights of the press since 2000.[42] The promises that the RUJ would necessarily continue the job, only better and more intensively, have never come true. Then again, through cautious manoeuvering between the interests of its rank and file and the wishes of the Kremlin, the RUJ leadership was slowly purged of the most politically active Secretaries, such as Yakovenko and Nadezhda Azhgikhina, to be replaced with

---

[39] 'Digital Television' (2010) 1 *IRIS Plus* 14 and 19–20.

[40] The Grand Jury has been inactive since 2005, while the Collegium has distanced itself from the RUJ: presscouncil.ru.

[41] '"Медиасоюз" встал под знамена Кремля. В Петербурге начал работу Медиафорум-2001', *Kommersant.ru*, 16 June 2001, available at: www.kommersant.ru/doc/563144.

[42] 'Центр экстремальной журналистики закрывается из-за Союза журналистов' *lenizdat.ru* (2 February 2012), available at: lenizdat.ru/articles/1102181.

'technocrats' and servile functionaries. By the time Bogdanov faced some sort of an ultimatum from the top in 2017, he had already lost his key supporters both in the RUJ governing body and the Kremlin. When he resigned, he was quickly replaced by the new breed of parachuted leaders who changed RUJ policies.

The focus was shifted to take care of the rights of journalists from Russian state-run media reporting from Ukraine, the Baltics, Poland and Moldova, who were then being expelled from those countries. This new course led, in particular, to a withdrawal of the RUJ from the European Federation of Journalists in the summer of 2021,[43] following the latter's solidarity campaign with oppressed Belarusian journalists, an end to the joint projects with the Organization for Security and Co-operation in Europe's Representative on Freedom of the Media and Ukrainian journalist associations,[44] while its self-regulation activity has been basically frozen. This downfall is symbolised by the Secretariat – right after the start of the open aggression in Ukraine – officially 'explaining' to journalists that blocking by Roskomnadzor of independent media outlets, such as Echo of Moscow and TV Dozhd, was caused by their 'hate speech', lack of verification of facts on the 'conflict' and 'repeated calls for violence'.[45]

As the Introduction to this book underlines, 'self-regulation can also help to achieve the goals of press regulation'. This was true in the initial phase of media regulation in Russia. Media freedom was then grounded on the understanding that journalists and media shared common professional standards. While in the 1990s numerous media outlets and associations of journalists adopted professional codes, only a dozen or so of the latter survive until now. Today, there are no publicly available editorial guidelines or codes of ethics for any mainstream news outlets, either commercial or state-run – including national television channels. Neither have the staff of major broadcasters acknowledged the Russian Union of Journalists' Code of Professional Ethics as a professional standard. For example, the charter of a must-carry national broadcaster, the Defence Ministry's television and radio company, Zvezda, stipulates that the company may engage in organising gambling but it fails to mention any professional standards in respect of journalism.[46] None of the other major broadcasters – Channel 1, Rossija-1, Rossija-24, Rossija-K, the 5th Channel, Match-TV, or TVC (all owned and/or run by the state) – have publicly accessible charters or editorial guidelines. The same is true for the notorious international services: RT and Sputnik. The conditions of

---

[43] 'Союз журналистов России покинул Европейскую федерацию журналистов для «оптимизации расходов»' *novayagazeta.ru* (9 June 2021), available at: novayagazeta.ru/articles/2021/06/09/ soiuz-zhurnalistov-rossii-pokinul-evropeiskuiu-federatsiiu-zhurnalistov-dlia-optimizatsii-raskhodov.

[44] L Voronova, 'Between Dialogue and Confrontation: Two Countries: One Profession Project and the Split in Ukrainian Journalism Culture' (2020) 13 *Central European Journal of Communication* 24.

[45] 'По поводу ограничения доступа к ресурсам «Эха Москвы», «Дождя»* и некоторых других СМИ' (*ruj.ru*, 2 March 2022), available at: ruj.ru/news/po-povodu-ogranicheniya-dostupa-k-resursam-ekha-moskvy-dozhdya-i-nekotorykh-drugikh-smi-17197?fbclid=IwAR2OqFjaPFHTfCDQdYVdccE-0FZpcGEbd8N5ZZyZy1M3Zp1zJFp0JWPs70E.

[46] 2009 Charter of the Zvezda television and radio company, available at: tvzvezda.ru/about/uchdocs.

their broadcast licences also do not refer to any editorial standards or accountability to the public. These broadcasters and other mainstream media habitually refuse to engage in available complaints procedures or self-regulation mechanisms.[47]

Formally, the Code of Professional Ethics of the Russian Journalist, adopted in 1994, remains one of the two key documents of the RUJ. Following its standards is still a condition for being a member. The current 'technocrat' RUJ leadership announced, in 2018, the need to revise it as an 'outdated' text for the new generation of tech-savvy media professionals. The Code has disappeared from the webpage of the organisation, as well as the references to the self-regulation body, the Grand Jury. Since then, no new draft has ever been compiled and put on the agenda. The only 'other' national association of journalists where the Code of Professional Ethics of the Russian Journalist is prominently displayed is the Trade Union of Journalists and Media Workers. It is a much smaller entity of some 600 members, which was established in 2016 after an attack on journalists and human rights activists in Chechenia.[48] After official registration in 2017, it became a member of the various international federations of journalists. In May 2022, following its anti-war statements, the Moscow Prosecutor's office started an inspection by its counter-extremism department of whether the trade union's (anti-war) information on its website fits its stated function and demanded its closure,[49] which was enforced in September 2022.

3.5. 'Abuse' of Media Freedom

Since its adoption in 1991, the Russian Statute on the Mass Media has undergone significant changes. From an Act that once provided a ban on censorship, freedom of private media and broad privileges for journalists, it has gone a long way. The best illustration of the transformation is one of its key provisions, Article 4, which lists instances when a media outlet 'abuses' freedom of the media, including such infractions as hate speech and incitement to terrorism. In such cases, says the statute in its other provisions, it shall be 'prescripted' (by Roskomnadzor), and eventually stopped from further activity. So, while in 1991 (and until 1995) the Article was 62 words long, at the time of writing this chapter it already contained 651 words, which is more than a tenfold increase.

Additional restrictions were recently added to the statute (Articles 16, 16(1), 25, 25(1), 49, 54 and 56), while its Article 57 on the privileges of journalists was amended in 2005 and 2013 to include conditions and exceptions to the rights of

---

[47] M Cappello (ed), *Media Reporting: Facts, Nothing but Facts?* (Strasbourg, European Audiovisual Observatory, 2018) 111–18.

[48] See: profjur.org/about-us.

[49] 'OSCE Media Freedom Representative Expresses Serious Concerns about Suspension of Independent Russian Trade Union of Journalists' Press release, 14 July 2022, available at: www.osce.org/representative-on-freedom-of-media/522709.

journalists, such as on fair reporting. In addition, writes Nathalie Maréchal,[50] a specific interpretation of restrictions has led 'to censorship well beyond what a literal reading of the law might suggest'. It all makes the argument that while in the 1990s the Statute on the Mass Media was indeed an instrument for media freedom, today it has become an instrument of oppression of the independent media and harassment of journalists into self-censorship.

3.6. The Sad Fate of Public Media

With the fall of the Communist regime in Russia, the mere ownership of the media by the state, even a new and democratic one, was generally considered a nonsense, a relic of the past. The press became independent from Soviet state ownership with the introduction of the new system of media registration by the 1990 and 1991 statutes. Independent broadcasters became popular on local frequencies all over the country. But the huge behemoth of national broadcasting has so far remained in the hands of the state. The remaining 'provisional' state control was explained by the ongoing discussion on whether to privatise the national system of state radio and television, or make it a public service media, on how to do it better, and with what instruments. For a while, the government played with the idea of limiting its media holding to just 'one newspaper, one newsagency, one television channel and one radio channel'; such a balancing act continued at least till 2002.[51] To reach a compromise for all stake-holders, the ill-fated broadcasting bill of 1997 envisioned the triad of state, public service and private broadcasters. Although it failed to be adopted, efforts intensified to persuade the Kremlin of the necessity for a public service broadcaster, more as a balance to the then oligarch dominated private broadcasting, than a replacement of state broadcasters.

In particular, research and lobbying for a bill on public service media renewed in 2001, with a Foundation to Develop Public Broadcasting, with its board of trustees that included Gorbachev and a number of cultural and political figures, and administrative coordination from the Russian Union of Journalists. In 2003, the bill was rejected by the State Duma. At about the same time, a number of local bills on public broadcasting were developed with the assistance of the Foundation in the constituencies of the Russian Federation (including the Moscow and Tomsk regions). They envisaged either the creation of a public television production company funded by a share of the regional budget, or the transformation of a local, state-owned broadcaster into a public television company. All these bills were rejected in 2006 by regional legislatures on the grounds that the regulation of

---

[50] N Maréchal, 'Networked Authoritarianism and the Geopolitics of Information: Understanding Russian Internet Policy' (2017) 5 *Media and Communication* 29, 32.

[51] N Rostova, 'Лесин хочет расформировать Минпечати' *Nezavisimaya gazeta* (20 June 2002), available at: www.ng.ru/politics/2002-06-20/1_lesin.html?id_user=Y.

broadcasting activities had 'suddenly' come within the exclusive competence of the federal authorities. The Foundation itself has been defunct since about that time, while the driving force behind its activities, Igor Yakovenko, the Secretary-General of RUJ, was soon forced to leave his post.[52]

The state firmly switched course to reinforcing state broadcasting and taking control of all independent voices on television.[53] It facilitated establishment of Gazprom-Media and the National Media Group and designated them as 'friendly' companies that would take over, one after another, independent national media outlets.[54] As to local broadcasting, the scenario, as it seems, was different. The switch-over to terrestrial digital television in Russia has led to a manifold decrease in the number of small broadcasters. Only one channel per constituency of the Russian Federation was supported in the switch-over process and received a slot on a free television multiplex, and that broadcaster in all cases turned out to be either a company owned or controlled by the regional authorities (that by that time had already fallen under strong dependence on the Kremlin). Others were left alone in finding resources for the switch-over and even when that turned out to be possible for them, they were forced out of the market by administrative means, as happened in 2014–15 with TV-2 in Tomsk.[55]

Then, suddenly, the idea of public television was brought back by President Medvedev in 2011, and a year later, he signed a decree to establish a national television channel Public Television of Russia (OTR). Its aim as declared is to inform the population 'in a timely, trustworthy and all-sided manner on current affairs of domestic and foreign policy, culture, education, sciences, spiritual life, as well as in other spheres'. A Council on Public Television was appointed by another decree of the President, to provide for 'public control over the activity of the television channel'. Formally, candidates for the Council are selected by the President from those presented to him by the Public Chamber of the Russian Federation.[56]

The Director-General of OTR, is appointed for a four-year term, also by the President of the Russian Federation. The Director-General also serves as the editor-in-chief.[57] This job turned out to be an august one, as the first Director-General started his term at the age of 75, and ended at his death at 84 (now his daughter, a medic, chairs the board), while the next, the current one, was appointed at the

---

[52] A Kornya, 'Журналистам не нравится генсек' *Vedomosti* (22 April 2008), available at: www.vedomosti.ru/newspaper/articles/2008/04/22/zhurnalistam-ne-nravitsya-gensek.

[53] I Zassoursky, *Media and Power in Post-Soviet Russia* (New York, ME Sharpe, 2004).

[54] See *The Digital Switchover* (Strasbourg, European Audiovisual Observatory, 2018) 9.

[55] M Bachina, 'Аномалия. История одной независимой телекомпании' (*Radio Svoboda*, 5 November 2018), available at: www.svoboda.org/a/29582894.html.

[56] The Public Chamber of the Russian Federation was created in 2005 by a federal law to facilitate interaction of citizens with the governmental bodies in order to take into account needs and interests of citizens as well as to protect their rights and freedom in the process of lawmaking.

[57] Общественное телевидение России, available at: council.gov.ru/media/files/41d4c 86963fb4131dc9f.pdf.

age of 80. Financing of the OTR comes from budget allocations and donations and has never been sufficient or sustainable. The channel has been criticised for lack of transparency on its programming goals, political bias and basically misinterpretation of the whole idea of public media, hence being compared to 'a suitcase without a handle'.[58]

As to state broadcasters, their mandate to exist initially depended upon availability of public scrutiny, or at least lip service to it. The Charter of the Russian State Television and Radio Company (VGTRK), adopted in 1998, still envisaged a public council at the office of its chair, composed from among 'outstanding personalities of science, culture and arts' to enable public control over the state media. In fact, the body has never been functional, and by 2000, the whole idea of state-run television had been revised. The concept prevailed that the state media belong primarily to the ruling elite, while the notion of a public asset created with and operating with public funds has disappeared from the public debate. Neither the Parliament, nor the government considered new attempts to reinvigorate public control over state broadcasting. The current Charter of VGTRK, approved in 2004, does not mention any guarantees of editorial or financial independence, while its Director-General is appointed and dismissed by the President of the Russian Federation without any procedural or qualification criteria (although, actually, it has been the same person since 2000).[59]

In today's Russia, the Kremlin effectively oversees all national broadcasters, directly or indirectly, through state-controlled private media companies, hiring and firing the top executives of all major state media outlets. Analysts traditionally say that state broadcasting chiefs are selected for their political reliability and personal loyalty to the President.[60] Russian state media pursue a programming policy that is based on the interests of the state – which generally means those of the country's elite. With the exception of the rights of approved candidates to free and paid access to state media during the four weeks prior to balloting, no public obligations exist in law for these outlets.[61] Effectively, one of the most important functions of state television and radio is to shape public opinion in support of the authorities. Most vividly this has been underlined by the consistent, since early 2014, daily television propaganda on all general interest channels of the

---

[58] I Yakovenko, 'Чемодан без ручки' *Yezhednevnyi zhurnal* (3 June 2013), available at: www.ej.ru/?a=note&id=12992; EV Abashina, 'Механизмы формирования Совета управления общественного вещателя в России и в странах Закавказья' *Mediascope* (2013) 3, available at: www.mediascope.ru/node/1378#22.

[59] The text of the Charter (approved by the Resolution of the Government of the Russian Federation of 16 February 2004, No 111) is available in Russian at: docs.cntd.ru/document/901889681?marker=6 5C0IR.

[60] *Media Sustainability Index 2004. The Development of Sustainable Independent Media in Europe and Eurasia* (Washington, IREX, 2005) 206.

[61] *Regulatory Framework* (n 29) 34–35.

narrative of the 'failed state' and 'Fascists' of Ukraine[62] and Russia's protection of compatriots all over the region.[63]

3.7. Stigmatising 'Foreign Agent' Media and Journalists

In the meantime, the Kremlin has become obsessed with the 'information security' of the country from voices which are foreign geographically, but most importantly, politically alien and fail to fall under its control. The notion of a 'foreign agent' was first introduced into Russian law and policy in 2012 by the 'Foreign Agents' Statute, the stated aim of which was to organise due public control over the work of certain public associations. The Statute established the conditions under which a non-commercial organisation (NCO) is considered to act as a foreign agent, as well as the obligations arising from this status, including labelling of the NCO's 'information materials'. The main criteria have been any, direct or indirect, foreign financing or other material assistance and engagement in the vaguely worded 'political activity'.[64]

Initially, the 'Foreign Agents' Statute was explained purely by the need for transparency of funds of NCOs, and was often presented as the Russian response to the 1938 American Foreign Agents Registration Act. But, as with other legal changes, its reasons and results were way more far-reaching. Amendments to the Mass Media Statute passed in 2017 expanded the requirements intended for 'foreign agent organisations' to 'foreign agent media'. Furthermore, in 2019 particular Russian private individuals involved in media-like activity became eligible to be included in the scope of these provisions as 'media performing the functions of a foreign agent'. Attempts in 2014 to challenge the constitutionality of some of these provisions, notably on the grounds that the status of foreign agent has a negative connotation and could be perceived as a manifestation of distrust or a desire to discredit and stygmatise entities qualifying as such, have failed. Roskomnadzor started to blacklist 'foreign agent media', slapping numerous fines on them, mostly for a failure to publish disclaimers on *all* their online materials, including the highest administrative fine in Russian history ever against a media publisher (at that time equal to about €300,000) in the 2018 case of *The New Times* online magazine.[65]

The initial list of 'foreign agent media' consisted of 10 outlets in 2017–20, mostly affiliated with the Radio Free Europe/Radio Liberty and Voice of America, only to jump to 53 by October 2022. The list of individuals with the status of

---

[62] V Gatov, Putin, *Maria Ivanovna from Ivanovo and Ukrainians on the Telly* (London, Henry Jackson Society, 2015) 13–14.

[63] Cappello (n 47) 113–15.

[64] A Richter, *'Foreign Agents' in Russian Media Law* (Strasbourg, European Audiovisual Observatory, 2020) 6–7.

[65] ibid 27.

'foreign agent media' increased from five in 2020 to 133 in October 2022, and in addition some 15 journalists have been entered into a general list of 'foreign agents'. The latest version of the 'foreign agent' law in Russia foresees that foreign funding is no longer necessary to be awarded this status: 'foreign influence' is enough. As a premature epilogue, in 2022 the European Court of Human Rights acknowledged the legal restrictions imposed by the 2012 statute, as amended, an infringement of freedoms of expression, saying 'the interference with the applicant organizations' rights had been neither prescribed by law nor "necessary in a democratic society"'.[66]

Furthermore, since 2015, several comparable federal statutes have been adopted, aimed at limiting the activities of foreign entities, including their media activities, as well as the distribution of information, both online and offline. These entities (today 55 of them) are carrying out 'undesirable activity' from the viewpoint of the authorities. Once found 'undesirable', the foreign or international NCOs have their activities suspended in Russia for an indefinite period, meaning also a ban on distributing their reports online and offline.[67]

3.8.   From Access to Information to a Monopoly on Information

Gorbachev's policy on *glasnost* envisioned a future law that would provide individuals with wide and free access to information held by public bodies. In a way it became a reality only in 2009, when President Medvedev signed into law the Federal Statute on Provision of Access to Information on Activity of the State Bodies and Bodies of Local Self-Government, earlier adopted by the State Duma. At the time, it was viewed by the President as a major instrument for the development of the Internet and Internet-based services.

The main aims of the Statute are transparency of the activities of governmental and municipal authorities, a wide use of modern technologies, and objective and full information for the public on the activities of the state. The Statute has led to the establishment and regular updating of official websites of state bodies and bodies of local self-government. It enumerates the types of information that may be provided online, including technical standards, information on the results of inspections conducted by the authorities, statistical data, information on the expenditure of public money and on vacancies. The exact type of information to be provided on official websites, though, is determined by the authorities

[66] 'European Court Rules that Russia's "Foreign Agents" Law Violates Human Rights Convention' *Le Monde* (14 June 2022), available at: www.lemonde.fr/en/international/article/2022/06/14/european-court-rules-that-russia-s-foreign-agents-law-violates-human-rights-convention_5986717_4.html.
[67] Richter, *'Foreign Agents'* (n 64).

that own these websites. In fact, the only obligatory items for official websites (according to the Statute) are the official email address for enquiries, working hours and news updates.[68] Neither an independent oversight body (like an information commission) was established, nor serious policy changes (like a training or publicity and information literacy campaign) were made. This led to systematic denials to provide information.

When I taught media law to some 250 undergraduates at Moscow State University, in 2010 and then in 2011, a condition for journalism students to pass the exam was to petition a public body for information and to chronicle the follow-up reactions. The result in the overall majority of cases was that the authorities attempted to ignore or even deny receiving requests for information, with at least one case in which a student was called to the prosecutor's office and made to explain why he would be interested in facts about a state-owned company. The prosecution tried to interpret his requests for information as a 'false report' on a committed crime, and was particularly interested in his professor who had given such 'suspicious' assignments to the students.

The Medvedev policy of open government and advancement of information openness online soon changed to an increase in the secrecy of official information. The most visible and challenged expansion of official secrecy happened in 2015, when a decree of the President made secret data on losses in the military in 'times of peace'. Their disclosure was to be treated as 'treason'.[69] Such losses, said the decree, might happen during 'special operations' (as if foreseeing the current one in Ukraine). The legality of the decree was appealed in the Supreme Court of Russia by a group of lawyers and journalists led by Ivan Pavlov, the leader of access to information NGOs, such as the Freedom of Information Foundation (that existed from 2004 to 2014, when it was assigned the status of 'foreign agent' and was forced to disband) and Team 29 (which existed from 2015 until 2021, when its leaders were assigned the status of 'foreign agents').[70] The appeal failed.[71] Meanwhile another decree, in 2017, 'prophetically' made secret other data relating to the plans of 'special operations'. Altogether, the list of secret information originally established in 1995, since 1998 has been expanded by 47 paragraphs, now listing 124 specific categories.[72]

---

[68] *Regulatory Framework* (n 29) 17.

[69] 'ВС подтвердил законность засекречивания военных потерь в мирное время' *RIA Novosti* (2 March 2020), available at: ria.ru/20151110/1317971053.html.

[70] '"The Kremlin Gets a Monopoly on Truth": A Lawyer Sets Out to Challenge Putin's Decree Classifying Russian Military Deaths' *Meduza* (17 June 2015), available at: meduza.io/en/feature/2015/06/17/the-kremlin-gets-a-monopoly-on-truth.

[71] While Pavlov, despite being a certified lawyer, was in an intensifying manner beaten, detained and otherwise harassed by the authorities, his wife expelled from Russia, banned to use internet, etc which taken together led to his self-exile to Georgia in 2021. In absentia, he was expelled from the barristers' chamber of St Petersburg.

[72] See: base.garant.ru/10105548/#friends.

These efforts were multiplied with the start of the open aggression in Ukraine in 2022. According to *The Bell*, an independent online medium in Russia, the country entered a 'data blackout'. It went on to explain:

> An unprecedented halt in the publication of official economic statistics since the start of the fighting means we now know much less about what's going on inside the economy. This lack of data has serious consequences: bad forecasting means rising costs and rising prices.[73]

The creation of the state monopoly on information, 'in blatant violation of Russia's international obligations', was specifically noted by the monitors of freedom of expression and freedom of the media for the United Nations, the African Commission of Human Rights, the Inter-American Commission for Human Rights, and the Organization for Security and Co-operation in Europe.[74]

3.9. A Ban on 'False News' in the Context of the War in Ukraine

To add to governmental control over information, in 2019, came the Law on Fake News, a set of amendments to prohibit publication of information deemed by the state to be false, to be followed by administrative and criminal liability for violation of the ban.[75] The amendments prohibit online dissemination of 'unreliable socially significant information', which would constitute a 'threat to life and/or health of citizens, property, threat of massive violations of public order and/or public security, or threat of establishing obstacles to the functioning of every-day supply objects, transport of social infrastructure, credit organisations, objects of power-supply, industry or communications'. As expected, the Law on Fake News provides additional powers to Roskomnadzor on blocking websites, without a court decision. Such blocking lasts at least until the unreliable information is removed. During the Covid-19 pandemic, under the pretext of protecting public health, Russian authorities successfully attempted to use the law both to monopolise the flow of public health information and to discriminate, harass and/or punish media and journalists that were holding officials accountable for their statements and actions in response to the pandemic.[76]

---

[73] 'Data Blackout' *The Bell* (16 May 2022), available at: thebell.io/en/data-blackout/?utm_source=The+Bell+%28Eng%29&utm_campaign=c78b27bac3-EMAIL_CAMPAIGN_2018_06_01_10_28_COPY_01&utm_medium=email&utm_term=0_cc8c2d1cde-c78b27bac3-74828914.

[74] Joint Statement on the Invasion of Ukraine and the Importance of Freedom of Expression and Information (2 May 2022), available at: www.osce.org/representative-on-freedom-of-media/517107.

[75] Federal Statute 'On Amendments to Article 15(3) of the Federal Statute on Information, Information Technologies and Protection of Information', 18 March 2019, No 31-FZ, available at: publication.pravo.gov.ru/Document/View/0001201903180031.

[76] See, eg, 'Chechnya Leader Launches Tirade Against Russian Investigative Journalist' *IPI* (15 April 2020), available at: ipi.media/chechnya-leader-launches-violent-tirade-against-russian-investigative-journalist.

These relatively modest efforts were multiplied with the start of the Russian aggression in 2022. On its first day, Roskomnadzor issued a general instruction to all media outlets, when reporting on the 'special operation' in Ukraine, to use information *only* from official Russian sources. This general warning, in particular, referred to Article 49 ('Duties of a Journalist') of the Statute on the Mass Media, requiring checking the authenticity of information prior to its dissemination. The specific examples of wrongdoing provided by Roskomnadzor were use of the words 'attack', 'invasion', and/or 'a declaration of war' instead of the official label of a 'special operation'. Dissemination of information about the shelling of Ukrainian cities and the death of civilians in Ukraine as a result of 'actions of the Russian Army', as well as 'mass losses' of Russian military personnel was also considered illegal. In its follow-up statements, Roskomnadzor blocked Internet resources that hosted 'false information', including those of Ekho Moskvy radio, InoSMI, Mediazona, New Times, TV-Dozhd, Svobodnaya Pressa, Krym.Realii, Novaya Gazeta, Journalist, Lenizdat and numerous other established media outlets. To protect their journalists, major Western news media suspended operations in Russia, while online access to their content was also blocked thereafter.[77]

In contrast to earlier practice, these resources were blocked without specific warnings or explanations of what exactly was to be considered false. Roskomnadzor also launched administrative investigations into the dissemination of unreliable, publicly significant information by the listed media. The offence is punishable with a fine of up to 5 million rouble (about €84,000 at the current exchange rate). In August 2022, the Prosecutor-General of Russia said that from the start of the war in February his office successfully demanded 340 times the taking down and/or blocking of online access in Russia to as many as 138,000 materials in connection with the 'special operation' in Ukraine.[78]

Then, amendments to the Statute on the Mass Media for the first time since its adoption in 1991 allowed for the closing down of a media outlet without a court decision. This happens when the prosecution notices a violation of a broad spectrum of bans that include, in particular, dissemination of any information 'directed to discredit the use of the Armed Forces of the Russian Federation in the aims of protection of the interests of the Russian Federation' or just 'an untruthful information' on such a use (even unintentional), including mobilisation and the situation at the theatre of operations, as well as calls to introduce sanctions against the Russian Federation and expressions of sheer disrespect towards Russian public bodies.[79] In practice, that means that liability starts if the media disseminates

---

[77] Harriet Sherwood and Dan Milmo, 'BBC, CNN and Other Global News Outlets Suspend Reporting in Russia' *Guardian* (5 March 2022), available at: www.theguardian.com/media/2022/mar/04/bbc-temporarily-suspending-work-all-news-journalists-russia.

[78] 'Не на бумаге, а на деле' *Kommersant* (8 August 2022), available at: www.kommersant.ru/doc/5501990.

[79] Art 56(2).

information from sources other than governmental ones on a growing number of politically sensitive topics.[80] Thus, the situation de facto brought the media back to the times of bans on 'anti-Soviet agitation' and on dissemination of 'fabrications discrediting the Soviet state'.

Finally, new Articles were added to the Criminal Code to introduce liability for 'public dissemination of knowingly false information on the use of the Armed Forces of the Russian Federation'. As becomes clear from the case law, it generally includes claims of atrocities committed by Russian forces in Ukraine, evaluation of the armed actions as a form of aggression or occupation by Russia, irregulatities during mobilisation of civilians, reporting on dissent in reation to Kremlin policies, such as in Ukraine. Starting with a fine of 700,000 rouble (about €12,000) the penalty may reach an imprisonment of 10–15 years. According to legal experts, now criminalised 'knowingly false information' is interpreted to mean any information which does not come from Russian official sources, establishing in a way a presumption that all information is false unless stated otherwise by governmental officials.[81] More importantly, criminal liability was introduced for public actions aimed at 'discrediting the use of the Armed Forces of the Russian Federation in the interest of the protection of interests of the Russian Federation and its citizens, and the sustainability of international peace and security, including through public calls to counteract'. If committed twice within a year, this offence is punishable with a fine of 100,000 rouble or imprisonment of up to five years. Finally, public calls by a Russian citizen for foreign or international economic sanctions against Russia, shall be punishable by a fine or imprisonment of up to five years.

3.10. Restrictions on Social Media

The Kremlin does not view Internet governance, cybersecurity and media policy as separate domains. Rather, everything here falls under Russian national 'information security'. Domestic surveillance, online content censorship and the switch of Internet governance to government jurisdiction are deeply connected to propaganda in Russia and disinformation campaigns abroad, and are 'used strategically to achieve geopolitical goals'.[82]

---

[80] According to the official data, in the March–June period of 2022, the courts issued decisions on 2,995 administrative cases relating to discreditation of the army. As a result, 2,496 individuals and eight legal entities were to pay monetary fines that averaged 34,237 rouble (€560); see: www.dw.com/ru/v-rossii-za-polgoda-rassmotreli-bolee-19-tysac-administrativok-izza-protestov/a-63451551.

[81] 'Understanding the Laws Relating to "Fake News" in Russia' *Committee to Protect Journalists and Thomson Reuters Foundation* (28 July 2022) 4, available at: cpj.org/2022/07/understanding-the-laws-relating-to-fake-news-in-russia. As of 19 October 2022, 124 persons were formally accused of the crime, reported the Prosecutor General's office, see: www.sibreal.org/a/genprokuratura-rf-soobschila-o-149-ugolovnyh-delah-vozbuzhdennyh-po-state-207-3/32091243.html.

[82] Maréchal (n 50) 38.

As social media has become one of the main forums for critical public debate in Russia,[83] its specific regulation is a good example of the focus of attention of the authorities. At the core of the regulation in Russia turned out to be various efforts to make the policies of global social networks fully compliant with national legislation and regulations, especially with regard to the availability and dissemination of content found to be illegal in Russia, and to ensure that this compliance is efficient and quick. Originally the policy appeared to reach its aims through forcing the social media companies to open formal branches in Russia and imposing on them significant monetary penalties.[84]

The developments with regard to access to global social networks in Russia should be understood in the context of the 'Sovereign Internet Law' which entered into force in 2019.[85] It is formally aimed at ensuring that the Russian segment of the Internet, the so-called Runet, can function independently of the global network in the event of certain threats, while providing to the public authorities technical possibilities necessary to effectively restrict access to certain online services and content.[86] Such threats were defined by the government in 2020 to include 'a threat of providing access to online information or information resources, access to which must be restricted in accordance with the legislation of the Russian Federation.'[87]

Specific to social media, violation of Russian legislation could include the lack of an obligatory twenty-four-words disclaimer on all statements (including on Twitter) identifying it as coming from 'foreign agent media' or a similar reference to the 'foreign agent' origin of the materials of 'foreign agent' NGOs. Another violation typical of the social networks is establishing 'limitations' to the online dissemination of information which is 'essential for the public', including materials of the Russian mass media, if such limitations discriminate on the basis of, for example, their property status, or are the result of sanctions imposed by foreign governments upon the Russian Federation, Russian citizens or companies. The nature of the 'limitations' has not been defined in law, but the administrative practice of Roskomnadzor points to the instances of marking the account as 'governmental media' or the content as 'violent' or the intentional removal of the account from 'most popular' lists.[88]

Huge pressure has been placed on all global social media networks, making the United Nations Special Rapporteur on Freedom of Expression, Irene Khan,

---

[83] 'Russia: Social Media Pressured to Censor Posts' (*Human Rights Watch*, 5 February 2021), available at: www.hrw.org/news/2021/02/05/russia-social-media-pressured-censor-posts.

[84] A Richter, 'New Rules on Social Networks: Blocking Permitted' (2021) 2:1/33 *IRIS* 27.

[85] A Richter, 'Sovereign Internet Law adopted' (2019) 6:1/22 *IRIS*.

[86] *Freedom on the Net 2020, Russia* (Freedom House, 2020), available at: freedomhouse.org/country/russia/freedom- net/2020#footnote12_g9flt86.

[87] On approval of the Rules of centralised command of the communication network of general use (Об утверждении Правил централизованного управления сетью связи общего пользования), Ordnance of the Government of the Russian Federation of 12 February 2020, No 127, available at: publication.pravo.gov.ru/Document/View/0001202002170013?index=0&rangeSize=1.

[88] Richter, 'New Rules on Social Networks' (n 84) 12–13.

in her 2021 report, single out Russia and two other countries which 'adopted laws that grant the authorities excessive discretionary powers to compel social media platforms to remove content that they deem illegal, including what they consider to be disinformation or "fake news" and sanction them with significant fines and/ or content blocking'. The report observed that 'such laws lead to the suppression of legitimate online expressions' and 'contradict Russia's commitments under the International Covenant on Civil and Political Rights'.[89] Until the 2022 aggression, the regulation took into account possible social discontent in the case of general blocking of access to major social networks, and technical difficulties in fully implementing such a block.

The Rubicon was crossed in 2022 as a court in Moscow issued its decision on the civil lawsuit of the First Deputy Prosecutor-General of the Russian Federation to the Meta Platforms Inc. Acting in the public interest, the plaintiff requested the court to ban the activities of the 'American transnational holding company' on the territory of the Russian Federation on the basis of its 'extremist activity', with the additional circumstance that the company's corporate policy 'is directed against the interests of the Russian Federation and its citizens, establishes a threat to public safety and to the life and health of the citizens of the Russian Federation, as well as state security'. The court noted the discriminatory measures taken by Meta in regard to Russian state media, earlier decisions of the Russian courts that proclaimed particular posts in Facebook and Instagram 'extremist', earlier demands by Roskomnadzor that Meta takes down posts found illegal, various fines imposed on Meta, calls to violence against Russians that were permitted after February 2022 despite the stated community policies, as well as dissemination of false information on the 'special military operation' against Ukraine. The court dismissed as 'declaratory' all arguments of the defendant and affirmed the lawsuit by banning the activity of Meta and the distribution of its products, Facebook and Instagram, on Russian territory.[90]

4. Discussion

A reflection of the short history of media freedom in contemporary Russia allows us to define a set of chapters, characterised by a certain main feature.

(1) *A period of booming guarantees of media freedom and journalists' rights* (1990–95). This was the time of adoption of the key national media statutes and the new Constitution to establish a ban on state censorship, privileges

---

[89] Disinformation and Freedom of Opinion and Expression, A/HRC/47/25, 13 April 2021, available at: undocs.org/A/HRC/47/25, para 57.

[90] 'Russian Court Labels Meta Platforms "Extremist", Effectively Outlawing Facebook, Instagram' (*RFE/RL's Russian Service*, 21 March 2022), available at: www.rferl.org/a/russia-facebook-instagram-outlawed-meta/31763417.html.

of journalists on access to information and freedom of private ownership of the news media. The laws deprived the state of its printed press, while private broadcasters were allowed to appear and prospered both in the provinces and Moscow. In their competition for power in 1993, both the President and the Parliament hurried to provide even more guarantees of freedom to the media, which later turned out to be generally empty promises.

(2) *The stalemate period* (1996–2002) started with the preparations to the 1996 presidential elections. Inspired by the concept of 'media management',[91] the Kremlin was slowly taking control of individual media through influence of its administrative power and persuasion. This process was formalised through the chief editors' weekly meetings.[92] The Kremlin was happy to provide specific benefits to certain news businesses, pushing – still without intimidation – the media to take on self-regulation obligations that more and more often resembled self-censorship. Apparently, at that time the authorities decided that the press had enough freedom and did not deserve any more. Joining the Council of Europe in 1996 without taking any obligations of further liberalisation of the media, persuaded the Kremlin that the West was already happy with the level of media freedom in the country.

(3) *The initial legal assault on freedom and independence of the media under the pretext of countering terrorism and extremism, protection of children and inefficiency of media self-regulation* (2002–12). Those laws established a speedy mechanism for declaring media stories prohibited and barring public access to them under the pretext of securing common public values. In 2002, the Kremlin facilitated establishing the Industrial Committee of the Mass Media to pretend that 'media captains' themselves wished tighter regulation of media freedom and a stronger self-organisation of the business for the sake of commercial success rather than the proclaimed rights of journalists.

This period included an inconsistent 'retreat' of the authorities during the time of Medvedev as President of Russia (May 2008–May 2012), when the grasp of Putin on power was not as direct as before and after that. During the break it became possible to establish some sort of a public service media and advance the right to access information law in Russia, as well as to decriminalise defamation. Also then, in 2010, the Supreme Court of Russia gave a liberal interpretation of media law by instructing the lower courts to respect press freedoms in judicial conflicts very much in line with the case law of the European Court of Human Rights.[93] However, through the 2011 amendments to the Statute on the Mass Media, broadcasting and online media were put under stricter governmental control.

---

[91] Gatov (n 62) 4–5.
[92] ibid 6.
[93] A Richter, 'Russia's Supreme Court as Media Freedom Protector' in P Molnar (ed), *Free Speech and Censorship around the Globe* (Budapest, Central European University Press, 2014).

(4) *The period of consistent measures to eliminate access to the free and independent media* (2012–21). Following public protests after Putin's re-election, the Kremlin intensified the rhetoric of an 'enemy encirclement' of Russia. It put forward a national agenda to counteract Western liberal messages through enforcing laws on 'foreign agents' and 'undesirable organisations', promoting 'sovereign Internet' law and stricter controls over information in social media, further concentration of national and regional broadcasting in the hands of the elites, the tolerance of impunity of attacks on independent media and journalists, the protection of the official narratives of Soviet/Russian history and severing all possible media support programmes that were outside the control of the authorities. In addition, the Covid-19 pandemic encouraged them to introduce general bans on 'false news' under the cover of threats they could make to public health.

(5) *The death of media freedom* (2022). Soon after the open start of the Russian aggression in Ukraine, a number of international media outlets suspended reporting from within the Russian territory, while the few remaining independent Russian media outlets stopped news reporting and even erased archives relating to the Russian war against Ukraine, citing the adoption of the amendments to the Criminal Code on 'false news'. Determination of what is true or not has become solely the mandate of public authorities. Legal prohibitions on 'discrediting' the army and public authorities, even in value judgements, has battered the last traces of freedom of political opinion in Russia. In this way the still existing small windows of pluralism in the country were forcibly shut, while privately owned media with messages that contradicted the official line either turned away from politics or folded. Having closed the remaining independent media within Russia and pushing free journalists beyond its borders, the authorities focused on blocking access to all independent voices in Russian, but increasingly also in foreign languages, from abroad, from both exile media and foreign news outlets.

I believe though that the end of the free press started with the changes in the country's political leadership from 1999 to 2000 and the resulting changes in media structure and regulation. These changes were initially taken by some media and political researchers as a rebirth or 'reconstruction of Russian mentality', wherein 'deeper levels of collective identity and mentality' do not depend any more on 'the power of the media to impose meanings' as 'television gradually came under government control'.[94] The 'new synthesis' that was applauded turned out to be a certainty of authoritarianism, thought control and aggression.

Under the ideology of the 'Russian World', with Moscow being the Third Rome, based on historical myths of the 'glorious' Soviet victories and using

---

[94] Zassoursky (n 53).

Bolshevik catch-phrases of 'enemy encirclement' and 'foreign agents',[95] the Kremlin-controlled propaganda – in the absence of competition from the free media – succeeded in establishing a society rallied around the infallible leader despite the irritative hardships and losses of everyday life.

The Russian example is quite demonstrative of what could happen in an authoritarian regime that aims to establish its monopoly on information, on the truth and eventually, on people's minds. The 'dictatorship of law' and 'stable vertical of power' ideas promoted in the early twenty-first century by state propaganda, set the stage for the ruling elite assuming the authority to judge the rightness and truthfulness of mass information, and of the friends and foes of the nation itself. The elite did so through establishing a firm and lasting control over the President's office (2000), the Parliament (2003), the government (2004), Russian provinces (2004), municipal self-governments (2009) and the courts, as well as over law enforcement, and over national television followed by other mass media, social media, education, arts, political sciences and so on.

The process of getting to the 'new censorship',[96] 'media, captured by the state'[97] or what we rather call state's 'monopolisation of truth'[98] – all went through various distinct and complementary steps. First, it focused on narratives and teachings that can be broadly labelled as 'extremist' and, thus, illegal; this included information on 'unsanctioned' protests or defaming the authorities. Second, the authorities defined which information is classified as 'disrespectful' to the state and to its symbols and introduced relevant liability. Third, the state became the sole arbiter of how recent and not so recent national and world historical events are to be interpreted, specifically those that serve as a source for the mandate and legitimacy of the nationalist and populist elite. Fourth, and most recently, any controversial information found 'dangerous to the public' enables servile judges to sanction dissent as 'unreliable information'.

---

[95] V Sazonov, 'The Ideology of Putin's Russia and its Historical Roots' in V Sazonov et al (eds), *Russian Information Warfare Against the Ukrainian State and Defence Forces: April–December 2014* (Tartu, Estonian National Defence College and NATO Strategic Communications Centre of Excellence, 2017).

[96] Gatov (n 62).

[97] T Besley and A Prat, 'Handcuffs for the Grabbing Hand? Media Capture and Government Accountability' (2006) 96 *American Economic Review* 720; M Petrova, 'Inequality and Media Capture' (2008) 92 *Journal of Public Economics* 183; A Mungiu-Pippidi, 'Freedom without Impartiality: The Vicious Circle of Media Capture' in P Gross and K Jakubowicz (eds), *Media Transformations in the Post-Communist World: Eastern Europe's Tortured Path to Change* (Lanham, MD, Lexington Books, 2013); S Gehlbach and K Sonin, 'Government Control of the Media' (2014) 118 *Journal of Public Economics* 163; M Dragomir, *Media Capture in Europe* (Budapest, Media Development Investment Fund, 2019); N Ryabinska 'Media Capture in Post-Communist Ukraine' (2014) 61(2) *Problems of Post-Communism* 46; A Szeidl and F Szucs, 'Media Capture through Favor Exchange' (2021) 89 *Econometrica* 281; A Shifrin (ed), *In the Service of Power: Media Capture and the Threat to Democracy* (Washington, National Endowment for Democracy, 2017) 67.

[98] A Richter, 'Post-Communist Media Freedom and a New Monopoly on Truth' (2021) 3(2) *Journal of Romanian Studies* 21.

In addition to the almost unchallenged state's media monopoly, the authorities introduced severe restrictions on information from sources still outside its control. These were either foreign-owned or labelled as 'foreign agent media', or 'unwanted' foreign non-governmental organisations. Extra-judicial blocking became routine in relation to online political information and websites, including foreign ones. 'Sovereign Internet' laws allowed the state to erect blocks over possibilities to access alternative foreign-based sources of information online.[99] The result is, in the words of hundreds of media organisations throughout the world, that the 'Russian people are being denied access to the truth'.[100]

Today we see the end of yet another experiment with media freedom in Russia. The first happened as a result of popular demand for human rights during the first Russian Revolution of 1905–07 and lasted until the Bolsheviks 'provisionally' suspended the liberal freedom of the press with one of its first decrees in November 1917. The second was a populist experiment with 'Soviet press freedom' for labourers only, which started in 1917 and ended with Stalin's grasp of power in the 1920s; while the third started with the *glasnost* policies in 1989 and legally ended in 2022.

I am an ardent supporter of the 'four theories of the press' and believe that the Russian model of the media in the last 35 years has drifted from the Soviet Communist to the libertarian and then to the authoritarian doctrines of freedom of the press. Authors of this classic book noted of the latter:

> The entire philosophical basis for a free exchange of ideas is foreign to authoritarian thinking. Since authority rests in the state and since the responsibility for the solution of public issues follows authority, the first duty of the press is to avoid interference with the objectives of the state. These objectives are determined by a ruler or by an elite rather than in the 'market place of ideas', as predicated by the libertarians. The idea that the press constitutes a check on government does not make sense to the authoritarian, who immediately asks the question – who checks the press?[101]

In my mind this observation strongly correlates with what Putin was saying about the press almost from the very start of his rule:

> They have stolen money, they bought mass media, and they manipulate public opinion ... They lie, they lie, they lie! Their logic is simple. They work on a huge audience and they do it to show ... the political leadership that we need them, that we should be afraid of them, yield to them, and let them go on plundering the nation ... That is the real aim of what they do.[102]

[99] M Domańska, *Gagging Runet, Silencing Society: 'Sovereign' Internet in the Kremlin's Political Strategy* (Warsaw, Center for Eastern Studies, 2019); Richter, 'Foreign Agents' (n 64).

[100] 'Perugia Declaration for Ukraine', 3 May 2022, available at: gfmd.info/perugia-declaration-for-ukraine.

[101] FS Siebert, T Peterson and W Schramm, *Four Theories of the Press: The Authoritarian, Libertarian, Social Responsibility, and Soviet Communist Concepts of what the Press should Be and Do* (Urbana, IL, University of Illinois Press, 1956) 28.

[102] *Moscow Times* (2 September 2000) v.

Such treatment of the independent media from the Kremlin's control was not exceptional and became visible at certain critical points that made Putin demonstrate his inner feelings. Those points, that allowed him to use the momenta of widespread fear and/or (often instigated) distaste and be bold in attacking free speech, were in follow-up to the siege of the hostages in the Nord-Ost theatrical centre (2002), the terrorist attack in Beslan (2004), and – apparently taken as a serious personal insult – the *Pussy Riot* performance (2012).[103]

I see no reason to believe in the existence of a 'sacred' Russian model or unique path in history, different from that of neighbouring civilisations. Russia has simply become an authoritarian country, and its media model could not but take the shape of the regime itself. We can easily detect similar if not the same stages of legal and political developments in shaping media models in Belarus, Ukraine (prior to March 2014), Azerbaijan, some of the Central Asian countries, as well as in the Central European countries, such as Hungary and Poland, which have already gone through the 'media capture' stage.

With sad feelings I close this chapter on the fate of free media in post-Communist Russia. It is clear that the key to understanding Russian media policy lies in the fact that it is part and parcel of an overall population control policy with the goal of the Kremlin to hold on to power and wealth. Since recently, it aims at the wealth and power of the whole post-Soviet region, if not the globe, through a combination of information aggression, blackmail and colonial wars. Whenever a new and brighter chapter of Russian history begins, a study of what happened from 1991 to 2022 will hopefully be of some use for reflection. Perhaps, an understanding of the patterns of change, at least in theory, could facilitate a future lasting liberation of the Russian media.

---

[103] Skillen (n 10) 299–303.

9

Press Freedom and Regulation in Slovakia

ANDREJ ŠKOLKAY

1. Introduction

For four decades (1948–89), there was a Marxist-Leninist perspective on press freedom in Slovakia. The press was supposed to serve as a collective propagandist (Marxism-Leninism was the final truth, thus there was no need to explore alternatives), to organise people (for instance, to achieve economic goals), and to agitate according to Marxist-Leninist standards.[1] This was reflected in the Press Act 184/1950, passed in 1950, which stipulated that the 'Press's mission is to help in creative efforts … and struggle for peace and cooperation and to cooperate in education to Socialism'. Thus, no plurality of opinions in the political-ideological and media spheres was either expected or welcome. Criticism by the press was possible, but it should be 'constructive' and focused on communal or personal life or work affairs, not on political life. During some periods of 'political thaw', slightly more press freedom was allowed, such as in 1956[2] (after the death of Stalin), in the 1960s[3] or in the late 1980s (during the *glasnost* period). Moreover, unexpectedly, total but short-lived press freedom was allowed during the spring and summer of 1968 for the period known as the Prague Spring.[4] In the latter case, this was the result of the legal abolition of censorship. All these short periods were accompanied by more or less intensive and more or less free discussions about the freedom of the press and freedom of speech (in the latter case, usually novelists and not journalists led the discussion).

---

[1] J Vojtek, 'Vznik socialistického charakteru tlače v revolučnom Rusku' (1986) 4 *Otázky žurnalistiky* 181.
[2] J Marušiak, *Slovenská literatúra a moc v druhej polovici päťdesiatych rokov* (Brno, Nakladatelství Prius, 2001).
[3] E Londáková, *Slovenská kultúra v rokoch 1968–1970* (Bratislava, Veda, 2015).
[4] E Londáková et al, *Rok 1968: Novinári na Slovensku* (Bratislava, Veda, 2008).

More discussions about press regulation, rather than discussion of a free press and free speech followed the fall of Communism. In the early 1990s, changes in the Penal Act eliminated threats to freedom of speech such as sedition committed by the media or subversion of the state through the media. To balance this, in the Civil Code, the right to privacy was introduced as well as financial compensation for non-pecuniary damages.[5] However, it took almost two decades and 30 drafts until a completely new Press Act was passed in 2008.[6] The major factors in this delay were internal politics and a lack of consensus among the major stakeholders: politicians, publishers and journalists.[7] Since then, the Press Act has been amended six times.[8] A new Press Act, the Act on Publications, was passed in 2022. There has also been ongoing discussion about drafting a general bill protecting journalists (between 2020 and 2021, but less so in 2022). It seems like in each decade or each two decades, there is some deeper motivation to support the media or journalists more vocally. For example, in 2002, the Parliament passed a not-legally binding document, the Declaration of the National Council (the Parliament) on Protection and Support of Media Development Environment.[9] In 2020, Igor Matovič, who was briefly the Prime Minister, came up with the idea of establishing a state fund supporting investigative journalism. A similar idea, a law on supporting the periodical press had been drafted in 1991.

2. Theories of Press Freedom

After the fall of Communism in 1989, two main approaches to the discussion of press freedom can be distinguished. The first perspective was defined by its origin (local or foreign) while the second centred on the type of regulatory powers envisioned (either self-regulation or public regulation, or rarely co-regulation). I will also briefly mention a third perspective, determined by the profession of the commentator. As just stated, the first perspective on freedom of the press is framed in terms of its origin – either finding inspiration about press freedom locally, or internationally. It can be said that those who searched for inspiration

---

[5] K Kirstová, 'Občianskoprávne aspekty slobody prejavu a ochrany individuálnych údajov' (1994) 46(12) *Justičná revue* 22.

[6] A Chlebcová Hečková, 'Politický proces prijímania mediálnej legislatívy v ČSFR a na Slovensku po roku 1989' (2013) 1 *Global Media Journal* 84, 85; see, eg, the commentary on one of the first changes in the existing Press Act in L Šefčák, 'O poslednej novelizácii tlačového zákona' (1991) 1 *Otázky žunalistiky* 12.

[7] I Sečík, 'Niektoré otázky mediálneho práva na Slovensku a v zahraničí' (1994) 2 *Otázky žurnalistiky* 119; S Nôtová-Tušerová, 'Mediálna problematika na Slovensku sa spája s kompromismi. Rozhovor' (2001) 3–4 *Otázky žurnalistiky* 147.

[8] See comprehensive analysis by J Vozár, P Kerecman and L Lapšanský, *Tlačový zákon. Komentár*, 2nd edn (Bratislava, CH Beck SK, 2021).

[9] L Šefčák, 'K návrhu Deklarácie Národnej rady SR o ochrane a zabezpečení rozvoja mediálneho prostredia' (2002) 10 *Fórum* 5.

locally usually ended up supporting authoritarian tendencies in government, contributing to shrinking press freedom and promoting propaganda in the media. It is difficult to determine whether this was solely due to their ideological affinity or was the effect of some psychological factors, or whether it was merely political or professional opportunism. Ľudovít Štúr, the founding father of Slovak political journalism, to whom these promoters sometimes referred, was often inconsistent in his ideas, adoring tsarist Russia and some features of feudalism while criticising the more liberal regimes in France and Germany (this will be discussed below). In contrast, those who attempted to find inspiration abroad focused mostly on liberal Western European and US examples and sources. Unlike the first group, the adherents of this group were critical of politicians in power, who found it difficult to understand why the press was critical of them. Similarly, until 2008 politicians found it difficult to adopt press regulations that were able to accommodate (with some public protests from the media and publishers) the perspectives of all major stakeholders in society.

The second broader perspective on freedom of the press can be defined by the type of regulatory powers envisioned – either soft power like ethical guidelines, or hard power, in the form of binding laws. In the context of the former, ethical self-regulation or co-regulation in the press was often discussed. In fact, a Code of Journalistic Ethics was adopted as early as 1990 by the Slovak Syndicate of Journalists (SSN), a major organisation of journalists. However, it was not until after 2000 that a weak form of self-regulation of the press at national level was established: the Press Council (later the Press and Digital Council). Thus, until then, with the brief exception of a period in the mid-1990s, priority was given (at a nationwide and especially political level) to discussion about hard regulation – by the law. However, such regulation was not necessarily only effected through press law as such. Instead, during the 1990s other forms of legal regulation were suggested or actually adopted, such as higher taxation of the tabloid press based on income from advertisements, or, for some time, a one-year period was set in which a decision by a court had to be made in cases of the protection of personality rights (impacted mostly by the press).[10] In addition, some attempts by authoritarian politicians to utilise the 1003 Resolution on Ethics in Journalism (1993) were evident.[11] Of course, as can be seen, these two perspectives or approaches have often been blurred or combined in public or professional discussions. For example, the very fact that the Press Council was finally established in 2002 was the result of a threat to incorporate this idea into one of many advanced draft press bills in 2001.[12] It should also be noted that the idea of a press council of ethics funded by the state was first raised back in 1995.[13] As a result of political pressure,

---

[10] A Školkay, 'The Media and Political Communication in Slovakia in the late 1990s' in N Schleicher (ed), *Communication Culture in Transition* (Budapest, Akadémiai, 2000) 175–76.

[11] See: assembly.coe.int/nw/xml/XRef/Xref-XML2HTML-en.asp?fileid=16414.

[12] Chlebcová Hečková (n 6) 88.

[13] A Remišová, *Etika médií* (Bratislava, Kalligram, 2010) 144.

an international conference on this self-regulatory option was organised by the SSN in 1996.[14] Similarly, press regulation was discussed in the journal *Otázky žurnalistiky* throughout 1996.

As already noted, a third perspective arose in this debate, based on profession. In various capacities, press regulation was discussed by members of a range of professions, including politicians, publishers, judges, lawyers, journalists and philosophers, to name just the most important potential stakeholders and discussants. However, in the local context philosophers contributed very little to the debate about freedom of speech and of the press. They mostly discussed metaphilosophical issues concerning the impact of the media, and in particular the electronic media, on society.[15] Only occasionally – such as in the work of Richard Sťahel[16] – could one find a contribution by a philosopher (who in this example was at the same time a former journalist), to the theoretical debate on ethics in journalism and the media. Interestingly, Sťahel pointed first of all to the business nature of media activities, including the one-sided character of major producers of news: political, non-governmental organisations and business stakeholders (as de facto public relationship activities). As a result, a journalist faces philosophical challenges such as having to consider what the truth is, noted Sťahel. Within the third perspective, one can identify the most important although least visible participants in the debate – judges. Their verdicts ultimately formulated the limits of the freedom of the press. Conversely, the most visible but least influential policy actors were the journalists and their organisation(s), as well as, indirectly, publishers.[17] Above all of them, politicians and affiliated state authorities, as the producers of the drafts of press regulations, played the key formative regulatory role. They established the boundaries within which both judges and journalists operated.

3. The Perspective of the Origins of Press Freedom

From the perspective of the origin of the international documents or ideas that may have inspired or impacted press regulation in Slovakia, initially (in the early 1990s), inspiration came almost exclusively from early British and American

---

[14] V Holina (ed), *Etika žurnalistiky a tlačové rady. Zborník z medzinárodnej konferencie* (Bratislava, SSN, 1997).

[15] S Gálik, *Úvod do filozofie médií* (Trnava, FMK UCM, 2011); V Gažová, 'Filozofia médií' in J Vopálenský (ed), *Médiá na prahu tretieho tisícročia: Človek v sieti mediálnej recepcie* (Trnava, FMK UCM, 2003); S Gáliková Tolnaiová, 'Človek a filozofia v čase elektronických médií (K aktuálnosti filozofie komunikácie a médií)' in L Čupková and J Skačan (eds), *Filozofia, kultúra a spoločnosť v 21. storočí Recenzovaný zborník vedeckých článkov* (Nitra, UKF, 2012).

[16] R Sťahel, 'Etika v médiách' (2002) 1–2 *Otázky žurnalistiky* 108.

[17] E Chmelár, 'Právo na odpoveď v slovenskom a európskom právnom poriadku' (2013) 1 *Global Media Journal* 64.

writings on freedom of the press,[18] including translations of classic works such as John Milton's *Areopagitica*. Similarly, the impact of US journalism schools and theories seems to have been widely present in practical journalism.[19] This know-how was transferred through US-based or funded establishments such as the Center for Independent Journalism in Prague or Bratislava. Furthermore, some ideas came from the International Federation of Journalists. For example, a 1999 guide published by the SSN envisaged a merger with the digital world in which 'free media still play a key social and cultural role in keeping democratic values'.[20] The document also argued against the 'dangers of concentration of media and power, and merger of telecom, IT and computer sectors, loss of plurality and public service values'. In the areas of regulation, it preferred flexible forms of regulation based on professional self-regulation.[21] As regards content regulation, on the one hand it called for differentiation in the regulation of content and, on the other, regulation of technical infrastructure as well as market regulation.[22] A separate section tackled public service broadcasting. Inspiration was also drawn from the case law of Austrian courts, especially as discussed at the European level and in the jurisprudence of the European Court of Human Rights (ECtHR).[23] At the theoretical level, there was occasionally analysis of the most important normative theories of the media, specifically those defined by Fred Siebert, Theodore Peterson and Wilbur Schramm,[24] Denis McQuail[25] and Andrej Školkay.[26] At the same time, reference was made to European norms, as defined by the Council of Europe (CoE) and its Parliamentary Assembly. Since the mid-1990s, attention has shifted towards the Convention for the Protection of Human Rights and Fundamental Freedoms (European Convention on Human Rights, ECHR) and its impact on freedom of the press through the case law of the ECtHR.[27]

---

[18] L Šefčák, 'On the Birth of Freedom of Speech and Press' (1996) 2 *Otázky žurnalistiky* 12; L Šefčák, 'Zrodslobody tlače v Anglicku' (1991) 17–18 *Žurnalistika* 125.

[19] H Burrell and KE Hug, *Nezávislá tlač* (Information Agency of the USA, 1992); MF Mallette, *Príručka pronovináře střední a východní Evropy* (Prague, Center of Independent Journalism, World Press Freedom Committee, 1991).

[20] A White and V Holina, *Premeny. Príručka pre novinárov a ich organizácie* (Bratislava, International Federation of Journalists and SSN, 1999) 8.

[21] ibid 10–11.

[22] ibid 11.

[23] J Vozár, 'Ochrana osobnosti a sloboda slova a tlače (Pohľad na problematiku cez súdne rozhodutia v Rakúsku)' (1993) 6 *Právny obzor* 632.

[24] FS Siebert, T Peterson, and W Schramm, *Four Theories of the Press: The Authoritarian, Libertarian, Social Responsibility, and Soviet Communist Concepts of what the Press should Be and Do* (Urbana, IL, University of Illinois Press, 1956).

[25] D McQuail, *Mass Communication Theory* (London, Sage, 1983).

[26] A Školkay, 'Normative Theories of the Media' (1996) 4 *Otázky žurnalistiky* 30.

[27] M Schefer, 'Štandardy tlačového práva v právnom rozhodovaní Európskeho súdneho dvora pre ľudské práva. Systém slobody prejavu v zmysle článku 10 Európskej konvencie pre ľudské práva – EMRK' (1997) 3 *Otázky žurnalistiky* 190; P Kerecman, *Sloboda prejavu novinára a ochrana pred jej zneužtím* (Bratislava, SSN, 2009); P Kerecman, *Novinári a sloboda tlače v rozhodnutiach Európskeho súdu pre ľudské práva* (Bratislava, Information Office of the Council of Europe, 2003); M Macovei, *Právo na slobodu prejavu* (Bratislava, Information Office of the Council of Europe, 2007); D Gomien,

On the topic of ethical press self-regulation, some examples from Swiss and German perspectives were discussed.[28] There was also discussion about the CoE Resolution on Ethics in Journalism. Interestingly, no author sought inspiration in Sweden, which has the longest history of freedom of the press. During Mikuláš Dzurinda's second term as Prime Minister (2002–04) the government struggled with an increasingly critical press. This prompted attempts to consult foreign experts about possible press regulation.[29] It should be noted that in 2002 a local law expert, Luboš Šefčák, questioned the usefulness of suggestions for the self-regulation and public regulation of journalism drafted by experts from Portugal and Denmark.[30] Perhaps the problem lay not in the country of origin of these experts (although this was specifically highlighted by the critic) but in the fact that these experts had been invited by the government, specifically, by the anti-corruption unit of the Office of the Government.

It is also true that the SSN (for which Šefčák was the key legal expert) rejected two ideas suggested by these foreign experts, namely, that journalistic cards should be issued by an institution established by the law and that there should be a media ethics council, funded by the state and created by Parliament (as is the case in Denmark and Portugal). Although this latter suggestion was omitted in its final reading in Parliament, the bill was still not passed. However, press legislation found inspiration in, or faced criticism from, more diverse sources, albeit mostly in the European context, including the International Press Institute in Vienna, Article 19, based in London in the 1990s,[31] or the Organization for Security and Co-Operation in Europe in Vienna in the early 2000s[32] and other international bodies such as the World Association of Publishers.[33]

In the second sub-group – from the perspective of origin of local heritage – the focus was on certain ideas in the writings of the founding father of Slovak

---

Krátky sprievodca Európskym dohovorom o ľudských právach (Bratislava, Ister Science, 1994); D Šváby, 'Z judikatúry Európskeho súdu pre ľudské práva' (2000) 2 *Ústavnosť a politika* 68; B Repík, 'Základné politické práva a slobody garantované Európskym dohovorom o ľudských právach a ich vzťah k trest-nému právu' (1994) 46(7–8) *Justičná revue* 5.

[28] R Blum, 'Strážcovia smerom dovnútra i navonok? (Problémy žurnalistickej samokontroly na príklade švajčiarskej tlačovej rady)' (1997) 3 *Otázky žurnalistiky* 183; L Hasler, 'Medzi obchodom a morálkou. Možnosti a hranice mediálnej etiky' (1997) 3 *Otázky žurnalistiky* 177.

[29] J Hrubala, *Investigatívna žurnalistika* (Bratislava, Úrad vlády, 2004).

[30] L Šefčák, 'K poslaneckému návrhu na vydanie zákona o masových médiách z roku 2002' (2002) 3–4 *Otázky žurnalistiky* 158.

[31] ibid 159–60.

[32] A Rikhter, 'Right Of Reply: International Standards and Slovak Press Law' (2019) 1–2 *Otázky žurnalistiky* 4.

[33] 'Sloboda tlače: Slovensko má problémy' *Euraktiv* (24 June 2008), available at: euractiv.sk/section/kultura-a-media/news/sloboda-tlace-slovensko-ma-problemy; 'OBSE žiada stiahnuť návrh sloven-ského tlačového zákona' *Euraktiv* (22 January 2008), available at: euractiv.sk/section/kultura-a-media/news/obse-ziada-stiahnut-navrh-slovenskeho-tlacoveho-zakona. Further discussion on the funda-mental ethical principles to be used by the journalists, based on international examples (mostly of US and German origin), could also be found in A Školkay, 'Teória a prax morálky žurnalistiky II' (2002) 1–2 *Otázky žurnalistiky* 2.

political journalism, Štúr, who was the founder of the first somewhat politically relevant newspaper (appearing bi-weekly) published in the Slovak language in the middle of the nineteenth century.[34] Another influential figure from the nineteenth century was Jozef Hurban, founder of a periodical published for a brief period in the middle of the century.[35] The fate of this latter periodical was symptomatic and is symbolically relevant for the early twenty-first century. The press regulation at that time required the payment of a large deposit, which the publisher was unable to secure. Thus, similarly to present day crowdfunding efforts and the support of online media by voluntary contributions, its editor appealed – unsuccessfully – for nationwide funding from wealthy sponsors. In a similar vein, the journal published by Štúr in the nineteenth century ceased publishing since it could not afford to pay a high one-off fee demanded by the government of the day.

As far as Štúr's ideological impact is concerned, he represented a populist and nationalistic version of nineteenth-century politics.[36] Indeed, Štúr's editorial policy was criticised by his contemporary and friend, Ján Francisci. In particular, Francisci decried the lack of liberal orientation and disliked the conservativism, as well as the priority given to nationalism, which typified the articles published in the journal edited by Štúr.[37] The excessively moderate style and even fear of the authorities of the editorial policy at that time was also criticised by his other peers. This editorial policy was defended by Štúr as a precautionary measure against censorship.[38] Importantly, Štúr's nineteenth-century journal acted as a substitute for a non-existent national or rather ethnic political party.[39] It should be noted for context that present-day Slovakia formed part of the Austro-Hungarian Empire until late 1918.

It was perhaps not an accident that his late twentieth-century followers supported the same populist and nationalist ideology and editorial policies.[40] However, according to Ľuboš Jurík, Štúr was compelled to make a stand against liberalism anyway – as his major opponents, the Hungarian authorities, were liberals (as opposed to the conservatives in imperial Vienna).[41] However, Fraňo Ruttkay pointed out that in any case Štúr did not trust the Hungarian elites of either the liberal or conservative persuasion.[42] Štúr realised that he

---

[34] F Ruttkay, *Ľudovít Štúr ako novinár* (Bratislava, TASR and Slovart, 2015); J Darmo, 'Journalism and Society' (1996) 4 *Otázky žurnalistiky* 35.

[35] F Ruttkay, 'K 150. výroču založenia slovenských pohľadov – II' (1996) 39(4) *Otázky žurnalistiky* 325.

[36] E Chmelár, 'Zrodenie národa' *Noveslovo* (19 September 2007), available at: www.noveslovo.sk/node/12018.

[37] V Jablonický, 'Sloboda v ponímaní štúrovcov' in I Sedlák (ed), *Ľudovít Štúr v súradniciach minulosti a súčasnosti* (Martin, Matica slovenská, 1997) 267.

[38] Ruttkay, *Ľudovít Štúr* (n 34) 175.

[39] ibid 7.

[40] J Darmo, 'Zvliekanie hadej kože alebo Slovensko od totality k demokracii (Masmédiá, politika, spoločnosť)' (Bratislava, Slovakia Plus and Stála konferencia slovenskej inteligencie, 1994); O Dostál, Z Fialová and M Vašečka, *Nacionalizmus a vybrané slovenské masmédiá* (Bratislava, Občiansky inštitút, 1992).

[41] Ľ Jurík, *Ľudovít Štúr, životný príbeh* (Martin, Vydavateľstvo Matice slovenskej, 2019).

[42] Ruttkay, 'K 150' (n 35) 330.

could not reach a political compromise with the Hungarian authorities nor with Hungarian revolutionaries.[43] In that sense, this approach or conflict was typical of the majority of smaller nations that prioritised language and ethnic rights over more advanced political rights – similar to the Czechs or other minor nations in Europe at that time. Jurík claimed that the Hungarian authorities and later revolutionaries favoured freedom of the press only for Hungarian language publications.[44] Overall, this historical intellectual heritage was rather controversial, as were the ideas of those journalists, lawyers, researchers and politicians who claimed to have found sources of inspiration for print media roles in nineteenth-century thinkers.

4. The Perspective of Normative Documents

From the perspective of normative documents, discussion initially remained on a more broadly philosophical or more narrowly ethical level (in the early-1990s and mid-1990s) based mostly on foreign ideas. Later, attempts were made to find a balance (and use normative power) between either ethical standards and/or increasingly authoritarian draft bills of legal regulations that were proposed (during the mid-1990s). Furthermore, throughout that period there was discussion about new legal regulation, which became increasingly in line with the CoE and the ECtHR normative guidelines or case law. For example, Šefčák criticised the draft press registration clause since it resembled to him the licensing that had been practised in the totalitarian regime.[45] Instead, the new press law should apply the democratic system of notification that allows only state authorities to register new titles in the press.

However, this was more of a semantic issue than a real problem. In practice it did not matter what it was called (whether it be 'registration' or 'evidence'), since in effect, initially, no publication could be published without a proper licence number (while later on publishing could start simply complying formally with this bureaucratic duty). These types of issues related to formalities were evident in a case that happened in late 2008 and early 2009, after the new press law entered into force. Publishers who did not notify the Ministry of Culture about the details of their ownership structure were deleted from the list of periodicals. This meant that they could no longer publish as they did not have a registration number. However, this temporary deadlock was quickly resolved with the help of legal advice from the Ministry of Culture.[46]

---

[43] J Demmel, *Ľudovít Štúr* (Bratislava, Kalligram, 2015) 287.

[44] Jurík (n 41) 313.

[45] L Šefčák 'Restrictions on the Periodical Press?' (1997) 3 *Otázky žurnalistiky* 219.

[46] See N Kališová, 'Obecné noviny zo zoznamu vymazali, no nezrušili' *Myorava* (20 March 2009), available at: myorava.sme.sk/c/4352593/obecne-noviny-zo-zoznamu-vymazali-no-nezrusili.html.

Ján Füle, who served for some time as chairperson of the SSN, highlighted the political interests of the new media owners, as well as the pressure coming from the government, as the most important issues facing journalists in the mid-1990s.[47] He considered discussion about ethics in journalism to be mere window dressing for political pressure on a critical press. Yet Füle supported giving a role to an ethics council – if the right time comes. He also called for a 'balanced' press law ('since power balance can change') and demanded that journalists support the idea of passing a bill supporting the press. Researcher Samuel Brečka called for legislation providing for transparency in print media ownership and for self-regulatory measures.[48] In addition, he suggested expanding the idea of the bill providing support to the press to all types of media.

It is not possible, due to space limitations, to discuss all the details of around 30 drafts of the press law. For those interested we recommend reading as a *pars pro toto* the draft from 2002 as summarised by Šefčák.[49] Concerning a more philosophical issue of a definition of truth in journalism, Šefčák argued that the authorities should not have the right to judge the truthfulness of journalism. The issue of truthfulness should be, according to Šefčák, an ethical issue in journalism.[50] A code of conduct should be established, along with a press council – Šefčák referred here to recommendations by the CoE. In retrospect, this opinion seems to be overly radical and applicable only to output based on opinions.

5. The Foundations of Press Regulation: Is the Free Press the Cornerstone of Democracy in Press Freedom Theory?

The answer to this question depends on whom one asks or which sources are consulted, and which period we are discussing. However, in general it can be claimed that the press has gained more rights and some limited duties since the fall of Communism. As mentioned above, the courts commonly refer in their verdicts to the role of the free press as the cornerstone of democracy. This is mainly done through referring to specific case law of the ECtHR. If one examines the case law relating to the press, the concept that the free press should be considered as being the cornerstone of democracy is heavily present (as will be discussed further). However, this concept is entirely missing in the (old) Press Law as well as in the Act on Publications and in some other strategic governmental documents. For example, Jozef Vozár and Ľubomír Zlocha compiled a collection of the case law

---

[47] J Füle, 'Čo rozumieme pod transformačným procesonm slovenskej žurnalistiky? Pokračovanie' (1996) 4 *Otázky žurnalistiky* 331.
[48] S Brečka, 'Slovenslý mediálny trh a potreba jeho ochrany II' (1996) 4 *Otázky žurnalistiky* 293.
[49] L Šefčák, 'K poslaneckému návrhu' (n 30); see especially his notes 1 and 2 for earlier drafts.
[50] L Šefčák, 'On the Truthfulness in Journalism' (1997) 1 *Otázky žurnalistiky* 23.

of the ECtHR, as well as that of Czech and Slovak courts.[51] It is clear from this collection of case law that the free press is seen as the cornerstone of democracy. However, as will be discussed further the local courts try to find a balance between personal or institutional rights on the one hand, and freedom of speech and the press on the other. There are two groups or two approaches of judges/courts in that respect.

In contrast, it is worth noting that the Press Act No 167/2008 Z.z. was written in rather bureaucratic or neutral language in that regard. There was nothing about the importance of a free press. In fact, the words 'journalist' or 'journalism' did not appear in the text. Thus, one can only deduce a philosophical meaning (theoretical foundations) of the freedom of the press either from the accompanying report (submitted with the draft legislation) and/or, indirectly, based on some of its fundamental features. From the former perspective, the key goal of the draft legislation was to 'bring to the forefront the quality of acquired information, the way of elaboration of information and the truthfulness of published information' as well as 'searching for an equilibrium between the right to freedom of speech on the one hand, and right to protection of personality of both natural and legal persons, on the other hand'.[52]

From the latter perspective, the Press Act was quite balanced. It provided two privileges to the press (although these were not necessarily granted directly to the journalists or editors but to the publishers), while it also asked the publishers to assume some responsibilities. Two key legal privileges were granted to publishers (as well as, somewhat unsystematically, to broadcasters): the right to receive information from public authorities; and the right (as well as a duty) to protect sources. Formally, the first right was not a privilege of journalists but of publishers. Moreover, it should be noted that this right was given in addition to the Freedom of Information (FOI) Act. Beyond this was the right to the protection of sources. This was actually formulated as a legal duty for publishers as well as for employees and other co-workers (and, as mentioned, for broadcasters). It should be noted that protection of sources is also mentioned as a responsibility of journalists in the Code of Ethics of a Journalist. The Code states in somewhat awkward language that '[a] journalist keeps promises of protection of identity of a source'.

The state authorities have the right to publish public announcements free of charge in the case of 'urgent public need'. Other stakeholders had the right to correction, the right to reply and the right to make additional announcements. An amendment to the Press Law passed during Iveta Radičová's government

---

[51] J Vozár and Ľ Zlocha, *Judikatúra vo veciach slobody prejavu a ochrany osobnosti* (Bratislava, Wolters Kluwer, 2014). This is a somewhat confusing collection since it suggests that the Czech case law may be seen as equally relevant to Slovakia. Although it is true that Slovak courts find inspiration in the Czech case law, normatively, Czech law should be seen as any other case law. Moreover, this collection of case law does not reflect the Press Law passed in 2008, but it deals with the case law based on Act 81/1966 Coll.

[52] Dôvodová správa k zákonu č. 167/2008 Z. z. o periodickej tlači a agentúrnom spravodajstve a o zmene a doplnení niektorých zákonov (tlačový zákon), available at: www.nrsr.sk/web/Dynamic/DocumentPreview.aspx?DocID=269991.

(2010–12) softened some of the obligations in relation to rights to reply or correction, and abolished some of the fixed financial compensation in the event of the breach of these rights. Specifically, since late 2011 it has not been possible to use both legal rights simultaneously. In addition, instead of fixed financial compensation the court can also decide in civil procedures (on the protection of personal rights) about possible financial compensation for non-pecuniary damages.

Interestingly, a follow-up attempt was made by 42 Members of Parliament (MPs) to specify in more detail the conditions of how the press should tackle this issue. The Constitutional Court decided that a request by the MPs, that there should be a stated condition that to request correction or reply should be further determined by the real potential for damage to be done to the reputation of a person, was not sufficient for demanding constitutional intervention (PL. ÚS 12/09-135). The Constitutional Court, in effect, ruled that whether there is potential damage to a personal reputation is to be decided by the individual decision of a specific person and not by a publisher.

Overall, these legal changes and reasonings can be seen as a positive move towards the free and independent work of the print media. It can also be argued, however, that some of these modifications represented steps that were neither necessary nor useful for rational public political discourse. For example, as mentioned previously the changes to the Press Act limited the legal rights of public figures to reply or comment on factual statements with respect to their public activity. This modification was demanded by the then opposition leaders (who had been in government during the preparation of this amendment). Obviously, the publishers were against any right to reply.[53] As will be discussed below, this changed a decade later (that is, the previously excluded professional group was included again).

It is instructive to compare the legal documents discussed above with other documents, to see how other stakeholders prioritised freedom of speech. For example, the official 551-page 'vision' and 'strategy of development' of Slovak society, prepared mostly by members of the Slovak Academy of Sciences in 2010, underlined only the negative aspects of the private media, while public service media was presented in idealistic terms.[54] The Ministry of Culture under the liberal ministers František Tóth (2005–06) and Rudolf Chmel (April–July 2006) drafted a Strategy of State Cultural Policy, including a blueprint for its Action Plan. In spite of its ambition to become a long-term programme, stretching across parliamentary terms, this strategy died when the new government came to power the same year. A previous effort, the even more voluminous Declaration of the Parliament on the Protection and Development of the Media Environment, prepared under the auspices of liberal minister Milan Kňažko in 2001, was also unsuccessful in

---

[53] A Školkay, M Ondruchová-Hong and R Kutaš, 'Case Study Report. Does Media Policy Promote Media Freedom and Independence? The Case of Slovakia' (2011), available at: www.academia.edu/7979203/Does_media_policy_promote_media_freedom_and_independence_The_case_of_Slovakia, 10.

[54] M Šikula et al, *Stratégia rozvoja slovenskej spoločnosti* (Bratislava, Ekonomický ústav SAV, 2010).

creating a consensus regarding long-term media policy. Thus, while there was no consensus among major political stakeholders at the turn of the century about an appropriate media policy – including, obviously, freedom of the press, the press legislation that was finally passed in 2008 (with later amendments) attempted to find a balance between the rights and duties of the key stakeholders.

Before discussing the 2022 version of the Press Act (as mentioned, this was labelled the Act on Publications) it may be instructive to discuss some of the media policies envisioned by arguably the three key political parties that formed the government after the 2020 general elections. Both the populist movements, Sme rodina (We are a Family) and OĽaNO (Ordinary People and Independent Personalities), had specific media policies in mind before the 2020 general elections, as suggested in their election manifestos.[55] However, there were few specific references to the printed media sector or to journalists. OĽaNO planned to revise 'unnecessary' media regulation. This appeared to be quite a liberal approach that committed, for example, to a 'new media act, as well as an act on protection of journalists' (Culture of Election Manifesto, Section 22(15)). Sme rodina planned, among other regulatory suggestions, to limit the abuses which result from the dominant position of oligarchs and financial groups in the media field. Another regulatory idea of theirs was a new framework for digital media to be set up that would aim to ensure higher transparency of the media's operations and decrease the possibility of disinformation being disseminated. For that purpose, the competencies of the regulatory authorities should be extended to encompass the new media. Finally, the Liberal party SaS (Freedom and Solidarity) wished to introduce grant schemes to support minority media as well as to introduce changes in the current system of sponsoring the audiovisual sector. Significantly, it planned the privatisation of the public service wire agency.

Overall, it is hard to make a final assessment of whether these suggested policies could be seen as having in mind a free press as a cornerstone of democracy. Certainly, these proposed media policies could be seen as legitimate policy aims, compatible with the standard media policies in a liberal democracy. In some aspects, they could also be seen as innovative or progressive and much needed (for example, the regulation of social media). In other aspects, they could be viewed as questionable within the local context, and possibly populist suggestions (for instance, changing the financing of public service media), although similar policies have been applied in some of the most developed liberal democracies. In 2022, only two new regulatory acts were passed in Parliament: the Media Services Act (MSA) and an Act on Publications. The former aims to introduce more transparency in media ownership with a duty to register firms in a repository of public partners, and provide for the regulation of online video platforms such as YouTube and providers of 'content services' (to be discussed further). The latter replaced the 2008 Press Act. It also covers, in addition to periodical press publishers and

---

[55] I Krasko, 'Volby 2020: Jak chtějí politici změnit slovenská média' *Mediaguru* (24 January 2020), available at: www.mediaguru.cz/clanky/2020/01/volby-2020-jak-chteji-politici-zmenit-slovenska-media.

wire agencies, the regulation of news web-portals. If the so-called alternative media (quite popular political news web-portals with little original news reporting but with heavy doses of low-quality, controversial content of a more commentary type), aim to enjoy the same rights as the legacy media, they have to meet certain conditions.

A trend appears to have emerged of regulating everything that looked like media in a similar (but not identical) manner. In that sense, either one should expand the meaning of 'free press' (for example, to include online media), or regard regulatory developments as shrinking the exclusivity of the 'free press'. As mentioned, in this regard there is – and always has been – the Press Act (now under different name). However, for libel, a citizen, or even a legal person, can use the Civic Code, or, if the intensity of breaching the law is high, the Penal Code.[56] Although the national penal law allows probably the harshest criminal penalty for libel in Europe, this option was not used in courts' judgments or prosecutors' decisions on media or journalists in the early 2010s. There was, however, a chilling effect of civil suits that throughout the early 2000s led to high non-pecuniary damages.[57]

6. Constitutional Press Freedom

Igor Palúš and his co-authors argue that the Constitution self-limits the state in matters of freedom of speech and of the press. First, in this regard there is Article 26(3) that forbids censorship. Second, Article 26(4) forbids publishing of the press from being based on the previous approval of the state.[58] Moreover, Tomáš Hubinák notes how Article 26(4) allows limitations to be put on the freedom of expression (including of the press) only by law (that is legal acts in force of highest importance save for constitutional law).[59] On the positive or active side, state authorities have a duty to inform the public about their activities in the official language of the state (Article 26(5)). Palúš and his co-authors include among 'positive' contributions to the freedom of speech also limitations put on freedom of speech such as the right to honour, dignity, reputation and goodwill. This reflects local efforts to balance fundamental rights, following the CoE documents and ECtHR case law. In addition, there are general positive guarantees of freedom of speech and the press/media in the Constitution.

There are actually two types of communicative freedoms and two types of communicative rights in the Constitution:[60] (1) freedom of thought (Article 24,

---

[56] O Repa, 'Trestný čin ohovárania vs prípustná (dovolená) kritika' *Pravne listy* (23 April 2018), available at: www.pravnelisty.sk/clanky/a649-trestny-cin-ohovarania-vs-pripustna-dovolena-kritika.

[57] P Hanák, 'Kriminalizácia žurnalistiky: Trestne stíhaní novinári na Slovensku v európskej perspektíve' (2016) 2 *Mediální studia* 245.

[58] I Palúš et al, *Ústavné právo SR* (Košice, UPJŠ, 2016).

[59] T Hubinák, 'Štát ako „nočný strážnik" vo vzťahu k slobode prejavu médií in T Majerčák (ed), *Sloboda prejavu a jej limity. IV. Ústavné dni* (Košice, UPJŠ, 2016).

[60] See: www.prezident.sk/upload-files/46422.pdf.

including the right to express one's own thoughts publicly); (2) freedom of expression (Article 26); (3) the right to information (Article 26); (4) and the right to petition (Article 27) – the three latter items are to be found within Political Rights. Thus, surprisingly from a constitutional point of view, freedom of expression is not considered to be a fundamental human right and freedom – it is 'just' a political right. Ján Drgonec pointed out that inclusion among political rights should be understood as a type of information.[61] Indeed, in practice the courts consider freedom of expression to be a fundamental right. At the same time, from a constitutional perspective, freedom of expression and the right to information are ranked at the same level. Indeed, it is noteworthy that Slovakia allows rather extensive access to information according to its FOI Law. The FOI Act was passed about a decade after the Constitution was adopted.

Interestingly, the Constitution does not separate free speech of individuals from that of the press. The Constitution does not differentiate between different types of media from the point of view of freedom of expression either: 'Everyone has the right to express his or her opinion in words, writing, print, images or by other means and also to seek, receive and disseminate ideas and information freely, regardless of the state borders' (Article 26). However, although the Constitution does not require approval for press publishing, radio and television broadcasting 'may be' subject to permission from the state. However, this regulation is limited to 'entrepreneurial activity' in the latter case. Thus, theoretically non-entrepreneurial broadcasting does not need permission. It should be noted that the Constitutional Court (PL.ÚS 15/98) pointed out that there is a difference in impact between print media and audiovisual media.

Despite such clear and liberal wording, initially, in the early 1990s, Slovak journalists neither had the right to publish untrue factual statements in error (as in the US system) nor were politicians accorded lower legal protection in comparison to other citizens, as in many Western European countries.[62] Nonetheless, since the adoption of the Charter of Fundamental Rights and Freedom in 1991[63] (before the break-up of Czechoslovakia and the establishment of an independent Slovakia), there has been a slow but increasing impact of the case law of the ECtHR in the country. At the same time (1992), the Constitution was written as a quite liberal constitution that provided the grounds for a wide interpretation of the freedom of the press (and the right to information). Overall, media policy in Slovakia attempts to balance various conflicting fundamental values both at the level of its formulation and at the level of its implementation. The Constitutional Court has shown a long-term, relatively consistent and increasingly liberal commitment towards the protection and promotion of freedom of expression in the media, as well as to

---

[61] J Drgonec, 'Sloboda prejav' (1996) 9 *KMIT* 22.

[62] A Školkay, 'An Analysis of Media Legislation: The Case of Slovakia' (1998–99) 2 *International Journal of Communications Law and Policy* 1.

[63] R Fico, 'Základné politické práva garantované vnútroštátnym právom SR' (1994) 46(7–8) *Justičná revue* 16.

access to information in Slovakia, to a large degree thanks to the case law of the ECtHR.[64]

7. Press Regulation, Achieved through State or Non-State Regulatory Bodies and Soft Law

Anna Sámelová compiled a list of the internal professional and ethical regulations of public service media.[65] The first accessible regulation was dated 1992, the last dated from 2011. Some of them were used in parallel. It is interesting to observe that all of these documents discussed journalistic professionalism (how to do) rather than journalistic ethics (why to do or not do). In other words, they reflected legal regulation (how to behave in a correct way) rather than ethical issues (such as what constitutes 'truth').

There are several typical challenges with respect to self-regulation of the press. The first problem is concerned with its general acceptance and enforcement. The second problem with non-state regulatory bodies, primarily the Press and Digital Council, is that some individuals tend to use such verdicts (in three categories of intensity of sanctions) before the courts to support their legal cases. It should also be mentioned that the Constitutional Court takes into consideration decisions made by the Press and Digital Council (Uznesenie I.ÚS132/2021-15, 30 March 2021). This may explain why, among the self-regulatory institutions, the most powerful tools for enforcing media self-regulation are those instruments outside journalism with a low degree of institutionalisation (online tools and individual initiatives by bloggers, for example).

In contrast, self-regulatory institutes outside journalism with a high degree of institutionalisation, such as research or education, contribute very little to media accountability in Slovakia. This can be seen as a paradox. An explanation can be found, on the one hand, in the low quality of media education and research, and on the other hand, in the rapid development of new online technologies that heighten the impact of individuals in monitoring and checking while at the same time happening more immediately.[66] Moreover, the initial unique composition of the members of the Press and Digital Council – respected and honest people from public life, but not peers – contributed to the low level of respect for the Council.[67] Under such conditions, it was the judiciary[68] as well as the state authorities in

---

[64] Školkay, *Ondruchová-Hong and Kutaš* (n 53).

[65] A Sámelová, *Normatívna regulácia verejnoprávnych médií. Mravy, cenzúra a editovanie v Rozhlase a televízii Slovenska* (Bratislava, Univerzita Komenského, 2016) 122.

[66] A Školkay, 'Slovakia: Conditional Success of Ethical Regulation via Online Instruments' in T Eberwein, S Fengler and M Karmasin (eds), *The European Handbook of Media Accountability* (London, Routledge, 2019).

[67] Remišová (n 13).

[68] E Kováčechová, 'Prístup súdov v Slovenskej republike' in P Wilfling and E Kováčechová, *Sloboda prejavu a žaloby na ochranu dobrej povesti* (Pezinok, Via Iuris, 2011).

general, including the government, that had to take the leading role in enforcing professional-ethical rules, but often with dubious results.[69]

Significantly, the MSA offers either a choice to adhere to the self-regulatory mechanism (de facto co-regulation) or to be under a public regulation. However, this must be determined a priori and in writing. Moreover, the MSA seems to be concerned primarily with self-regulation in relation to harmful low-quality food and alcohol content aimed at minors. In any case, the public regulator monitors self(co-)regulatory activities and can intervene in case of failure. In contrast, the current version of the Act on Publications includes a section on self-regulation relating to advertising only.

8. Press and Media Freedom

It is first useful to summarise the constitutional principles in this area as they have been defined by the Constitutional Court. First, the Constitutional Court in its finding IV. ÚS 107/2010 explicitly and unquestionably gave priority to freedom of expression in some cases. More importantly, this priority should be given, the Constitutional Court argued, even when a certain performance or result may have certain deficiencies from the point of view of the traditional legal protection of personality. This is in line with previous argumentation employed by the Supreme Court (see Ruling of the SC 5 Cdo 55/2008 from 25 February 2009). In the words of the former chairperson of the Constitutional Court:

> The Constitutional Court of the Slovak Republic respects also certain specifics of the standard periodical print media for the mass public (in contrast to professional publications) which in certain cases, especially when taking into account the scope of individual contributions and readers' interest, must accept certain simplifications … What matters is always the overall meaning of the information, which should correspond with the truth.[70]

Moreover, the chairperson of the Constitutional Court argued that

> not every publication of an untrue 'fact' may by definition mean an illegal intervention into personal rights. An illegal intervention into personal rights can be seen in such cases only under two conditions: (1) where there exists a direct correlation between intervention and breaking into the personal sphere and (2) where this intervention in a concrete case overstepped a certain qualitative level in such a manner that it would be impossible to tolerate in a democratic society.

---

[69] A Školkay, 'The freedom of expression in the media and the Slovak judiciary' in E Psychogiopoulou (ed), *Media Policies Revisited: The Challenge for Media Freedom and Independence* (London, Palgrave Macmillan, 2014).

[70] I Macejková 'Sloboda prejavu v ústavných prameňoch práva a v judikatúre súdov' in T Majerčák (ed), *Sloboda prejavu a jej limity. IV. Ústavné dni* (Košice, UPJŠ, 2016).

Second, in the opinion of the Constitutional Court (finding of the CC I. ÚS 155/07, 3 December 2008), possible legal (co-)responsibility by a person supplying information to the media can be established only if (1) the media make this information public; (2) the media learned about this information in an official way from the authorities (or, as it expanded it later, from a public source); and (3) the information infringed the rights of other persons. The Constitutional Court argued that the above-mentioned criteria cannot be applied if the information provided is commented on or supplemented, including its interpretation in a misleading way and context. Thus, this legal approach also protects sources in cases where the media interpret their words in the wrong context. This case also shows that due to the differing legal opinions of the district (lower) and regional (higher) courts, and ultimately of the Constitutional Court (or the ECtHR), as well as due to procedural mistakes, it can take up to 10 years to reach a final verdict.

Third, the Constitutional Court guaranteed legal immunity to information provided by the official state authorities. In the view of the Constitutional Court (finding of the CC IV. ÚS 107/2010, 28 October 2010), the publishers of the periodical press are not obliged to decide on the trustworthiness of information provided by a state authority. Otherwise, the right of the public to receive comprehensive information on issues of public interest would be denied. The Constitutional Court referred in its rulings both to previous decisions of the ECtHR and to its own rulings (namely finding of the CC III ÚS 83/01 which states that the presumption of innocence is not violated by statements that only express the situation of suspicion of commission of a criminal act by a person).

Fourth, the Constitutional Court also indirectly differentiates between tabloid and serious media, giving higher societal value to the latter. This was apparent in finding I. ÚS 155/07, when the Constitutional Court underlined the importance of the professional competencies of journalists, including their impartiality (in the sense of not giving preferential treatment to interests or rights) as well as the value of not pursuing worthless sensationalism and at the same time taking care regarding possible irreparable harm which could be caused to another person.

Fifth, the Constitutional Court also accepted the criticism of the judiciary by the media in its decision (II. ÚS 152/08) of 15 December 2009. The chairperson of the Constitutional Court stated that the Constitutional Court 'accepts the trend towards a shifting position of judges who seem to be located somewhere between politicians and common citizens'. At the same time, the chairperson of the Constitutional Court underlined that judges have severely limited opportunities to react to occasional criticism or to resist potential media pressure.

Finally, the chairperson differentiated between criticism and offence.[71] Previously, the Constitutional Court had been more balanced in its approach

---

[71] ibid 21–22.

towards freedom of speech and the media and the protection of personality. This could be seen in its ruling CC I. ÚS 67/06:

> If there is a collision between the basic political right to freedom of speech and the right to information and its dissemination on the one hand, and the right to the protection of personality on the other hand, that is between equal basic constitutional rights, it will always be an issue for independent courts, having in perspective the specifics of each particular case, to carefully balance, whether one right was not unjustifiably preferred.

There are also differences between how the impact of the press is understood compared with that of the audiovisual media. In short, audiovisual media are seen as having a potentially greater impact emotionally and within its scope as well as with respect to immediacy. This was noted in the case law of the Supreme Court and the Constitutional Court. Moreover, as mentioned business in broadcasting has been strictly regulated since the beginning, and its production is monitored by a semi-state authority or sui generis authority – the Broadcasting Board (the Board for Media Services since 2022). Formally, there was a Press Act (currently the Act on Publications) and there has been legislation that tackles audiovisual media, and, most recently, partly social media (the MSA). However, the two key rights – the protection of sources and the right to information – were identical for publishers, the wire agency and for broadcasters. One difference was that in the audiovisual legislation there was provision only for a right to correction (currently the rights are identical to those in the Act on Publications, that is a right to expression and a right to additional announcement, in addition to other rights such as a right to information in the MSA).

The Press Act (167/2008, updated in 2011, 2016, 2018 and 2019) as well as the Act on Publications (2022) formally do not mention journalists. They both stated that they addressed the rights and duties of publishers of the periodical press as well as of the wire agency (a singular) and, later on, of broadcasters (this part of the Press Act was formerly part of the Broadcasting Act), when acquiring and further disseminating information. Moreover, the Press Act defined the rights and duties of persons (legal and natural) when enforcing their rights to correction, to reply and to additional announcement in both the periodical press and via the wire agency. The Act on Publications merged the rights to correction and to reply into a right to expression, as well as keeping the right to additional announcement. However, the right to expression is defined more widely. It allows feedback not only about untruthful statements but also to correct incomplete factual statements. The right to additional announcement deals with cases such as when a person was discussed in the media as being related to criminal or similar activities and there is a final verdict by a public authority on that particular issue.

Furthermore, both Acts discuss formal 'evidence' of the periodical press as well as sanctions for breaching this law. Similarly to the previous Press Act (valid even under Communism), it stated 'the right to information' and, at the same time, the duty of public authorities (and some organisations established by law by public authorities) to provide to a publisher and wire agency, on an equal basis, truthful, timely and complete information about 'their activities' in order to keep the public informed. The law then stipulated in a footnote that there are further rights, such as those stated in the FOI Act or duties relating to the protection of classified information. The Act on Publications extended this right to news web-portals.

The next right, which has been effectively defined as a positive duty, related to the 'protection of source of information'. Again, this duty primarily applied to publishers and the wire agency, not to individual journalists. It was subsequently extended to news web-portals by the Act on Publications. However, this duty is binding for (all) employees as well as on 'other persons' according to the Act on Publications. Previously, it was valid only for those who have signed a business or civil law contract with a publisher or a wire agency 'to provide information in a professional manner'.

Thus, while theoretically anyone can claim to be a journalist, only institutionalised journalists have specific privileges and duties. In practice, however, since it is difficult to check who is an 'institutionalised' journalist, the authorities do not strictly differentiate between them. Moreover, as mentioned above the requirements of the FOI further dilute the difference between institutionalised and non-institutionalised journalists. It should also be noted that a somewhat fuzzy and relatively new condition included in the Press Act stating that '[i]nformation that could breach the rights of other persons should not be revealed by the content' was not included in the Act on Publications. Although the (old) Press Act had stipulated that the publisher or wire agency are responsible for content published, the new Act on Publications states that the publisher or provider of news on a web-portal are actually meant to be those who are editorially responsible for the content. In other words, while previously it was a top manager, currently it can be the editor-in-chief who is responsible for the content. In any case, the authors of content can be sued under civil law or even criminal law, or other law (for instance, the law that defines classified information).

Until 2019, the level of taxation on newspapers in Slovakia was among the highest in the European Union (EU). Since then, with taxation at 10 per cent, it is at the EU average level of taxation. However, in spite of the government's proposal, Parliament lowered press taxation only for daily newspapers. All other periodicals (weeklies and magazines) are taxed at a rate of 20 per cent, which is among the highest rates in the EU Member States. Slovakia is one of only two states within the EU to have two levels of taxation of the press.

As mentioned earlier, the right to reply was included in the Press Act (2008–22). There was quite a detailed procedure for this and various conditions had to be met if one wanted to apply for this right. The right to reply was defined as concerning an 'untruthful factual statement'. Between 2019 and 2022, this right could be used by public authorities again (after a decade when it had been dropped from the law). The right to correction can be applied if 'there is an untruthful, incomplete, or truth-twisting factual statement that concerns the honour, dignity, or privacy of natural person, or the name or goodwill of a legal person, on the basis of which one can correctly identify such person'. The right to an additional announcement was somewhat specific. It concerned reporting on 'factual statements' stated before the public authorities during their formal activities. In other words, if a court or the police came to a final conclusion or verdict about a specific person, that person can ask the publisher or a wire agency to publish this final conclusion or verdict. As noted earlier, this latter right has been preserved in the Act on Publications.

Darina Malová and Max Steuer conducted interesting research into the test of proportionality versus the reference to fundamental rights, namely the Constitution and the ECHR.[72] In this legal context, they compared ontological and philosophical justifications of verdicts reached by courts with their more theo-retical justifications. They found that courts or judges who referred to ontological or philosophical arguments were more likely (by a 2:3 ratio) to prefer freedom of speech. However, this was only a minority of all the cases examined. In general, only in about half of the examined cases (27 out of 60), did the courts mention the principle of proportionality. Interestingly, if a court mentioned the test or principle of proportionality, in three-quarter of the cases it decided in favour of freedom of speech. Of 60 verdicts examined, 45 referred either to the Constitution or to the ECHR. In such cases, in 71 per cent of the cases the courts decided in favour of freedom of speech while in 29 per cent it ruled in favour of the protection of personality rights. Thus, according to the authors there are two different interpre-tations of freedom of speech.

According to the first interpretation, the verdicts are supported first of all by legislation (for instance, by the Articles of the Constitution or the ECHR). This leads to the balancing of different rights. However, more criticism by the media is allowed for political speeches and statements by public figures. The principle of proportionality is applied in such cases. In the second interpretation, proportion-ality is accorded lower priority than personal rights. This type of legal reasoning is supported by the Civic Code and partially by the case law of the ECtHR. However, the supporters of this line of reasoning tend to ignore the most relevant case law of the ECtHR or Article 26 of the Constitution. This leads to the conflation of factual and value-based statements. In this line of reasoning, the principle of proportion-ality is often ignored or openly rejected. As a result, the test of proportionality is not applied. An earlier study also concluded that local courts often only formally referred to the case law of the ECtHR.[73]

There are several differences between the regulation of the press and that of broadcasting, starting from their differentiation in the Constitution. In general, broadcasting is regulated in much more detail, and is much more strictly supervised by the sui generis authority. The courts follow the ECtHR dictum that broadcast-ing has a much wider possible impact. It can be asserted that while the content of

---

[72] D Malová and M Steuer, 'Sloboda prejavu v Slovenskej republike: Analýza vybraných súdnych rozhodnutí' (2014) 4 *Právnik* 309.

[73] P Wilfling and E Kováčechová, *Sloboda prejavu a žaloby na ochranu dobrej povesti* (Pezinok, Via Iuris, 2011).

broadcasting is legally regulated heavily and in detail a priori, the content of the press tends to be legally regulated instead *post factum* (when the press breaches someone's rights) and a priori only via specific ethical rules. With the exception of the Code of Ethics of a Journalist (and the right to urgent public announcement as well as the right to protection of sources), there is no content-specific regulation of the press (for example, no requirement for impartial news coverage). Of course, the case law plays an increasingly important role here. Although formally, with the exception of EU law, there is no case law in Slovakia, in practice, the courts tend to refer in their verdicts to case law of foreign (EU case law, or usually Czech or German case law) or local origin. The rules against ownership concentration are only mentioned in the broadcasting regulation, and these, indeed, include possible mergers with printed press publishers. In such cases, the Anti-monopoly Authority can become involved.

9. Press Freedom and Platform Regulation

As mentioned above, in 2022, the Parliament passed a new and fairly lengthy Media Services Act (consisting of 184 pages), which also addressed video-sharing platform services such as YouTube. The MSA is very much territorially focused: the location of either the seat (headquarters), the localisation of an enterprise, or its domicile are seen as key principles for the inclusion of platforms under the regulations. The MSA also regards it as important whether a platform is of local origin and whether it has a 'stable and efficient' connection with the economy of the country. For general video-on-demand, 'editorial responsibility' is seen as a core regulatory principle, supplemented by the localisation either of the workforce in the territory or the use of the terrestrial or satellite capacity of the country.

The core regulatory idea is the limited editorial responsibility of video-platform providers. In general, the law laid out two partially overlapping sets of exceptions (based on the related and earlier Act on electronic commerce) under which a platform would be exempt from legal responsibility. These conditions include common sense rules such as having no previous knowledge of illegal content. If the platform was notified, removal or blocking is compulsory within five days. However, the regulator has 90 days to act. In specific cases, such as those relating to the protection of minors or the general public in cases concerning terrorism, child pornography or the endorsement of war crimes, suggested regulatory measures are stipulated to be adopted by the platform (time slot, age control, etc). These measures must be both feasible and suitable for the service provided. At the same time, no control measures or content filtering should be applied when recording. The final supervision will be guaranteed by the (formerly audiovisual media) regulator which has expanded its competencies and has changed its name. The platform will have to provide any information requested by the regulator.

In contrast to other by and large more liberal developments and ideas, there was ongoing critical discussion at the intergovernmental level throughout 2021 about the possibility of bringing criminal charges against the spreading of disinformation. After the outbreak of the Russian–Ukrainian war in early 2022, the National Security Authority used a general and vague right to block certain news web-portals (both local and foreign) without a court order. This temporary blocking was justified as being based on identified 'harmful activity' (Act on Cybersecurity No 69/2018).[74] No specific details about these harmful activities were provided. Two foreign news portals (RT and Sputnik) were blocked at the request of the NSA, following an EU-wide ban.[75] The majority of commentaries on this questioned the legality of such an action.[76] As a result, in May 2022 the National Security Authority came up with its own legal initiative, bringing more transparency and court authority to the process.[77]

10. Conclusion

The debate about the free press can be traced back to various professional participants and sources, both to the more authoritarian period (1993–98) and to the other, more liberal periods in Slovakia's recent history. Among the participants, we have identified the key stakeholders in press regulation – formally or practically these include politicians (usually advised by lawyers) who have a major ability to shape or to postpone the passing of legislation, the main organisation of journalists, and the publishers. It should be mentioned that in the early 1990s and later occasionally in the 2000s, there was also a discussion about a comprehensive media law that would merge both press and audiovisual media.[78]

Among the sources or inspiration for regulation, we can differentiate those of local and international origin, and those of a hard law and a soft law nature. With regard to the former group, local heritage, although marginal, led during a short period in the mid-1990s to rather restrictive measures for freedom of speech and of the press. In contrast, international case law, especially that of the ECtHR and CoE in general, provided more liberal inspiration. Concerning the contrast between hard law versus soft law (ethical regulation), in the final analysis, the hard law prevailed, although some aspects of ethical self-regulation have been adopted (Press and Digital Council).

---

[74] See: www.nbu.gov.sk/urad/o-urade/hybridne-hrozby-a-dezinformacie/zoznam-blokovanych-subjektov/index.html.

[75] See: www.nbu.gov.sk/2022/03/10/stopka-pre-sputnik-a-russia-today/index.html.

[76] P Šamko, 'Slovenské cúvanie z demokracie cenzúrou internetu (pójde Slovensko pri blokovaní webových stránok tureckou cestou?)' *Pravne listy* (13 March 2022), available at: www.pravnelisty.sk/clanky/a1071-slovenske-cuvanie-z-demokracie-cenzurou-internetu-pojde-slovensko-pri-blokovani-webovych-stranok-tureckou-cestou; dsl.sk/article.php?article=25911.

[77] See: zive.aktuality.sk/clanok/ojGBOYE/nbu-ma-blokovat-webovy-obsah-az-po-suhlase-sudu-co-sa-ma-zmenit-podla-chystanej-novely.

[78] M Černák, 'Podnety prípravy masmediálneho zákona a jej stručná chronológia' in *Právne a ekonomické predpoklady slobody a plurality médií* (Bratislava, Article 19, 1995).

The Constitution is seen as a liberal document, or it is interpreted as such by the Constitutional Court. In day-to-day life it is the judiciary that specifies the concrete limits of the freedom of the press and attempts to balance the fundamental rights of stakeholders. Interestingly, the judiciary does not appear to have a homogeneous approach to the freedom of the press. In general, the judiciary is highly (but selectively) influenced by the case law of the ECtHR and secondarily by the guidelines set by the Constitutional Court as well as by the Supreme Court.

Although it is true that the philosophical foundations of the press are based on the historical role of the press, this was not acknowledged directly in the Press Act but only in accompanying documents. In fact, neither the (old) Press Act nor the new Act on Publications explicitly mention journalists, but both instead focus on publishers, a wire agency and most recently on providers of news web-portals – that is, institutionalised stakeholders. Not even the professional body of journalists is mentioned there. One new term is introduced, however – 'community media'. Similarly, news web-portals have to be registered only if their content is made accessible from the territory of the state. In practice, this means that some 'alternative' news and current affairs web-portals – also based on their negative experience with the arguably unconstitutional, albeit short-lived ban by the National Security Authority – moved their registration and access to webhosting abroad. It should be mentioned that the regulation is a bit fuzzy here – it seems to include news web-portals accessible in Slovakia from abroad even if the owner lives or does business in the country.

Some attempts were made to grant a special legal status or privileges to journalists or the media in the early 1990s, and later around 2000, and then in the period around and after 2018, following the murder of the journalist Ján Kuciak, when the idea was discussed in Parliament but nothing came of it in the 2018 session. In 2021, this idea was discussed again at the level of departments (at the Ministry of Justice, based on a suggestion by the Ministry of Culture). However, a problem emerged with definition of a journalist. In addition, intergovernmental bodies discussed changes to the definition of the term 'slander'. The idea was to limit the possibility of bringing such criminal charges against journalists, or to lower the possible length of jail sentences. Similarly, while in 2021 the Ministry of Justice suggested introducing a new crime – spreading untruthful information, to be sanctioned by one to five years' imprisonment, or in extreme cases by up to eight years' imprisonment – in 2022 this idea evaporated.

Several new media regulatory laws and measures were passed in 2022, with their content sometimes seen as making the transparency of regulation even more blurred, which in some aspects were more liberal (for example, protection of sources), while in other aspects they were arguably less liberal or at least balancing rights or protecting rights according to others (right to expression, temporarily an arguably unconstitutional ban on selected alternative news portals), and in general more detailed in regulation, and cross-referenced. There is a constitutional difference between the roles, rights and duties of the press and those of broadcasters, although social media and online-only news media seem to blur this line further, as the new legislation and related public professional discussion and restrictive measures suggest.

In conclusion, media policy in Slovakia attempts to balance naturally conflicting fundamental values, both at the level of its formulation and at the level of its implementation. There is no absolute preference given to freedom of the press. Indeed, journalists and the media are usually not even mentioned in the legislation, and references to media or journalists as a cornerstone of democracy are to be found only – if at all – in accompanying documents to a draft legislation. At the same time, there have been some attempts to give more protection and support to journalists and the media in separate, exclusively legal as well as declaratory documents.

10

Press Regulation in the United Kingdom in a Changed Media Ecosystem

PETER COE

1. Introduction

Much has already been written about the state of the United Kingdom's (UK) press as an industry,[1] and how our press is, and perhaps should, be regulated. On the one hand, in his Inquiry into the Culture, Practices and Ethics of the Press Lord Justice Leveson was clear that the *regulatory ideal* for the press is independent self-regulation.[2] On the other hand, commentators such as Paul Wragg have convincingly argued that this form of regulation does not work and that it should be substituted for a mandatory regime.[3] This debate is fuelled by ongoing press malfeasance in relation to both its newsgathering and publication activities, that has caused, and continues to cause, what Leveson LJ referred to as 'real harm … to real people'.[4]

The concern of this debate has almost exclusively been the institutional press (that is, our established newspapers). This is perhaps not surprising when one considers that our newspapers have historically been the subject of regulation because of their amplification effect – in other words, their ability to 'control the message' that is received by the public. However, the dawn of the Internet and the ubiquity of social media platforms has changed all of this. This technology has permanently altered the media ecosystem by enabling citizen journalism and other forms of independent publishers to flourish. These new media actors have entered

---

[1] See, eg, DF Cairncross, *The Cairncross Review: A Sustainable Future for Journalism. Department for Digital, Culture, Media and Sport*, 12 February 2019, available at: assets.publishing.service.gov. uk/government/uploads/system/uploads/attachment_data/file/779882/021919_DCMS_Cairncross_ Review_.pdf.

[2] LJ Leveson, *An Inquiry into the Culture, Practices and Ethics of the Press: Report* (HC 780, November 2012) 1758, [4.1].

[3] P Wragg, *A Free and Regulated Press: Defending Coercive Independent Press Regulation* (Oxford, Hart Publishing, 2020).

[4] Leveson (n 2) 50, [2.2].

the media marketplace and are able to exercise their control over the message. In doing so, they are playing an increasingly important role in public discourse by creating and publishing news content and by acting as a source of news for the institutional press and wider mainstream media.[5]

What this means is that 'real harm to real people' is no longer being caused solely by our established newspapers. Citizen journalists and independent publishers are just as capable of causing the type of harm to 'real people' that was once only associated with the press industry.[6] Therefore, any satisfactory regulatory solution must surely be one which extends to the institutional press *and* this new breed of journalist. Indeed, in his Inquiry, Leveson LJ himself was of the view that it is 'abundantly clear that, for a regulatory regime to be effective, it must be capable of delivering any perceived benefits to online publication as much as to print'[7] and that membership of a regulatory body 'should be open to all publishers on fair, reasonable and non-discriminatory terms, including making membership potentially available on different terms for different publishers'.[8] Yet, despite these statements, perhaps rather shortsightedly, his Inquiry was exclusively concerned with the established printed press.[9]

The purpose of this chapter is not to rehearse the arguments that have already been made about the state of UK press regulation in respect of the institutional press. This has already been covered eloquently and comprehensively by other commentators.[10] Rather, I intend to consider press regulation within the context of the media ecosystem that has been created by the Internet. To this end I begin the

---

[5] See generally, P Coe, *Media Freedom in the Age of Citizen Journalism* (Cheltenham, Edward Elgar, 2021).

[6] Indeed, the Alliance of Independent Press Councils of Europe has, until relatively recently, only been concerned with the institutional printed press. In recent years, however, its remit has been widened to cover online iterations of the press and citizen journalists. This is because, according to the Alliance, complaints made by the public against citizen journalists for alleged breaches of journalistic ethical standards to its Councils have increased rapidly. See A Hulin, 'Citizen Journalism and News Blogs: Why Media Councils don't Care (yet)' (*LSE*, 14 June 2016), available at: blogs.lse.ac.uk/medialse/2016/06/14/citizen-journalism-and-news-blogs-why-media-councils-dont-care-yet.

[7] Leveson (n 2) 1587, [2.9].

[8] ibid 1761, [4.13].

[9] ibid; LJ Leveson's Inquiry did no more than 'observe' the ascendance of citizen journalism (see 168, [4.3]–[4.4], 173, [5.2] respectively). Although it may be defensible that his Inquiry was limited in this way, as the institutional press were the 'wrongdoers' in the context within which he was reporting, arguably his regulatory solution to press malfeasance ought to have recognised the increasing influence that citizen journalists are having on the public sphere and what this means for the future of press regulation.

[10] eg, see the body of work by Wragg, including *A Free and Regulated Press* (n 3); P Wragg, 'The Legitimacy of Press Regulation' (2015) April *Public Law* 290; P Wragg, 'Leveson's Vision for Press Reform: One Year On' (2014) 19 *Communications Law* 6; P Wragg, 'Time to End the Tyranny: Leveson and the Failure of the Fourth Estate' (2013) 18 *Communications Law* 12; the work of Hacked Off: hackinginquiry.org/; and the work of Lara Fielden, including L Fielden, *Regulating the Press: A Comparative Study of International Press Councils* (Oxford, Reuters Institute for the Study of Journalism, 2012), available at: reutersinstitute.politics.ox.ac.uk/sites/default/files/2017-11/Regulating%20the%20Press.pdf.

chapter with a discussion on the concept of press freedom. In setting out its justifi-cations and its normative bases, which in the UK largely derive from the European Court of Human Rights' (ECtHR, Strasbourg Court) interpretation of Article 10(1) of the Convention for the Protection of Human Rights and Fundamental Freedoms (European Convention on Human Rights, ECHR), I consider how it protects the press, and what is expected of the press in return for this protection. In essence, I suggest that the press is not fulfilling its side of the *bargain*, which has contrib-uted to press malfeasance and the need for effective regulation. The problem, I go on to say, is that the current regulatory regime is not satisfactory for the institu-tional press, let alone independent and citizen journalism. Although the problems I identify in this chapter are perhaps obvious, I recognise that a solution is not. I suggest that although a mandatory regime may work for the institutional press, it is not suitable for citizen journalists. Bearing this, and the deficiencies of the current voluntary self-regulatory regime in mind, what, then, is the alterna-tive? In my view, as I explain at the end of the chapter, an overhauled voluntary self-regulatory scheme may provide *some* of the answers.

2. Press Freedom

2.1. Justifying Press Freedom

The concept of press freedom is founded on the notion that as 'the Fourth Estate' the primary function of the press is to act as a 'public watchdog',[11] in that it operates as the general public's 'eyes and ears' by investigating and reporting abuses of power.[12] Thus, pursuant to the liberal theory of the media, the press is free and independent; it is committed to the discovery and reporting of truth, the advancement of knowledge and, ultimately, to strengthening democracy.[13] This liberal ideal is reflected in the observations made by Leveson LJ in his Inquiry that in recent years the press has played a critical role in informing the public on matters of public interest and concern.[14] The Inquiry cites a number of examples of valuable public interest journalism, relating to a wide variety of stories, submitted by Associated Newspapers Limited,[15] *The Guardian,*

---

[11] *The Observer and The Guardian v the United Kingdom* (1992) 14 EHRR 153, [59].

[12] *Attorney-General v Guardian Newspapers Ltd (No 2)* [1990] 1 AC 109, 183 (Sir John Donaldson MR); see also, E Barendt, *Freedom of Speech* 2nd edn (Oxford, Oxford University Press, 2005) 418; D Weiss, 'Journalism and Theories of the Press' in S Littlejohn and K Foss (eds), *Encyclopedia of Communication Theory*, Vol 2 (New York, SAGE, 2009) 577.

[13] J Charney, *The Illusion of the Free Press* (Oxford, Hart Publishing, 2018) 3.

[14] Leveson (n 2) 451–55.

[15] Associated Newspapers Limited has been known as DMG Media since 2013. It publishes the *Daily Mail, Mail on Sunday, MailOnline, Metro* and *Metro.co.uk*. DMG Media is part of the Daily Mail and General Trust plc (DMGT). In November 2019, DMGT purchased JPI Media Publications Limited and, in doing so, the '*i*' newspaper. The takeover was cleared by the UK government in March 2020.

Northern & Shell,[16] *The Sun, The Times* and *Sunday Times* and *The Telegraph.*[17] This type of journalism, that is driven by a commitment to professionalism and the public interest, is undoubtedly adopted and replicated by the press and its journalists around the world and has led to the communication of some of the most important stories of our time.[18]

In much the same way, citizen journalists and independent publishers are playing their part in disseminating vitally important information, thereby often stepping into the watchdog shoes of the institutional press.[19] They too, through their reporting, continue to have a positive impact on the public sphere. Although their contribution to public discourse can relate to any story or context, arguably it is most obvious in conflict or crisis situations that present significant dangers and/or accessibility challenges to the institutional press. In recent years these journalists have provided vital 'on-the-ground' coverage of, for instance, the spread of Covid-19 in Wuhan (and how the rising number of cases was being concealed to the rest of the world by the Chinese government), the Arab Spring Uprising, the Iraq conflict,[20] and, most recently, Russia's invasion of Ukraine. Thus, the value of the press, in so far as it plays a critical role in free speech and democracy by engaging in this type of activity, is undeniable. In turn, this 'value' is, understandably, used in political and legal commentary, and by the press themselves, to justify press freedom.[21]

2.2. The Concept of Press Freedom: What is its Normative Basis? What does this Freedom Cost the Press? And what is the Press Free to do?[22]

Press freedom, and more broadly media freedom, is mentioned explicitly in a variety of international treaties and domestic laws. For example, pursuant to Article 11(2) of the Charter of the Fundamental Rights of the European Union

---

[16] Northern & Shell published the *Daily Express, Sunday Express, Daily Star* and *Daily Star Sunday*, and the magazines *OK!, New!* and *Star* until these were sold to Trinity Mirror in February 2018. Northern & Shell also owned three entertainment television channels: Channel 5, 5* and 5USA until 2015.

[17] eg, amongst others, these stories include the *Daily Mail's* Stephen Lawrence campaign; *The Sunday Times'* Thalidomide Campaign against Distillers; and its investigation that exposed corruption in the FIFA voting process for determining which nation will host the football World Cup. See Leveson (n 2) 455–70.

[18] Coe, *Media Freedom* (n 5) 18. For examples from the US, see the Pulitzer Prize winners at: www.pulitzer.org/prize-winners-by-year. For further examples from the UK, see *The Cairncross Review* (n 1) 19.

[19] Coe, *Media Freedom* (n 5) 93.

[20] ibid 3–7.

[21] See Wragg, *A Free and Regulated Press* (n 3) ch 1.

[22] For more detailed discussion on the extent of the protection afforded to the press and wider media by the concept of press (and media) freedom, see Coe, *Media Freedom* (n 5) 103–22; D Tambini, *Media Freedom* (Cambridge, Polity Press, 2021) ch 2.

(CFR),[23] 'freedom and pluralism of the media shall be respected'.[24] Similarly, in the United States (US), the First Amendment states that '[c]ongress shall make no law ... abridging the freedom of speech, or of the press'.[25] Within a UK context, the normative basis for press freedom is now, largely, drawn from Article 10(1) of the ECHR, and its protection of *freedom of expression*.[26]

As you will note if you look at Article 10(1), unlike, for instance, the CFR and the First Amendment to the US Constitution, it does not explicitly provide for the protection of press (or media) freedom[27] in distinction to that of private individuals and non-media institutions. Rather, in interpreting Article 10(1) the ECtHR has attached great importance to the role of the press (and wider media),[28] and in doing so its jurisprudence has clearly established the press's contribution to democracy,[29] and its 'role of public watchdog'.[30] Indeed, its case law recognises a duty on the press to 'contribute to public debate'[31] by conveying information and ideas on political issues and public interest,[32] and the right of the public to receive this information.[33] As a consequence of this, the ECtHR affords the press preferential treatment, in that it interprets Article 10(1) to contain privileged protection of the press even in the absence of express provisions to that effect.[34] It has even

[23] The Charter was initially solemnly proclaimed at the Nice European Council on 7 December 2000. At that time, it did not have any binding legal effect. However, on 1 December 2009, with the entry into force of the Treaty of Lisbon, the Charter became legally binding on the EU institutions and on national governments: ec.europa.eu/justice/fundamental-rights/charter/index_en.htm.

[24] Art 5(1)2 of the German Basic Law provides a separate provision for the specific protection of media expression, thus creating a clear distinction with free expression guarantees for private individuals: 'Freedom of the press and freedom of reporting by means of broadcasts and films shall be guaranteed'; Art 21(2) of the Italian Constitution, Art 25(1) of the Belgian Constitution and the media clauses in Art 17 of the Swiss Constitution, the Swedish Constitution Freedom of the Press Act, Law of 29 July 29 1881 on the Freedom of Press (French Press Freedom Law). See generally, J Oster, 'Theory and Doctrine of 'Media Freedom' as a Legal Concept' (2013) 5 *Journal of Media Law* 57, 59; Barendt (n 12) 417–19.

[25] However, despite a specific free press clause, the US position is very different from the ECHR jurisprudence of the ECtHR; see below (n 30).

[26] The concept of press freedom was recognised in UK courts long before the introduction of the Human Rights Act 1998 and its incorporation of the ECHR into domestic case law; see above (nn 11 and 12).

[27] This also applies to Art 19 of the United Nations International Covenant on Civil and Political Rights and Art 13 of the American Convention on Human Rights.

[28] See, eg, *Bladet Tromsø and Stensaas v Norway* (2000) 29 EHRR 125, [59]; *Bergens Tidende v Norway* (2001) 31 EHRR 16, [48]; *Busuioc v Moldova* (2006) 42 EHRR 14, [64]–[65]; *Jersild v Denmark* (1995) 19 EHRR 1; *Janowski v Poland (No 1)* (2000) 29 EHRR 705, [32].

[29] See, eg, *Perna v Italy* (2004) 39 EHRR 28.

[30] *The Observer and The Guardian* (n 11) [59]; *Goodwin v the United Kingdom* (1996) 22 EHRR 123, [39]; *Thorgeirson v Iceland* (1992) 14 EHRR 843, [63]; *Bladet Tromsø* (n 28) [62].

[31] *Wojtas-Kaleta v Poland* [2009] App no 20436/02, [46].

[32] ibid. *Thorgeirson v Iceland* (n 30); *Lingens v Austria* (1986) 8 EHRR 103, [26]; *Oberschlick v Austria (No 1)* (1991) 19 EHRR 389, [58]; *Castells v Spain* (1992) 14 EHRR 445, [43]; *Jersild v Denmark* (1995) 19 EHRR 1 [31].

[33] *The Sunday Times v the United Kingdom* (1979) 2 EHRR 245, [65]; *Fressoz and Roire v France* (2001) 31 EHRR 2, [51]; *Bergens Tidende* (n 28) [52].

[34] See, eg, *Busuioc* (n 28); *Wojtas-Kaleta* (n 31); *Vejdeland and Others v Sweden* [2012] ECHR 242. For analysis of these cases, see Coe, *Media Freedom* (n 5) 98–99. For a detailed discussion on the

said, in *Thorgeirson v Iceland*,[35] that '[r]egard must therefore be had to the pre-eminent role of the press in a State governed by the rule of law'.[36] Thus, pursuant to its jurisprudence, and unlike the dominant position in the US,[37] press freedom is *special* (and distinct from that of freedom of expression) because a journalist or newspaper is, as Jan Oster explains, 'governed by a different set of factors concerning the scope and intensity of protection when preparing, editing or issuing a publication, compared to freedom of expression afforded to private individuals or non-media entities'.[38] Therefore, the fact that a statement can be classed as media expression, as opposed to expression by a private individual or non-media institution, adds to the burden of justifying its restrictions.[39]

Vejdeland and Others v Sweden[40] provides an illustration of how the Court elevates press (and media) freedom above personal freedom of expression.[41] The applicants, who were not associated with the press, had been convicted for distributing homophobic leaflets in a secondary school. The ECtHR unanimously held that there was no violation of Article 10, whilst in a concurring opinion, Judge Zupančič observed: 'If exactly the same words and phrases were to be used in public newspapers ... they would probably not be considered a matter for criminal prosecution and condemnation'.[42] On this interpretation it follows that the special protection afforded to media expression permits the use of wide discretion as to the methods and techniques adopted to report on matters, and how that material is subsequently presented.[43] Moreover, it allows the media to have recourse to exaggeration and even provocation,[44] including the use of strong terminology

---

arguments relating to whether press (and media) freedom is distinct to that of freedom of expression, see Coe, *Media Freedom* (n 5) 96–103, 123–26; Barendt (n 12) 419–24.

[35] (1992) 14 EHRR 843.

[36] ibid [63].

[37] Although beyond the scope of this chapter, it is worthy of note here that despite commentators such as Justice Potter Stewart, Melvin Nimmer, Randall Bezanson, Floyd Abrams, Vincent Blasi and Sonja West, and dissenting Supreme Court judgments, arguing that the specific free press clause 'or of the press' in the First Amendment to the US Constitution creates a similar distinction between press freedom and personal freedom of expression from that recognised by the ECtHR, this claim has been opposed by commentators such as Eugene Volokh, and resisted by the Supreme Court. For detailed commentary on this (and the views of the commentators and the Supreme Court), see Coe, *Media Freedom* (n 5) 96–103, 123–26; Barendt (n 12) 419–24.

[38] Oster (n 24) 59. However, see below (nn 41 and 65).

[39] ibid.

[40] *Vejdeland* (n 34) 242.

[41] See also, eg, *Busuioc* (n 28); *Wojtas-Kaleta* (n 31). Although this is perhaps the dominant view that comes from the Strasbourg Court's jurisprudence, it is not the *only* view; eg, in *Magyar Helsinki Bizottság v Hungary*, App no 18030/11, judgment of 18 November 2018, [168], although the Court made explicit reference to the watchdog function of the press, it was clear that a right to access to information does not apply exclusively to the press. From the UK, see *AG v Observer Ltd* (1990) 1 AC 109, 201. See also below (n 65) and Wragg, *A Free and Regulated Press* (n 3) chs 3 and 4.

[42] *Vejdeland* (n 34) [12].

[43] *Jersild v Denmark* (1995) 19 EHRR 1 [31]; *Bladet Tromsø* (n 28) [63]; *Bergens Tidende* (n 28) [57].

[44] *Prager and Oberschlick v Austria* (1995) 21 EHRR 1, [38]; *Thoma v Luxembourg* (2003) 36 EHRR 21, [45]–[46]; R Clayton and H Tomlinson, *Privacy and Freedom of Expression*, 2nd edn (Oxford, Oxford University Press, 2010) 271 [15.254].

or polemic formulations.[45] Additionally, the ECtHR has held that this protection extends beyond the dissemination of the journalist's or media organisation's own opinions, to encapsulate those expressed by third parties in the context of, for example, interviews.[46]

The ambit of press freedom is not just limited to stronger protection for press speech; instead it extends to rights that are not, in any way, available pursuant to freedom of expression guarantees. Consequently, press freedom and freedom of expression differ in relation to the intensity of the protection they offer, and in respect of the scope of the protected action. This position equates to institutional protection of the media that, in turn, guarantees rights that are not exclusively concerned with expression; it extends to the press's and wider media's newsgathering or editorial activities,[47] and even to the existence of an independent media.[48] This institutional protection afforded to the press can be categorised as being both defensive, in that it protects the media against interference by the state, and positive, as it entitles the media to state protection.[49]

In relation to the defensive category, undoubtedly effective journalism is dependent upon the use of sources, who tend to be insiders working in or associated with the subject matter of the publication, to provide the most effective information.[50] Accordingly, case law from the ECtHR and the UK is clear that a fundamental tenet of press freedom is the protection of journalistic sources, because '[w]ithout such protection, sources may be deterred from assisting the press in informing the public on matters of public interest'.[51]

---

[45] *Thorgeirson v Iceland* (n 30) [67]; *Oberschlick v Austria (No 2)* (1998) 25 EHRR 357, [33]; Oster (n 24) 59.

[46] *Jersild v Denmark* (1995) 19 EHRR 1.

[47] Editorial freedom has been consistently recognised as a fundamental element of the right to freedom of expression, and the enhanced right to media freedom, pursuant to Art 10 ECHR (eg, see *Melnychuk v Ukraine* [2005] App no 28743/03, decision of 5 July 2005, 6; *Manole and Others v Moldova*, App no 13936/02, judgment of 17 September 2009, [98]; *Centro Europa 7 SRL and Di Stefano v Italy*, App no 38433/09, judgment of 7 June 2012, [133]). Furthermore, it has been held by the ECtHR, and in the UK, that editorial judgement allows the press to determine the technique of reporting adopted and the form in which the ideas and information are conveyed. From the ECtHR, see *Jersild v Denmark* [1994] App no 15890/89, [31]; *News Verlags GmbH & Co KG v Austria* (2000) 31 EHRR 246, [39]. From the UK, see *Flood v Times Newspapers Ltd* [2012] UKSC 11 Lord Mance [132], [170] and Lord Dyson [194], [199]; [2010] EWCA Civ 804 (Moore-Bick LJ) [100]; *Re Guardian News and Media Ltd* [2010] AC 697 (Lord Rodger) [63]; *In re British Broadcasting Corporation* [2010] 1 AC 145 (Lord Hope of Craighead) [25]; *Jameel and Others v Wall Street Journal Europe Sprl* [2006] UKHL 44 (Lord Hoffman) [51]; *Campbell v Mirror Group Newspapers Ltd* [2004] 2 AC 457 (Lord Hoffman) [59].

[48] *Manole* (n 47) [98]; *Centro Europa* (n 47) [133]; Oster (n 24) 60.

[49] Oster (n 24) 60.

[50] Coe, *Media Freedom* (n 5) 116.

[51] *Goodwin v United Kingdom* [1996] App no 17488/90, [39]. See also (from the ECtHR): *Roemen and Schmit v Luxembourg* [2003] App no 51772/99, [57]; *Cumpǎnǎ and Mazǎre v Romania* [2004] App no 33348/96, [106]; *Radio Twist as v Slovakia* [2006] App no 62202/00, [62]; *Voskuil v the Netherlands* [2007] App no 64752/01, [65]; *Tillack v Belgium* [2007] App no 20477/05, [53]; *Financial Times Ltd and Others v the United Kingdom* [2009] App no 821/03, [59]; *Sanoma Uitgevers BV v the Netherlands* [2010] App no 38224/03, [50]; *Nagla v Latvia* [2013] App no 73469/10. From the UK, see *Ashworth Hospital Authority v MGN Ltd* [2002] 4 All ER 193.

As Lord Denning observed in *Attorney-General v Mulholland and Foster*,[52] the journalist 'can expose wrong-doing and neglect of duty which would otherwise go unremedied ... the mouths of his informants will be closed to him if it is known that their identity will be disclosed'.[53] The importance of this protection is illustrated by the fact that the Strasbourg Court has consistently held that journalistic rights pursuant to press freedom are interfered with by virtue of the very existence of an order to disclose a source's identity, regardless of whether or not the order is actually enforced.[54] Furthermore, if the sole or predominant purpose of the search of press or media premises and the seizure of journalistic material is to identify sources, then the search and seizure are in direct conflict with the right to press (and media) freedom, as they have 'an intolerable chilling effect on journalistic work and may also deter informants from providing information that they are only willing to provide confidentially'.[55] Indeed, the Strasbourg Court has held that the mere threat to search media premises causes a 'chilling effect' and is, prima facie, irreconcilable with media freedom.[56]

This defensive protection afforded by press freedom extends further than source protection: its beneficiaries are protected against unjustified interferences with activities related to all forms of newsgathering. Thus, in *Társaság a Szabadságjogokért v Hungary*,[57] the ECtHR stated that 'the law cannot allow arbitrary restrictions which may become a form of indirect censorship should the authorities create obstacles to the gathering of information, [which] is an essential and preparatory step in journalism and ... an inherent, protected part of press freedom'.[58] And in *Halis Dogan and Others v Turkey*, the Court found that press freedom includes the protection of the newspaper distribution infrastructure.[59] It has also been held that journalists cannot be made to give evidence concerning

---

[52] *Attorney-General v Mulholland and Foster* [1963] 2 QB 477.

[53] ibid 489.

[54] *Financial Times Ltd* (n 51) [56]; *Sanoma Uitgevers BV* (n 51) [50]; *Roemen and Schmit* (n 51) [57]; *Telegraaf Media Nederland Landelijke Media BV and Others v the Netherlands* [2012] App no 39315/06 [127]. See also the House of Lords case of *British Steel Corporation v Granada Television Ltd* [1981] 1 All ER 417.

[55] Oster (n 24) 54.

[56] *Sanoma* (n 51) [71].

[57] *Társaság a Szabadságjogokért TASZ) v Hungary* [2009] App no 37374/05, [27].

[58] ibid. It is important to note that Társaság a Szabadságjogokért is a non-governmental organisation. According to the ECtHR, [27]: 'The function of the press includes the creation of forums for public debate. However, the realisation of this function is not limited to the media or professional journalists. In the present case, the preparation of the forum of public debate was conducted by a nongovernmental organisation. The purpose of the applicant's activities can therefore be said to have been an essential element of informed public debate. The Court has repeatedly recognised civil society's important contribution to the discussion of public affairs ... The applicant is an association involved in human rights litigation with various objectives, including the protection of freedom of information. It may therefore be characterised, like the press, as a social "watchdog" ... In these circumstances, the Court is satisfied that its activities warrant similar Convention protection to that afforded to the press'.

[59] *Halis Dogan and Others v Turkey* [200] App no 50693/99, [24]. See also, *Gsell v Switzerland* [2009] App no 12675/05, [49].

confidential information or sources, even if it has been obtained illegally.[60] They are also exempt from certain data protection and copyright provisions.[61] With regard to the positive category, states are required to protect journalists from acts of violence in the course of their work,[62] and from undue influence by financially powerful groups[63] or the government.[64]

2.3. The Deal-Breaking Press?

On the face of it the ECtHR's *deal* for the press is straightforward: in exchange for the press fulfilling a public watchdog role by contributing to discourse on matters of public interest, and by acting ethically and in accordance with the tenets of responsible journalism, the Court provides the press, through its interpretation of Article 10(1), and its concept of press freedom, with enhanced protections distinct from those provided to individuals by the right to freedom of expression. The press's side of this *bargain* has been consistently articulated by the Strasbourg Court as a 'duty', or its 'duties and responsibilities'.[65] For instance, in *Axel Springer v Germany* it said:[66] 'The press plays an essential role in a democratic society … [I]ts duty is … to impart – in a manner consistent with its obligations and responsibilities – information and ideas on all matters of public interest'.[67] Not only does the press have the task of imparting such information and ideas; the public also has a right to receive them. Were it otherwise, the press would be unable to play its vital role of 'public watchdog'.[68] And in *Bladet Tromsø and Stensaas v Norway*[69] it held:

> By reason of the 'duties and responsibilities' inherent in the exercise of the freedom of expression, the safeguard afforded by Article 10 to journalists in relation to reporting on issues of general interest is subject to the proviso that they are acting in good faith in order to provide accurate and reliable information in accordance with the ethics of journalism.[70]

---

[60] *Goodwin v United Kingdom* (1996) 22 EHRR 123, [39]; *Radio Twist as v Slovakia* [2006] ECHR 1129, [62]; *Sanoma* (n 51) [50].

[61] See, eg, Art 85 of the General Data Protection Regulation and sch 2(5)(26) of the Data Protection Act 2018. See also, Art 9 Data Protection Directive 95/46/EC [1995] OJ L281/31; Art 5(3)(c) Copyright Directive 2001/29/EC [2001] OJ L167/10, 19.

[62] *Ozgur Gundem v Turkey* [2000] ECHR 104, [38 ff].

[63] Art 21(4)(2) EC Merger Regulation 139/2004 [2004] OJ L24/1; Part 5(2) Communications Act 2003 c 21.

[64] *Manole* (n 47) [109]; *Centro Europa* (n 47) [133].

[65] This duty-right construct that runs through Strasbourg jurisprudence is not without its critics. Chiefly among them is Wragg, who provides an excellent counter argument to this dominant jurisprudential narrative. Indeed, as Wragg acknowledges, even the ECtHR has, by virtue of some of its own jurisprudence, undermined it. See (n 41) and Wragg, *A Free and Regulated Press* (n 3) 85–95.

[66] *Axel Springer v Germany* [2012] EMLR 15.

[67] ibid [43].

[68] ibid [79]. See also, *De Haes and Gijsels v Belgium* [1998] 25 EHRR 1, [39].

[69] *Bladet Tromsø* (n 28).

[70] ibid [65]. See also, *Bédat v Switzerland* (2106) 63 EHRR 15, [50].

This principle resonates in press regulatory codes across Europe,[71] and in the UK, in his Inquiry, Leveson LJ based his explicit reference to the 'duty of the press to hold power to account'[72] on the Strasbourg Court's jurisprudence.[73] Yet despite this, although as demonstrated by the examples in section 2.1 above, there are journalists and newspapers engaging in high quality public interest journalism, certain sections of the press, it seems, choose to ignore, or perhaps (because of the perilous financial state of much of the industry) must ignore, its side of the press freedom bargain.[74] History tells us that the power associated with the privileged position that the press enjoys is very often abused, for reasons such as financial gain, political leverage, or ideological advancement.[75] Indeed, an increasing number of newspapers are choosing to engage in and publish lucrative clickbait, rather than reporting on matters of public concern.[76] This has led to a number of commentators arguing that the press's public watchdog role gradually diminished towards the end of the twentieth century as its focus shifted onto commercially viable, and often self-serving, stories.[77] Moreover, newspaper ownership, and the power derived from it, and the expectations placed on the modern mass media (including newspapers) such as the need for 24-hour news coverage,[78] means that

[71] eg, as Wragg explains, the Danish Pressenævnet refers to the press's duty 'to publish information correctly and promptly'. The word duty is also used in the respective codes of conduct of Austria's Österreichischer Presserat, Norway's Pressens Faglige Utvalg, the Press Council of Ireland, the German Deutscher Presserat, and Belgium's and the Nederlands' Raad voor de Journalistiek. The Swedish Allänhetens Pressombudman justifies the obligations it imposes on the press by reason of 'the role played by the mass media in society and the trust of the public of these media'. The Belgian Raad voor de Journalistiek refers to 'the public's right to know the truth' (which is similarly used by the Finnish Julkisen Sanan Neuvosto). See Wragg, *A Free and Regulated Press* (n 3) 85.

[72] Leveson (n 2) 1495, [8.7]. The re-drafted IMPRESS Standards Code and Guidance (at page 2) says that '[i]t has been developed to enable those regulated by IMPRESS to produce high-quality journalism in the public interest'. The guidance to Clause 5 ([5.12]) makes explicit reference to the press's 'watchdog role'. In contrast, the IPSO Editors' Code of Practice does not refer to press duties or the watchdog role of the press. See section 3 below for detailed discussion of IMPRESS and IPSO and the UK's regulatory system.

[73] ibid 1848, [2.18]; 1863, [2.71]; 1884, [3.104].

[74] See Coe, *Media Freedom* (n 5) chs 1 and 2.

[75] ibid 178.

[76] Numerous examples are provided in Leveson (n 2) 539–91.

[77] See, eg, T Aalberg and J Curran (eds), *How Media Inform Democracy: A Comparative Approach* (London, Routledge, 2012); C Calvert and M Torres, 'Putting the Shock Value in First Amendment Jurisprudence: When Freedom for the Citizen-Journalist Watchdog Trumps the Right of Informational Privacy on the Internet' (2020) 13 *Vanderbilt Journal of Entertainment and Technology Law* 323, 341; J Curran and J Seaton, *Power Without Responsibility: Press, Broadcasting and the Internet in Britain* 7th edn (London, Routledge, 2010) 96–98; T Gibbons, 'Building Trust in Press Regulation: Obstacles and Opportunities' (2013) 5 *Journal of Media Law* 202, 214; T Gibbons, 'Freedom of the Press: Ownership and Editorial Values' [1992] *Public Law* 279, 296; T Gibbons, 'Conceptions of the Press and the Functions of Regulation' (2016) 22(5) *Convergence: The International Journal of Research into New Media Technologies* 484, 485; R McChesney, *Rich Media, Poor Democracy Communication Politics in Dubious Times* (Champaign, IL, University of Illinois Press, 1999) 275; A Kenyon, 'Assuming Free Speech' (2014) 77 *Modern Law Review* 379, 387–91.

[78] Gibbons, 'Building Trust in Press Regulation' (n 77) 214.

there is a constant conflict between the press's watchdog role, or gatekeeper, and commercial reality.[79] It has been observed that during the twentieth and twenty-first centuries investigative journalism has been negatively affected by an increased concentration of newspaper ownership,[80] which is now vested in a relatively small number of wealthy individuals or large and powerful companies,[81] and the commercial pressures imposed by this corporate ownership model,[82] that has in turn resulted in the proliferation of 'churnalism'[83] – the recycling of news from other sources by journalists.[84]

Undoubtedly, this situation that the press industry finds itself in contributes to press malfeasance which, as I explained in the Introduction to this chapter, Leveson LJ acknowledged in his Inquiry causes 'real harm to real people'.[85] By this he meant that press abuses not only affect a small minority, such as celebrities, sportsmen and women, or politicians, but also ordinary people. These people do not tend to have the financial resources required to fund litigation, nor do they have access to lawyers or reputation management and public relations advisers to help them respond to and spin negative stories.[86] Accordingly, as Wragg observes, 'these are people that the press become fascinated with, often briefly, and whose lives are destroyed or irrevocably damaged for reasons of titillation, curiosity or prurience'. Consequently, he says, these victims alone are reason enough to seek a satisfactory regulatory solution to the problem.[87]

This brings me on to following section, in which I explain three things: first, the rationale and theory behind the UK's voluntary self-regulatory system; second, why the UK's current regime does not offer an adequate solution to the challenges posed by ongoing press malfeasance, and why it is ill-suited for regulating modern journalism; and third, why mandatory regulation is not a viable alternative, at least for regulating citizen journalists.

---

[79] CE Baker, *Human Liberty and Freedom of Speech* (Oxford, Oxford University Press, 1989) 250.

[80] Gibbons, 'Freedom of the Press' (n 77) 286; SL Carter, 'Technology, Democracy, and the Manipulation of Consent' (1983–84) 93 *Yale Law Journal* 581, 600–07; P Garry, 'The First Amendment and Freedom of the Press: A Revised Approach to the Marketplace of Ideas Concept' (1989) 72 *Marquette Law Review* 187, 189; OM Fiss, 'Free Speech and Social Structure' (1985) 71 *Iowa Law Review* 1405, 1415. See also Leveson LJ's assessment of the commercial pressures on the press, Leveson (n 2) 93–98; Media Reform Coalition, *Who Owns the UK Media?* (12 March 2019).

[81] P Thomas, 'Media Democracy' in S Littlejohn and K Foss (eds), *Encyclopedia of Communication Theory*, Vol 2 (New York, SAGE, 2009) 628; Media Reform Coalition, *Who Owns the UK Media?* (n 80). Media ownership and the impact that the dominant proprietor and corporate ownership models have had on press freedom are discussed in detail in Coe, *Media Freedom* (n 5) ch 2.

[82] N Fenton, 'Regulation is Freedom: Phone Hacking, Press Regulation and the Leveson Inquiry – The Story So Far' (2018) 23(3) *Communications Law* 118, 119.

[83] See generally, N Davies, *Flat Earth News* (New York, Vintage Books, 2009).

[84] See generally, Coe, *Media Freedom* (n 5) for a discussion on the symbiotic relationship that now exists between 'traditional' institutional journalists and citizen journalists.

[85] Leveson (n 2) 50, [2.2]. See also Wragg, *A Free and Regulated Press* (n 3) 60–61.

[86] Wragg, *A Free and Regulated Press* (n 3) 60–61.

[87] ibid 61.

3. Press Regulation in the United Kingdom

3.1. Voluntary Self-Regulation: A Brief History of Libertarianism versus Social Responsibility

Voluntary self-regulation as we know it today is underpinned by social responsibility theory.[88] The origins of this theory can be found in the work of William Hocking,[89] and two reports published on either side of the Atlantic Ocean in the 1940s: the Royal Commission on the Press in the UK,[90] and the Hutchins Commission on Freedom of the Press in the US.[91] Both reports were born out of diminishing faith in libertarianism's optimistic notion that its self-righting process[92] carried efficacious 'built-in correctives' for the press. This disillusionment gave rise to an extreme anti-libertarian movement, grounded in paternalism, that resulted in increased pressure on the UK and US governments to regulate the press.[93]

Ultimately, in the US, because the Hutchins Commission feared that the imposition of compulsory regulation could act as a catalyst for official control of the press,[94] it was clear in its report that the press should regulate itself.[95] However, it left the door ajar for government intervention in press practices by stating: 'Without intruding on press activities ... government may act to improve the conditions under which they take place so that the public interest is better served'.[96] It went on to say that any such laws or preventions should be permissive rather than restrictive, in that they should not be 'subtractions from freedom' but rather a 'means of increasing freedom, through removing impediments to the practice and repute of the honest press'.[97] Thus, the upshot of the Commission's adoption of social

---

[88] See section 3.2 below.

[89] WE Hocking, *Freedom of the Press: A Framework of Principle* (Chicago, IL, University of Chicago Press, 1947).

[90] *Royal Commission on the Press, 1947–1949, Report* (Cmnd 7700).

[91] *The Commission on Freedom of the Press, A Free and Responsible Press* (Chicago, IL, University of Chicago Press, 1947).

[92] This process underpins libertarianism. It was laid down in the sixteenth century by John Milton in *Areopagitica*. The process dictates that everyone should be free to express themselves and, ultimately: 'The true and sound will survive; the false and unsound will be vanquished. Government should keep out of the battle and not weigh the odds in [favour] of one side or the other. And even though the false may gain a temporary victory, that which is true, by drawing to its [defence] additional forces, will through the self-righting process ultimately survive'. See F Siebert, T Peterson and W Schramm, *Four Theories of the Press: The Authoritarian, Libertarian, Social Responsibility, and Soviet Communist Concepts of what the Press should Be and Do* (Urbana, IL, University of Illinois Press, 1956) 45.

[93] ibid 77.

[94] See generally, D Davis, 'News and Politics' in D Swanson and D Nimmo (eds), *New Directions in Political Communication* (New York, SAGE, 1990); J McIntyre, 'Repositioning a Landmark: The Hutchins Commission and Freedom of the Press' (1987) 4 *Critical Studies in Mass Communication* 95.

[95] *The Commission on Freedom of the Press* (n 91) 126.

[96] ibid 127. In making this recommendation the Commission drew on the work of Hocking (n 89).

[97] *The Commission on Freedom of the Press* (n 91) 127–28.

responsibility theory was its formulation of a compromise between libertarian ideology and paternalism. This compromise was founded on faith placed in the press by the Commission's members, who emphasised that the press needed to refocus its efforts on serving the public which would 'obviate governmental action to enforce' its public responsibility through regulation.[98]

In the UK, this faith placed in the press to *do the right thing*, and a dogmatic resistance to anything other than voluntary self-regulation as a means to prevent state control of the press, has run consistently through government policy from 1949, when the Royal Commission on the Press presented its findings, right up to the recommendations made by Leveson LJ at the conclusion of his Inquiry and the present day.[99] The result of the first government inquiry was the creation of the Press Council, whose primary function

> should be to safeguard the freedom of the Press; to encourage the growth of the sense of public responsibility and public service amongst all engaged in the profession of journalism; ... and to further the efficiency of the profession and the well-being of those who practice in it.[100]

If we fast forward to the publication of Leveson LJ's Inquiry in 2012, the same sentiments come through in his ideal outcome for the press: 'What is required is independent self-regulation. By far the best solution to press standards would be a body, established and organised by the industry, which would provide genuinely independent and effective regulation of its members and would be durable'.[101]

Unfortunately, despite the commendable rationale that underpins the idea of voluntary self-regulation of the press, a devotion by successive UK governments to a blunt and self-serving version of the system (more on this in the following section) represents nothing more than an idealistic *hope* that the press will fulfil its side of the press freedom bargain; a hope that has been, and continues to be, consistently undermined by the behaviour of the press and its ongoing malfeasance.[102] Thus, in the final section of this chapter I will set out my ideas for a regulatory scheme that, although draws on social responsibility theory and operates within a voluntary and approved self-regulatory model, differs significantly from the current regime. However, before considering this 'solution' I will explain the state of press regulation in the UK today, and why it is not fit for purpose.

---

[98] ibid 91.

[99] Coe, *Media Freedom* (n 5) 159.

[100] *The Royal Commission, Report* (n 90) ch XI, [683]–[684].

[101] Leveson (n 2) 1758, [4.1]. As Wragg observes, this 'sanguinity' has not just been found in either public inquiries (Wragg, *A Free and Regulated Press* (n 3) 66). eg, in 2012, Lord Chief Justice Igor Judge endorsed the idea that self-regulation is the 'only' way to ensure independence from government. See Lord Judge, 'Press Regulation', 13th Annual Justice Lecture (19 October 2011).

[102] Coe, *Media Freedom* (n 5) 159. For examples of recent 'press harm', see Press Recognition Panel, Annual Report on the Recognition System, 10 February 2022, available at: pressrecognitionpanel.org. uk/wp-content/uploads/2022/02/Annual-Recognition-Report-Feb-2022-FEB-For-web.pdf, ch 6.

3.2. An Overview of Regulation in the United Kingdom Today

As I have alluded to in the previous section, among the key recommendations made by Leveson LJ in his Inquiry was the creation of a system of voluntary self-regulation that is 'genuinely independent' from the government and the press industry.[103] In the words of the Press Recognition Panel (PRP), Leveson LJ 'proposed a genuinely independent and effective system of self-regulation, with processes in place to ensure that regulators met the minimum required levels of independence and effectiveness'.[104] As a result, the Royal Charter on Self-Regulation of the Press (Royal Charter) was granted on 30 October 2013,[105] which subsequently created the PRP,[106] a body corporate empowered to approve press regulators that meet the conditions set out in the Recognition Criteria pursuant to Schedule 3 of the Charter. In line with Leveson LJ's recommendation for genuine independence from the government and the press industry, Schedule 3(1) prescribes that an

> independent self-regulatory body should be governed by an independent Board. In order to ensure the independence of the body, the Chair and members of the Board must be appointed in a genuinely open, transparent and independent way, without any influence from industry or Government.[107]

As things currently stand, the UK has two press regulators: the Independent Press Standards Organisation (IPSO) and IMPRESS. Of the two regulators, IMPRESS is the only one approved by the PRP and therefore regarded as being 'Leveson-compliant'.[108] It has the power to fine members who breach its Code, and it offers an arbitration service that settles disputes without the need for litigation. IPSO has the power to fine,[109] but it has yet to exercise that power,[110] much to the

---

[103] Leveson (n 2) 1758, [4.1]. However, although he was clear he was not recommending it at the time, Leveson LJ did leave open the possibility of a statutory backstop regulator being established by the government if self-regulation failed, Leveson (n 2) 1758, [3.34]–[3.35].

[104] Press Recognition Panel, Annual Report (2022) 7. Pursuant to sch 4(1) of the Royal Charter on Self-Regulation of the Press a 'regulator' means 'an independent body formed by or on behalf of relevant publishers for the purpose of conducting regulatory activities in relation to their publications'.

[105] ibid.

[106] The Press Recognition Panel came into existence on 3 November 2014.

[107] Pursuant to Paragraph 2, the Chair of the Board must be nominated by an appointment panel that must also be independent of government and industry. Paragraph 3 sets out the composition requirements for the Panel, including that a substantial majority of the members are 'demonstrably independent' of the press. Paragraph 5 prescribes the composition of the Board, according to which the majority of the members should be independent of the press, it should not include any serving editor, and members must be independent of government and politics.

[108] IMPRESS was recognised by the Press Recognition Panel as the first 'Leveson-compliant' independent press regulator on 25 October 2016, see: www.impress.press/about-us/faq.html.

[109] See: www.ipso.co.uk/monitoring/standards-investigations.

[110] Indeed, IPSO's annual reports of 2015 to 2020 show that it has not yet even launched a 'standards investigation' – the process that would lead to the imposition of a fine. The reports are available at: www.ipso.co.uk/monitoring/annual-reports.

frustration of commentators given the press's ongoing tendency for malfeasance.[111] Common to both schemes is their reliance on members of the press to voluntarily join them.

3.3. Why is the System Problematic?

IPSO's apparent lack of desire to fine its members aside, why, then, is this system problematic? First, despite the voluntary self-regulatory nature of IMPRESS and IPSO, there is a framework in place for a more incentivised, and arguably more coercive, regime. In light of Leveson LJ's recommendations to 'encourage' press membership of a regulator approved by the PRP (which, as I have said above, is currently IMPRESS), section 34 of the Crime and Courts Act 2013 enables a court to award exemplary damages against any 'relevant publisher'[112] in litigation who is *not* a member of 'an approved regulator'. Among the requirements for approved status that are prescribed by the Royal Charter is that the regulator will have a low-cost arbitration system to reduce legal costs for both claimants and the press.[113] Section 40 *could* be at the core of this 'costs incentives regime' as it empowers the court to award adverse costs against non-members of an 'approved regulator' by forcing the 'relevant publisher' to pay the claimant's legal costs even if the publisher is successful in defending the claim, subject to certain exceptions.[114] However, section 40 has not been enacted, and is likely to be repealed, meaning that Leveson LJ's recommendations have only been partially implemented.[115]

Consequently, as stated in the PRP's latest Annual Report on the Recognition System, the approved regulation system is frustrated by political involvement in that section 40 is dormant and remains unenforceable until it is activated by

---

[111] Wragg, *A Free and Regulated Press* (n 3) 261–62; Paul Magrath, 'Bob the Builder: Can IPSO Fix It?' (*Inforrm*, 8 November 2018), available at: inforrm.org/2018/11/08/bob-the-builder-can-ipso-fix-it-paul-magrath; Brian Cathcart, 'Manchester United, the Sun and that complaint to the "press regulator" IPSO' (*Inforrm*, 11 February 2020), available at: inforrm.org/2020/02/11/manchester-united-the-sun-and-that-complaint-to-the-press-regulator-ipso-brian-cathcart/; Brian Cathcart, 'IPSO: The Toothless Puppet Rolls over for its masters (again)' (*Inforrm*, 26 October 2018), available at: inforrm.org/2018/10/26/ipso-the-toothless-puppet-rolls-over-for-its-masters-again-brian-cathcart/; Brian Cathcart, 'Sam Allardyce, the Telegraph and another IPSO failure' (*Inforrm*, 3 September 2018), available at: inforrm.org/2018/09/03/sam-allardyce-the-telegraph-and-another-ipso-failure-brian-cathcart.

[112] Section 41 sets out what is meant by 'relevant publisher'. This is qualified by sch 15 which excludes certain persons and organisations from this definition and, therefore, from the ambit of Sections 34 to 42. The scope of Section 41 is discussed below.

[113] Royal Charter (nn 104 and 105) sch 3, [22].

[114] These exceptions are dealt with below.

[115] At the time of writing, on 10 May 2022, the annual Queen's Speech to the House of Commons revealed a number of legislative changes that will affect the UK media, including the Media Bill. If enacted in its current form the Bill will repeal s 40. See Queen's Speech 2022: Background briefing notes, 10 May 2022, available at: /www.gov.uk/government/publications/queens-speech-2022-background-briefing-notes, 41–42.

the Secretary of State for Digital, Culture, Media and Sport,[116] which as I have explained is unlikely in light of the government's recently announced proposals to repeal it.[117] The effect of this is that it renders approved regulation a blunt instrument as it disincentivises membership of an approved regulatory scheme and it ultimately, and fundamentally, undermines its purpose, thereby effectively inverting approved regulation into a self-serving system.[118] As the PRP states, not only has this contributed to a large number of significant publishers choosing not to join IMPRESS, it can also have serious implications for the press and the public:

> The failure to commence Section 40 also means there are limited incentives to encourage publishers to sign up to the recognition system and no low-cost way for the public to raise legal complaints against the vast majority of news publishers … the absence of Section 40 means there is limited incentive in place for people bringing complaints against its member publishers to use IMPRESS's arbitration scheme to settle disputes. This maintains the chilling effect on free speech (which Section 40 would remove) as it means that even IMPRESS publishers may still have to defend costly libel actions through the courts rather than through IMPRESS's arbitration process.[119]

Furthermore, the PRP argues that the fact the recognition system is (at least at the time of writing) in a state of limbo has, paradoxically, maintained a political presence within press regulation; a situation that undermines a self-regulatory system and Leveson LJ's recommendation that politicians should not be involved in press regulation, other than in legislating for a 'backstop' regulator.[120] In the view of the PRP '[f]ull implementation of the recognition system would safeguard against ongoing political interference'.[121]

Secondly, citizen journalists rarely join the various regulatory schemes that exist across Europe.[122] Indeed, in his Inquiry, Leveson LJ acknowledged that technological changes in the past few decades have led to a fragmentation of the media (and its audience), as it has introduced new actors, such as citizen journalists, who do not tend to engage with voluntary regulation.[123] He states that the Internet is an 'ethical vacuum … [that] does not claim to operate by express ethical standards, so that bloggers and others may, if they choose, act with impunity'[124] and, specifically, '[b]logs and other such websites are entirely unregulated'.[125] Consequently regulators, such as IPSO and IMPRESS, that can only deal with complaints against

---

[116] Press Recognition Panel (n 104) 8–9, ch 5.
[117] See above (n 97).
[118] Coe, *Media Freedom* (n 5) 268.
[119] Press Recognition Panel (n 104) 19.
[120] Coe, *Media Freedom* (n 5) 268; see Leveson (n 2) 1758, [3.34]–[3.35].
[121] Press Recognition Panel (n 104) 19.
[122] Hulin (n 6).
[123] Leveson (n 2) 165–66, [3.7]–[3.8].
[124] ibid 736, [3.2].
[125] ibid 171, [4.20].

their members, are hamstrung when it comes to investigating complaints against non-members.[126]

In the UK, this issue has not been helped by IPSO's Code of Practice[127] and the Crime and Courts Act 2013. In respect of IPSO, which as explained above is not a PRP-approved regulator, citizen journalists are only covered by its Code if they submit material to the publishers that it regulates.[128] This requirement would seem to exclude most citizen journalists as the very nature of citizen journalism dictates an inherent tendency to eschew the mainstream media, including members of the institutional press that make up the bulk of IPSO's membership.[129]

As explained above, sections 34 and 40 of the 2013 Act apply to any 'relevant publisher'. According to section 41(1) a 'relevant publisher' is a person who, in the course of a business,[130] publishes news-related material that is written by different authors and is subject to editorial control. Section 41(2) tells us that this means that a person, who does not have to be the publisher, has editorial or equivalent responsibility for the content and presentation of the material, and the decision to publish it. Crucially, section 41 has the potential to exclude a large number of citizen journalists for two reasons. By definition, many citizen journalists are not publishing news-related material 'in the course of a business'. Moreover, citizen journalists tend to be both the author and publisher of their material, as opposed to publishing material 'written by different authors'.[131] Thus, the Act's definition of 'relevant publisher' is fundamentally flawed, and seems to go against Leveson LJ's view that greater press regulation is required to prevent 'real harm caused to real people', and that membership of a regulatory body 'should be open to all publishers … including making membership potentially available on different terms for different publishers'.[132] This situation therefore begs two (currently unanswered) questions: first, why should a member of the institutional press, whether it publishes material in print, or online, be captured by sections 34 and 40 (if it were enacted), yet a citizen journalist, by virtue of not publishing in the course of a business, and being both the author and publisher of the material, not be? Second, surely, a citizen journalist who is gathering and publishing news should be eligible to join the same regulatory scheme(s), albeit perhaps on 'different terms', as a member of the institutional press?[133]

---

[126] Coe, *Media Freedom* (n 5) 269. eg, the Austrian and Dutch Councils and the French and Flemish Councils in Belgium will investigate complaints about any media content, regardless of the publisher. Norway's Council has recently enacted a rule change to enable it to deal with complaints against non-members.

[127] Although the same cannot be said for IMPRESS' Code which does cover citizen journalists.

[128] See: www.ipso.co.uk/faqs/editors-code.

[129] Coe, *Media Freedom* (n 5) 269. See also: www.ipso.co.uk/complain/who-ipso-regulates.

[130] Whether or not carried on with a view to make a profit.

[131] Coe, *Media Freedom* (n 5) 269–70.

[132] ibid; Leveson (n 2) 1761, [4.13].

[133] Coe, *Media Freedom* (n 5) 269–70.

3.4. Why is Mandatory Regulation Not a Solution for Citizen Journalists?

As I said in the Introduction above, Wragg has convincingly argued for mandatory regulation of the institutional press.[134] He gives three reasons why this form of regulation would offer better protection for individuals. First, although the 'market' provides adequate protection of rights against press malfeasance, via causes of action such as defamation, misuse of private information, and data protection law, it still fails most ordinary people. This is because 'accessing' this market is 'significantly curtailed' by the financial costs (and let us not forgot the emotional and mental toll) involved in pursuing these claims; especially against members of the institutional press who benefit from a well-stocked armoury of lawyers, and an ability, through their publications, to control narratives to their advantage. As Wragg says,

> in the UK ... we can point to a broad range of legal measures, but none of that is any comfort to the press victim who simply cannot afford to pursue a legal action ... [M]edia law is a luxury that very few can afford.[135]

Rather, he says that regulation offers a solution by providing inexpensive and fast complaints handling (which he also argues should be supplemented by the regulator being given the power to award compensation),[136] and an arbitration service to settle disputes without the need to involve the courts.[137]

The second reason relates to the first and is something I have already alluded to: in addition to the financial burden of bringing a claim, all litigation, relating to any cause of action, against any defendant, can be emotionally and mentally draining. Arguably however this 'cost' is exacerbated when suing members of the institutional press because of their ability to control the message, both during and after litigation, through their outlets, and because the would-be claimant risks 'painting a target on their back'.[138] In Wragg's opinion regulation could alleviate this burden, through not only the faster and more efficient resolution of complaints but primarily because it creates 'a barrier between the victim and the oppressor', chiefly by the regulator having the power to initiate claims against publishers of its own volition, which 'presents an opportunity for victims to be shielded from the press's bullying behaviour'.[139] The final reason he advances relates to the second. Regulation makes press wrongdoing transparent in a way that litigation cannot. It does this because the market relies on individuals 'championing' their own individual rights to hold malfeasance to account.

---

[134] Wragg, *A Free and Regulated Press* (n 3) ch 9.
[135] ibid 279–80.
[136] ibid ch 9.
[137] ibid 280.
[138] ibid. This issue was also acknowledged by Leveson LJ in his Inquiry, see Leveson (n 2) 481, [2.39]–[2.40], 516–17, [4.35], 704–09.
[139] Wragg, *A Free and Regulated Press* (n 3) 281.

These individuals, therefore, are not able to come together as a 'homogenous mass' to tackle press wrongdoing. Because of the inequality of arms between them and the press they are often isolated and easily picked-off by a would-be defendant in a far superior bargaining position. This means that the success of an individual's claim often comes down to their 'resolve and capacity to ensure the stultifying effect of the defendant's litigation strategy' rather than the merits of their claim. Consequently, these individual claims are often settled before trial, so the public is unaware of the wrongdoing, and/or they are portrayed by the press as isolated incidents, rather than systemic abuses (if that is the case). Thus, in Wragg's view, regulation provides the only means of holding this power wielded by the press to account, because, unlike individuals, it is not susceptible to the same pressures, and it cannot be 'bought off'.[140]

Despite these valid arguments, as I have previously explained in my book, *Media Freedom in the Age of Citizen Journalism*, there are practical reasons why mandatory regulation is not a viable alternative to voluntary self-regulation for *citizen journalists*, which I will summarise here.[141] First, Wragg suggests that mandatory regulation should be created by legislation that would 'determine the field of members'.[142] With the institutional press, identifying those members would be easily achievable by virtue of their corporate status. To the contrary, the same cannot be said for citizen journalists because: (i) citizen journalists do not tend to operate 'in the course of a business', therefore they are not identifiable as corporate entities; and (ii) the sheer number of citizen journalists operating at any one time, and the transient nature of citizen journalism, in that they may dip in and out of journalism, and may publish in an irregular or ad hoc manner, would arguably make it impossible for a regulator to implement a system of regulation that takes regulation *to* the subject (in other words, imposes mandatory regulation on the citizen journalist), and is able to monitor their journalistic activity.

Secondly, if citizen journalists perceive regulation as being restrictive by virtue of it being forced upon them they are less likely to engage with it, regardless of whether it is mandatory, and irrespective of whether it is, in fact, permissive and beneficial. Of course, the same argument could be made in respect of institutional journalists. However, for the reasons discussed in the previous paragraph, unlike institutional journalists that are readily identifiable, enforcing mandatory regulation on citizen journalists would be at best extremely difficult, and at worst impossible. The combination of these two factors may lead to many citizen journalists falling through the cracks of regulation as it would encourage them to participate in 'underground' and unregulated journalism. This would be detrimental to both the public, in that it would further limit the protection they have

---

[140] ibid. 282.
[141] For more detailed analysis of this, see Coe, *Media Freedom* (n 5) 270–73.
[142] Wragg, *A Free and Regulated Press* (n 3) 256.

against the malfeasance of citizen journalists, and citizen journalists themselves, as they would be denied the opportunity to engage with regulation that, contrary to their perception, may be empowering. Taking this argument a step further, this is a situation that could negatively impact public discourse. If citizen journalists feel forced to participate in journalism that avoids regulation then, because of the 'risks' associated with practising journalism in this way (I am thinking here, predominantly, of the risk of liability for participating in journalism whilst not being a member of a mandatory scheme) this, in itself, is likely to reduce the number of citizen journalists and therefore the voices that are able to contribute to the public sphere. It could also impact upon the quality of their journalism, by virtue of them not being able to take advantage of the beneficial services provided by a regulator, or simply because they cannot conduct their journalistic activities in the same way, and using similar resources, as their regulated (and 'legal') counterparts. A combination of these factors is likely to limit the size of the audience that journalism undertaken in this way can reach. Of course, others may be discouraged entirely from participating in public discourse for fear of being subjected to forced regulation.[143]

4. (Desperately) Seeking a Regulatory Solution

In the previous sections I hope I have made three things clear: first, putting our trust in the press to fulfil its side of the press freedom bargain is idealistic. Ongoing press malfeasance serves as a clear reminder of the need for regulation. Secondly, despite this need for regulation, the current version of the UK's voluntary self-regulatory system does not work (and arguably never has worked) and is certainly not appropriate for citizen journalists. As Wragg has said,

> the twenty-first century press shows no remorse for not only decades of public distrust but also, moreover, the shame, in the strongest sense, arising from the litany of unethical – and illegal – practices that Leveson uncovered in his inquiry. Quite obviously, reliance solely upon self-directed, ethical decision-making is a poor means of improving press standards.[144]

Thirdly, therefore, we need to find a suitable regulatory solution. Mandatory regulation may work for the institutional press, but it does not work for citizen journalists. Because this new type of journalist now plays such an important role in the gathering and publication of news in the UK (and, I would argue, worldwide), any regulatory 'solution' must, as Leveson LJ acknowledged (and I have already referred to), extend to 'all publishers',[145] including citizen journalists.

---

[143] Coe, *Media Freedom* (n 5) 271–72.
[144] Quoted by Coe, ibid 65.
[145] Leveson (n 2) 1587, [2.9], 1761, [4.13].

I have previously advanced a blueprint for a 'reimagined', and robust, approved self-regulatory framework that addresses the question of how citizen journalists could be regulated alongside their institutional counterparts.[146] This framework has been finessed by my involvement with IMPRESS, and my work with the regulator in re-drafting its Standards Code and Guidance.[147] Setting out this scheme in totality is beyond the scope of this chapter. Rather, in the following section I have provided a sketch of its core principles.[148]

4.1. Voluntary Approved Self-Regulation: Version 3.0

4.1.1. *Influence from Other Jurisdictions*

This modified scheme of regulation is informed by reviews, recommendations and regulatory schemes from other countries. It draws on Lara Fielden's extensive *Comparative Study of International Press Councils*,[149] and it pays close attention to three wide-ranging reviews of the press from Australia (the Australian government's Finkelstein Report)[150] and New Zealand (the New Zealand Law Commission's Report),[151] as they have, to varying degrees, considered the impact of online news publishers, including citizen journalists, on their respective regulatory frameworks, whilst taking into account Leveson LJ's recommendations in his Inquiry.

4.1.2. *Eligibility*

In advancing this reimagined regulatory scheme, I rely on a new conceptual foundation for the media that I call the media-as-a-constitutional-component concept.[152] This concept adopts a functional, as opposed to institutional, approach to defining media, as it focuses on the functions that are performed by media actors, as opposed to their inherent characteristics. In essence, it determines that adherence to certain norms of public discourse (in other words the *type* of speech

---

[146] Coe, *Media Freedom* (n 5) ch 9.

[147] At the time of writing, the public consultation on the re-drafted Code and Guidance had just closed: www.impress.press/page/code-consultation.html.

[148] For a detailed explanation of the scheme, see Coe, *Media Freedom* (n 5) ch 9.

[149] Fielden (n 10).

[150] The Finkelstein Report and the Convergence Review are reviews of Australia's media and its regulatory framework. Both were published by the Australian government in 2012: Australian Government, *The Report of the Independent Inquiry into the Media and Media Regulation*, 28 February 2012 (Finkelstein Report); *Convergence Review* (Final Report to the Minister for Broadband, Communications and the Digital Economy, Sydney, 2012).

[151] New Zealand Law Commission, *The News Media Meets 'New Media' Rights Responsibilities and Regulation in the Digital Age. March 2013, Report 128* (NZLC).

[152] Coe, *Media Freedom* (n 5); P Coe, 'Redefining "Media" Using a "Media-as-a-constitutional-component" Concept: An Evaluation of the Need for the European Court of Human Rights to Alter its Understanding of "Media" Within a New Media Landscape' (2017) 37 *Legal Studies* 25.

conveyed by the actor) and standards of professional behaviour (for example, acting ethically and in good faith, and publishing content that is based on appropriate research to verify the provenance of it and its sources), rather than the education, training or employment of the actor, can help to identify who is a 'journalist', and therefore who should benefit from the enhanced right to press freedom and be subject to its concomitant duties and responsibilities. Thus, pursuant to this concept press freedom can apply to any actor that conforms to the definition, which is: (i) a natural and legal person; (ii) engaged in the process of gathering information of public concern, interest and significance; (iii) with the intention, and for the purpose of, disseminating this information to a section of the public; and (iv) whilst complying with objective standards governing the research, news-gathering and editorial process.[153]

The Finkelstein Report and the New Zealand Law Commission recommended that their proposed models of regulation should only apply when publication is regular and, in the case of the Finkelstein Report, meets threshold figures. To my mind, this is over exclusive. Actors can fulfil the definition of media that I have advanced, and make a valuable contribution to the public sphere, on one-off occasions or on an ad hoc basis.[154] Significantly, this can be the case within a citizen journalism context, in which valuable contributions to public discourse can be made intermittently, and via different platforms. Thus, an individual can be acting as media, and therefore be subject to the right to press freedom and its duties and responsibilities, even if they are publishing on an irregular basis.

A further recommendation made by the New Zealand Law Commission is that any actor wishing to join its regulatory scheme must be willing to comply with its code of practice, complaints process and any subsequent rulings.[155] The regulatory scheme that I propose would adopt a similar expectation in that it too would require its members to adhere to, and be accountable to, a standards code. This raises three questions: first, because citizen journalists are not necessarily socialised into the norms of professional journalism, should they be subject to the same law and regulation as their institutional counterparts? Secondly, should citizen journalists be subject to the same or similar duties and responsibilities as the institutional press? The functional rather than institutional definition of the press I have set out above determines that the answer to these questions is 'yes', albeit that when law or regulation is applied the nature of citizen journalism should be taken into account.[156] Any actor fulfilling the definition of media under the

---

[153] Coe, *Media Freedom* (n 5) 281.

[154] *Editions Plon v France*, App no 58148/00, judgment of 18 May 2004, [43]; *Lindon, Otchakovsky-Laurens and July v France*, App nos 21279/02 and 36448/02, judgment of 22 October 2007, [47].

[155] New Zealand Law Commission (n 151) 182, [7.121].

[156] To a large extent, this accords with the Court of Appeal's judgment in *Economou v de Freitas* [2018] EWCA Civ 2591; [2019] EMLR 7 in respect of the application of the Defamation Act 2013 s 4 defence of 'publication on a matter of public interest'. The judgment, and its implications for citizen journalists, is discussed in Coe, *Media Freedom* (n 5) ch 8, s 3.2.2.

media-as-a-constitutional-component concept's definition would be expected to adhere to the same standards, or duties and responsibilities, including the same standards code, regardless of whether they are a citizen journalist or a member of the institutional press.

This leads to the final question: because they should be subject to the same law and regulation as institutional journalists, should the nature of citizen journalism, and the needs of citizen journalists, at least be considered for the purposes of implementing regulation? In respect of the practical operation of a standards code my answer to this question is 'yes'. To encourage participation in the regulatory scheme the standards need to be applicable and accessible to citizen journalists. Significantly, this does not mean that they should be subject to *different* standards from institutional journalists, or that they need to be. Rather, and quite simply, the standards should be accompanied by clear guidance on their application to citizen journalists who are predominantly operating in an online environment. Taking the modified IMPRESS Standards Code (which as I have said, is currently subject to public consultation)[157] as an example, it provides significant contextual guidance on each Code clause, and the nuances associated with each clause, and on aspects of journalistic practice that citizen journalists may not be immediately familiar with.[158]

4.1.3. Incentivising Membership

In respect of statutory incentives, my reimagined scheme contains incentives similar to sections 34 and 40 of the Crime and Courts Act 2013.[159] However, the issues associated with these provisions would be remedied, as they would: (i) (in the case of section 40) be enacted and operational; and (ii) unlike the 2013 Act, apply to citizen journalists, as they would capture actors that are operating as the author and publisher of material and those that are not publishing in the course of a business, in the same way as those that are.

As I said have alluded to throughout this chapter, the concern of regulation is protecting the public from 'real harm' being caused to 'real people'. Yet, incidentally, the quality of discourse within the public sphere can be improved, and journalists themselves can, to an extent, be shielded from liability, and even empowered, by virtue of the non-statutory incentives, or 'services' offered by a regulatory scheme.[160] Thus, my scheme proposes a number of such incentives, or services, as follows:[161]

(1) The Cairncross Review has recommended the introduction of a government innovation fund to develop new approaches and tools to improve the supply

---

[157] See above (n 147).
[158] For further analysis of these issues, see Coe, *Media Freedom* (n 5) ch 9, s 6.2.2.
[159] See section 3.2 and section 3.3 above.
[160] Coe, *Media Freedom* (n 5) 291.
[161] ibid. These are explained in detail at 291–93, but are summarised here.

of public interest news. It also recommends the introduction of new forms of tax relief, including extending zero-rated VAT to digital newspapers and magazine, as well as digital only publications.[162] This scheme would take this one step further, in that members could access public funding for publications adhering to its standards code.[163]

(2)   A mediation service would be accessible to both complainants and members of the scheme to encourage the cost-effective and efficient settlement of cases which may otherwise proceed to court.

(3)   Members would be able to access training,[164] education resources, law and policy updates, and advice to help them to develop their journalistic practice, apply for funding, understand and to comply with the scheme's standards code and, for instance, to provide them with a requisite level of knowledge to report appropriately on court proceedings (and therefore to avoid allegations of contempt of court). This incentive would also help them to meet, for instance, the statutory requirements of Defamation Act 2013 defences, and to comply with data protection law. This incentive would be particularly attractive to citizen journalists who are unlikely to have had any 'formal' journalistic or legal training or have access to a legal team. Although not a complete shield, access to training, education and advice is likely to reduce members' risk of liability. At the same time, a member's engagement with these incentives indicates to the public that they are making every effort to operate professionally and within the law, and in doing so that they are trying to insulate themselves from unnecessary litigation risks, which leads on to the following incentive.

(4)   Membership of this scheme would provide reputational, or brand, advantages. It would demonstrate to the outside world that members are journalists that place a high value on, and have bound themselves to act, responsibly. It says that they will abide by the scheme's standards of professional behaviour and norms of discourse and are, ultimately, prepared to be accountable for their actions. Something akin to a 'kitemark' could be awarded to members to enable them to demonstrate membership of, and compliance with, the scheme's standards code. This will also enable anonymous actors to advertise their membership without having to be named.

(5)   Many citizen journalists choose to operate anonymously or pseudonymously.[165] To encourage membership of the scheme from these actors, and to ensure they can continue to publish in this way, it would 'protect' their anonymity and pseudonymity so long as they adhered to its standards. This 'protection' would manifest in different ways. For instance,

---

[162] *The Cairncross Review* (n 1) 90–102.

[163] A similar recommendation was made by the New Zealand Law Commission (n 151) 181, [7.115]–[7.117].

[164] T Gibbons, 'Conceptions of the Press' (n 77) 487.

[165] P Coe, 'Anonymity and Pseudonymity: Free Speech's Problem Children' (2018) 22(2) *Media & Arts Law Review* 173.

these journalists would not be named (or their pseudonym would be used) on the regulator's website and in correspondence, briefings or reports etc, and it would extend to any proceedings relating to alleged breaches of its code. Only in extreme cases, such as in the event of criminal conduct, would the actors be named.[166] This means that not only can anonymous and pseudonymous citizen journalists join the scheme and take advantage of its incentives, safe in the knowledge that their identities are protected, but the audience will know that these actors are members of a scheme committed to responsible journalism by virtue of the award of a kitemark.

4.1.4. *The Regulator: Powers and Sanctions*

The regulator with oversight of the scheme would have the power to impose sanctions on members for breaches of its code. These include the issuing of fines and/or requirements to: (i) publish an adverse decision in the publication concerned, with the regulator having the power to determine its prominence and positioning (including the placement on a website and the period for which it will be displayed); (ii) take down specified material from a website; (iii) correct incorrect material; (iv) grant a right of reply to a person; and (v) publish an apology, with the regulator having the power to direct its prominence and positioning. In exceptional cases the regulator would have the power to suspend or terminate the membership.[167]

5. Conclusion

In the above, I have explained the current status of the approved voluntary self-regulatory system in the UK, and why I think it needs to be overhauled. My starting point is that I do not think that approved voluntary self-regulation is a lost cause. Far from it. If we accept that most (although certainly not all) members of the press cannot be trusted to *do the right thing* and fulfil their side of the press freedom bargain, and if our government and our press regulators are prepared to reimagine a voluntary self-regulatory system with more 'teeth', and that is adaptable to our changed media ecosystem, I firmly believe that we can repair what is so evidently broken. The scheme that I have summarised in the preceding section could regulate members of the institutional press and citizen journalists without compromising the right to freedom of expression and the enhanced right to

---

[166] DK Citron, *Hate Crimes in Cyberspace* (Cambridge, MA, Harvard University Press, 2014) 239.
[167] For further analysis, and for consideration of non-members, see Coe, *Media Freedom* (n 5) 293–95.

press freedom.[168] However, despite this optimism that a workable regulatory solution is possible, I am forced to end this chapter on a pessimistic note. The UK government's continued reluctance to enact section 40, and its recently published, and it must be said, unsurprising intention to repeal it, provides further evidence that unfortunately ours is a government that remains in the thrall of our institutional press. And for that reason, despite the possibilities and the benefits that regulation could bring to bear on the institutional press, citizen and independent journalists and, perhaps most importantly, us as ordinary members of the public, a scheme of regulation that would meaningfully discourage, and could intervene in, press malfeasance, and ultimately help to protect the public and public discourse, is a long way away.

---

[168] By sketching the contours of this scheme I have undoubtedly created new questions that are beyond the scope of this chapter to answer, but are nevertheless vitally important for any potential regulator to consider, eg, it leaves open questions relating to how these non-statutory incentives, or services, could be offered: does the regulator have the expertise, resources and capacity to offer these services, or would they need to be contracted to a third party? Either way, would this expose the regulator to liability and, if so, how would this risk be managed? The composition of the standards code, and its contextualisation for citizen journalists also need to be determined. Indeed, these questions, amongst others, have been considered by IMPRESS in its recent Code and Guidance re-drafting exercise. See above (n 147).

11

The Press Freedom Jurisprudence of the European Court of Human Rights

JAN OSTER

1. Introduction

The European Court of Human Rights (ECtHR, Strasbourg Court) can rightly be regarded as a 'norm entrepreneur', not only for press and media freedom but also for freedom of expression in general: with its jurisprudence, the Court has significantly contributed to the development of pan-European standards and the extent to which these standards have been internalised by national actors and institutions.[1] Moreover, the ECtHR engages in a constant 'judicial dialogue' with international courts and tribunals from within and outside Europe in which the courts mutually inspire each other.[2] Finally, the Strasbourg Court has had a significant influence on the development of human rights protection in the European Union (EU) and – even after the entering into force of the Charter of Fundamental Rights of the Euroepan Union (CFR) – is frequently referred to by the Court of Justice of the European Union in Luxembourg.[3]

---

[1] J Oster, 'On "Balancing" and "Social Watchdogs": The European Court of Human Rights as a Norm Entrepreneur for Freedom of Expression' in LC Bollinger and A Callamard (eds), *Regardless of Frontiers: Global Freedom of Expression in a Troubled World* (New York, Columbia University Press, 2021); on the concept of norm entrepreneurship, see M Finnemore and K Sikkink, 'International Norm Dynamics and Political Change' (1998) 52 *International Organization* 887.

[2] *Satakunnan Markkinapörssi Oy and Satamedia Oy v Finland* [2017] App no 931/13, [150]; *Stoll v Switzerland* [2007] App no 69698/01, [111] and *Magyar Helsinki Bizottság v Hungary* [2016] App no 18030/11, [146], referring to the IACtHR; in turn, see the following references to the ECtHR: IACtHR, *Ivcher-Bronstein v Peru* [2001] Case no 11.762, [152]; *Herrera-Ulloa v Costa Rica* [2004] Case no 12.367, [113] and [126]; AfCtHR, *Alex Thomas v United Republic of Tanzania* [2015] App no 005/2013, [97]; *Wilfred Onyango Nganyi & 9 Others v United Republic of Tanzania* [2016] App no 006/2013, [136].

[3] See, eg, C-288/89 [1991] *Stichting Collectieve Antennevoorziening Gouda and Others v Commissariaat voor de Media*, [23]; C-260/89 [1991] *ERT v DEP and Others*, [41]; C-23/93 [1994] *TV 10 SA v Commissariaat voor de Media*, [24]; C-368/95 [1997] *Familiapress v Heinrich Bauer Verlag*, [25]–[26].

At the same time, the Court's potential for norm entrepreneurship has limits. International human rights conventions, such as the Council of Europe's Convention for the Protection of Human Rights and Fundamental Freedoms (European Convention on Human Rights, ECHR), are subsidiary to the national protection of human rights. This means that the Convention States are initially responsible for securing human rights, and the ECtHR's task is limited to reviewing under the ECHR the decisions domestic authorities have taken.[4] As a consequence, the Strasbourg Court exercises some self-restraint if the domestic authorities seem to be in a better position to assess the factual or normative circumstances of a case, for example, in cases involving alleged threats to national security[5] or cases in which morals are at stake.[6] A narrow margin of appreciation therefore leads to a higher degree of harmonisation of norms on a pan-European level; a broad margin of appreciation maintains national fragmentations. In particular, the margin of appreciation is limited where restrictions on speech relating to a matter of public concern are at issue.[7] In any case, the exercise of the Convention States' discretion goes 'hand in hand' with the Court's scrutiny.[8] Yet the consistency of this margin of appreciation doctrine is not beyond reproach.[9]

Decisions from Strasbourg have an effect beyond the individual case at hand. The Convention States – and not only the Convention State that was the defendant in a particular case – have had to readjust their standards of balancing freedom of expression, press and media freedom with conflicting rights. This has led partly to stronger freedom of expression protection,[10] and partly to stronger protection of conflicting rights, in particular the right to respect for private live in Article 8 of the ECHR with its sub-categories of privacy and reputation.[11]

---

[4] ECHR, Art 35(1); *Handyside v the United Kingdom* [1976] App no 5493/72 [49]; *The Sunday Times v the United Kingdom (No 1)* [1979] App no 6538/74, [59].

[5] cp *Sürek v Turkey (No 1)* [1999] App no 26682/95, [61]; *Şener v Turkey* [2000] App no 26680/95, [40]; *Erdoğdu v Turkey* [2000] App no 25723/94, [62].

[6] See, eg, *Handyside* (n 4) [48].

[7] See, eg, *Lingens v Austria* [1986] App no 9815/82; *Flux v Moldova (No 1)* [2006] App no 28702/03, [32].

[8] See, eg, *Editions Plon v France* [2004] App no 58148/00, [42]; *Egeland and Hanseid v Norway* [2009] App no 34438/04, [48].

[9] See S Greer, '"Balancing" and the European Court of Human Rights: A Contribution to the Habermas–Alexy Debate' (2004) 63 *Cambridge Law Journal* 412, 425; H Fenwick and G Phillipson, *Media Freedom under the Human Rights Act* (Oxford, Oxford University Press, 2006) 82–86; I de la Rasilla del Moral, 'The Increasingly Marginal Appreciation of the Margin-of-Appreciation Doctrine' (2006) 6 *German Law Journal* 611; V Filipova, 'Standards of Protection of Freedom of Expression and the Margin of Appreciation in the Jurisprudence of the European Court of Human Rights' (2012) 17 *Coventry Law Journal* 64; J Oster, *Media Freedom as a Fundamental Right* (Cambridge, Cambridge University Press, 2015) 119–23.

[10] Such as the development of the 'qualified privilege' defence in the English tort of defamation; see *Reynolds v Times Newspapers Ltd* [2001] 2 AC 127, now s 4 of the Defamation Act of 2013.

[11] See *Campbell v MGN* [2004] UKHL 22; *OBG Ltd and Others v Allan and Others* [2007] UKHL 21. The ECtHR's *Von Hannover v Germany (No 1)* ([2004] App no 59320/00) decision on privacy protection of public figures induced German courts to abandon the concept of a 'public figure par excellence' (see D Dörr and E Aernecke, 'A Never Ending Story: Caroline v Germany' in D Dörr and L Weaver (eds), *The Right to Privacy in the Light of Media Convergence* (Berlin, De Gruyter, 2012) 124.

2. Theory of Press Freedom

Unlike the CFR in Article 11(2), the ECHR does not include an express provision protecting the press or the media. Article 10(1)3 of the ECHR mentions broadcasting, television and cinema enterprises, but only with a view to the authorisation of Member States to license these entities, not by affording special protection to them. However, the ECtHR has derived the 'freedom of the press',[12] and the freedom of the media in general,[13] from the freedom of expression provision in Article 10 of the ECHR. Since the Strasbourg Court infers press and media freedom from the provision protecting freedom of expression, the Court's theoretical assumptions about press and media freedom can only be understood against the backdrop of its free speech theory. In its seminal decision *Handyside v the United Kingdom*,[14] the ECtHR revealed its theoretical justification of freedom of expression:

> Freedom of expression constitutes one of the essential foundations of [a democratic] society, one of the basic conditions for its progress and for the development of every man. Subject to paragraph 2 of Article 10 (art 10-2), it is applicable not only to 'information' or 'ideas' that are favourably received or regarded as inoffensive or as a matter of indifference, but also to those that offend, shock or disturb the State or any sector of the population. Such are the demands of that pluralism, tolerance and broadmindedness without which there is no 'democratic society'.[15]

The Court has reiterated these principles in all cases involving freedom of expression ever since, albeit with one terminological modification: it replaced 'the development of every man' with 'each individual's self-fulfilment'.[16] The Strasbourg Court has thus positioned its freedom of expression theory on both the consequentialist argument from democracy[17] and the liberal argument from individual autonomy and self-fulfilment.[18] The liberal argument – 'each

---

[12] See, eg, *Lingens* (n 7) [42]; *Oberschlick v Austria (No 1)* [1991] App no 11662/85, [58]; *Thoma v Luxembourg* [2001] App no 38432/97, [45]; *Cumpănă and Mazăre v Romania* [2004] App no 33348/96, [93]; *Rumyana Ivanova v Bulgaria* [2008] App no 36207/03, [58].

[13] *Jersild v Denmark* [1994] App no 15890/89, [31]; *Radio France and Others v France* [2004] App no 53984/00, [33].

[14] *Handyside* (n 4).

[15] ibid [49]; reiterated in, amongst many other decisions, *Sunday Times* (n 4) [65]; *Lingens* (n 7) [41]; *Axel Springer AG v Germany (No 1)* [2012] App no 39954/08, [78].

[16] See, eg, *Lindon, Otchakovsky-Laurens and July v France*, [2007] App nos 21279/02 and 36448/02, [45]; *Frankowicz v Poland* [2008] App no 53025/99, [38].

[17] See, in particular, A Meiklejohn, *Free Speech and its Relation to Self-Government* (New York, Harper Brothers, 1948); A Meiklejohn, 'The First Amendment is an Absolute' [1961] *Supreme Court Review* 245; RH Bork, 'Neutral Principles and some First Amendment Problems' (1971) 47 *Indiana Law Journal* 1; CR Sunstein, 'Free Speech Now' (1992) 59 *University of Chicago Law Review* 255, 263; J Weinstein, 'Participatory Democracy as the Central Value of American Free Speech Doctrine' (2011) 97 *Virginia Law Review* 633.

[18] *cf* V Blasi, 'The Checking Value in First Amendment Theory' [1977] *American Bar Foundation Research Journal* 521, 545; CE Baker, 'Scope of the First Amendment Freedom of Speech' (1978) 25 *UCLA Law Review* 964, 996; TM Scanlon, 'Freedom of Expression and Categories of Expression' (1979) 40 *University of Pittsburgh Law Review* 519, 533 ff; MH Redish, 'The Value of Free Speech' (1982) 30

individual's self-fulfilment' – regards freedom of speech not as a means to an end but as an end in itself. Consequently, the Court seems to regard freedom of speech as valuable not because of its consequences but because of its intrinsic value as an essential feature of a person's individual autonomy: individuals must *as such* be able to express themselves. By contrast, the consequentialist component of the Court's justification of freedom of expression – 'one of the essential foundations of [a democratic] society, [and] one of the basic conditions for its progress' – explains freedom of speech because of its instrumental value, not because of its intrinsic one. A consequentialist theory of freedom of expression emphasises the social interest of freedom of expression rather than the individual.

It would go far beyond the scope of this contribution to discuss the extent to which the two free speech rationales – the liberal argument from self-fulfilment and the consequentialist argument from democracy – are empirically reflected in the Court's case law on freedom of expression. It is remarkable, however, that the Court's jurisprudence on press and media freedom are informed *exclusively* by the consequentialist rationale, and not by the argument from self-fulfilment. The Court regularly emphasises that:

> Although the press must not overstep certain bounds, in particular in respect of the reputation and rights of others, its duty is nevertheless to impart – in a manner consistent with its obligations and responsibilities – information and ideas on all matters of public interest. Not only does the press have the task of imparting such information and ideas; the public also has a right to receive them. Were it otherwise, the press would be unable to play its vital role of 'public watchdog'.[19]

Moreover, '[f]reedom of the press ... affords the public one of the best means of discovering and forming an opinion of the ideas and attitudes of political leaders and on other matters of general interest'.[20] The Court thus emphasises not the right of the press to express itself but its 'duty' and 'task' to impart information and ideas on 'matters of public interest', and the public's right to receive that information and form its opinion. This culminates in the metaphor of the press as 'public watchdog'.

As a consequence of its instrumental understanding of press and media freedom, pan-European press freedom is *different* from freedom of expression, and it is *conditional*: it is different, because the press and other journalistic media receive privileged protection that is not included in freedom of expression; and it is conditional, because these privileges are subject to the media fulfilling certain duties and

---

University of Pennsylvania Law Review 591, 593; RC Post, 'Meiklejohn's Mistake: Individual Autonomy and the Reform of Public Discourse' (1993) 64 *University of Colorado Law Review* 1109; V Moore, 'Free Speech and the Right to Self-Realisation (2005) 12 *UCL Jurisprudence Review* 95; CE Baker, 'Autonomy and Hate Speech' in I Hare and J Weinstein (eds), *Extreme Speech and Democracy* (Oxford, Oxford University Press, 2009).

[19] See only *Axel Springer (No 1)* (n 15) [79]; *von Hannover v Germany (No 2)* [2012] App nos 40660/08 and 60641/08, [102].

[20] *Lingens* (n 7) [42]; reiterated in, eg, *Oberschlick (No 1)* (n 12) [58]; *Thoma* (n 12) [45]; *Scharsach and News Verlagsgesellschaft mbH v Austria* [2003] App no 39394/98, [30]; *Cumpănă and Mazăre* (n 12) [93].

responsibilities. Unlike freedom of expression, media freedom is not natural and inherent but has to be 'earned' in the first place.[21]

3. Media Privileges and their Beneficiaries

3.1. Who are 'the Media'?

Subject to the fulfilment of certain conditions (see section 4 below), the ECtHR grants privileged protection (see section 3.2 below) to 'the press' and 'the media'. This raises the question who or what 'the press' and 'the media' actually are. To begin with, the Court seems to use the terms 'press' and 'media' interchangeably, referring to 'the press' in cases of the print media,[22] and 'the media' in cases of audiovisual media.[23] Other than that, the Court's legal doctrines have been identical,[24] save for regulatory questions relating to the underlying technology (see section 3.3 below). However, the Strasbourg Court has never provided a succinct definition of its notion of 'press' or 'media'. The Court grants privileged protection, and requires the fulfilment of enhanced duties and responsibilities from *journalists*. For the Court, 'press freedom' and 'media freedom' are thus identical with 'journalistic freedom'. This has several consequences.

First, the Court applies 'press' and 'media' freedom to content providers, but not to mere speech intermediaries, such as Internet Service Providers (ISPs). Contrary to linguistics, 'media' is thus not to be regarded as the plural of 'medium' but as the journalistic media. Media freedom requires the exercise of some editorial control. The mere conduit of information and the dumping of raw data without any analytical input do not amount to a journalistic activity.[25] Second, the medium of communication is irrelevant,[26] as long as the content provider conducted journalistic work prior to publication. This explains why it would not make sense for the Court to draw a distinction between 'press freedom' and 'broadcasting freedom', as

---

[21] A Koltay, *Freedom of Speech: The Unreachable Mirage* (Budapest, CompLex, 2013) 45; Oster, *Media Freedom* (2015) 25; A Koltay, *New Media and Freedom of Expression* (Oxford, Hart, 2019) 45, 55; D Tambini, *Media Freedom* (Cambridge, Polity Press, 2021) 137.

[22] See, eg, *Sunday Times* (n 4) [66]; *Bergens Tidende and Others v Norway* [2000] App no 26132/95, [60]; *Perna v Italy* [2003] App no 48898/99, [39].

[23] See, eg, *Purcell and Others v Ireland* [1991] App no 15404/89; *Jersild* (n 13) [31]; *Centro Europa 7 SRL and Di Stefano v Italy* [2012] App no 38433/09, [131].

[24] See *Radio France* (n 13) [33].

[25] *Satakunnan* (n 2) [175].

[26] *Engels v Russia* [2020] App no 61919/16, [30]. See, on the one side, internet publications enjoying press freedom: *Times Newspapers Ltd v United Kingdom* (Nos 1 and 2) [2009] App nos 3002/03 and 23676/03, [27]. See, on the other side, internet publications denied press freedom: *Perrin v United Kingdom* [2005] App no 5446/03; *Willem v France* [2009] App no 10883/05. See also, eg, *Verlagsgruppe Droemer Knaur GmbH & Co. KG v Germany* [2017] App no 35030/13, [44]: application of journalistic duties to a book publisher.

does, for example, the German Constitution. For the Strasbourg Court, as long as it is journalistic, it is all 'media freedom'. Third, the crucial question underlying the Court's case law is not the question 'what is press?' or 'what is media?' but 'what is journalism?' Here the Court's more recent case law suggests a functional, rather than formal, understanding. The Court's jurisprudence in this regard is still in development, but two critical, interrelated factors can already be identified. First, the influence on the audience: does the audience have a reasonable expectation as to the veracity of the published information, or, in other words, does the audience expect the publisher to have adhered to some standards of information gathering before publishing the information? Second, the publisher's appearance: does the publisher claim enhanced credibility?

Against this backdrop, the privileges and obligations of the journalistic media do not only apply to professional journalists, as is suggested by the Court's earlier case law and by Council of Europe documents.[27] Rather, the Court's more recent decisions indicate that the Court extends the media's privileges to anyone who regularly contributes to matters of public concern and abides by certain stand-ards of conduct, such as non-governmental organisations, journalist-like bloggers, online news portals and other 'social watchdogs'.[28] As stated before, the privileges of media freedom have to be earned (see section 2 above), and anyone who fulfils certain duties and responsibilities with a level of diligence comparable to that of traditional news media organisations has earned media freedom.

3.2. What are the Media's Privileges?

Media freedom affords particular privileges to the journalistic media, which do not apply to freedom of expression in general. The fact that an impugned state-ment is 'media speech', rather than speech by any other individual or institution, adds to the burden of justifying its restrictions.[29] Journalistic freedom protects both the substance of the ideas and information expressed and the form in which they are conveyed, including a certain degree of provocation and exaggeration,[30]

---

[27] See *Sürek and Özdemir v Turkey* [1999] App nos 23927/94 and 24277/94, [63]; *Şener* (n 5) [42]; *Wizerkaniuk v Poland* [2011] App no 18990/05, [68]; *Kaperzyński v Poland* [2012] App no 43206/07, [70]; Council of Europe, Recommendation No R (2000) 7 on the right of journalists not to disclose their sources of information, Appendix, para 38.

[28] See, eg, *GRA Stiftung gegen Rassismus und Antisemitismus v Switzerland* [2018] App no 18597/13, [57]; *Orlovskaya Iskra v Russia* [2017] App no 42911/08, [107 ff], where the Court applied freedom of the press to an NGO's newspaper without even attempting to make a distinction; by contrast, see *Nix v Germany* [2018] App no 35285/16 on a private blogger, *Savva Terentyev v Russia* [2018] App no 10692/09, [81] for user-generated content. For a general overview and reference to the academic debate, see J Oster, *European and International Media Law* (Cambridge, Cambridge University Press, 2017) 9–12.

[29] Oster, *Media Freedom as a Fundamental Right* (n 9) 48–51.

[30] See, eg, *Prager and Oberschlick v Austria* [1995] App no 15974/90, [38]; *De Haes and Gijsels v Belgium* [1997] App no 19983/92, [46]; *MAC TV sro v Slovakia* [2017] App no 13466/12, [49].

immoderate statements,[31] the use of strong terms,[32] or polemic formulation,[33] vulgar phrases or a satirical style.[34] It is for journalists, and not for courts, to decide on the methods and techniques of their reporting.[35] Moreover, freedom of the media does not only protect the dissemination of a journalist's own opinions but it also includes the publication of opinions of a third party, irrespective of whether the publisher associates themselves with the content of the publication.[36] The Court has recently extended that principle to hyperlinks provided by online news portals.[37]

In addition, media freedom provides privileged institutional protection to the media that goes beyond protection of media publications. The media may invoke rights relating to journalistic newsgathering, editorial or distribution process, or even to the mere existence of an independent media. The institutional protection of the media includes, for example, the pluralism and independence of the (broadcasting) media,[38] especially of public broadcasters,[39] the protection of journalistic research and investigation,[40] the confidentiality of journalistic sources[41] and of journalistic communication,[42] as well as the liberty of the press to invite and open discussion via online comment sections.[43] Yet these protections are not absolute but subject to a balancing exercise (see section 4 below).

By contrast, the ECtHR still refuses to accept a general and intrinsic right of access to information.[44] Although documents of the Council of Europe encourage the Convention States to establish such freedom of information acts,[45] the

---

[31] *Mladina dd Ljubljana v Slovenia* [2014] App no 20981/10, [40].

[32] *Thorgeir Thorgeirson v Iceland* [1992] App no 13778/88, [67]; *July and SARL Liberation v France* [2008] App no 20893/03, [75].

[33] *Oberschlick v Austria (No 2)* [1997] App no 20834/92, [33]; *Unabhängige Initiative Informationsvielfalt v Austria* [2002] App no 28525/95, [43].

[34] *Tuşalp v Turkey* [2012] App nos 32131/08 and 41617/08, [48].

[35] See, eg, *Jersild* (n 13) [31]; *Bladet Tromsø and Stensaas v Norway* [1999] App no 21980/93, [63]; *Schweizerische Radio- und Fernsehgesellschaft SRG v Switzerland* [2012] App no 34124/06, [64].

[36] See, eg, *Jersild* (n 13) [36]; *July and SARL Liberation* (n 32) [70].

[37] *Magyar Jeti Zrt v Hungary* [2018] App no 11257/16, [80].

[38] Thus far, the cases relating to pluralism were all decided in the context of broadcasting. It remains to be seen whether pluralism as applied to the press and/or online content services will be an issue for the ECtHR's future case law (see section 3.3 below). See, eg, *VgT Verein gegen Tierfabriken v Switzerland (No 1)* [2001] App no 24699/94, [72]; *Animal Defenders International v United Kingdom* [2013] App no 48876/08 [112].

[39] See, eg, *Wojtas-Kaleta v Poland* [2009] App no 20436/02, [47]; *Manole and Others v Moldova* [2009] App no 13936/02 [98].

[40] See, eg, *Cumpănă and Mazăre* (n 12) [96]; *Dammann v Switzerland* [2006] App no 77551/01, [52].

[41] See, eg, *Goodwin v the United Kingdom* [1996] App no 17488/90, [39]; *Sanoma Uitgevers BV v the Netherlands* [2010] App no 38224/03, [50]; *Becker v Norway* [2017] App no 21272/12, [76].

[42] See, eg, *Roemen and Schmit v Luxembourg* [2003] App no 51772/99, [57]; *Nagla v Latvia* [2013] App no 73469/10, [95]; *Big Brother Watch and Others v United Kingdom* [2021] App nos 58170/13, 62322/14 and 24960/15, [448].

[43] *Standard Verlagsgesellschaft mbH v Austria* (No 3) [2021] App no 39378/15, [73]–[74].

[44] See, eg, *Leander v Sweden* [1987] App no 9248/81, [74]; *Matky v Czech Republic* [2006] App no 19101/03, [10]; *Társaság a Szabadságjogokért (TASZ) v Hungary* [2009] App no 37374/05, [35].

[45] See Council of Europe, Committee of Ministers, Convention on Access to Official Documents, adopted on 27 November 2008; Recommendation No R (81) 19 on the access to information held by

Court has, in principle, restricted the right to receive information and ideas in Article 10(1)2 of the ECHR to publicly available information disseminated by others. Certainly, since 2006,[46] the Court has interpreted the notion of freedom to receive information more broadly as a right of access to information. However, the Court requires access to the information to be 'instrumental' for the exercise of freedom of expression.[47] In other words, a right of access to information is dependent on the purposes of the applicant, and thus not intrinsic.[48] This is different in the EU, where Article 42 of the CFR and – with some reservations – Article 15(3) of the Treaty on the Functioning of the European Union grant such an unconditional right. The Grand Chamber clarified the Court's principles of access to information in the 2016 decision *Magyar Helsinki Bizottság v Hungary*. Accordingly, Article 10 of the ECHR does not, in principle, 'confer on the individual a right of access to information held by a public authority nor oblige the Government to impart such information to the individual'. But such a right or obligation may arise, inter alia, 'in circumstances where access to the information is instrumental for the individual's exercise of his or her right to freedom of expression, in particular "the freedom to receive and impart information" and where its denial constitutes an interference with that right'.[49] This is the case if the gathering of the information is a relevant preparatory step for contribution to a public debate, the information itself is of public interest, and the applicant is a journalist or an organisation contributing to the discussion of public affairs.[50]

3.3. Are there Differences between Press and Broadcasting Regulation?

As has been shown before, the Court's approach to press and media freedom is technology-neutral: the extent to which a certain publication or the newsgathering process towards that publication is protected by Article 10 of the ECHR depends mainly on the fulfilment of certain duties and responsibilities. However, the medium of communication can influence *which* duties and responsibilities the publisher has to fulfil in the first place.[51] According to the Court, enhanced

---

public authorities; Recommendation No R (91) 10 on the communication to third parties of personal data held by public bodies; Recommendation No R (97) 18 concerning the protection of personal data collected and processed for statistical purposes; Recommendation No R (2000) 13 on a European policy on access to archives; Recommendation Rec(2002)2 on access to official documents.

[46] The first decision in which the ECtHR considered (but eventually rejected) to derive a right to access to public documents from Art 10 of the ECHR was *Matky* (n 44).

[47] *Studio Monitori and Others v Georgia* [2020] App nos 44920/09 and 8942/10, [39].

[48] See *TASZ* (n 44) [38]; *Kenedi v Hungary* [2009] App no 31475/05, [43]; *Gillberg v Sweden* [2012] App no 41723/06, [93].

[49] *Magyar Helsinki Bizottság* (n 2) [156], [161] and [166].

[50] ibid [158].

[51] Koltay, *New Media and Freedom of Expression* (n 21) 50.

duties and responsibilities apply to audiovisual media, which have a particularly important role regarding the dissemination of information and ideas. The television's position as a source of information and entertainment 'in the intimacy of the listener's or viewer's home further reinforces [its] impact.'[52] For the Court, even the Internet does not have the same impact as broadcast information.[53]

The Court also distinguishes between the media of communication as far as the press is concerned, namely between written texts, on the one side, and photographs, on the other. For the Court, if a written article is accompanied by a photograph intruding into a person's private life, the publication of the photograph must be necessary to ensure the credibility of the story.[54] Moreover, the Court scrutinises the content of pictures, especially whether the images contain very personal or even intimate information about an individual.[55] The non-consensual publication of pictures of nakedness, wardrobe malfunctions, sexual activity, ill or dead persons usually violates this person's privacy or even dignity.[56] Finally, the Court examines the circumstances under which pictures have been taken (see section 4.2 below).[57] Yet these examples should not disguise the fact that the Court focuses in the first place on the content and not on the medium of publication.

This is different, however, with regard to the regulation of the underlying technology itself and independently of the content that is being disseminated. While the Court has been generally reluctant to accept, albeit not entirely prohibited, compulsory licensing requirements for newspapers and their representatives (see section 5 below), licensing requirements for broadcasting are more easily justified by the need to manage scarce resources, such as the electromagnetic wavelength spectrum.[58] Sentence 3 of Article 10(1) of the ECHR expressly states that freedom of expression shall not prevent states from requiring the licensing of broadcasting, television or cinema enterprises.

Similar considerations apply to requirements of media pluralism. The Court has not yet had the opportunity to develop a consistent body of case law with regard to press pluralism. Where such cases come under the Court's purview, it can be expected that the Court would emphasise the Convention States' positive

---

[52] *Manole* (n 39) [97], citing *Jersild* (n 13) [31].

[53] *Animal Defenders* (n 38) [119].

[54] See *Fressoz and Roire v France* [1999] App no 29183/95, [54]; *MGN Ltd v United Kingdom* [2011] App no 39401/04, [151].

[55] See, eg, *Von Hannover (No 1)* (n 11) [59]; *Mosley v United Kingdom* [2011] App no 48009/08, [115]; see also, mutatis mutandis, *Krone Verlag GmbH and Co KG v Austria (No 1)* [2002] App no 34315/96, [37]; *Eerikäinen and Others v Finland* [2009] App no 3514/02, [62].

[56] See, eg, *Hachette Filipacchi Associés v France* [2007] App no 71111/01, [46]; *US Supreme Court, National Archives & Records Administration v Favish* 124 SCt 1570 (2004).

[57] *Von Hannover (No 2)* (n 19), [103]. See, eg, *Von Hannover (No 1)* (n 11), [59]; *Hachette Filipacchi Associés ('Ici Paris') v France* [2009] App no 12268/03, [40]; mutatis mutandis, *Fontevecchia and D'Amico v Argentina* [2011] no 12.524, [68].

[58] Council of Europe, Committee of Ministers, Recommendation CM/Rec(2011)7 on a new notion of media, app, para 77.

obligation to safeguard media pluralism and to prevent influential economic or political groups from obtaining a dominant position over the media.[59] By contrast, the Court's jurisprudence on pluralism in broadcasting is much more refined. The Strasbourg Court expressed that '[i]t is of the essence of democracy to allow diverse political programmes to be proposed and debated, even those that call into question the way a State is currently organised, provided that they do not harm democracy itself'.[60] The Court thus found, for example, that there is no longer a 'pressing social need' for Convention States to maintain a public broadcasting monopoly, in particular because technological progress made available a number of frequencies and channels.[61] If a state decides to create a public broadcasting system, the domestic law and practice has to safeguard that the public broadcaster provides a pluralistic programme.[62] The requirement of a plurality of opinions in broadcasting applies both to the broadcasting landscape as a whole and to plural-ism within a particular media organisation.[63] Media pluralism might even require broadcasters to grant transmission time for third parties.[64]

4. Duties and Responsibilities

According to Article 10(2) of the ECHR, the exercise of freedom of expression is subject to 'duties and responsibilities'. Although applicable to speech of both media and non-media actors, the main purpose of the 'duties and responsibilities' clause is to offer Member States a tool to prevent abuse of power by the modern mass media.[65] From the ECtHR's own theoretical standpoint (see section 2 above), the extent to which media freedom is protected is to a much lesser extent deter-mined by the individual liberty of the publisher than by the role that the media plays for a democratic society, or in other words, by the extent to which the media fulfils its 'duties and responsibilities'. The media's 'freedom' and its 'duties and responsibilities' thus stand in a relationship of conditionality.[66] These duties and

---

[59] cp *Informationsverein Lentia and Others v Austria* [1993] App nos 13914/88, 15041/89, 15717/89, 15779/89 and 17207/90, [32]–[34]; *Tierfabriken* (n 38) [77]; *TV Vest AS & Rogaland Pensjonistparti v Norway* [2008] App no 21132/05, [78].

[60] *Manole* (n 39) [95], reiterated in *Centro Europa* (n 23) [129]; see also *United Communist Party of Turkey and Others v Turkey* [1998] App no 133/1996/752/951, [57].

[61] *Informationsverein Lentia* (n 59) [39].

[62] *Manole* (n 39) [101]. See also Council of Europe, Committee of Ministers, Recommendation No R (96) 10 on the guarantee of the independence of public service broadcasting; Recommendation No R (94) 13 on measures to promote media transparency.

[63] *Manole* (n 39) [100].

[64] See, eg, *Tierfabriken* (n 38); *Murphy v Ireland* [2003] App no 44179/98; *TV Vest* (n 59); *Animal Defenders* (n 38).

[65] cp JM Bossuyt, *Guide to the 'Travaux Préparatoires' of the International Covenant on Civil and Political Rights* (Dordrecht, Martinus Nijhoff Publishers, 1987) 386.

[66] Tambini (n 21) 137, 165.

responsibilities are manyfold, but they can be roughly divided into three main categories: the degree to which the reporting at issue is of public concern; the extent to which the media abided by certain standards of conduct; and whether the publisher acted in good faith.

4.1. Public Concern

The public concern criterion is already implied in the Court's theoretical justification of media freedom: It is the media's 'duty ... to impart ... information and ideas *on all matters of public interest*', and freedom of the media 'affords the public one of the best means of discovering and forming an opinion of the ideas and attitudes of *political leaders and on other matters of general interest*'.[67] These are not merely lofty words, but the Court takes them very seriously, not only in what they include but also in what they exclude. On the one side, the Court grants relatively strong protection to publications that the Court considers to be of public concern. Certainly, the Court has never committed itself to one specific definition of 'public concern', but rather takes an 'I know it when I see it' approach.[68] More recently, however, the Court explained that public concern, or public interest,

> ordinarily relates to matters which affect the public to such an extent that it may legitimately take an interest in them, which attract its attention or which concern it to a significant degree, especially in that they affect the well-being of citizens or the life of the community. This is also the case with regard to matters which are capable of giving rise to considerable controversy, which concern an important social issue, or which involve a problem that the public would have an interest in being informed about. The public interest cannot be reduced to the public's thirst for information about the private life of others, or to an audience's wish for sensationalism or even voyeurism.[69]

More importantly than definitional questions, the Court has developed a voluminous body of precedents that allows categorisations of matters of public concern, such as political matters,[70] matters of public administration,[71] businesses,[72] criminal offences and their prosecution,[73] the protection of animals,[74] historical

---

[67] See *Lingens* (n 7) [42]; emphasis added.

[68] Phrase borrowed from the famous dictum of Justice Potter Stewart in *Jacobellis v Ohio* 378 US 184, 197 (1964).

[69] *Satakunnan* (n 2) [171] (reference to other case law omitted).

[70] See, eg, *Lingens* (n 7) [42]; *Feldek v Slovakia* [2001] App no 29032/95, [74]; *Gutiérrez Suárez v Spain* [2010] App no 16023/07, [26]; *Lykin v Ukraine* [2017] App no 19382/08, [27].

[71] See, eg, *Thorgeir Thorgeirson* (n 32); *Nilsen and Johnsen v Norway* [1999] App no 23118/93, [44]; *Kasabova v Bulgaria* [2011] App no 22385/03, [56].

[72] See, eg, *Steel and Morris v the United Kingdom* [2005] App no 68416/01.

[73] See, eg, *White v Sweden* [2006] App no 42435/02, [29]; *Salumäki v Finland* [2014] App no 23605/09, [54].

[74] See, eg, *Bladet Tromsø* (n 35); *PETA Deutschland v Germany* [2012] App no 43481/09, [47]; *Animal Defenders* (n 38) [102].

debates[75] and sport-related issues.[76] People who expose themselves by virtue of their role as a 'public figure', as a participant in a public debate on a matter of public concern, or by otherwise entering the public scene, may claim weaker protection of their personality rights than a private person.[77] In particular, the limits of acceptable public scrutiny are wider in relation to professional politicians acting in their public capacity than in relation to private individuals.[78]

On the other side, the natural opponent of a matter of 'public concern' is obviously a matter of 'private concern'. Yet these two terms should not be regarded as binary but as operating on a scale; the Court investigates *to what extent* a publication relates to a matter of public concern, and *to what extent* it is private. Privateness, or privacy, encompasses the institutions mentioned in Article 8 of the ECHR: family, home and correspondence, furthermore, a person's name[79] or picture,[80] a person's physical intimacy, such as nakedness, illness or injury,[81] a person's sexuality, sexual life and orientation,[82] the personality of each individual in his or her relations with other human beings,[83] and personal data.[84] The Court has expressed particular disdain for sensational and lurid news 'intended to titillate and entertain, which are aimed at satisfying the curiosity of a particular readership regarding aspects of a person's strictly private life',[85] serving only to 'entertain' and not to 'educate'.[86] In stark contrast to US jurisprudence, the Strasbourg Court accepts that a person can be private even in public places.[87]

The notion of the media's 'duty' to report on matters of public concern should be understood as an ethical duty, not as a legally enforceable duty. The media is thus not under a legal obligation to publish exclusively on matters of public concern. Newspapers and magazines are, in principle, at liberty to publish whatever they like. Nevertheless, where the Court balances media freedom with *conflicting* rights

---

[75] See, eg, *Feldek* (n 70) [80]; *Karsai v Hungary* [2009] App no 5380/07, [35].

[76] See, eg, *Société de Conception de Presse et d'Edition et Ponson v France* [2009] App no 26935/05, [55].

[77] See, amongst many other authorities, *Lingens* (n 7) [42]; *Oberschlick (No 1)* (n 12) [59]; *Armonienė v Lithuania* [2008] App no 36919/02, [47].

[78] See, eg, *Lingens* (n 7); *Oberschlick (No 1)* (n 12) [59].

[79] See, eg, *Burghartz v Switzerland* [1994] App no 16213/90, [24]; *Standard Verlags GmbH v Austria (No 3)* [2012] App no 34702/07, [36].

[80] See, eg, *Schüssel v Austria* [2002] App no 42409/98; *Von Hannover (No 1)* (n 11) [50 ff]; *Eerikäinen* (n 55) [61].

[81] See, eg, *X and Y v Netherlands* [1985] App no 8978/80, [22]; *Raninen v Finland* [1997] App no 152/1996/771/972, [63]; *Biriuk v Lithuania* [2008] App no 23373/03, [43].

[82] See, eg, *Biriuk* (n 81) [34]; *Peck v the United Kingdom* [2003] App no 44647/98, [57]; *Ruusunen v Finland* [2014] App no 73579/10, [50].

[83] *Botta v Italy* [1998] App no 153/1996/772/973, [32]; *Von Hannover* (No 1) (n 11) [50].

[84] *S and Marper v the United Kingdom* [2008] App nos 30562/04 and 30566/04, [41].

[85] *Mosley* (n 55) [114]; see also, eg, *Von Hannover (No 1)* (n 11) [65]; *Hachette* ('Ici Paris') (n 57) [40]; *MGN* (n 54) [143]; *Alkaya v Turkey* [2012] App no 42811/06, [35].

[86] *Mosley* (n 55) [131]; see also Council of Europe, Parliamentary Assembly, Resolution 1165 (1998) on the right to privacy, para 6.

[87] *Von Hannover (No 1)* (n 11) [77]; *Satakunnan* (n 2) [134].

and interests, the 'weight' attached to media freedom depends on the extent to which the media reports on matters of public concern.

4.2. Standards of Conduct

When balancing media freedom with conflicting rights and interests, the Strasbourg Court not only scrutinises the content of the publication but also the media's behaviour prior to publication. In particular, the media has to act according to the 'ethics of journalism' and the principles of 'responsible journalism', which does not only refer to the content of a publication but also to journalistic information gathering and the way in which material is presented. Such ethical restraints are often included in codes of conduct of media self-regulation. This cuts both ways: even when publishing truthful information, the method of obtaining that information or the tone of the publication might weigh against media freedom, whereas the media may be exculpated from disseminating wrongful information if it conducted a reasonable amount of research prior to publication.

Information, even if true and in the public interest, must not be obtained by subterfuge or other illicit means, or through the use of secret recording devices.[88] In particular, where the right to privacy is affected, the Court has condemned that

> photos appearing in the 'sensationalist' press or in 'romance' magazines, which generally aim to satisfy the public's curiosity regarding the details of a person's strictly private life, are often taken in a climate of continual harassment which may induce in the person concerned a very strong sense of intrusion into their private life or even of persecution.[89]

Moreover, the media has to abide by certain standards of conduct when reporting on criminal proceedings,[90] particularly the respect for presumption of innocence.[91] Particular vigilance is called for where the interests of children are concerned.[92] Finally, media freedom does not give licence to illegal activity or violations of public safety rules that apply to everyone.[93]

---

[88] See, eg, *Hachette ('Ici Paris')* (n 57) [47]; *Flinkkilä and Others v Finland* [2010] App no 25576/04, [81]; *Saaristo and Others v Finland* [2010] App no 184/06, [65]; *Satakunnan* (n 2) [185].

[89] *Von Hannover (No 2)* (n 19) [103] (references omitted). See, eg, *Von Hannover (No 1)* (n 11) [59]; *Hachette ('Ici Paris')* (n 57) [40].

[90] See, eg, *Eerikäinen* (n 55); *Egeland and Hanseid* (n 8); *News Verlags GmbH and Co KG v Austria* [2000] App no 31457/96; Council of Europe, Committee of Ministers, Recommendation Rec(2003)13 on the provision of information through the media in relation to criminal proceedings.

[91] ECHR, Art 6(2). See, eg, *Bladet Tromsø* (n 35) [65]; *White v Sweden* (n 73) [21]; *Axel Springer (No 1)* (n 15) [96]; Council of Europe, Committee of Ministers, Recommendation Rec(2003)13 on the provision of information through the media in relation to criminal proceedings.

[92] *S and Marper* (n 84) [124]; *Kurier Zeitungsverlag und Druckerei GmbH v Austria (No 2)* [2012] App no 1593/06, [57]; *Ageyevy v Russia* [2013] App no 7075/10, [175].

[93] cp *Pentikäinen v Finland* [2015] App no 11882/10, [114]; *Erdtmann v Germany* [2016] App no 56328/10, [22]; *Amaghlobeli and Others v Georgia* [2021] App no 41192/11, [37].

Media publications must be based on an accurate factual basis.[94] The ECtHR has accepted it as principally compatible with freedom of expression to place the onus of proving the truth of defamatory statements even concerning a public figure on a defendant in libel proceedings.[95] However, under Strasbourg case law, there is no absolute obligation on a defendant in libel proceedings to establish the truth of a publication.[96] Instead, the media may be exculpated if it has taken all reasonable steps to verify the accuracy of its statements prior to publication[97] and if it has communicated remaining doubts.[98]

4.3. Good Faith

The journalistic media must always act in good faith.[99] 'Good faith' consists of two components: first, journalists must not intentionally disseminate false, harmful information or act with a grossly negligent disregard for the truth;[100] second, the media must not publish a statement with improper motives or intentions, for instance, to stigmatise someone, or to stir up violence and hatred.[101] Where journalists lack such good faith, there is no need for an examination of whether they can be exempted from their obligation to verify factual statements (see section 4.2 above). Rather, civil liability for a false, defamatory statement made in bad faith is always justified.[102]

5. Press Regulation

Unlike the regulation of press content via the 'duties and responsibilities' clause (see section 4 above), regulation of the press as a technology has not yet been subject to much scrutiny by the ECtHR thus far – in contrast to broadcasting. The extent to which the press is in that sense 'free and regulated',[103] particularly

---

[94] See, eg, *Bladet Tromsø* (n 35) [65]; *Fressoz* (n 54) [54]; Council of Europe, Parliamentary Assembly, Recommendation 1215 (1993) on the ethics of journalism.

[95] See, eg, *McVicar v United Kingdom* [2002] App no 46311/99 [87]; *Steel and Morris* (n 72) [93].

[96] See, eg, *Thorgeir Thorgeirson* (n 32) [65]; *Dalban v Romania* [1999] App no 28114/95, [49]; *Gutiérrez Suárez v Spain* (n 70) [37].

[97] See, eg, *Prager and Oberschlick* (n 30) [37]; *Europapress Holding doo v Croatia* [2010] App no 25333/06, [68].

[98] *Pedersen and Baadsgaard v Denmark* [2003] App no 49017/99, [77 ff]; *Wizerkaniuk* (n 27) [66].

[99] See, eg, *Bladet Tromsø* (n 35) [65]; *Fressoz* (n 54) [54]; *Novaya Gazeta and Borodyanskiy v Russia* [2013] App no 14087/08, [37].

[100] cp *Alithia Publishing Company Ltd and Constantinides v Cyprus* [2008] App no 17550/03, [66]; *Gutiérrez Suárez v Spain* (n 70) [38].

[101] See, eg, *Nilsen and Johnsen* (n 71) [50]; *Selistö v Finland* [2004] App no 56767/00, [68]; *Lindon, Otchakovsky-Laurens and July* (n 16) [57].

[102] *Alithia* (n 100) [67]; see also *Pedersen and Baadsgaard* (n 98) [78].

[103] P Wragg, *A Free and Regulated Press: Defending Coercive Independent Press Regulation* (Oxford, Hart Publishing, 2020).

through self-regulation, has thus largely remained a domestic issue. The Court's case law permits fewer inferences as to what domestic authorities – and press self-regulatory bodies – are not allowed to do than what they are allowed to do under the ECHR. For example, the European Commission of Human Rights (EComHR) and the Strasbourg Court have accepted compulsory official registration requirements for journalists.[104] Moreover, since the EComHR's seminal decision in *Ediciones Tiempo SA v Spain*, Strasbourg has not raised any objections on principle against domestic requirements for the media to publish a reply or a counterstatement.[105] The Court emphasised that the right of reply of an aggrieved person is itself protected by Article 10 of the ECHR, and may as such give rise to a positive obligation on the state to enforce this right through its courts.[106]

As a further example of the Court's reluctance to intervene with press regulation, the majorities of the Strasbourg Court have consistently held that Article 10 of the ECHR does not generally prohibit the imposition of prior restraints.[107] Without doubt, the Court has held that ex post facto damages usually provide an adequate remedy.[108] However, the legality of prior restraints is, according to the Court, evidenced by the words 'conditions', 'restrictions', 'preventing' and 'prevention' in Article 10(2) of the ECHR.[109] Accordingly, prior restraints may be 'justified in cases which demonstrate no pressing need for immediate publication and in which there is no obvious contribution to a debate of general public interest'. However, the Strasbourg Court also conceded that 'news is a perishable commodity', and even a short delay of its publication may deprive it of all its value.[110] As a consequence, 'the dangers inherent in prior restraints are such that they call for the most careful scrutiny on the part of the Court'.[111]

The provision on which the preventive measure is based must be formulated with sufficient precision to clarify the types of restrictions authorised, their purpose, duration, scope and control, and to enable the citizen to foresee the consequences of a violation of the prior restraint.[112] Restraints that are not imposed on

---

[104] *Loersch and Nouvelle Association du Courrier v Switzerland* [1995] App nos 23868/94 and 23869/94, [3]; cf *Gawęda v Poland* [2002] App no 26229/95, [48], in which the Strasbourg Court struck down a Polish registration scheme for registration of periodicals only because it was not 'prescribed by law'.

[105] *Ediciones Tiempo SA v Spain* [1989] App no 13010/87, [253]; see also, eg, *Kaperzyński* (n 27) [66].

[106] *Kaperzyński* (n 27) [66]; *Melnychuk v Ukraine* [2005] App no 28743/03, [6].

[107] For dissenting opinions, see *Observer and Guardian v the United Kingdom* [1991] App no 13585/88, partly dissenting opinion of Judge De Meyer (concerning prior restraint), joined by Pettiti, Russo, Foighel and Bigi JJ; *Wingrove v United Kingdom* [1996] App no 17419/90, dissenting opinion of Judge De Meyer, [1].

[108] *Wizerkaniuk* (n 27) [83].

[109] *The Sunday Times v the United Kingdom (No 2)* [1991] App no 13166/87, [51]; see also *Association Ekin v France* [2001] App no 39288/98, [56]; *Mosley* (n 55) [117]; *Wizerkaniuk* (n 27) [65]. However, see also the partly dissenting opinion of Judge De Meyer (concerning prior restraint), joined by Pettiti, Russo, Foighel and Bigi JJ in *Observer and Guardian* (n 107).

[110] *Mosley* (n 55) [117].

[111] See, eg, ibid; *Observer and Guardian* (n 107) [60]; *Wizerkaniuk* (n 27) [81].

[112] *RTBF v Belgium* [2011] App no 50084/06, [107]–[115].

particular types of news reports or articles but on the future publications of entire newspapers, are usually not 'necessary' in a democratic society.[113] The wholesale blocking of a website disregarding the distinction between the legal and illegal information the website may contain can therefore be justified only under exceptional circumstances.[114] Finally, the Court has rejected a legal duty for the media to notify the affected persons in advance of a publication allegedly violating their right to respect for their private life.[115]

6. Press Freedom and Internet Regulation

Thus far, cases involving the regulation of platforms and of ISPs in general have been relatively scarce. This is to no small extent owed to the fact that the regulation of ISPs and, even more so in the future, of online platforms, is to a large extent harmonised by EU law.[116] For the citizens of the 27 Convention States which also happen to be EU Member States, in such areas the road to Strasbourg, initially paved by Article 6(2) of the Treaty on European Union, has been blocked again by Opinion 2/13 of the Court of Justice of the European Union (CJEU).[117] But that does not change the fact that the Strasbourg Court has also left its impression on ISP regulation and Internet communication in general.[118] To begin with, the Court has accepted the importance of the Internet for communication.[119] But this has not induced the Court to downgrade the importance of traditional journalism, on the contrary: 'In a world in which the individual is confronted with vast quantities

---

[113] See *Ürper and Others v Turkey* [2009] App nos 14526/07, 14747/07, 15022/07, 15737/07, 36137/07, 47245/07, 50371/07, 50372/07 and 54637/07, [42]-[44]; *Güdenoğlu and Others v Turkey* [2013] App nos 42599/08, 30873/09, 38775/09, 38778/09, 40899/09, 40905/09, 43404/09, 44024/09, 44025/09, 47858/09, 53653/09, 5431/10 and 8571/10, [19].

[114] *Yıldırım v Turkey* [2012] App no 3111/10, here in particular the instructive concurring opinion by Judge Pinto de Albuquerque; *Kablis v Russia* [2019] App nos 48310/16 and 59663/17, [94]; *OOO Flavus and Others v Russia* [2020] App nos 12468/15, 23489/15 and 19074/16, [38].

[115] *Mosley* (n 55) [129].

[116] See Arts 12–14 of the e-Commerce Directive (Directive (EU) 2018/1808 of the European Parliament and of the Council of 14 November 2018 amending Directive 2010/13/EU on the coordination of certain provisions laid down by law, regulation or administrative action in Member States concerning the provision of audiovisual media services (Audiovisual Media Services Directive) in view of changing market realities [2018] OJ L303/ 69); Art 17 of the DSM Directive (Proposal for a Regulation on a Single Market For Digital Services (Digital Services Act) and amending Directive 2000/31/EC, COM/2020/825 final; Proposal for a Regulation on contestable and fair markets in the digital sector (Digital Markets Act), COM/2020/842 final).

[117] CJEU, Opinion 2/13. On the limited scope of judicial review of CJEU decisions by the Strasbourg Court, see *Bosphorus Hava Yolları Turizm ve Ticaret Anonim Şirketi v Ireland* [2005] App no 45036/98, [156]; confirmed in, eg, *Povse v Austria* [2013] App no 3890/11, [77].

[118] In addition, see Council of Europe, Committee of Ministers, Recommendation CM/Rec(2018)2 to Member States on the roles and responsibilities of internet intermediaries.

[119] See, eg, *Tamiz v the United Kingdom* [2017] App no 3877/14, [90]; *Magyar Jeti* (n 37) [66]; *Vladimir Kharitonov v Russia* [2020] App no 10795/14, [33].

of information circulated via traditional and electronic media and involving an ever-growing number of players, monitoring compliance with journalistic ethics takes on added importance'.[120]

Media freedom and its connected duties and responsibilities may only apply to content providers, and not to mere disseminators of third-party speech such as ISPs (see section 3.1 above). Intermediaries who merely provide platforms for other people's speech are not to be categorised as 'media' according to the concept of media freedom. Therefore, they cannot rely on the rights deriving from media freedom, but do not have to fulfil its concomitant duties and responsibilities either. Particular problems thus arise where an online platform provides both journalistically edited and user-generated content, such as news portals providing readers' comments sections. The leading case in this context is *Delfi AS v Estonia*.[121] The fact that the Strasbourg Court dealt with this case in the first place was in itself problematic. Given that the case largely depended on the interpretation of the e-Commerce Directive,[122] a reference to the CJEU by the domestic courts might have been called for[123] (but this is not to be discussed here).

The applicant company, Delfi, had integrated a comment section into its news portal, and invited users to post comments, many of which were defamatory and insulting. The ECtHR accepted the relatively strict standards the domestic courts had imposed on Delfi. The applicant company 'was expected to exercise a degree of caution in the circumstances of the present case in order to avoid being held liable for an infringement of other persons' reputations',[124] particularly with a view to the fact that the applicant's news portal had a notorious reputation for publishing defamatory and degrading comments. Yet the joint concurring opinion to *Delfi* remarked that the Court 'should have stated more clearly the underlying principles leading it to find no violation of Article 10 [of the ECHR]', having left 'the relevant principles to be developed more clearly in subsequent case law'.[125]

The ECtHR added one such principle in *Tamiz v United Kingdom*,[126] where the Court found that the exclusion of ISPs from the English concept of 'publisher' did not violate the applicant's rights under Article 8 of the ECHR, whose defamation claim against a host provider had been rejected for that reason.[127] The Court also distinguished more recent cases by highlighting that, in contrast to *Delfi*, the

---

[120] See, eg, *Novaya Gazeta and Borodyanskiy* (n 99) [42]; *Magyar Jeti* (n 37) [64]; see also Koltay, *Freedom of Speech* (n 21) 75.

[121] *Delfi AS v Estonia* [2013] App no 64569/09.

[122] Directive 2000/31/EC of the European Parliament and of the Council of 8 June 2000 on certain legal aspects of information society services, in particular electronic commerce, in the Internal Market ('Directive on electronic commerce').

[123] See *Delfi* (n 121) [43].

[124] ibid [86].

[125] ibid, joint concurring opinion of Raimondi, Karakas, De Gaetano and Kjølbro JJ, [8].

[126] *Tamiz* (n 119).

[127] ibid [90].

impugned speech did not amount to hate speech or incitement to violence, which is why Article 10 of the ECHR weighed stronger in favour of the ISP.[128]

The Court also had to deal with Internet blocking orders. In *Yıldırım v Turkey*,[129] the applicant had published content allegedly insulting the memory of Mustafa Kemal Atatürk on his website, which was hosted by 'Google Sites'. The domestic court did not only order the restriction of access to the applicant's website, but of all of Google's sites. As the Act on which the Turkish court based its decision did not satisfy the 'foreseeability' requirement,[130] and did not afford the applicant the degree of protection to which he was entitled, the Court found that the interference was not 'prescribed by law' within the meaning of Article 10(2) of the ECHR.[131] Judge Pinto de Albuquerque in his concurring opinion went even further than the majority and established several criteria for Convention-compatible legislation on Internet-blocking measures.[132] In the remarkable decision *Cengiz and Others v Turkey*,[133] the Strasbourg Court then decided that the right of two Turkish academics to *receive* information had been violated because a Turkish court order had requested to block access to YouTube.

The Strasbourg Court has also had the opportunity to leave its mark on the notorious 'right to be forgotten' (RTBF). Certainly, that right gained its notoriety because of a decision by the CJEU.[134] It is now codified in EU data protection law[135] and is, as such, outside the jurisdiction of the Strasbourg Court. Nevertheless, with a view to Article 8 of the ECHR, the ECtHR had already developed its own case law on an RTBF, and on a similar concept that might be termed a 'right to be vindicated', with regard to Internet archives. According to the ECtHR, Internet archives

> constitute an important source for education and historical research, particularly as they are readily accessible to the public and are generally free. While the primary function of the press in a democracy is to act as a 'public watchdog', it has a valuable secondary role in maintaining and making available to the public archives containing news which has previously been reported ... The maintenance of Internet archives is a critical aspect of this role.[136]

---

[128] See *Magyar Tartalomszolgáltatók Egyesülete and Index.hu Zrt v Hungary* [2016] App no 22947/13, [64]; *Pihl v Sweden* [2017] App no 74742/14, [25].

[129] *Yıldırım* (n 114).

[130] On the requirement of 'foreseeability' see, eg, *Sunday Times* (n 4) [49]; *Hashman and Harrup v the United Kingdom* [1999] App no 25594/94, [41]; *Sanoma* (n 41) [81].

[131] *Yıldırım* (n 114) [67].

[132] See ibid, concurring opinion by Judge Pinto de Albuquerque.

[133] *Cengiz and Others v Turkey* [2015] App nos 48226/10 and 14027/11.

[134] Case C-131/12 [2014] *Google Spain SL v AEPD and Others*; on the geographical scope of the 'right to be forgotten', see Case C-507/17 [2019] *Google v CNIL*.

[135] Regulation on the protection of natural persons with regard to the processing of personal data and on the free movement of such data, and repealing Directive 95/46/EC (Data Protection Directive) Art 17.

[136] *Węgrzynowski and Smolczewski v Poland* [2013] App no 33846/07, [59]; see also *Times Newspapers* (n 26) [45]; *Fuchsmann v Germany* [2017] App no 71233/13, [39].

Yet 'maintenance' does not only mean to keep such archives available but also to keep them up to date. As a consequence, newspapers may be obliged to add a notice or qualification to content stored in an archive that turns out to be false and defamatory.[137] The Court also upheld a domestic court order to anonymise an article in a newspaper's archive that reported on a fatal accident from 20 years before.[138] In *Biancardi v Italy*,[139] the Court recently held that an online newspaper my be obliged to de-index an article. Within the balancing exercise between freedom of expression and the right to respect for one's private life, one decisive factor was that the interference did not consist of an obligation to remove the article but merely to make it less easily accessible via search engines.[140]

7. Conclusion

The ECtHR is a court of law, not a policymaker. Or, perhaps, it is more appropriate to say: as a court of law, the ECtHR is different from other policymakers. It cannot set its own agenda, but has to wait for appropriate cases by which it can set its precedents. Despite – or perhaps even because of – the necessarily incremental character of the ECtHR's jurisprudence, the Court has been able to establish itself as the most authoritative pan-European institution in matters relating to press and media freedom. The Court's principles and doctrines on media and press freedom are by now firmly and reliably established, ensuring a certain level of predictability for cases to follow. The next seminal decisions of the Court can be expected with regard to online platforms and perhaps cases on algorithmically generated speech. It is not for the Court to choose when it has to engage with such questions. But once such cases reach Strasbourg, the Court will certainly not shy away from leaving its impression once more.

---

[137] *Times Newspapers* (n 26) [47]; *Węgrzynowski and Smolczewski* (n 136) [66]; see also, mutatis mutandis, *ML and WW v Germany* [2018] App nos 60798/10 and 65599/10.
[138] *Hurbain v Belgium* [2021] App no 57292/16.
[139] *Biancardi v Italy* [2021] App no 77419/16.
[140] ibid [59], [70].

12

Conclusion: European Visions of a Free and Regulated Press

PAUL WRAGG

1. Introduction: Our Shared History

The overriding theme that emerges from the contributions to this book relates to a wider thematic trend in the broader literature, and that is the tension in narrative voice when we speak of the press. For, as we know, the press has the capacity for heroism and villainy in its actions. Yet when commentators speak of press freedom, invariably they focus, sometimes exclusively, on the power of the press to do good, as if that is the natural or ultimate end of press freedom, and so describe the press in noble terms. Accordingly, we see the journalist lionised as the supreme combatant, speaking truth to power, bringing wrongdoing into the light, and risking reputation, livelihood and, sometimes, life itself to ensure justice is done.

The reason why we tend to speak of the press in positive terms is, I think, a result of our shared history. As Europeans, ours is a history of conflict, turmoil, oppression and revolutionary change. This pattern explains the near constant alterations to the geographical map of Europe, from the decline of the Habsburg Empire, the unification of Germany, and the end of the Ottomans to, in our time, the dismantling of the Union of Soviet Socialist Republics, the aftermath of civil war in Yugoslavia, and the peaceful separation of Slovakia from the Czech Republic. This pattern follows from, usually, the bloody end to an oppressive, tyrannical regime.

In amongst these political tumults, we find the press more often than not acting as the champion of popular interests. When the press is free, it can galvanise the public against tyranny, as when Jean-Paul Marat's *L'Ami du peuple* provided the means by which to undermine Louis XVI's control over popular opinion,[1] or it can achieve great political change, as when the Chartist Movement, spurred on by *The Poor Man's Guardian* and the *Northern Star and Leeds General Advertiser*, provoked the British government into extending the political franchise, first in 1832 and then again in 1867. It was this facet of press activity – to galvanise popular

---

[1] See, eg, E Hobsbawm, *The Age of Revolution, 1789–1848* (Abacus, [1962] 1977).

support and effect political change – that motivated Karl Marx's lifelong belief that newspapers held the key to realising his communist dream.[2] When, however, the press is not free, its power is either diminished to the point of pusillanimity or else becomes merely a conduit of state propaganda. As Sten Schaumburg-Müller explains, this was the experience of Denmark until 1849.[3]

For the British and French, the position was more complicated: the inability of newspapers to achieve maximal reach resulted not from overt censorship as such, but, indirectly, from restrictive financial policies that made them relatively expensive to produce. It was not until, in France, Napoleon III's Decree of 1870,[4] and, in the United Kingdom (UK), the abolition of the Stamp Act in 1855, that newspapers could be published cheaply, and thus more widely circulated. The Eastern European experience, though, was very different from the West's – and for these purposes we can include both Germany and Italy in our definition of the East. There, newspapers became vehicles for state manipulation of popular opinion as both Benito Mussolini and Joseph Goebbels demonstrated, and with heinous effect, as both Udo Fink[5] and Pietro Dunn and Oreste Pollicino[6] allude to. Whereas, for Germany, Italy and Western Europe, these restrictions on press freedom ceased with the end of the Second World War, and were strengthened by the introduction of the Convention for the Protection of Human Rights and Fundamental Freedoms (ECHR) in 1950, they continued, in varying degrees, in the Eastern Bloc countries, as both Joanna Kulesza[7] and Andrej Školkay[8] explain. In Russia, the idea of the press as the untrustworthy agent of state propaganda has never really disappeared, and indeed, *Pravda*, the Russian newspaper, has gained such notoriety that the word has entered the lexicon as a synonym for such state manipulation, which is ironic given that its literal translation is 'truth'.

Yet, *Pravda*'s origins, as the official voice of Lenin's revolutionary aims, are not inconsistent with the common experience at that time. For example, the UK's *Daily Worker* was owned by the Communist Party of Britain (whilst the US *Daily Worker* was owned by the Communist Party USA); *Vorwärts* was founded by the Sozialdemokratische Partei Deutschlands (Social Democratic Party of Germany (SDP); similarly, the *Hamburger Morgenpost* was founded by the SDP in 1949); *Avanti!* by the Partito Socialista Italiano (Italian Socialist Party) in 1896; whilst the *Heraldo de Madrid* in Spain was owned by a succession of politicians and came to embrace, first, liberalism and then republicanism until its demise in 1939. Likewise, the centrist party of Sweden, Centerpartiet, acquired several titles during

---

[2] See, eg, G Stedman Jones, *Karl Marx: Greatness and Illusion* (London, Penguin, 2016).

[3] See Sten Schaumburg-Müller, 'Danish Perspectives on Press Regulation', ch 2, section 2.2 in this volume.

[4] See Guilhem Gil, 'Freedom of the Press in France', ch 3, section 2 in this volume.

[5] See Udo Fink, 'German Constitutional Rules Concerning the Press', ch 4, section 3 in this volume.

[6] See Pietro Dunn and Oreste Pollicino, 'Freedom of the Press in Italy', ch 6, section 1 in this volume.

[7] See Joanna Kulesza, 'Freedom of the Press and Press Regulation in Poland', ch 7, section 1 in this volume.

[8] See Andrej Školkay, 'Press Freedom and Regulation in Slovakia', ch 9, section 3 in this volume.

the latter half of the twentieth century, including *Hallands Nyheter, Södermanlands Nyheter, Östersunds-Posten* and *Hudiksvalls Tidning.*

Britain's history of party-owned newspapers is, perhaps, less well known than it should be. For example, *The Sun* newspaper, 1792–1876 (not to be confused with the *Sun* newspaper of today), was funded by the Tories and used by William Pitt the Younger as a vehicle with which to promote the Party's aims. Similarly, the *Daily Citizen* (1912–15) was owned by the Labour Party and served as the Party's means of educating the public about its aims. Perhaps the most egregious example occurred during the General Strike of 1926 when the state produced the *British Gazette* which, with Winston Churchill as its editor, ran with the explicit aim of being no more, but no less, than a vehicle by which to attack the popular unionist activity of that time.[9]

We must never forget the atrocities of our shared history, yet neither must we be blinded by them. Whereas, for most of Europe, politician-owned or party-owned newspapers are no more, yet newspaper partisanship is thriving. Accordingly, we live in an age in which deliberative democratic processes are threatened not so much by the state manipulating the press, but by the press manipulating the state. Whereas the point should not be taken too far, still we should recognise that such manipulation sits uneasily with our neat theories of civic discourse, of the sort that Habermas has long advocated.

In an important sense, of course, press influence over state policy is a triumph of deliberative democracy. For example, the newspaper, aligned to popular feeling, which demands that government takes climate change seriously would, if the state acted so, be a paradigm of healthy democracy in action. This, though, has not been the uniform experience of Europe. For example, in the UK, where the newspaper scene is dominated by right-wing voices, climate change has been, at best, downplayed and, at worst, denied – as it has in other European countries. Accordingly, climate change activists are typically denounced as delusional, alarmist or dangerous. Similarly, we have seen how the campaign for Brexit played to right-wing agendas – as have other popular Eurosceptic movements, past and present, such as Italexit in Italy, Alternative für Deutschland in Germany, Marine Le Pen's Front National, Geert Wilder's Partij voor de Vrijheid in the Netherlands, and Austria's Freiheitliche Partei Österreichs. These movements have proved popular thanks to right-wing press support.

The problem, if it is not obvious, is that it is by no means clear that the influence of the right-wing press on state policy is a reflection or manipulation of popular sentiment. Accordingly, it is not clear whether the press is driven by actual popular feeling, an impressionistic or caricatured account of it, or else by powerful but elite interests, that is, those of the owner, advertisers, etc. The result is the distinct possibility of a discourse driven by propaganda not that far removed from that which

---

[9] On the history of the British press, see further, M Conboy, *Journalism: A Critical History* (New York, SAGE, 2004).

characterised the European experience of the 1930s. As with all propaganda, such movements succeed where the underlying message taps into a prevailing concern or phenomenon and so achieves the ring of truth. The information is not literally true but sounds plausible because it speaks to intuition or common experience. Deborah Lipstadt has written of this tactic amongst holocaust deniers: 'Truth is mixed with absolute lies, confusing readers who are unfamiliar with the tactics of the deniers. Half-truths and story segments, which conveniently avoid critical information, leave the listener with a distorted impression of what really happened'.[10]

A British climate change campaigner, Bob Ward, has spoken of a similar experience concerning climate change denial coverage in UK newspapers:

> Most of the authors of these articles had track records of promoting false information about climate change, and many had undeclared affiliations with the Global Warming Policy Foundation, a campaign group set up in 2009 which lobbies against policies to reduce greenhouse gas emissions from the consumption of fossil fuels. The Foundation, well-funded by secret donors since it was launched by Lord Lawson of Blaby in 2009, denies that climate change poses a significant risk. It was sanctioned in 2014 for the dissemination of propaganda that broke the Charity Commission's rules.[11]

These behaviours are common in populist politics, in which the appeal to feelings, intuition and belief trump logic, reason and expertise.[12]

If, then, there is a problem with accuracy, such that public and private decision-making is ill-informed, the question remains: what can be done about it? As our contributors have said, with one voice, our conception of press freedom is driven by the innate belief that a free press undergirds our shared vision of a free society, one in which the citizen is all powerful in the ultimate analysis. Školkay,[13] Andrei Richter[14] and Kulesza[15] all refer to the press as the 'cornerstone' of democracy. The press has a 'primary function', says Peter Coe, to act as a public watchdog.[16] This is echoed by Dunn and Pollicino, who refer to 'the fundamental role played by the press for the good functioning of democracy'.[17] The press, says Richter, is 'mediator between the state and society'[18] for, says Fink, 'access to independent

---

[10] D Lipstadt, *Denying the Holocaust: The Growing Assault on Truth and Memory* (London, Penguin, [1993] 2016) 2–3.

[11] Bob Ward, 'The Climate Crisis Cover-Up', available at: hackinginquiry.org/special-report-chapter-one-the-climate-crisis-cover-up.

[12] See, eg, J-W Müller, *What is Populism?* (London, Penguin, 2016); T Zick, *The First Amendment in the Trump Era* (Oxford, Oxford University Press, 2019).

[13] Školkay (n 8) section 5.

[14] Andrei Richter, 'The Legal Death of Media Freedom in Russia', ch 8, section 2 in this volume.

[15] Kulesza (n 7) section 3.

[16] Peter Coe, 'Press Regulation in the United Kingdom in a Changed Media Ecosystem', ch 10, section 2.1 in this volume.

[17] Dunn and Pollicino (n 6) section 5.

[18] Richter (n 14) section 2.

and trustworthy information ... is a prerequisite for social discourse'.[19] Kulesza calls this the 'role of journalists ... to disseminate information and ideas about matters of public interest'.[20] Here, then, are the familiar arguments that we say in the established literature, especially the work of Alexander Meiklejohn, Robert Post and Jürgen Habermas.

As the preceding chapters make clear, these ideas have found their way into judicial thinking. As Jan Oster explains, this finds expression in the European Court of Human Rights' (ECtHR) constant refrain that

> although the press must not overstep certain bounds ... its duty is nevertheless to impart – in a manner consistent with its obligations and responsibilities – information and ideas on all matters of public interest. Not only does the press have the task of imparting such information and ideas; the public also has the right to receive them.[21]

In my own work, I have speculated about the meaning of this principle.[22] At times, it seems to me to act as a sort of apologia. For example, in cases where the speech appears harmful – because, say, it is morally offensive, as in *Jersild v Denmark*,[23] or threatens to undermine the authority of the judiciary, as in *De Haes and Gijsels v Belgium*,[24] the principle gives extra weight or significance to the speech despite its unappetising qualities. It only seems to be mentioned though in negative rather than positive terms: that is, it is never used (so far as I can tell) to attack the press – to criticise it, for example, for non-performance or under-performance of this so-called duty – but, instead, to defend the press in circumstances where public interest expression is at stake. Thus, it operates as a sort of veneer that provides public watchdog activity with special radiance.

Certainly, it is difficult to make the ECtHR's use of 'duty' (of the press) and 'right' (of the public) fit the classic Wesley Hohfeldian right–duty dynamic.[25] For, if the public does have a 'right' to public interest journalism then how is it secured or enforced? Consider, for example, the UK scandal known colloquially as 'Partygate'. Allegations that former Prime Minister Boris Johnson, and his staff, had broken strict Covid-19 rules prohibiting social gatherings (by holding parties at No 10 Downing Street – official residence of the Prime Minister) in 2020 and 2021 was not reported by the press until 30 November 2021. Dominic Cummings (Johnson's aide at the time) subsequently alleged that the delay in reporting was explainable by the fact that political journalists were at these parties and had sought

---

[19] Fink (n 5) section 1.

[20] Kulesza (n 7) section 3.

[21] Jan Oster, 'The Press Freedom Jurisprudence of the European Court of Human Rights', ch 11 in this volume.

[22] See P Wragg, *A Free and Regulated Press: Defending Coercive Independent Press Regulation* (Oxford, Hart Publishing, 2020) 85–88.

[23] *Jersild v Denmark* (1995) 19 EHRR 1, [33]–[37].

[24] *De Haes and Gijsels v Belgium* (1998) 25 EHRR 1, [39].

[25] WN Hohfeld, *Fundamental Legal Conceptions* (New Haven, CT, Yale University Press, 1919).

'to bury' them.[26] A subsequent public inquiry into these allegations resulted in a damning report which confirmed that these gatherings had taken place, in breach of Covid-19 restrictions in place at that time,[27] but since the attendees of these events were not named we cannot know for sure whether or not Cummings's claims about press involvement are authentic. Nevertheless, this episode raises an important practical point about this so-called duty to act as a public watchdog, for if members of the press either knew about these flagrant breaches of the law (because they were there) or ought to have known (because the political reporting community is tight-knit), then there are good grounds to argue that the duty had been breached.

In this sense, Poland sits as something of an outlier. For, as Kulesza explains, under Polish law, there is a positive duty upon the press to provide 'reliable' information. Whereas, as she says, there is some latitude in respect of objective information, we can see that the provision of 'subjective truth' (Kulesza's term) may be the subject of court proceedings when the information breaches common standards of due professional care. This misrepresentation of facts is considered a criminal matter. Arguably, this arrangement is incompatible with Article 10 for, although consistent with the literal wording of the Strasbourg principle (this notion of a 'duty' to provide information), it is, surely, inconsistent with its spirit. Admittedly, it depends upon how the law is applied. If it operates as a palliative alongside libel laws, and so applies when reputation is at stake (as the good faith doctrine does in French law),[28] it would be more defensible than if it acted to quell polemical speech about political issues. For example, an argument that exaggerated the benefits of Britain's exit from Europe whilst obscuring the (considerable) detriments would represent, according to theory, a valid contribution to deliberative democratic debate that called for greater speech in response rather than suppression.

2. Press Freedom and Press Regulation

Press freedom, whether conceived as a superior or equivalent right to freedom of speech,[29] should be taken seriously. Whereas the threat to press freedom is overt in places like Russia, as Richter makes clear, the rest of Europe is not immune. As Dunn and Pollicino remind us, defamation is a criminal matter in Italy, as it is elsewhere on the continent; similarly, as Kulesza explains, the failure to maintain

---

[26] Rowena Mason, 'Dominic Cummings: "Very Unwise for No 10 to Lie" about Christmas Parties' *Guardian* (6 December 2021), available at: www.theguardian.com/politics/2021/dec/06/dominic-cummings-very-unwise-for-no-10-to-lie-about-christmas-parties.
[27] Cabinet Office, *Findings of Second Permanent Secretary's Investigation into Alleged Gatherings on Government Premises During COVID Restrictions* (25 May 2022).
[28] See discussion in Gil (n 4) section 4. See also, Oster (n 21) section 3.
[29] This literature is discussed in Wragg, *A Free and Regulated Press* (n 22) 24–31.

the secrecy of certain confidential information is a criminal offence in Poland.[30] Yet, it is not the fact of interference with press speech, however, that constitutes unconstitutional behaviour but the degree. The question is whether the interference is unjustified. That the press can play the part of hero *and* villain is explicit in Schaumburg-Müller's view that 'on the one hand ... the role of the press is paramount to democracy and freedom, and on the other hand ... the press is a power which in itself must be contained'.[31]

Thus, any measure, either through hard or soft law, which curbs press speech must be justified. In my own work, I have sought to make that distinction clear through the dichotomy of press malpractice and press freedom.[32] If, as I maintain, we can separate journalistic activities into these two spheres of behaviour, then we can speak sensibly of regulating press malpractice without undue interference (or, indeed, any interference at all) with press freedom itself. This requires us to be clear on what counts as press malpractice, not least so that we avoid being trapped in a circular argument that press freedom stops where press malpractice begins and vice versa.

We can think of press malpractice as the breach of obligations owed by the press, collectively or individually, to others. These obligations may be contractual, such as is found in the terms of a confidentiality agreement by which the journalist promises not to disclose the identity of a whistleblower, for example, or tortious, such as where the journalist defames or else unduly invades the privacy rights of others. These obligations are not noble promises to do good for society at large but instead speak to that sense of responsibility (more accurately: accountability) by which wrongs must be made good (or otherwise avoided). These are the 'duties and responsibilities' that Dunn and Pollicino speak of in their chapter;[33] they include, in Germany, obligations relating to personal honour and the protection of youth, under Article 5(2) of the Basic Law;[34] the right to reply, in Slovakia, that Školkay discusses;[35] and the Danish prohibition on unwarranted recordings of intrusion into secluded places, which Schaumburg-Müller surveys.[36]

These obligations are also apparent in the various press regulatory codes operating across Britain, Ireland and mainland Europe.[37] As I have said elsewhere, these codes can be divided into three discrete groups, which speak to the peculiar interests of victims (of press malpractice), readers and wider society.

Prior to delineating these provisions in finer terms, I should explain the term 'regulation' given that, as the preceding chapters make clear, it is sufficiently

---

[30] Kulesza (n 7) section 4.
[31] See Schaumburg-Müller (n 3) section 2.1.
[32] See Wragg *A Free and Regulated Press* (n 22) especially Part III.
[33] Dunn and Pollicino (n 6) section 2.
[34] Fink (n 5) section 12.4.
[35] Školkay (n 8) section 5.
[36] Schaumburg-Müller (n 3) section 2.3.1.
[37] See discussion in András Koltay, 'On European Press Freedom: An Introduction', ch 1, section 2 in this volume.

flexible to capture the positive law. The idea of a regulator in a soft law context is, of itself, controversial.[38] For our purposes, though, it is sufficient to think of it as a non-judicial body invested with the power to direct that its members comply with a code of practice such that failure to do so attracts rebukes and/or penalties. France lacks such a body, though the Syndicat National des Journalistes operates a 'charter' of professional ethics which is said to be binding (*engagent*) upon all journalists. This charter lists the 'pillars of journalistic action' as critical thinking, veracity, accuracy, integrity, fairness and impartiality' (*l'esprit critique, la véracité, l'exactitude, l'intégrité, l'équité, l'impartialité*).

As Guilhem Gil explains, there have been moves, in France, to create the sort of regulatory body we see elsewhere in Europe, but without success. With the exception of Denmark, and, to a limited extent, Ireland (where members are said to be 'incentivised' to join and cooperate), membership of these regulatory bodies is voluntary. Nevertheless, the most that Denmark's Pressenævnet can do is recommend that the state prosecutes members who refuse to publish an adverse regulatory adjudication. To ensure compliance with the codes they operate, such schemes tend to rely upon publishers reacting with sufficient shame or embarrassment if and when adverse adjudications occur.[39] Such compliance is achieved with varying success. Whereas, for example, the Finnish press regulator, Julkisen sanan neuvosto seems to be remarkably effective in achieving compliance, the German experience is more mixed whilst the picture in Britain is rather depressing.[40]

Here, membership is entirely voluntary with the *Guardian*, *Financial Times* and the *Independent* (all major national daily titles) sitting outside the scheme of independent regulation altogether. Whereas, in principle, the press's preferred regulator – the Independent Press Standards Organisation (IPSO) – has the power to issue financial sanctions for serious and systematic breaches of the Editors' Code of Practice, it has never even commenced an investigation (the necessary preliminary stage of the process) let alone issued such sanctions. As I argue elsewhere, this is unsurprising, and the chances of a sanction being issued highly unlikely, for the simple reason that IPSO depends upon the continued support of its members for its existence.[41] Given that members are not obliged to remain with IPSO (and, although unlikely, could move to IMPRESS, which is the UK's only officially recognised regulator, through a process established post-Leveson),[42] then the more onerously the terms of membership are enforced, the less incentive there is to remain. (I discuss this in more detail below.)

---

[38] See discussion in, eg, A Ogus, *Regulation: Legal Form and Economic Theory* (Oxford, Oxford University Press, 1994) ch 1; R Baldwin, M Cave and M Lodge, *Understanding Regulation: Theory, Strategy, and Practice*, 2nd edn (Oxford, Oxford University Press, 2012) ch 1.

[39] See discussion in L Fielden, *Regulating the Press: A Comparative Study of International Press Councils* (Oxford, Reuters Institute for the Study of Journalism, 2012), available at: reutersinstitute. politics.ox.ac.uk/sites/default/files/2017-11/Regulating%20the%20Press.pdf.

[40] See discussion in Wragg, *A Free and Regulated Press* (n 22) 57–61.

[41] ibid 258–63.

[42] Royal Charter on Self-Regulation of the Press. See further, P Wragg, 'The Legitimacy of Press Regulation' [2015] *Public Law* 290.

Generally, press regulation works through the enforcement of a code of conduct by the regulator, either following a complaint by an affected group or individual or else of the regulator's own volition. Codes of conduct vary across Europe, but speak to three distinct interest groups: victims (of press malpractice), readers and society at large. To my mind, the legitimacy of enforcing codes of conduct by coercive means, that is, financial sanctions, depends upon the proximity of the code provision to its analogue in law. Accordingly, provisions which speak to the sort of Article 8 of the ECHR rights to privacy or reputation that we find in domestic law, and at supranational level, cause no problems of legitimacy, at least, not in principle, when enforced by a regulatory body.

Conceptual difficulties arise, though, where the provision imposes an obligation of accuracy in terms that exceed reputational rights and speak, instead, to those familiar democratic participation norms, of the sort we find in, say, Habermas, Post or Cass Sunstein.[43] We see this expressed in various forms. The Belgian Raad voor de Journalistiek's Code says 'a journalist must report information accurately. This comes from the public's right to know the truth'.[44] The Danish Pressenævnet's Code says that '[b]reach of sound press ethics also includes the withholding of rightful publication of information of essential importance to the public'.[45] The German Presserat's Code says: 'Respect for the truth, preservation of human dignity and accurate information of the public are the overriding principles of the Press'.[46] The Swedish Allmänhetens Pressombudsman's Code says: 'The role played by the mass media in society and the trust of the public of these media call for accurate and objective news reporting'.[47] The Finnish Julkisen sanan neuvosto's Code says that '[a] journalist is primarily responsible to the readers, listeners and viewers, who have the right to know what is happening in society'.[48] Similarly, IPSO's Editors' Code speaks of 'the public's right to know' in its preamble, whilst the Irish Code commences with the statement that '[t]he freedom to publish is vital to the right of the people to be informed'. The Norwegian is the only European code, so far as I know, to require journalists to report on the performance of others in fulfilling its public watchdog role. Its Clause 1.4 says: 'It is a press obligation to shed critical light on how media themselves exercise their role'.[49]

Enforcing these provisions is problematic, in the ultimate analysis, for several reasons, including those which John Stuart Mill gave us in the nineteenth century. If we are to ensure that society – either directly, as readers, or indirectly, through readers – receives the information it 'needs' rather than 'wants' then we must have

---

[43] See Koltay (n 37) section 1.
[44] Raad voor de Journalistiek, December 2016. Code of Practice.
[45] Pressenævnet, May 2013. The Press Ethical Rules.
[46] Deutsher Presserat, March 2017. German Press Code – Guidelines for journalistic work as recommended by the German Press Council.
[47] Pressens Opinionsnämnd.
[48] Guidelines for Journalists, January 2014. Clause 1.
[49] Pressens Faglige Utvalg, June 2015. Ethical Code of Practice for the Press.

clear and unequivocal standards about the difference between the two. In other words, we must be able to recognise essential information when it arises and be capable of differentiating it from the inessential. Similarly, we must know the authentic from the inauthentic. Not only is this the 'assumption of infallibility' that Mill warned against in *On Liberty*, it relies upon a further rationale that it cannot sustain, which is that members of society accept truth when it arises. It is for this reason that I disagree entirely with those, like Onora O'Neill, who argue that the press is an institution of trust and that our mission should be to inculcate public trust in such institutions by developing systems of responsibility that underpin trust.[50]

To my mind, realising such an aim would be an intellectual disaster of epic proportions for it would destroy or otherwise undermine the critical faculties that all autonomous beings should develop if they are to realise truth. Popularism, as overt fascism did before it, relies upon the cult of personality to realise its aims. Its charismatic leaders succeed by fooling their followers into suspending their critical distrust – theirs is the language of flattery, division and flawed logic, which relies upon half-truths and plausible (but inaccurate) statements in which the subverted realise only too late that they have been duped.

The Italians and Germans saw this in the 1940s. The British are seeing it now as the 'dream' of Brexit manifests its nightmarish self. That famous promise, on the side of a bright red bus, that £350 million *per week* would be spent on the National Health Service post-Brexit – a sum total of £18.2 billion – was revealed as a lie the day after the vote when leading Brexit campaigner, Nigel Farage, announced on breakfast television that the promise was a 'mistake' and could not be realised.[51] Nevertheless, even the most deluded Brexiteer must realise something is amiss when, as now, the Royal College of Nursing is lobbying government for an inflation-matching pay rise for its members only to be told that there is insufficient public funding available to meet it. The total cost of such a rise, says the government, is £9 billion and simply unaffordable[52] – despite being well within the so-called £350 million saving per week following our exit from the EU. The problem is, of course, that the hardened Brexiteer does not see the truth or else refuses to accept it. The epitome of this, of course, is Farage himself who refuses to accept that leaving the EU is the cause of our woeful economic prospects, instead pointing the blame at everything from executive incompetence (the government secured, he says, the wrong sort of Brexit) to Vladimir Putin's illegal war in Ukraine, from the Covid-19 pandemic to an unspecified Remainer conspiracy to make Brexit a failure.[53]

---

[50] See, eg, O O'Neill, *A Question of Trust* (Cambridge, Cambridge University Press, 2002).

[51] 'Nigel Farage labels £350m NHS promise "a mistake"' *ITV* (27 June 2016), available at: www.itv.com/goodmorningbritain/articles/nigel-farage-labels-350m-nhs-promise-a-mistake.

[52] Emily Craig, '£150 Billion-a-Year NHS Will get Even MORE Money in Tomorrow's Budget, Health Secretary Steve Barclay Says ... but It WON'T be Dished Out to Nurses' (*Mailonline*, 16 November 2022), available at: www.dailymail.co.uk/health/article-11434269/150billion-year-NHS-money.html.

[53] See: twitter.com/Nigel_Farage/status/1580902437988495369; Adrian Zorzut, 'Nigel Farage Reminded of Claim that "Acid Test of Brexit" Surrounds Fishing after clip Resurfaces' *New European*

These anecdotes resonate with our shared experience of civic society of late and speak to an essential problem of causality. If we follow the logic of regulating inaccurate information, for the benefits it provides to democratic participation, then the most plausible justification is that inaccuracy harms civic discourse. We see this justification often enough in the literature. For example, the so-called 'Hutchins Commission', back in 1947, was adamant that press inaccuracy was 'dangerous'[54] since 'not only positive misdeeds but omissions and inadequacies of press performance have now a bearing on general welfare'.[55] The argument goes that since 'accurate information is a pre-requisite for arriving at informed political and social judgements' the public should be 'protected' from the 'damaging consequences' that misinformation and disinformation have.[56]

In the liberal tradition, the fact of harm is insufficient to justify coercion. So, if we are to penalise newspapers for publishing inaccurate information, and if we are to be consistent with those traditions, then it must be that the harm is *caused* by the wrongdoing. Reading across the law, we see this tradition manifest in, say, European consumer protection laws that penalise inaccurate information in the form of advertisements.[57] The justification for this, if it is not obvious, is that the defective information *causes* harm, usually in the form of financial loss but also physical injury. In the Consumer Protection from Unfair Trading Regulations 2008/1277, which implement the Unfair Commercial Practices Directive 2005/29, this causality is explicitly stated in Regulation 5(2)(b): a commercial practice breaches the material provisions of the Regulations only if it 'causes or is likely to cause the average consumer to take a transactional decision he would not have taken otherwise'.

Admittedly, we can think of analogous circumstances in which the press might disseminate false information which satisfies the causality test. In fact, IPSO's Code of Conduct envisages such a scenario, for example, by prohibiting journalists

---

(26 January) 2021, available at: www.theneweuropean.co.uk/brexit-news-westminster-news-nigel-farage-clip-on-fish-and-brexit-resurfaces-7073308; Emilio Casalicchio and Jack Blanchard, 'The Brexit Cult that Blew Up Britain' (*Politico*, 21 October 2022), available at: www.politico.eu/article/conservative-libertarian-brexit-cult-wont-be-dead-for-long-liz-truss; Katie Harris, 'Nigel Farage Calls for "Brexit 2.0" as He Issues Dire Warning to Tories Over Election' *Daily Express* (16 August 2022), available at: www.express.co.uk/news/politics/1656179/nigel-farage-brexit-tories-general-election-migrant-channel-crossings; Rowena Mason, 'Nigel Farage Denies Being Conspiracy Theorist after Far-Right Talkshow Appearances' *Guardian* (7 May 2019), available at: www.theguardian.com/politics/2019/may/07/nigel-farage-denies-being-conspiracy-theorist-after-far-right-talkshow-appearances; Ivan Rogers, 'Why even the Brexiteers Are in Despair over Brexit' *New Statesman* (22 June 2022), available at: www.newstatesman.com/politics/uk-politics/2022/06/ivan-rogers-why-boris-johnson-failed-brexiteers.

[54] The Commission on Freedom of the Press, *A Free and Responsible Press* (Chicago, IL, University of Chicago Press, 1947) 115.

[55] ibid 124.

[56] T O'Malley and C Soley, *Regulating the Press* (London, Pluto Books, 2000) 145. See further, Koltay (n 37) section 4.

[57] See, eg, the Unfair Commercial Practices Directive 2005/29 and the Misleading and Comparative Advertising Directive 2006/114. See discussion in P Wragg, 'Advertising, Free Speech and the Consumer' in J Devenney and M Kenny (eds), *European Consumer Protection: Theory and Practice* (Cambridge, Cambridge University Press, 2012).

from using financial information for their own profit (Clause 13). This clause was breached in 1991 when business journalists at the *Daily Mirror* used their column to promote companies that they owned shares in.[58] Nevertheless, enforcement of the accuracy clause is generally problematic, in terms of causality, not least from a remoteness perspective. To say that false information on societal issues causes readers to adopt positions that they would not otherwise adopt requires proof that is not easily met. For it has been said that right-wing press supporters read such newspapers not for new viewpoints but to have their pre-existing viewpoints reinforced.[59] Thus, when newspapers like the *Daily Mail* pursue its transparent agenda that immigration harms society, Muslims are a threat to national security, benefits seekers are lazy, the gay or trans community are a threat, single mothers are a scourge, etc, the causality question looks like this: do readers share these viewpoints because they *read* positive reinforcement of them in their newspaper or because they *want* to read such? Thus, if newspapers were prevented or otherwise penalised for publishing such gross inaccuracies, would the viewpoints of these readers change materially? Likewise, there is the very real problem that newspapers are not the uniform cause of such viewpoints for, as we have seen already, politicians themselves perpetuate these myths to serve their own political agendas, as our shared recent history tells us only too well.

Accordingly, to achieve the grand aim of optimal democratic participation by means of press regulation is, to my mind, highly doubtful from a pragmatic perspective and deeply problematic from a principled one. In the final analysis, it is simply unachievable for its failure to respect the sanctity of individual autonomy. No one is forced to read newspapers, much less believe them. The patent failure to engage the critical faculties so as to distrust the press speaks to a shared, civic failing for which society itself is to blame, and for which society must look to itself to find a solution. When newspapers exploit this gullibility, they do so, in the main, by exercising their right to freedom of expression under Article 10.

Coercive regulation – that is, regulatory systems that would penalise or otherwise prevent breaches of its code of conduct – is on a safer footing when protecting reader interests. The causality nexus is less sharply strained in these scenarios. Nevertheless, there is an issue, I think, in terms of establishing loss, especially where that loss seems remote. We have already seen one example of this, in the UK context, concerning financial journalism. We can find others which prohibit, say, plagiarism (for example, Clause vii(1) of the Slovakian Code), digital manipulation of images (Clause 12 of the Swedish Code), or to avoid conflicts of interest (Clause A of the Dutch Code). Sometimes these take an idiosyncratic form, as when, in the Austrian Code, journalists are required to ensure that '[t]ravelogues or reports of touristic nature shall include ... information about the social and

---

[58] *PCC v Mirror City Slickers*: www.pcc.org.uk/cases/adjudicated.html?article=MTc4NQ.
[59] For a detailed and sustained examination of this issue see, eg, N Davies, *Flat Earth News* (London, Chatto & Windus, 2008).

political background and conditions prevailing in the country or region in question (such as serious human rights violations),[60] and that '[e]nvironmental, transport and energy policy matters shall ... be given adequate consideration in the paper's motor section.[61] In such cases, the loss, such as it is, seems to me to be purely personal and confined to the purchase price, if at all.

By far the safest ground on which to use coercive powers is the regulation of provisions which speak to victims' rights. These rights relate both to content and conduct, that is, published material as well as the newsgathering process. It is surely no coincidence that Europe's most overtly coercive regulatory scheme, found in Denmark, contains a code that speaks almost exclusively to victims' rights and little else. These provisions either find their analogue in law (for example, rights to privacy or reputation under Article 8 of the ECHR, and rights to a fair trial under Article 6 of the ECHR) or else satisfy liberalism's basic formula of wrongdoing–causation–undue harm. An example of the latter is the prohibition on using clandestine methods to obtain information unless it is in the public interest to do so. This prohibition is common throughout Europe (Denmark, Clause B7; Finland, Clause 9; Germany, Clause 4; Belgium, Clause 17; Switzerland, Clause 4; Norway, Clause 3.10; Netherlands, Clause B.1; Ireland, Clause 3.2; Slovakia, Clause V1-6).

3. Voluntary Self-Regulation[62]

Most European press regulation operates on a strictly voluntary basis (Denmark is a notable exception). Members are not compelled to join a regulator but are encouraged to do so. These incentives may be political – in Ireland, and to some extent Britain, it is said to be the fear of government implementing a more coercive regime that prompts relative compliance[63] – or commercial – in Scandinavian countries, journalists seem fearful of reputational damage caused by poor regulatory compliance.

In a voluntary scheme, though, compliance with regulatory codes of conduct is, in the ultimate analysis, an indulgent submission of the will by members rather than an imposition of will by the regulator. It is contingent upon members realising some incentive to do so. In short, it is an exercise in risk-based decision-making in which the benefit/burden of compliance is weighed against that of non-compliance.

---

[60] Österreichischer Presserat, Guiding Principles for Journalistic Activities, June 2014. Clause 9.1.

[61] ibid Clause 9.2.

[62] This section comprises a modified version of that which appears in Wragg, *A Free and Regulated Press* (n 22) 258–72 and is reproduced here with permission and thanks.

[63] This, at least, is what the Irish Press Ombudsman, John Horgan, told Lord Justice Leveson in 2011. Lord Justice Leveson, *An Inquiry into the Culture, Practices and Ethics of the Press: Report* (HC 780, 2012) 1669, [5.4]. According to Leveson 'the one incentive that we have heard about that has been demonstrated to be effective is the realistic threat of press standards legislation if an adequate voluntary body with full coverage is not forthcoming', ibid 1782, [7.10].

Consequently, the regulator operates in circumstances of sub-optimal leverage over the member. We see this vividly enough in the UK context. Despite having the power to sanction members for serious or systematic breaches of the code, IPSO has yet to do so in its eight years of existence. This is entirely unsurprising. Disgruntled members can be expected to leave. This sort of antagonism towards regulation occurred in Germany when, as Fielden tells us, the Bauer Media Group failed to renew its pledge to comply with the Standards Code in 2011, after the Presserat issued 13 public reprimands against it.[64]

Given these obvious and chronic deficiencies in the voluntary model of press regulation, it is surprising that mandatory regulation is not commonplace throughout Europe. Admittedly, our reticence towards compulsory modes of press regulation is understandable given the shared history I outlined above. Yet, our common fear of totalitarianism is neither inevitable should we regulate the press compulsorily nor unrealisable if we do not. In short, the threat to press freedom inherent in mandatory press regulation depends entirely on *what* is regulated compulsorily and not the fact of it.

In defence of this claim, though, I should like to spend the remainder of this concluding chapter speaking to the British experience of implementing an enhanced regulatory regime following the well-known Leveson Inquiry. Given that readers are bound to be familiar with that Inquiry, at least in passing, I shall not say much about it other than to mention that it was set up in light of shocking evidence that a British tabloid – the now defunct *News of the World* – had engaged in serious and sustained illegal phone hacking so as to obtain information stored in the mobile phone messaging services of not only the rich and famous but also, and perhaps most shockingly of all, ordinary members of the public, including, in 2002, the then missing schoolgirl, Millie Dowler.[65] Police enquiries into her disappearance were hampered by this interference; her parents were given false hope that their daughter was still alive, listening to her messages. Tragically, she was already dead.

The subsequent inquiry into press malpractice concluded, in 2012, with a series of recommendations for an independent system of self-regulation, which resulted in both IPSO and IMPRESS being created. Sadly, Leveson was wedded to the idea that this new system must be voluntary in nature. The reasons for this are rather opaque. Although accepting that if the industry did not reform itself sufficiently, the government would have 'no alternative but to provide in legislation for a [mandatory] regulator to apply and enforce a Code,'[66] he identified (and, ultimately, accepted) four arguments against state imposition of mandatory

---

[64] Fielden (n 39) 42.

[65] See discussion in T Watson and M Hickman, *Dial M for Murdoch: News Corporation and the Corruption of Britain* (London, Penguin, 2012) 171–88; N Davies, *Hack Attack* (London, Chatto & Windus, 2014) 375–77.

[66] Leveson Report (n 3) 1782, [7.10].

regulation. The first of these is pragmatic: that a mandatory scheme would be ineffective because it would be repulsive to the press; only a scheme commanding industry approval would produce 'genuinely willing participants'.[67] Secondly, that mandatory regulation is, or else risks degenerating into, state control of the press. Even if the scheme itself did not unduly threaten press freedom, such legislation would be the 'thin end of the wedge' allowing more censorial measures to be passed more easily in the future. Thirdly, that statute is too cumbersome: 'Any mandatory system would require some form of legislation; it is argued that this would make the resultant system inflexible and unable to move to react to changes in the market or in technology'[68] or, as Lord Black put it, 'keep pace with a fast-moving industry in the way that self-regulation could'.[69] Finally, that mandatory regulation generates irresolvable definitional issues.

The fourth objection strikes me as sleight of hand. The VAT exemption for the press, in the UK, has caused no definitional issues so far as I can tell, and neither has Denmark experienced any great difficulties through its use of definitions to determine who counts as 'the press'. The third is also easily dismissed, for we can say, with Eric Barendt, that, fundamentally, it misunderstands the point of statute, which is to establish the structure not the substance of press regulation.[70] Of the two remaining objections, the first lacks normative content. It is not a claim about the compatibility of regulation with press freedom; it simply describes an attitude towards compulsion: that press petulance will scupper it. The second claim is normative, but its contingency diminishes its significance. For the root of this concern lies in the *perception* of what mandatory, statutory regulation represents, and how it could be used. When we look, not only at Leveson but the established literature, and other inquiries, we see this perception at work. People hear the phrase 'statutory regulation' or 'mandatory regulation' and they project some dark meaning upon it. In this way, the phrase takes on a meaning that is never acknowledged lucidly, candidly and comprehensively, but only hinted at darkly. In other words, the common reaction is one of seeing what we want to see, of imposing an order or a meaning upon a form that is not necessarily true. Psychologists call this phenomenon 'pareidolia'. We look at the moon and see a face. We look at shadows cast from some innocuous object and see a monster. It is this phenomenon, of seeing what we want to see or expect to see, which characterises the debate on press freedom and press regulation. Hannah Arendt could have been describing this phenomenon when she said: 'it certainly is a category of the mind to bring order into all sensory data, whatever their nature may be, and thus it makes experience possible'.[71] We think these terms stand for something and, consequently, this

---

[67] ibid 1656, [4.2].

[68] ibid 1656, [4.3].

[69] ibid 1674, [7.3].

[70] E Barendt, 'Statutory Underpinning: A Threat to Press Freedom?' (2013) 5 *Journal of Media Law* 189, 195.

[71] H Arendt, *Between Past and Future* (London, Penguin Books, [1954] 2006) 143.

something then determines both the limits of state action in relation to that thing and the nature of the guarantees that the thing provides. It strikes me that if we are alive to this phenomenon's presence, in the debate, we can make progress.

During the Leveson Inquiry, participants saw in the phrase 'mandatory regulation' their worst fears realised: that 'Parliament is itching to control the press and that this would be an opportunity to do so';[72] that it would 'make it easier to amend an existing Act than to bring in a new one';[73] that it is bound to have a 'chilling effect on free speech or press freedom';[74] and that it portends 'freedom of expression Armageddon'.[75] We see this pareidolia elsewhere. For example, we see it in Parliament's reaction to Leveson in 2012. We see it also in its reaction in 1946, when sections of the House of Commons feared that the appointment of a Royal Commission into press practices would lead to some legislative solution:

> It was this implied threat of legislation which evoked thunderous denunciation from some of the newspapers … They can scarcely have thought that a British Labour Government in 1946 was in the least likely to imitate the methods of totalitarian countries, to nationalise the press, or to institute a censorship. But in evoking the principle of 'the freedom of the press' they were sure of a ready response from Liberal England.[76]

We see it in the Royal Commission's response: 'we [do not] see a solution in any form of state control of the Press'.[77] We see it also in Lord Black's conclusion that statutory regulation would be 'repugnant to a proper view of the freedom of the press',[78] and post-Leveson, the press's response that it would end '300 years of press freedom' and imperil serious investigative journalism.[79] Clearly, there is a perception here of some insidious force lurking in the idea of statutory regulation.

In an important sense, the fear of state control is unjustifiably alarmist. Specifically, the claim that mandatory regulation amounts to 'licensing' is a powerful but manipulative trope to generate unwarranted sympathy for the press, intended to reference not the sort of scheme that applies in the broadcasting context but that censorious system that prevailed in the UK until 1695. Under this system, the Star Chamber, that most pernicious of judicial bodies, during the reign of the Stuarts, utilised terrifying methods to punish heresy and criticisms

---

[72] Leveson (n 63) 1780, [6.38].

[73] ibid [6.39].

[74] ibid 1782, [7.8].

[75] ibid 1783, [1.3].

[76] K Martin, *The Press the Public Wants* (London, The Hogarth Press, 1947) 20.

[77] *Royal Commission on the Press, 1947–49, Report* (Cmnd 7700), Chapter XI, [683].

[78] Leveson (n 63) 67, [5.11].

[79] See, eg, 'Keep the Press Free' *Spectator* (31 December 2016), available at: www.spectator.co.uk/article/keep-the-press-free/; 'Daily Mail Comment: After 300 Years, the Freedom of Britain's Press Is in Peril. YOU Can Save It' *Daily Mail* (9 January 2017), available at: www.dailymail.co.uk/debate/article-4100518/DAILY-MAIL-COMMENT-300-years-freedom-Britain-s-Press-peril-save-it.html; Gordon Rayner, 'Investigative Journalism to Be "Stopped Dead in Tracks" by 'Menacing' Laws after Leveson Inquiry' *Independent* (15 October 2015), available at: www.telegraph.co.uk/news/uknews/leveson-inquiry/11933515/Investigative-journalism-to-be-stopped-dead-in-tracks-by-menacing-laws-after-Leveson-Inquiry.html.

of royal policy, as when the puritan William Prynne was branded on both cheeks with the letters S and L to indicate his crime of seditious libel against the Crown.[80] Mandatory press regulation is no more comparable to the Star Chamber than the Clergy Discipline Commission is to the Spanish Inquisition.

Nevertheless, the source of this pareidolia is not merely paranoia but emerges through the common perception that the press exists to perform a function. We have already seen this type of teleological ambition for press freedom in the various European codes we have examined, all of which claim some fundamental role for the press in a democratic society. Given statements like this, it is understandable that the press should fear regulatory function creep. The commentary feeds this pareidolia through its insistence upon the existence of a press 'duty' to serve the public good and, likewise, that it must act 'responsibly' in the use of power. Thus, the phrase press freedom becomes overburdened, which in turn pollutes our perceptions of press regulation with this pareidolia. This, in turn, drives the libertarian fear that unwarranted interference with press speech could occur unchecked because we would lack the language to articulate the unconstitutionality of the function creep.

Yet, this fear is misplaced. We have the language by which to ensure this eventuality does not happen. The press must be accountable for the wrongs it causes, but its obligations are no greater than that. It has the duty to make good, not do good. By rejecting purposive interpretations of press freedom, as a duty owed to democracy, the range of permissible regulatory codes becomes much more limited than those caught in the grip of pareidolia fear. Accordingly, it would not be legitimate to operate provisions ostensibly regulating 'truth', 'the public's right to know', or indeed any clauses imposing 'duties' to enable democratic participation, educate the public or check on power. Such provisions are beyond the scope of legitimate regulation. As the preceding has sought to argue, regulatory codes of conduct are themselves subject to rules of design. All provisions must correspond to the formula of wrongdoing–causation–harm that the liberal tradition recognises. It is only if these governing rules are followed that the provision is compatible with press freedom. Thus, the fear that, say, press criticism of the state could be penalised – now, or in the future – does not arise by virtue of linguistic vulnerability, and cannot, therefore, arise from function creep, because we have the language to designate it an unconstitutional act. The fact that we can both articulate the nature of press freedom and the limits of legitimate regulatory rules of conduct means that we have the critical vocabulary by which to identify mandate breaches by the regulator or government. We can say what is a legitimate use of coercive power, and what is not. Consequently, the pareidolia is rendered nugatory. Accordingly, the state could enact legislation to create a mandatory scheme of coercive independent press regulation without compromising press freedom.

---

[80] LW Levy, *Emergence of a Free Press* (Oxford, Oxford University Press, 1985) 132; M Kishlansky, 'A Whipper Whipped: The Sedition of William Prynne' (2013) 56(3) *The Historical Journal* 603.

Yet, the press is bound to think this controversial. In Black's testimony to the Leveson Inquiry, we see esoterism creep into his description of the task of drafting the code for, according to him, 'only serving editors would have the practical day-to-day understanding of what life was like in newsrooms'.[81] Quite why only serving editors are uniquely qualified is not clear. Leveson rejected that claim, albeit he did not altogether dismiss it. On several occasions, we see him say that a 'strong editorial voice' on standards was 'important',[82] 'invaluable'[83] and 'obviously necessary'.[84] This conclusion is worth scrutinising, for what is the unique contribution that serving editors make? Consider a different regulatory context – say, medicine or law. In those fields, the input of members *is* 'obviously necessary' for we cannot say what amounts to medical or legal malfeasance unless we have knowledge of those professions.[85] This is not true of journalism. It does not involve the same sort of 'special skill' that would necessitate practitioner input. Of course, editors are bound to hold views on what is useful or desirable, but, clearly, that is not the same thing. The reason for this is apparent from previous chapters: that the only code provisions that can be enforced coercively against the press are those that protect *rights*. These, then, are questions of law, not journalism. The regulator is not required to know – to be on the inside of – journalism to determine these standards. Not only are journalists unnecessary in this process, they are irrelevant, and, quite possibly, a hindrance. For what can they say about the realities of newsgathering and the intricacies of reporting technique that is vital to the rights claims at stake?

4. Conclusion

Despite the sustained argument for mandatory press regulation, there remains a constant need for vigilance to ensure that neither the regulator nor the government exceeds their mandate. We must always guard against complacency. The government's self-interest in a subdued press should never been forgotten. Neither should we think that the mature democracies of the West are somehow immune to corruption, incompetence, or abuse of power. We know all too well that they are not. Nor should we think that independent regulation is beyond such either. This concern, though, is not an unassailable argument against the creation of a coercive, independent press regulator. Far from it. Instead, it is an argument in favour of ensuring the proper safeguards exist to monitor or otherwise address the possibility of regulatory failings. To ensure that the regulator's power is not

---

[81] Leveson (n 63) 1624, [3.4].

[82] ibid [3.6].

[83] ibid 1527, [3.30].

[84] ibid 1529, [3.39].

[85] See, eg, *Montgomery v Lanarkshire Health Board* [2015] UKSC 11; *Bolam v Friern Hospital Management Committee* [1957] 1 WLR 582.

abused, its actions should be subject to some sort of oversight or transparency – and, of course, the usual means of doing this is judicial review, so that instances of errant regulatory decision-making can be remedied.[86] Ireland's regulatory scheme, for example, contains an additional layer of transparency by operating an appeals process in which first-instance decisions by the press ombudsman can be overturned and replaced by decisions of the press council on appeal.[87] The Royal Charter provides a different, important, safeguard against, especially, systematic failings by the regulator. This arises in the form of the 'recognition body' – a separate entity that is independent of the state, the industry and the regulator itself – which is tasked with appointing the regulator, in the first place, according to specific criteria set out in the Royal Charter,[88] and with conducting reviews of the regulator's performance, at least once every three years after the regulator has been appointed,[89] but also on an 'ad hoc' basis, either because the recognition panel suspects that there has been a serious breach (or breaches) of the recognition criteria or because there is a 'significant public interest' in such a review.[90]

Given the arguments above, that mandatory press regulation is legitimate where its provisions reflect the law or otherwise mirror its structure, it may be questioned what value regulation adds that the legal system does not already possess. After all, those defamed or whose privacy is unduly interfered with can bring legal actions if they wish.

To my mind, regulation represents an important alternative to legal action for three reasons. First, the financial costs of legal proceedings are a significant deterrent to all but those rich enough to risk losing their action and, thus, paying their own costs and their opponents. As Lord Justice Leveson recognised in his Inquiry, the press continues to cause real harm to real people – by which he meant it vilifies, defames and intrudes upon the private lives of not only the rich and famous but also ordinary members of the public. Regulation represents an important alternative means of achieving justice, even if the outcome amounts only to an apology and/or adverse adjudication that recognises, publicly, the wrongdoing done by the press.

Secondly, regulation alleviates the emotional burden of pursuing a claim against the press. Partly, this is achieved through the faster resolution of complaints, in which an outcome is reached in months instead of years. Chiefly, though, it can be achieved through recognition that breaches of the code are matters which affect the regulator itself and not only the complainant. Whereas, for example, breaches of the civil law are matters between litigants in which the state is merely adjudicator, the regulator has a vested interest in ensuring that the

---

[86] The PCC was also subject to judicial review, see *R v PCC ex parte Stewart-Brady* [1997] EMLR 185.
[87] Press Council of Ireland. June 2015. Code of Practice. See discussion in Daithi Mac Síthígh, 'Press Freedom in Ireland: Laggard or Innovator?', ch 5 in this volume.
[88] N 42, Sch 3.
[89] ibid. These are known as cyclical reviews, under Clause 5, Sch 2.
[90] ibid Clause 8, Sch 2.

standards it imposes are met. Accordingly, the regulator can, in effect, step into the shoes of the complainant after the complaint is initiated. In this way, victims can be shielded from press bullying to much greater effect than can occur in judicial proceedings. Thirdly, and relatedly, the crucial feature of press regulation is its capacity for realising public accountability of the press. For, unlike in civil claims, regulation provides the sort of transparency about press malfeasance that the legal system cannot. Civil suits are of limited public record. Proceedings may be threatened but never initiated. Litigants with strong claims but weak resolve or limited resources may settle claims that ought to be litigated in the public interest. Some may be forced to drop even meritorious claims for fear of financial ruin in the unlikely event of loss. Accordingly, the true picture of malfeasance remains unknown. Regulation guards against this sort of opaqueness. The press, as public watchdog, rarely reports on itself and, thus, regulation provides the sort of public accountability that is otherwise missing.

INDEX